Oracle Press™

D0771574

Oracle
High-Performance
SQL Tuning

Oracle Press™

Oracle High-Performance SQL Tuning

Donald K. Burleson

Osborne/**McGraw-Hill**

New York   Chicago   San Francisco
Lisbon   London   Madrid   Mexico City   Milan
New Delhi   San Juan   Seoul   Singapore   Sydney   Toronto

Osborne/**McGraw-Hill**
2600 Tenth Street
Berkeley, California 94710
U.S.A.

To arrange bulk purchase discounts for sales promotions, premiums, or fund-raisers, please contact Osborne/**McGraw-Hill** at the above address. For information on translations or book distributors outside the U.S.A., please see the International Contact Information page immediately following the index of this book.

Oracle High-Performance SQL Tuning

1234567890 FGR FGR 01987654321

ISBN 0-07-219058-2

Publisher
   Brandon A. Nordin

Vice President & Associate Publisher
   Scott Rogers

Acquisitions Editor
   Lisa McClain

Senior Project Editor
   Carolyn Welch

Acquisitions Coordinators
   Ross Doll
   Paulina Pobocha

Technical Editor
   Mike Ault

Copy Editor
   Bob Campbell

Proofreader
   Pat Mannion

Indexer
   Donald K. Burleson

Computer Designers
   Allan Shearer
   Roberta Steele

Illustrators
   Michael Mueller
   Alex Putney

Series Design
   Jani Beckwith

Cover Designer
   Will Voss

Cover Photo
   Damir Frkovic/Masterfile

This book was composed with Corel VENTURA™ Publisher.

This book is dedicated to my wife, Janet,
whose love and support made it possible
for me to write this text.

About the Author

Donald Keith Burleson is one of the world's top Oracle Database experts with more than 20 years of full-time experience. He specializes in creating database architectures for very large online databases and he has worked with some of the world's most powerful and complex systems. A leading database author, Don has written 12 books, published more than 60 articles in national magazines, and serves as Editor-in-Chief of Oracle Internals, a leading Oracle Database journal. Don's professional Web sites include http://www.dba-oracle.com/and http:// www .remote-dba.net/.

Donald Burleson also provides remote DBA support and consulting services, specializing in Oracle database tuning, Oracle data warehousing, and design of Oracle databases on the Web. Don is also a former adjunct professor and has taught more than 100 graduate-level computer courses. Don is a popular lecturer and teacher and is a frequent speaker at Oracle Openworld and other international database conferences.

Don also writes the Oracle Answers column at TechRepublic.com and publishes the weekly Oracle tech-tips e-mail.

In addition to his services as a consultant, Don also is active in charitable programs to aid visually impaired and blind individuals. Don pioneered a technique for training tiny pigmy horses as guide animals for the blind and manages a nonprofit corporation called The Guide Horse Foundation, which is dedicated to providing guide horses to blind people free of charge.

The Web site for The Guide Horse Foundation is http://www.guidehorse.org/.

Don Burleson's books include:
Oracle Internals: Tips, Tricks, and Techniques for DBAs (CRC Press, 2001)
Oracle High-Performance SQL Tuning (**Osborne/McGraw-Hill**, Oracle Press, 2001)
High Performance Oracle tuning with STATSPACK (**Osborne/McGraw-Hill**, Oracle Press, 2001)
Unix for the Oracle DBA (O'Reilly & Associates, 2000)
Oracle SAP Administration (O'Reilly & Associates, 1999)
Inside the Database Object Model (CRC Press, 1998)
High Performance Oracle Data Warehousing (Coriolis Publishing, 1997)
High Performance Oracle 8 Tuning (Coriolis Publishing, 1997)
High Performance Oracle Database Applications (Coriolis Publishing, 1996)
Oracle Databases on the Web (Coriolis Publishing, 1996)
Managing Distributed Databases (John Wiley & Sons, 1994)
Practical Application of Object-Oriented Techniques to Relational Databases
   (John Wiley & Sons, 1993)

Contents at a Glance

PART III
Advanced SQL Tuning

Contents

PART I
Background

PART III

Advanced SQL Tuning

Acknowledgments

There is always a team effort in the creation of any technical book, and this book was created as the direct result of the dedicated efforts of many individuals. I would like to thank Lisa McClain for her diligent efforts in helping with the concept and fruition of the idea for this book, and Ross Doll, Carolyn Welch, and Paulina Pobocha, who were instrumental in coordinating the editing and graphics efforts. I would also like to thank Jennifer Burleson for doing a superb job on the index.

Introduction

he tuning of Oracle SQL is more important than any other area of Oracle tuning, and proper tuning of SQL statements can dramatically improve the performance of an entire Oracle database. Unfortunately, many Oracle professionals do not know the correct method to ensure that their SQL is optimally tuned.

This comprehensive guide to Oracle SQL is intended to be a valuable aid to all Oracle professionals who must write SQL statements. This text directs the reader through all of the SQL tuning steps and provides expert tips and techniques for tuning any type of SQL.

Topics include a detailed discussion of Oracle's optimizer modes, techniques for displaying the execution plan for SQL, and a wealth of methods improving the performance of any SQL statement. This book takes a very complex and technical task and explains each SQL tuning step in plain, easy to understand methods.

Because Oracle SQL is a "declarative" language, the user only needs to specify the data columns they want, the tables that contain the data, and any constraints on the data. Because of the innate power of SQL, it is possible to write an identical query in many forms, each with widely varying performance. This book show how to take any SQL statement, view the internal execution plan, and change the execution plan to improve the performance of the statement. This is an exciting topic that can greatly improve the performance of any Oracle database.

This book incorporates proven techniques for identifying offensive SQL statements and tuning the statements for optimal performance. All of the techniques in this book use standard Oracle utilities, so no special products are required to tune any SQL statement. This text is also intended to be comprehensive, covering every aspect of SQL tuning from a simple SELECT statement to a complex noncorrelated Subquery. This text also includes expert tips and techniques that have been developed by the author that will dramatically improve SQL performance.

As Oracle SQL evolves and becomes more complex, this book will continue to evolve. You are encouraged to send me any of your comments and ideas for future editions, and you can e-mail me at don@burleson.cc with any useful information.

PART
I

Background

CHAPTER
1

Introduction to SQL

he acronym "SQL" is short for Structured Query Language. Unfortunately, SQL is not structured, SQL is not only for queries, and SQL is not a language, per se, because SQL is embedded within other languages such as C and COBOL. Regardless of the mistaken name, SQL has emerged as the dominant access method for relational databases.

This chapter will introduce the nature of Oracle SQL and lay the foundation for techniques that we will be using throughout this book. In this chapter, we will cover the following topics.

- **The basic nature of SQL**   This section will compare SQL to navigational database query languages.

- **The beginning of SQL**   This section will show how SQL has evolved as the de facto standard for database access.

- **The SQL optimizer**   This will be a brief introduction to the process of SQL optimization.

- **The goals of SQL tuning**   This will cover the overall goals of SQL tuning.

- **SQL tuning as a phase of Oracle tuning**   This section will explore how SQL tuning fits into the overall tuning model.

- **The barriers to SQL tuning**   This section discusses the problems encountered when attempting to tune Oracle SQL.

- **The process of SQL tuning**   This section will explore the general goals for tuning an individual SQL statement.

- **Our SQL tuning toolkit**   This section will introduce the toolkit that we will be using throughout the book for examining SQL statements for tuning.

The Basic Nature of SQL

The SQL standard proposal was originally created as an alternative to the cumbersome navigational languages of existing databases. In the 1960s, the IBM IMS database was the only large-scale commercial database management system. Unlike databases on the relational model, IMS is a hierarchical database with an internal pointer structure used for navigating between database records.

The navigational database access tools required the programmer to navigate through the data structures by means of pointer chasing. Here is an actual example of a query from the popular IDMS database, an early CODASYL network database:

```
MOVE 'JONES' TO CUST-DESC.
    OBTAIN CALC CUSTOMER.
    MOVE CUSTOMER-ADDRESS TO OUT-REC.
    WRITE OUT-REC.
    FIND FIRST ORDER WITHIN CUSTOMER-ORDER.
        PERFORM ORDER-LOOP UNTIL END-OF-SET.
    ***********
    ORDER-LOOP.
    ***********
        OBTAIN FIRST ORDER-LINE-REC WITHIN ORDER-LINE.
        PERFORM ORDER-LINE-LOOP UNTIL END-OF-SET.
        FIND NEXT ORDER WITHIN CUSTOMER-ORDER.
    ***********
    ORDER-LINE-LOOP.
    ***********
        OBTAIN NEXT ORDER-LINE-REC WITHIN ORDER-LINE.
        MOVE QUANTITY-ORDERED TO OUT-REC.
        WRITE OUT-REC.
        OBTAIN OWNER WITHIN ORDER-LINE-PRODUCT
        MOVE PRODUCT-NAME TO OUT-REC.
        WRITE OUT-REC.
```

Here we see that the query navigates between data records, accessing the record, finding a pointer, and moving between pointers according to the pointer values (as shown in Figure 1-1). The point is that this type of database query requires knowledge of the internal structures of the database in order to extract data.

The equivalent statement in SQL is quite different in syntax and function. Unlike a navigational database access language, SQL is designed to require only a specification of the columns you want to display, the tables that contain the data, and the join criteria for the tables.

```
select
    customer_address,
    product_name,
    quantity_ordered
from
    customer c,
    order o,
    order_line l,
    product
where
    customer_name = 'JONES'
and
    c.cust_nbr = o.cust_nbr
and
    o.order_nbr = l.order.nbr
and
    l.product_nbr = p.product_nbr
;
```

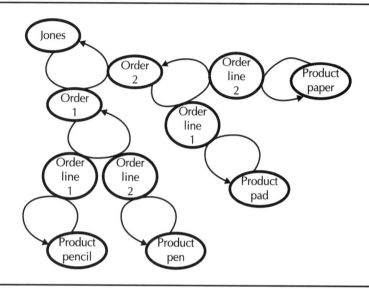

FIGURE 1-1. *A navigational database query*

We will take a closer look at the basic structure of SQL later in this chapter. While SQL is generally associated with relational databases, it is important to note that SQL is also popular in nonrelational databases. The IDMS network database developers renamed their product to IDMS/R after they created a SQL engine, and several object-oriented databases now offer SQL front ends that make their databases appear to be relational.

The Beginnings of SQL

In 1970, Dr. Edgar Codd of IBM and Chris Date developed a relational model for data storage. In the model, data would be stored in simple linear structures called "relations" or "tables." One of the best improvements of the relational model over its predecessors was its simplicity. Rather than requiring users to know dozens of navigational data manipulation Language (DML) commands, the relational model introduced a declarative language called SQL to simplify data access and manipulation.

   In Codd and Date's model, the tables are represented as two-dimensional arrays of "rows" and "columns." Rows were called "tuples" (rhymes with "couples"), and columns were called "attributes." A table will always have a field or several fields that make a "primary key" for a table. In their relational database model, the tables are independent, unlike in hierarchical and network models, where they are pointer-connected.

The relational database model offered the following improvements over the existing hierarchical and network databases:

■ **Simplicity**   The concept of tables with rows and columns is extremely simple and easy to understand. End users have a simple data model. Complex network diagrams used with the hierarchical and network databases are not used with a relational database.

■ **Data independence**   Data independence is the ability to modify data structures (in this case, tables) without affecting existing programs. Much of this ability comes because tables are not hard-linked to one another. Columns can be added to tables, tables can be added to the database, and new data relationships can be added with little or no restructuring of the tables. A relational database provides a much higher degree of data independence than do hierarchical and network databases.

■ **Declarative Data Access**   The SQL user specifies what data is wanted, and then the embedded SQL, a procedural language, determines how to get the data. In relational database access, the user tells the system the conditions for the retrieval of data. The system then gets the data that meets the selection conditions in the SQL statements. The database navigation is hidden from the end user or programmer, unlike in a CODASYL DML language, where the programmer had to know the details of the access path.

In the marketplace, the declarative data access capability was far more interesting than the internal storage components of the relational database, and SQL became synonymous with the relational model.

A Model for SQL

The first model of SQL can be thought of as having three categories of function: Define, Manipulate, and Authorize.

■ **Define**   refers to the data definition language (DDL) that performs object create, drop, and alter functions.

■ **Manipulate**   refers to the data manipulation language (DML) that performs select, insert, update, and delete functions.

■ **Authorize**   refers to the control that performs grant and revoke functions.

Within the Manipulate functions, we see three dimensions to SQL, *select, project,* and *join.* These three simple metrics define the whole functionality of SQL.

Select Operation

A *select* operation reduces the length of a table by filtering out unwanted rows. By specifying conditions in the *where* clause, the user can filter unwanted rows out of the result set, as shown in Figure 1-2. In sum, the *select* operation reduces the results vertically.

Project Operation

Just as the *select* operation reduces the number of rows, the *project* operation reduces the number of columns. The column names specified in the SQL select determine those columns that are displayed, as shown in Figure 1-3. In sum, the project operation reduces the size of the result set horizontally.

Join Operation

A *join* operation such as is shown in Figure 1-4 is used to relate two or more independent tables that share a common column. In a join, two or more independent tables are merged according to a common column value.

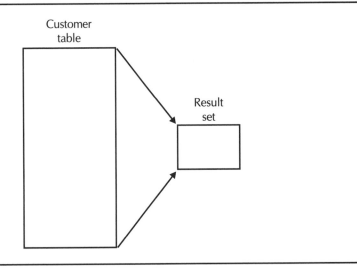

FIGURE 1-2. *A select filter reduces the number of returned rows*

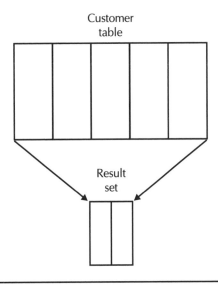

FIGURE 1-3.   *The project operation removes unwanted columns*

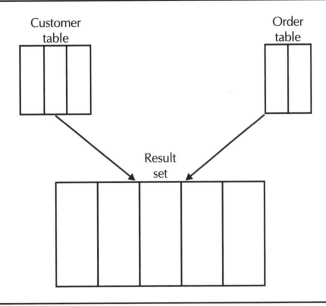

FIGURE 1-4.   *A join operation*

Within this simple framework we see that a query in SQL is a "state-space" type of query. That is, the person who writes the query does not need to be concerned with the navigation path to the data. The SQL optimizer handles the navigation path to the data tables internally.

The SQL Optimizer

In a perfect world, the SQL optimizer should be able to generate the most efficient method to service the data request. If the SQL optimizer has all of the information about all of the tables involved in the query (e.g., the number of rows, the distribution of values within a column), the optimizer should always choose the best execution plan for accessing the data.

In the real world, the SQL optimizer requires human assistance. It is the responsibility of the Oracle DBA to ensure that all of the object statistics are available to the SQL optimizer, and the overwhelming complexity of SQL optimization makes it very difficult for any vendor to deliver an optimizer that always chooses the best access path to the data. Hence, we need a book such as this to understand how to help the optimizer choose the most efficient path to the data.

The Goals of SQL Tuning

SQL tuning is the most time-consuming and challenging of all Oracle tuning activities. Unlike SGA tuning, which is performed only once, SQL tuning is an ongoing process. Each SQL statement must be individually tuned, and the tuning must be made permanent by using hints or with the new Oracle8i optimizer plan stability feature. For details on using optimizer plan stability, please see Chapter 13.

Also, SQL tuning has the most immediate positive impact on Oracle performance. When the Oracle optimizer chooses a less-than-optimal execution plan, human tuning can often triple the speed of the query. For queries that are executed thousands of times per day, this can result in a dramatic improvement of database throughput and extend the life of the hardware on the database server. The following list summarizes the goals of SQL tuning:

- **To ensure that all SQL has been "approved" for performance** It is important to note that the goals of the programmers who write the SQL are very different from the goals of the person charged with tuning the SQL. The programmers are concerned with getting a query with the correct result as quickly as possible, and it is not uncommon to find SQL that is less than optimal from a performance perspective.

- **To create Oracle statistics and indexes that will benefit all SQL** The Oracle SQL optimizer does not exist in a vacuum, and it is the goal of the Oracle DBA to create appropriate indexes and object analysis techniques to ensure that all SQL will perform in an optimal fashion.

- **To lock down the execution plan for all SQL** Adding a new index can sometimes result in a change to dozens of SQL statements, and a primary goal of SQL tuning is to make the tuning changes permanent. For any SQL statement, there is only one optimal execution plan, and once that is identified, it is the goal of the Oracle DBA to make the execution plan permanent by adding hints to the query or by using optimizer plan stability.

We will be discussing these goals as a central theme throughout the body of this book.

SQL Tuning as a Phase of Oracle Tuning

The tuning of SQL is a very integral component of Oracle tuning, and one that can have an immediate impact on performance. However, it is very tempting to dive into SQL tuning without performing the prerequisite tuning activities.

There is a very specific order to Oracle tuning. All Oracle database are organized as a hierarchy, with global components affecting subcomponents, as you can see in Figure 1-5.

This hierarchy is very important because any bad tuning at a high level will affect all activities at the level beneath it. Here are the details about the Oracle tuning hierarchy:

- **Environmental tuning** Environmental tuning involves the tuning of the database server, the network, and the disk I/O subsystem. Only after these components are tuned can the Oracle DBA begin tuning the Oracle database.

- **Database server tuning** The tuning of the Oracle database server is a prerequisite for all Oracle tuning. If the database server experiences shortages of RAM or CPU, no amount of Oracle tuning will remedy the problem.

- **Network tuning** The network substrate must be tuned to ensure that there are no packet shipping issues at the network protocol level. For details on tuning Oracle network communications, see *Oracle High-Performance Tuning with STATSPACK*, Chapter 7.

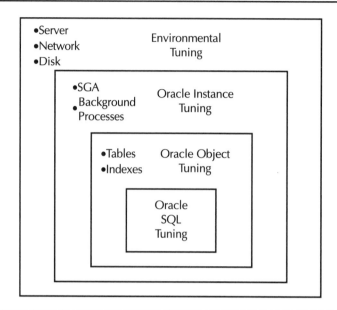

FIGURE 1-5. *The Oracle tuning hierarchy*

■ **Disk tuning**   The tuning of the disk I/O subsystem is an absolute prerequisite to Oracle tuning. Disk I/O bottlenecks and disk access problems must be addressed before Oracle tuning begins.

■ **Instance tuning**   Once the external environment is tuned, the next phase is the tuning of the Oracle instance. This involves tuning the SGA memory region and tuning the behavior of the Oracle background processes. With regard to SQL tuning, this is the step where the default *optimizer_mode* for all SQL in the database is set. For details about Oracle's *optimizer_mode* parameter, see Chapters 14 and 15.

■ **Object tuning**   Once the instance is tuned, each Oracle object must be tuned for optimal performance. This phase involves getting the proper setting for all storage parameters, especially those storage parameters that affect I/O. The settings for pctfree, pctused, and freelists all have an important impact on SQL performance.

■ **SQL tuning**   Once all of the general tuning has been accomplished, you are ready to embark on SQL tuning. This phase involves the identification of high-use SQL statements, tuning the statements, and ensuring that the optimal execution plan is made permanent.

Database Design and SQL Performance

Note that we have deliberately left out one of the most important factors in SQL speed, the design of the original data structures, outlined in Figure 1-6. The amount of data normalization and the amount of planned redundancy within the Oracle tables will have a dramatic impact on the speed of the queries. As you will learn later in this text, by adding redundant columns to tables (denormalization), you can avoid expensive SQL joins and improve performance.

We have omitted this discussion because it is rarely possible for the Oracle DBA to change the table design once the application has gone into a production environment. However, we will be discussing column replication techniques in a later chapter, to show you how you can avoid a SQL table join by replicating a data column from one table to another (as shown in Figure 1-7), and how you can provide a trigger to keep the replicated data item up to date.

Next, let's look at the challenges that are faced by the Oracle DBA when undertaking SQL tuning.

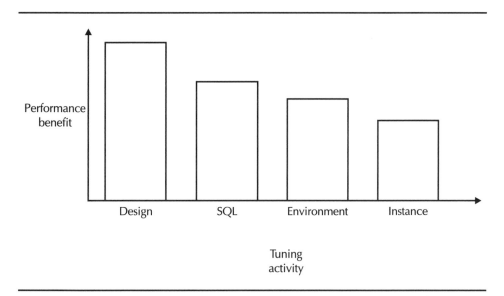

FIGURE 1-6. *The relative performance benefits of different tuning activities*

A denormalized table

Product_ID	Product_Name	Order_NBR	Customer_ID
661	Pen	123	Jones
427	Pencil	123	Jones
873	Paper	123	Jones
661	Pen	456	Smith

FIGURE 1-7. *Improved performance with column replication*

The Barriers to SQL Tuning

The tuning of Oracle SQL is one of the most time-consuming, frustrating, and annoying areas of Oracle tuning. There are several factors that make SQL tuning a maddening undertaking.

- **Locating the offensive SQL statement** Later in this book we will explore techniques for fishing SQL out of the Oracle library cache and tuning the statement. However, if you have an early release of Oracle8 that does not support optimizer plan stability, you must find the location of the SQL source code in order to make your tuning changes permanent. As we know, SQL source code can exist in a variety of locations, including PL/SQL, C programs, and client-side Visual Basic code.

- **Resistance from management** SQL tuning is a time-consuming and expensive process, and it is not uncommon for managers to be reluctant to invest in the time required to tune the SQL. In many cases, the DBA must prepare a cost-benefit analysis showing that the saving in hardware resources justifies the costs of tuning all of the SQL in a database.

- **Tuning with ad hoc SQL generators** Products such as the SAP application dynamically create the Oracle SQL inside the SAP ABAP programs, and it is often impossible to modify the SQL source code.

- **Resistance from SQL programmers** Many programmers are reluctant to admit that they have created a suboptimal SQL statement. This can make it quite difficult when the Oracle DBA determines that the statement must be rewritten to improve performance.

- **Tuning nonreusable SQL statements**   Many third-party applications generate SQL statements with embedded literal values (e.g., *select * from customer where name = 'JONES';*). In these cases, the library is flooded with tens of thousands of nonreusable SQL statements, with many identical SQL statements that cannot be reused because they have no host variables (e.g., *select * from customer where name = :var1;*). In these cases, *cursor_sharing* must be implemented, and sometimes the library cache must be downsized or flushed with the *alter system flush shared pool* command.

- **Diminishing marginal returns**   As the Oracle DBA identifies and tunes high-use SQL statements, it becomes harder to locate SQL statements for tuning. For example, there may be many dozens of infrequently executed SQL statements that would greatly benefit from tuning, but their sporadic appearance in the library cache makes them difficult to locate. Hence, we see a point where the marginal benefit from tuning will become less than the Oracle DBA effort in locating the statements, as Figure 1-8 illustrates.

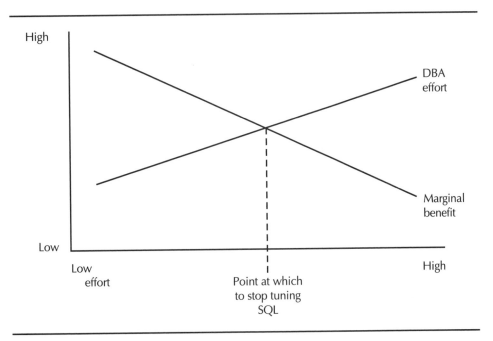

FIGURE 1-8.   *The marginal benefits of SQL tuning*

Despite these difficulties and challenges, the tuning of Oracle SQL can make the Oracle DBA a hero, both to management and to the programming staff. Enlightened companies always make the programmers submit SQL statements with their current execution plans to the DBA for a review, prior to placing the SQL into their production environment.

Next, let's take a high-level tour of the steps involved in SQL tuning.

The Process of SQL Tuning

Once all of the prerequisite tuning has been done to the server, network, disk, instance, and objects, the process of SQL tuning can begin. Although we will be covering this subject in greater detail later, let's take a high-level tour of the steps of SQL tuning.

It is critical to remember that SQL tuning is an iterative activity. The Oracle DBA is challenged to perform the following activities:

- **Locate high-use SQL statements** The first step in SQL tuning is locating the frequently executed SQL. This involves using STATSPACK or fishing through the library cache.

- **Tune the SQL statement** The tuning of a SQL statement involves generating an execution plan and evaluating alternative execution plans by:

  - **Adding indexes** You can add indexes (especially bitmapped and function-based indexes) to remove unwarranted full-table scans.

  - **Changing the optimizer mode** You can try changing the optimizer mode to *rule*, *all_rows*, or *first_rows*.

  - **Adding hints** You can add hints to force a change to the execution plan.

- **Make the tuning permanent** Once you have tuned the SQL statement, you must make the change permanent by locating and changing the SQL source code or by using optimizer plan stability.

Let's take a close look at these steps.

Locate the High-Use SQL

The first step is to locate the most frequently executed SQL statements. Since SQL may enter Oracle from a variety of sources (Pro*C programs, Visual Basic code, etc.), the Oracle DBA must prepare an approach to sample the SQL that is currently in the library cache. There are two approaches to locating candidate SQL statements for tuning:

■ **Use STATSPACK**   The STATSPACK approach involves using the *stats$sql_summary* table to capture SQL statements.

■ **Fish through the library cache**   This approach involves using utilities to explain all of the SQL that is currently in the library cache.

Let's take a close look at each of these approaches.

Using STATSPACK to Capture SQL

When using STATSPACK, you will find that the *stats$sql_summary* table is the most highly populated of all of the STATSPACK tables. If your threshold values are set very low and you have a busy database, it's not uncommon to get several hundred rows added to the *stats$sql_summary* table each and every time STATSPACK requests a snapshot. Hence, it is very important that the DBA remove unwanted rows from the *stats$sql_summary* table once they are no longer used for SQL tuning. Remember though, that the SQL stored in the *stats$sql_summary* table is filtered by the thresholds stored in the *stats$statspack_parameter* table.

■ *executions_th*   This is the number of executions of the SQL statement (default 100).

■ *disk_reads_th*   This is the number of disk reads performed by the SQL statement (default 1,000).

■ *parse_calls_th*   This is the number of parse calls performed by the SQL statement (default 1,000).

■ *buffer_gets_th*   This is the number of buffer gets performed by the SQL statement (default 10,000).

Remember, a SQL statement will be included in the *stats$sql_summary* table if *any one* of the thresholds is exceeded. Most Oracle DBAs will schedule an hourly STATSPACK sample so that they will get a sample of all of the SQL that resides in the library cache at the time that the snapshot was gathered.

The major drawback to using STATSPACK for collecting SQL statements is the need to adjust the threshold values as your SQL tuning progresses. As you identify and tune SQL statements, you will need to lower the threshold values so that you can continue to tune the the less frequently executed SQL statements. Lowering the threshold causes more rows to be placed into the *stats$sql_summary* table and will cause the STATSPACK tablespace to fill rapidly. Most Oracle DBAs will periodically delete the *stats$sql_summary* rows once they have tuned those SQL statements.

Fishing Through the Library Cache

Another popular approach to SQL tuning is to randomly extract SQL statements from the library cache. These are several techniques that are used to do this:

■ **Using a third-party tool**   Third-party GUI tools can be used to quickly display the SQL in the library cache and extract the most frequently executed and resource-intensive statements. These tools include Oracle's Enterprise Manager Performance Pack, SQL*Lab, Q Diagnostic Center, SQL Expert, and many others.

■ **Using SQL*Plus scripts**   We will also explore a script called access.sql that will extract and explain all of the SQL that is currently in the library cache. We will go into greater detail on access.sql in Chapter 9.

Once we have located the candidates for tuning, we proceed to individually tune each SQL statement.

Tune the SQL Statement

The process of tuning the SQL statement involves several activities. SQL tuning moves from a global level to a specific one. The goal of SQL tuning is to verify that the execution plan is optimal for the statement. Verifying the speed to SQL execution is normally done by using SQL*Plus with the *set timing on* command and actually timing the speed of the query.

■ **Changing the optimizer mode**   You can try changing the optimizer mode to *rule, all_rows,* or *first_rows.* This will normally result in several execution plans, and each must be timed to determine the plan with the fastest execution time.

■ **Adding indexes**   You can add indexes (especially bitmapped and function-based indexes) to remove unwarranted full-table scans. However, be aware that adding an index can change the execution plan for many other SQL statements. It is not uncommon to add an index only to find that the speed of other SQL statements changes.

■ **Adding hints**   You can force a change to the execution plan by adding hints to the select statement. Oracle provides dozens of hints to change the execution plan for SQL, and we will be going into detail on hint-based SQL tuning in Chapter 12.

Make the Tuning Permanent

Once tuned, it is critical that the tuning change become permanent. There are several methods for doing so. Making a SQL tuning change permanent is especially important in an environment where global changes such as changing the *optimizer_mode* initialization parameter or adding indexes could potentially change the execution plans for many SQL statements.

Optimizer Plan Stability

Oracle8*i* provides a new package called OUTLINE that allows the DBA to store a ready-to-run execution plan for any SQL statement. This utility has several features:

- Parsing and execution time is sometimes reduced because Oracle will quickly grab and execute the stored outline for the SQL.

- Tuning of SQL statements can easily be made permanent without locating the source code.

- SQL from third-party products (e.g., SAP, Peoplesoft) can be tuned without touching the SQL source code.

Optimizer plan stability enables you to maintain the same execution plans for the same SQL statements, regardless of changes to the database such as reanalyzing tables; adding or deleting data; modifying a table's columns, constraints, or indexes; changing the system configuration; or even upgrading to a new version of the optimizer.

To use optimizer plan stability, you must run the *dbmsol.sql* script from $ORACLE_HOME/rdbms/admin. When the script is executed, a new Oracle user called OUTLN is created (with DBA privileges) and a package called OUTLN_PKG is installed to provide procedures used for managing stored outlines.

Oracle provides the CREATE OUTLINE statement to create a stored outline. The stored outline contains a set of attributes that the optimizer uses to create an execution plan. Stored outlines can also be created automatically by setting the initialization parameter *create_stored_outlines=true*. For more details on using stored outlines, see your Oracle8*i* documentation and Chapter 13.

Change the SQL Source

In pre-Oracle8*i* environments, the SQL source code must be located in order to make the tuning change permanent. This can be a challenging problem for an application where the SQL is distributed in client-side applications, systems that use ODBC to communicate with Oracle, and systems that generate dynamic SQL.

The Guidelines for SQL Tuning

The cardinal rules of SQL tuning are very straightforward.

1. There exists only one optimal execution plan for any SQL statement. It is the job of the Oracle DBA to find that execution plan.

2. Because SQL comes to the Oracle database from external programs, the Oracle DBA must continually monitor the library cache for untuned SQL.

3. A properly tuned SQL statement will always have the fastest wall-clock execution time. This is usually associated with the execution plan that has the least amount of table I/O.

In practice, the Oracle DBA should strongly advocate removing all SQL from application programs. This is normally achieved by placing all SQL inside stored procedures, and then placing the stored procedures inside Oracle packages. This approach makes the SQL source easy to locate because it is in the Oracle data dictionary. It also has the side benefit of making all remote applications portable, because all calls to Oracle are encapsulated into function and stored procedure calls.

Before we get into the details of this SQL tuning text, let's review some of the tools that we will be using in this book. In order to make this book useful for everyone, we are going to use standard Oracle utilities and scripts for all of our SQL analysis. This alleviates the need for expensive third-party products and ensures that every reader can analyze and tune all SQL.

The Goals of SQL Tuning

Oracle SQL tuning is a phenomenally complex subject, and we will begin with a high-level statement of the goals of SQL tuning and get into detail in later chapters.

Now that we have stated the goals, let's examine some of the specific goals of SQL tuning. There are some general guidelines that all Oracle DBAs must follow in order to improve the performance of their systems. The goals of SQL tuning are simple:

■ **Remove unnecessary large-table full-table scans** Unnecessary full-table scans cause a huge amount of unnecessary I/O and can drag down an entire database. The tuning expert first evaluates the SQL in terms of the number of rows returned by the query. If the query returns less than 40 percent of the table rows in an ordered table, or 7 percent of the rows in an un-ordered table, the query can be tuned to use an index in lieu of the full-table scan. The most common tuning remedy for unnecessary full-table scans is adding indexes. Standard B-tree indexes can be added to tables, and bitmapped and function-based indexes can also eliminate full-table scans. The decision about removing a full-table scan should be based on a careful examination of the I/O costs of the index scan versus the costs of the full-table scan, factoring in the multiblock reads and possible parallel execution. In some cases an unnecessary full-table scan can be converted to an index scan by adding an index hint to the SQL statement.

- **Cache small-table full-table scans**   In cases where a full-table scan is the fastest access method, the tuning professional should ensure that a dedicated data buffer is available for the rows. In Oracle7, you can issue *"alter table xxx cache."* In Oracle8 and beyond, the small table can be cached by forcing it into the KEEP pool.

- **Verify optimal index usage**   This is especially important for improving the speed of queries. Oracle sometimes has a choice of indexes, and the tuning professional must examine each index and ensure that Oracle is using the proper index. This also includes the use of bitmapped and function-based indexes.

- **Verify optimal JOIN techniques**   Some queries will perform faster with NESTED LOOP joins, others with HASH joins.

These goals may seem deceptively simple, but these tasks make up 90 percent of SQL tuning, and they don't require a thorough understanding of the internals of Oracle SQL. Next let's look at a series of tools that we can use to tune SQL statements.

The SQL Tuning Toolkit

The scripts for this book are located at www.Osborne.com. The basic scripts that we will introduce in this chapter include the following:

- **access.sql**   This is a script that will explain all of the SQL from the library cache and create a series of reports showing the type of table access and table names for all SQL that currently exists in the library cache.

- *Access_report.sql*   This is a set of reports that will show various summaries of SQL activity. This includes reports on full-table scans, full-index scans, index range scans, and accesses by ROWID.

- *get_sql.sql* This is a simple script that will list all matching SQL statements from the library cache.

- *plan.sql* This is a generic script that is used to display the execution plan for any SQL statements.

We will be returning to these scripts many times during the course of this book, so this is a good time to become familiar with these scripts.

Reporting on SQL from the Library Cache

The Oracle DBA must always be on the lookout for new SQL statements that may appear in the library cache. This section explores a technique that runs the Oracle *explain plan* statement on all SQL statements in the library cache, analyzes all the execution plans, and provides reports on all table and index-access methods.

At first glance, it may be hard to fully appreciate the value of this technique and the information produced by the reports. But if your database has a large library cache, you can get some great insights into the internal behavior of the tables and indexes. The information also offers some great clues about what database objects you need to adjust. The reports are invaluable for the following database activities:

- **Identifying high-use tables and indexes** See what tables the database accesses the most frequently.

- **Identifying tables for caching** You can quickly find small, frequently accessed tables for placement in the KEEP pool (Oracle8) or for use with the CACHE option (Oracle7). You can enhance the technique to automatically cache tables when they meet certain criteria for the number of blocks and the number of accesses. (I automatically cache all tables with fewer than 200 blocks when a table has experienced more than 100 full-table scans.)

- **Identifying tables for row resequencing** You can locate large tables that have frequent index-range scans in order to resequence the rows, to reduce I/O.

- **Dropping unused indexes** You can reclaim space occupied by unused indexes. Studies have found that an Oracle database never uses more than a quarter of all indexes available or doesn't use them in the way for which they were intended.

- **Stopping full-table scans by adding new indexes** Quickly find the full-table scans that you can speed up by adding a new index to a table.

Here are the steps to execute the access.sql script:

1. Download the access.sql, *access_report.sql*, and plan.sql scripts.

2. Issue the following statements for the schema owner of your tables.

```
grant select on v_$sqltext to schema_owner;
grant select on v_$sqlarea to schema_owner;
grant select on v_$session to schema_owner;
grant select on v_$mystat to schema_owner;
```

3. Go into SQL*Plus, connect as the schema owner, and run access.sql.

You must be signed on as the schema owner in order to explain SQL statements with unqualified table names. Also, remember that you will get statistics only for the SQL statements that currently reside in your library cache. For very active databases, you may want to run this report script several times—it takes less than 10 minutes for most Oracle databases.

The access.sql Reports

As we noted, the access.sql script grabs all of the SQL in the library cache and stores it in a table called sqltemp. From this table, all of the SQL is explained and placed into a single PLAN table. This PLAN table is then queried.

You should then see a report similar to the one listed next. Let's begin by looking at the output this technique provides, and then we'll examine the method for producing the reports. For the purpose of illustration, let's break the report up into several sections. The first section shows the total number of SQL statements in the library cache, and the total number that could not be explained. Some statements cannot be explained because they do not indicate the owner of the table. If the value for statements that cannot be explained is high, then you are probably not connected as the proper schema owner when running the script.

Report from access.sql

```
PL/SQL procedure successfully completed.

Mon Jan 29
page 1
                        Total SQL found in library cache

    23907
```

```
Mon Jan 29
page 1
                    Total SQL that could not be explained

     1065
```

The Full-Table Scan Report

This is the first report from *access_report.sql*, and it is the most valuable report of all. Next we see all of the SQL statements that performed full-table scans, and the number of times that a full-table scan was performed. Also note the "C" and "K" columns. The "C" column indicates if an Oracle7 table is cached, and the "K" column indicates whether the Oracle8 table is assigned to the KEEP pool. As you will recall, small tables with full-table scans should be placed in the KEEP pool.

```
Mon Jan 29
page 1
                    full table scans and counts
```

OWNER	NAME	NUM_ROWS	C	K	BLOCKS	NBR_FTS
SYS	DUAL		N		2	97,237
SYSTEM	SQLPLUS_PRODUCT_PROFILE		N	K	2	16,178
DONALD	PAGE	3,450,209	N		932,120	9,999
DONALD	RWU_PAGE	434	N		8	7,355
DONALD	PAGE_IMAGE	18,067	N		1,104	5,368
DONALD	SUBSCRIPTION	476	N	K	192	2,087
DONALD	PRINT_PAGE_RANGE	10	N	K	32	874
ARSD	JANET_BOOKS	20	N		8	64
PERFSTAT	STATS$TAB_STATS		N		65	10

In the preceding report, we see several huge tables that are performing full-table scans (e.g., donald.page). For tables that have less than 200 blocks and are doing legitimate full-table scans, we will want to place these in the KEEP pool. The larger table full-table scans should also be investigated, and the legitimate large-table full-table scans should be parallelized with the ALTER TABLE PARALLEL DEGREE nn command.

An Oracle database invokes a large-table full-table scan when it cannot service a query through indexes. If you can identify large tables that experience excessive full-table scans, then you can take appropriate action to add indexes. This is especially important when you migrate from Oracle7 to Oracle8, because Oracle8 offers indexes that have built-in functions. Another cause of a full-table scan is when the cost-based optimizer decides that a full-table scan will be faster than an index-range scan. This occurs most commonly with small tables, which are ideal for caching in Oracle7 or placing in the KEEP pool in Oracle8. This full-table scan report is critical for two types of SQL tuning.

For a small-table full-table scan, cache the table by using the *alter table xxx cache* command, which will put the table rows at the most recently used end of the data buffer, thereby reducing disk I/O for the table. (Note that in Oracle8 you should place cached tables in the KEEP pool by issuing the *alter table xxx buffer_pool keep* command.)

For a large-table full-table scan, you can investigate the SQL statements to see if the use of indexes would eliminate the full-table scan. Again, the original source for all the SQL statements is in the SQLTEMP table. We will talk about the process of finding and explaining the individual SQL statements in the next section.

Next we see the index usage reports. These index reports are critical for the following areas of Oracle tuning:

- **Index usage** Ensuring that the application is actually using a new index. DBAs can now obtain empirical evidence that an index is actually being used after it has been created.

- **Row resequencing** Finding out which tables might benefit from row resequencing. Tables that have a large amount of index range scan activity will benefit from having the rows resequenced into the same order as the index. Resequencing can result in a tenfold performance improvement, depending on the row length. For details on row resequencing techniques, see Chapter 10.

Next, let's look at the index range scan report.

The Index Range Scan Report
Next we see the report for index range scans. The most common method of index access in Oracle is the index range scan. An index range scan is used when the SQL statement contains a restrictive clause that requires a sequential range of values that are indexes for the table.

 Mon Jan 29
page 1

                        Index range scans and counts

OWNER   TABLE_NAME   INDEX_NAME   TBL_BLOCKS
NBR_SCANS

--------- -------------------- -------------------- ------------ -----------
-

DONALD   ANNI_HIGHLIGHT   HL_PAGE_USER_IN_IDX   16
7,975

```
DONALD      ANNI_STICKY          ST_PAGE_USER_IN_IDX          8
7,296
DONALD      PAGEER               ISBN_SEQ_IDX               120
3,859
DONALD      TOC_ENTRY            ISBN_TOC_SEQ_IDX            40
2,830
DONALD      PRINT_HISTORY        PH_KEY_IDX                  32
1,836
DONALD      SUBSCRIPTION         SUBSC_ISBN_USER_IDX        192
210
ARSD        JANET_BOOK_RANGES    ROV_BK_RNG_BOOK_ID_I         8
170
PERFSTAT    STATS$SYSSTAT        STATS$SYSSTAT_PK           845
32
12 rows selected.
```

The Index Unique Scan Report

Here is a report that lists index unique scans, which occur when the Oracle database engine uses an index to retrieve a specific row from a table. The Oracle database commonly uses these types of "probe" accesses when it performs a join and probes another table for the join key from the driving table. This report is also useful for finding out those indexes that are used to identify distinct table rows, as opposed to indexes that are used to fetch a range of rows.

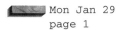Mon Jan 29
page 1

```
                         Index unique scans and counts

OWNER      TABLE_NAME           INDEX_NAME              NBR_SCANS
---------  -------------------- --------------------    ------------
DONALD     BOOK                 BOOK_ISBN                  44,606
DONALD     PAGEER                ISBN_SEQ_IDX              39,973
DONALD     BOOK                 BOOK_UNIQUE_ID              6,450
DONALD     ANNI_EAR             DE_PAGE_USER_IDX            5,339
DONALD     TOC_ENTRY            ISBN_TOC_SEQ_IDX            5,186
DONALD     PRINT_PERMISSIONS    PP_KEY_IDX                  1,836
DONALD     RDRUSER              USER_UNIQUE_ID_IDX          1,065
DONALD     CURRENT_LOGONS       USER_LOGONS_UNIQUE_I          637
ARSD       JANET_BOOKS          BOOKS_BOOK_ID_PK               54
DONALD     ERROR_MESSAGE        ERROR_MSG_IDX                  48
```

The Full-Index Scan Report

The next report shows all full-index scans. As you will recall, the Oracle optimizer will sometimes perform a full-index scan in lieu of a large sort in the TEMP tablespace. You will commonly see full-index scans in SQL that have the ORDER BY clause.

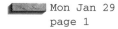

```
Mon Jan 29
page 1
                         Index full scans and counts

    OWNER       TABLE_NAME                INDEX_NAME                NBR_SCANS
    ---------   -------------------       --------------------      ------------
    DONALD      BOOK                      BOOK_ISBN                     2,295
    DONALD      PAGER                     ISBN_SEQ_IDX                    744
```

The Oracle database engine commonly uses full-index scans to avoid sorting. Say you have a customer table with an index on the *cust_nbr* column. The database could service the SQL command *select * from customer order by cust_nbr;;* in two ways:

■ It could perform a full-table scan and then sort the result set. The full-table scan could be performed very quickly with the *db_file_multiblock_read_count* parameter set, or the table access could be parallelized by using a parallel hint. However, the result set must then be sorted in the TEMP tablespace.

■ It could obtain the rows in customer-number order by reading the rows via the index, thus avoiding a sort.

Limitations of the access.sql Reports

The techniques for generating these reports are not as flawless as they may appear. Because the "raw" SQL statements must be explained in order to obtain the execution plans, you may not know the owner of the tables. One problem with native SQL is that the table names are not always qualified with the table owner. To ensure that all the SQL statements are completely explained, many DBAs sign on to Oracle and run the reports as the schema owner.

A future enhancement would be to issue the following undocumented command immediately before each SQL statement is explained so that any Oracle database user could run the reports:

```
Alter session set current_schema = 'table_owner';
```

This would change the schema owner immediately before explaining the SQL statement.

Now that we have covered the SQL reporting, let's move on to look at how the individual SQL statements are extracted and explained.

Conclusion

The purpose of this chapter is to introduce you to the benefits and challenges of Oracle SQL tuning and introduce some of the tools we will be using to easily tune SQL statements. As we proceed through this text, we will be looking at detailed techniques for ensuring that your database performs at optimal levels.

Oracle SQL tuning is one of the most rewarding activities in Oracle database tuning. There is nothing like the feeling of tuning a SQL statement and taking it from a two-hour execution time to a 20-second execution time. With the proper approach and diligence, the Oracle DBA can become the hero and dramatically improve the performance of the entire database.

CHAPTER
2

Overview of Oracle SQL Extensions

his chapter will investigate some of the SQL extensions that are
unique to Oracle. While the Oracle SQL implementation adheres to
the ANSI standard for the SQL languages, Oracle has added numerous
features to improve the productivity of SQL. While many of these
features are a significant departure from the ANSI standard for SQL,
there are numerous Oracle-centric extensions to SQL that greatly enhance the
usability of Oracle SQL as a development language. These SQL extensions can
be categorized into three general areas:

- **In-line views** In an exciting departure from the ANSI standard, Oracle
  allows queries to be substituted in the place of table names in the FROM
  clause. This non-ANSI extension to SQL is extremely useful when you need
  to compare ranges of summed table values in a single query.

- **Built-in functions (BIFs)** Oracle offers a wealth of built-in functions that will
  transform the display format of column values. These BIFs are most often used
  to transform DATE datatypes and to manipulate character columns.

- **Object-oriented extensions** Starting with Oracle8, Oracle enhanced SQL
  to allow for the use of abstract datatypes, nested tables, and repeating items
  within table columns.

Each of these areas improves the functionality of Oracle SQL but also impacts
the way that Oracle services the execution plans for these classes of statements. For
each of these areas, we will explore the syntax change to Oracle SQL and look at
how the Oracle professional can tune the statements for maximum efficiency. Let's
begin by looking at in-line views.

Oracle In-Line Views

In a radical departure from the SQL standard, Oracle allows a query to be substituted
in the place of a table name in the SQL *from* clause. This is a fascinating extension to
SQL because it allows for queries to be formed in a variety of exotic ways. It is also
mind-boggling because it is very difficult to imagine a result set being treated as a
table name in a SQL *from* clause.

To see how this works, let's start with a simple example. Here are two examples
of a simple SQL query, both of which count the number of customers in the Southern
region. The first query uses standard SQL:

```
select
    count(*)
from
```

```
       customer
where
    region= 'south';
```

This same query can be written with an in-line view:

```
select
    count(*)
from
    (select * from customer where region= 'south')
;
```

A common use for in-line views in Oracle SQL is to simplify complex queries by removing join operations and condensing several separate queries into a single query. The best example of the in-line view is the common Oracle DBA script that is used to show the amount of free space and used space within all Oracle tablespaces. Let's take a close look at this SQL to see how it works. Carefully note that the *from* clause in this SQL query specifies two subqueries that perform summations and grouping from two views, *dba_data_files*, and *dba_free_space*.

tsfree.sql

```
column "Tablespace" format a13
column "Used MB"      format 99,999,999
column "Free MB"      format 99,999,999
colimn "Total MB"     format 99,999,999
select
    fs.tablespace_name                          "Tablespace",
    (df.totalspace - fs.freespace)              "Used MB",
    fs.freespace                                "Free MB",
    df.totalspace                               "Total MB",
    round(100 * (fs.freespace / df.totalspace)) "Pct. Free"
from
    (select
       tablespace_name,
       round(sum(bytes) / 1048576) TotalSpace
    from
       dba_data_files
    group by
       tablespace_name
    ) df,
    (select
       tablespace_name,
       round(sum(bytes) / 1048576) FreeSpace
    from
       dba_free_space
```

```
group by
   tablespace_name
) fs
where
   df.tablespace_name = fs.tablespace_name;
```

This SQL quickly compares the sum of the total space within each tablespace to the sum of the free space within each tablespace. Here is a sample of the output:

 SQL> @tsfree

Tablespace	Used MB	Free MB	Total MB	Pct. Free
RANNOD	6	44	50	88
RANNOX	5	45	50	90
RBOOKX	5	0	5	0
SGROUPD	2	8	10	80
SGROUPX	2	8	10	80
BRBS	68	32	100	32
RDRUSERD	2	18	20	90

Basically, this query needs to compare the sum of total space within each tablespace with the sum of the free space within each tablespace. In ANSI standard SQL, it is quite difficult in a single query to compare two result sets that are summed together (see Figure 2-1). Without the use of an in-line view, several separate SQL queries would need to be written, one to compute the sums from each view and another to compare the intermediate result sets.

This use of in-line views becomes even more convoluted when we remember that the *dba_free_space* and *dba_data_files* views are built upon underlying internal Oracle structures. Regardless of the complexity, the *tsfree.sql* script runs very quickly to get the tablespace report. The execution plan for this simple query is mind-boggling, as shown in the next listing. You will learn about interpreting the output from Oracle execution plans in Chapter 4, but this listing is shown so you can appreciate the complexity of the Oracle optimizer in determining the best execution plan for this query. Obviously, the Oracle optimizer is performing a very sophisticated analysis of the query to arrive at this access method.

OPERATION
```
------------------------------------------------------------------------
OPTIONS                       OBJECT_NAME                     POSITION
----------------------------  ----------------------------  ----------
SELECT STATEMENT
                                                                 819
   MERGE JOIN
                                                                   1
```

```
          VIEW
                                                          1
            SORT
GROUP BY                                                  1
              VIEW
                              DBA_FREE_SPACE              1
                UNION-ALL
                                                          1
                  NESTED LOOPS
                                                          1
                    NESTED LOOPS
                                                          1
                      TABLE ACCESS
FULL                          TS$                         1
                      TABLE ACCESS
CLUSTER                       FET$                        2
                  INDEX
UNIQUE SCAN                   I_FILE2                      2
                    NESTED LOOPS
                                                          2
                      NESTED LOOPS
                                                          1
                      TABLE ACCESS
FULL                          TS$                         1
                        FIXED TABLE
FIXED INDEX #1                X$KTFBFE                     2
                  INDEX
UNIQUE SCAN                   I_FILE2                      2
        SORT
JOIN                                                      2
          VIEW
                                                          1
            SORT
GROUP BY                                                  1
              VIEW
                              DBA_DATA_FILES              1
                UNION-ALL
                                                          1
                  NESTED LOOPS
                                                          1
                    NESTED LOOPS
                                                          1
                      FIXED TABLE
FULL                          X$KCCFN                      1
                      TABLE ACCESS
BY INDEX ROWID               FILE$                        2
                        INDEX
UNIQUE SCAN                   I_FILE1                      1
                      TABLE ACCESS
CLUSTER                       TS$                         2
                  INDEX
```

```
UNIQUE SCAN                          I_TS#                    1
                NESTED LOOPS
                                                              2
                    NESTED LOOPS
                                                              1
                      NESTED LOOPS
                                                              1
                        FIXED TABLE
FULL                                 X$KCCFN                  1
                      TABLE ACCESS
BY INDEX ROWID                       FILE$                    2
                    INDEX
UNIQUE SCAN                          I_FILE1                  1
                    FIXED TABLE
FIXED INDEX #1                       X$KTFBHC                 2
                    TABLE ACCESS
CLUSTER                              TS$                      2
                  INDEX
UNIQUE SCAN                          I_TS#                    1
```

Again, it is not necessary to fully understand this execution plan other than to appreciate all of the complex work that the SQL optimizer has done to formulate the best execution plan for this query.

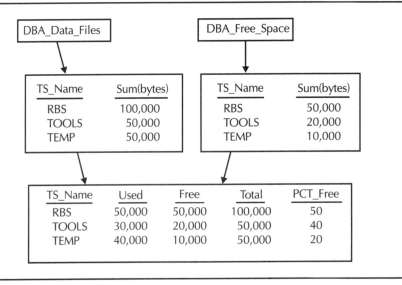

FIGURE 2-1. *Comparing the sums of two grouped queries with SQL*

Next, let's look at another class of extensions to Oracle SQL that has been with us since the earliest release of Oracle. By using built-in functions, Oracle SQL has been extended to allow for the easy manipulation of column data.

Oracle Built-in Functions

Oracle offers a wealth of built-in functions (BIFs) that are used to transform table column data. SQL developers and programmers find these functions extremely useful because they can avoid having to perform cumbersome translations of incoming column values from Oracle. In many cases, Oracle BIFs are used to translate column data into the appropriate datatype (e.g., *update customer set date_of_birth = to_date('03-25-1956','MM-DD-YYYY');*), and BIFs are also used to reformat nondisplayable native datatypes such as DATE into readable formats. It is also common to use Oracle BIFs inside SQL that queries for table values.

While there are many dozens of Oracle BIFs for everything from date manipulation to string conversion, we will focus on some of the most common BIFs used in SQL queries and see how they simplify the query and affect the execution plan for the SQL. We will also examine the impact of BIFs on the execution plans for SQL statements and see how function-based indexing can improve the speed of these queries.

Here is a list of some frequently used Oracle SQL BIFs:

- **to_char** The *to_char* function is especially useful for translating DATE datatypes and converting numeric columns to character representations.

- **upper** The *upper* function is often used in queries that search text columns and ensure that retrievals of case-sensitive data are properly serviced.

- **lower** The *lower* function is used to convert text to a lowercase representation and is quite useful when searching for strings in text.

- **substr** The *substr* function is used to extract substrings in a large character column. This is commonly used to extract subsets from large character datatype columns such as subsets of telephone numbers.

- **decode** The *decode* function is used to translate values in a SQL statement from a cryptic abbreviation to a readable value. For example, the *decode* function can translate two-digit State names into the full name of the State.

From the perspective of Oracle SQL tuning, you must remember that these BIFs will often cause the SQL optimizer to perform a full-table scan unless a function-based index is created to match the BIF.

The most common example of an Oracle BIF is the use of the *to_char* function to translate a column with a DATE datatype. For example, the following query will display the number of STATSPACK snapshots that occurred in the month of January.

```
select
    count(*)
from
    perfstat.stats$snapshot
where
    to_char(snap_time,'Mon') = 'Jan'
;
```

If we were using a generic index on the *snap_time* column, the *to_char* function would not be able to utilize the DATE index. However, with the use of built-in functions, an index can be built on *to_char(snap_time,'Mon')* and the SQL query could avoid a full-table scan.

BIFs and Function-Based Indexes

In almost all cases, the use of a BIF in a SQL query will cause a full-table scan of the target table. To avoid this problem, many Oracle DBAs will create corresponding indexes that make use of function-based indexes. If a corresponding function-based index matches the built-in function of the query, Oracle will be able to service the query with an index range scan, thereby avoiding a potentially expensive full-table scan.

To illustrate, let's take a simple example. We start by running the *access.sql* script to explain all of the SQL in our library cache. The first report from *access.sql* shows all full-table scans and indicates the table size in rows as well as data blocks.

```
              Full table scans and counts
       Note that "?" indicates in the table is cached.

OWNER         NAME                     NUM_ROWS C K   BLOCKS  NBR_FTS
------------- ------------------------ -------- - - -------- --------
SYS           DUAL                              N        2        412
SYSTEM        SQLPLUS_PRODUCT_PROFILE           N        2        344
DONALD        CUSTOMER                  461,232 N     71,192       89
```

From this report we see that the customer table is quite large (71,192 blocks) and has experienced 89 full-table scans. To be pragmatic, we will assume that the Oracle DBA has no knowledge of the SQL and must locate the statement from the library cache. Our next step is to see if these full-table scans are legitimate or if the query speed could be improved by using a function-based index.

We do this by running *get_sql.sql* and checking for SQL that references the subscription table and has a value of 89 for *executions*.

Get_sql.sql

```
set lines 2000;

select
   sql_text,
   disk_reads,
   executions,
   parse_calls
from
   v$sqlarea
where
   lower(sql_text) like '% customer %'
order by
   disk_reads desc
;
```

From the output of this script, we can easily identify the SQL that has 89 executions and we can cut and paste this SQL to get the execution plan. Here is the SQL statement that we extracted from the output of the *get_sql.sql* script. After examining the SQL, we clearly see that it is accessing a customer by converting the customer name to uppercase using the *upper* BIF.

```
select
   c.customer_name,
   o.order_date
from
   customer c,
   order    o
where
upper(c.customer_name) = upper(:v1)
and
   c.cust_nbr = o.cust_nbr
;
```

Running the *explain plan* utility confirms our suspicion that this query is responsible for the full-table scans. Here is the output from running the *plan.sql* script after explaining the statement:

```
OPTIONS                           OBJECT_NAME                       POSITION
------------------------------    ------------------------------    ----------
SELECT STATEMENT
                                                                           4
   NESTED LOOPS
                                                                           1
     TABLE ACCESS
FULL                              CUSTOMER                                 1
```

```
    TABLE ACCESS
BY INDEX ROWID                  ORDER                                  2
        INDEX
RANGE SCAN                      CUST_NBR_IDX                           1
```

The *table access full customer* option confirms our suspicion that the BIF has caused a full-table scan. Since we know that a matching function-based index may change the execution plan, we add a function-based index on *upper(customer_name)*. Note that it is often dangerous to add indexes to tables, because the execution plans of many queries may change. However, we do not have this problem with a function-based index, because Oracle will only use this type of index when the query uses a matching BIF.

```
create index
    upper_cust_name_idx
on
    customer
    (upper(customer_name))
    tablespace customer
    pctfree 10
    storage (initial 128k next 128k maxextents 2147483645 pctincrease 0);
```

Now we can re-explain the SQL and see that the full-table scan has been replaced by a index range scan on our new function-based index. For this query, we have changed the execution time from 45 seconds to less than 2 seconds.

```
OPERATION
--------------------------------------------------------------------------
----
OPTIONS                         OBJECT_NAME                       POSITION
------------------------------  ------------------------------  ----------
SELECT STATEMENT
                                                                       5
  NESTED LOOPS
                                                                       1
    TABLE ACCESS
BY INDEX ROWID                  CUSTOMER                               1
        INDEX
RANGE SCAN                      CUST_NBR_IDX                           1
    TABLE ACCESS
BY INDEX ROWID                  ORDER                                  2
        INDEX
RANGE SCAN                      UPPER_CUST_NAME_IDX                    1
```

This simple example serves to illustrate the foremost SQL tuning rule for BIFs. Whenever a BIF is used in a SQL statement, a function-based index must be created.

Next let's look at another popular extension that allows Oracle to support some object-oriented constructs. Starting with Oracle8, Oracle has made a commitment to adding object-oriented extension to the database, and Oracle also was required to make corresponding changes to Oracle SQL.

Oracle SQL and Object-Oriented Extensions

The movement of Oracle toward object orientation resulted in some significant changes to Oracle SQL syntax. As the Oracle DBA charged with tuning, it is important that you understand these extensions to Oracle SQL syntax and see how they affect performance. The object-oriented extensions of Oracle SQL fall into three areas.

■ **Abstract datatypes**   Oracle8 allows for the creation of abstract datatypes (sometime known as user-defined datatypes). These datatypes greatly simplify Oracle table structure and help to create uniformity within a database.

■ **Repeating columns within Oracle tables**   Oracle8 now allows non–first normal form tables with repeating groups of *varray* data items within a single row.

■ **Nested tables and SQL**   Oracle8 introduced a new data structure whereby a column in a table has a pointer to a nested table.

We will take a closer look at each of these constructs and see how Oracle SQL has been extended to manage this new functionality.

Abstract Datatypes and Oracle SQL

Unlike pre-object releases of Oracle (Oracle7), which only provided for primitive datatypes such as INT and VARCHAR, Oracle8 allows for the creation of abstract datatypes (ADTs). Oracle also calls them user-defined datatypes or UDTs, and the Oracle documentation calls these constructs by both names.

Oracle database designers are now beginning to realize that the ability to create abstract datatypes can greatly simplify their Oracle database design. Although abstract datatypes have been used for decades within programming languages, they have been slow to catch on within the Oracle8 database.

As you may know, Oracle8 implements support for abstract data typing by extending Oracle SQL syntax to allow for a *create type* definition. At the most basic level, abstract datatypes are nothing more than a collection of smaller, basic datatypes that can be treated as a single entity (see Figure 2-2).

Customer_Name		Customer_Address			
First_Name	Last_Name	Street	City	State	ZIP

FIGURE 2-2. *An abstract datatype*

There are several reasons why ADTs are useful within an Oracle8 database:

- **Encapsulation** Because each abstract datatype exists as a complete entity, it includes the data definitions, default values, and value constraints. Adding abstract datatypes ensures uniformity and consistency across the whole Oracle database. Once defined, an abstract datatype may participate in many other abstract datatypes, such that the same logical datatype always has the same definition, default values, and value constraints, regardless of where it appears in the database.

- **Reusability** As a hierarchy of common data structures is assembled, these can be reused within many definitions, saving coding time and ensuring uniformity. For example, a datatype called *full_mailing_address_type* may be included in a *customer* table, an *employee* table, and any other table that requires a person's full address.

- **Flexibility** The ability to create real-world representations of data allows the Oracle database object designer to model the real world and create robust datatypes that can be uniformly applied to the design.

One of the shortcomings of Oracle7 databases was the inability to model grouped data columns. For example, if we want to select all of the address information for a customer, we are required to select and manipulate *street_address, city_address,* and *zip_code* as three separate column statements in our SQL. With abstract data typing, we can create a new datatype called *full_mailing_address_type,* and manipulate it as if it were an atomic datatype. While this may seem like an advanced new feature, it is interesting to note that prerelational databases supported this construct, and the ancient COBOL language (circa A.D. 1959) had ways to create data "types" that were composed of subtypes. For example, in COBOL, we could define a full address as follows:

```
05   CUSTOMER-ADDRESS.
        07 STREET-ADDRESS       PIC X(80).
        07 CITY-ADDRESS         PIC X(80).
        07 ZIP-CODE             PIC X(5).
```

We can then manipulate the *customer-address* as if it were an individual entity:

```
MOVE CUSTOMER-ADDRESS TO PRINT-REC.
MOVE SPACES TO CUSTOMER-ADDRESS.
```

Fortunately, Oracle8 allows us to do the same type of grouping with their new create type syntax:

```
CREATE OR REPLACE TYPE full_mailing_address_type AS OBJECT
( Street         VARCHAR2(80),
  City           VARCHAR2(80),
  State          CHAR(2),
  Zip            VARCHAR2(10) );
```

Once it is defined, we can treat *full_mailing_address_type* as a valid datatype and use it to create tables:

```
CREATE TABLE
    customer
    (
      full_name                 full_name_type,
      full_address              full_mailing_address_type,
    );
```

Now that the Oracle table is defined, we can reference *full_mailing_address_type* in our SQL just as if it were a primitive datatype:

```
insert into
    customer
```

```
values (
    full_name_type('ANDREW','S.','BURLESON'),
    full_mailing_address_type('123 1st st','Minot','ND','74635');
```

Next, let's select from this table. Here you see a very different output than from an ordinary *select* statement:

```
SQL> select * from customer;

FULL_NAME(FIRST_NAME, MI, LAST_NAME)
-------------------------------------
FULL_ADDRESS(STREET, CITY, STATE, ZIP)
---------------------------------------------------------------------------
FULL_NAME_TYPE('Andrew', 'S', 'Burleson')
FULL_MAILING_ADDRESS_TYPE('123 1st st', 'Minot', 'ND', '74635')
```

Again, the point of this exercise is to show the difference in syntax for this new construct. The execution plans for these ADTs will be the same as for any other intrinsic datatype, and the introduction of ADTs does not have any effect on SQL performance.

Next let's look at the most revolutionary change to Oracle8 SQL, the ability to place repeating groups within a table row.

Violating the Relational Rules— Lists of Repeating Data Items

For many years, the idea of repeating data items within an object has been repugnant to relational database designers. The foremost tenet of relational theory dictated that the removal of repeating data items was the very first step toward a clean data model. During normalization, the removal of repeating groups in a relation was the very first step in relational database design, and a table without any repeating values was said to be in first normal form (1NF). Hence, the reintroduction of repeating values into Oracle8 tables is said to be a non–first normal form table, or 0NF for short. Oracle8 implemented repeating groups within tables by allowing a *varray* datatype.

In fact, the widespread adoption of non–first normal form datatypes in Oracle and other relational databases caused C.J. Date to reconcile his definition of the relational data model. Date introduced a new concept into the relational model called a "set," to allow for 0NF relations to fit into the relational paradigm.

However, there are some rules when deciding to introduce a repeating group into an Oracle8 table:

■ The repeating data items should be small in size.

- The data item should be static and rarely changed.

- The repeating data should never need to be queried as a "set."

You should note that Oracle has provided us with two ways to introduce repeating groups in a table design. We can either use the *varray* construct or a nested table. While both *varray* tables and nested tables serve the same purpose, they are completely different in terms of internal structures and SQL syntax.

There are several differences between nested tables and *varray* tables, and the characteristics of the data determine which should be implemented.

- **Number of repeating groups**   Nested tables can have an infinite number of subordinate rows, whereas *varrays* have a maximum size. Hence, small numbers of repeating groups normally utilize *varray* tables.

- **Element control**   Individual elements can be deleted from a nested table, but not from a *varray*. Therefore, nested tables are best for highly dynamic data, while *varray* tables are best for static repeating groups such as prior employer information.

- **Internal Storage**   *Varray* rows are stored by Oracle in-line (in the same tablespace), whereas nested table data is stored out-of-line in a stored table, which is a system-generated database table associated with the nested table.

- **Sequencing**   Nested tables do not retain their ordering and subscripts, whereas *varray* rows will always retain their original sequences.

- **Index capabilities**   Nested table entries support indexes, while *varray* rows do not support indexes. Hence, repeating items that require index-based SQL should always be implemented with nested tables.

To show how repeating groups are implemented, let's use a simple example. Suppose that we are designing an employee database and we notice that every employee has a history of prior employers. Since we only need to keep the employer's name, it does not make sense to create a subordinate table to represent this structure (see Figure 2-3).

Since the *employer_name* column is the only prior employer information that we need to keep, we can simplify the Oracle table structure and remove an extra table join by including the previous employer names in the *employee* table. Oracle provides a construct that allows us to embed the names of all prior employers within a single table row (see Figure 2-4).

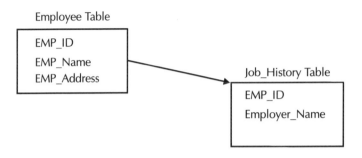

FIGURE 2-3. *Normalization of repeating groups into subordinate tables*

Varray Tables

Before Oracle8, we would need to represent repeating groups in a table in a very clumsy and nonelegant fashion. Here is the syntax we use to create the table in Oracle7:

```
create table employee (
    full_name               full_mailing_address_type,
    last_name               varchar(40),
    previous_employer_one   varchar(40),
    previous_employer_two   varchar(40),
    previous_employer_three varchar(40)
);
```

Employee Table		Repeating VARRAY		
EMP_ID	EMP_Name	Prev_EMP	Prev_EMP	Prev_EMP
123	Jones	IBM	Oracle	AT&T
124	Smith	Revlon	TUSC	
126	Doll	CNN	ABC	NBC

FIGURE 2-4. *Adding a repeating group to an Oracle8 table*

We begin by creating a Oracle type to hold the repeating group of prior employers:

```
CREATE OR REPLACE TYPE
    employer_name
AS OBJECT
(e_name varchar(40))
;
CREATE OR REPLACE TYPE
   prior_employer_name_arr
AS
   VARRAY(10) OF employer_name;
```

Next, we create the *employee* type, embedding our *varray* of prior employers:

```
CREATE OR REPLACE TYPE employee AS OBJECT
(
    last_name                varchar(40),
    full_address             full_mailing_address_type,
    prior_employers          prior_employer_name_arr
);
```

Next, we create the *emp* table, using the *employee* type.

```
SQL> create table emp of employee;
Table Created.
```

Now we insert rows into the object table. Note the use of the *full_mailing_address_type* reference for the ADT and the specification of the repeating groups of previous employers.

```
insert into emp
values
(
   'Burleson',
   full_mailing_address_type('7474 Airplane Ave.','Rocky
Ford','NC','27445'),
   prior_employer_name_arr(
      employer_name('IBM'),
      employer_name('ATT'),
      employer_name('CNN')
   )
);
insert into emp
values
(
```

```
          'Lavender',
          full_mailing_address_type('7474 Bearpond Ave.','Big Lick','NC','17545'),
          prior_employer_name_arr(
               employer_name('Oracle'),
               employer_name('Sybase'),
               employer_name('Computer Associates')
          )
);
```

Next, we perform the select SQL. Note that we can select all of the repeating groups with a single reference to the *prior_employers* column.

```
select
     p.prior_employers
from
     emp p
where
     p.last_name = 'Burleson';

PRIOR_EMPLOYERS(E_NAME)
-------------------------------------------------------------------------------
----
PRIOR_EMPLOYER_NAME_ARR(EMPLOYER_NAME('IBM'), EMPLOYER_NAME('ATT'),
EMPLOYER_NAM
E('CNN'))
```

This output can be difficult to interpret because of the nature of the repeating groups. In the next example, we use a new BIF called table that will flatten out the repeating groups, redisplaying the information:

```
column l_name      heading "Last Name"      format a20;

SELECT
     emp.last_name               l_name,
     prior_emps.*
FROM
     emp                         emp,
     table(p.prior_employers) prior_emps
WHERE
     p.last_name = 'Burleson';
```

Here we see a flattened output from the query, and the single information is replicated onto each table row:

```
Last Name              E_NAME
-------------------- ---------------------------------------
Burleson               IBM
```

```
Burleson              ATT
Burleson              CNN
```

Execution Plans for varray Tables

The execution plans for the preceding simple query reveal some of the new access methods that were added to Oracle SQL to manage objects. Note the *pickler fetch* and *collection iterator* operations. The pickler code is very new in Oracle8, and there are several reported memory leak issues with pickler fetches. As for performance, the collection iterator operation is used to extract the embedded repeating group from the row. Remember, rows with *varray* items are stored in-line, so that a fetch for the data block that contains the row will also contain the repeating groups. Hence, the performance of tables with *varray* columns is comparable to standard row select statements.

```
OPERATION
-------------------------------------------------------------------------------
----
OPTIONS                         OBJECT_NAME                        POSITION
------------------------------- ----------------------------- ----------
SELECT STATEMENT

                                                                        33

   NESTED LOOPS

                                                                         1

     TABLE ACCESS
FULL                            EMP                                      1

     COLLECTION ITERATOR
PICKLER FETCH                                                            2
```

Next, let's continue with our discussion of repeating groups and look at a unique object-oriented concept that is exclusive to Oracle8. A *nested table* is a special construct that allows for another table to be embedded within a master table.

Nesting of Tables

Now let's take this concept one step further and consider how Oracle implements a nested table. Unlike a table with embedded repeating groups, the nested table creates a subordinate table structure to give the appearance of embedding (see Figure 2-5). Internally, we see embedded pointers that are used to navigate between the master table and the nested table.

In this example, we will use a nested table to represent a repeating group for previous addresses. Whereas a person is likely to have a small number of previous

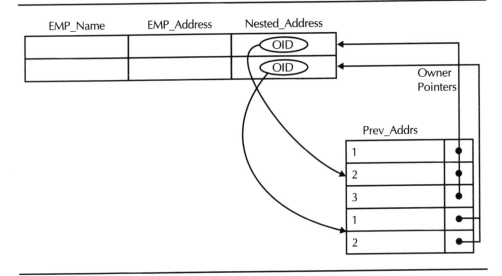

FIGURE 2-5.   *A nested table with pointer links*

employers, most people have a larger number of previous addresses. First, we create a type using our *full_mailing_address_type:*

```
create type prev_addrs as object
(
    prior_address        full_mailing_address_type
);
```

Next, we created the nested object:

```
create type nested_address as table of prev_addrs;
```

Now, we create the parent table with the nested table:

```
create table
    emp1
(
    last_name        char(40),
    current_address  full_mailing_address_type,
    prev_address     nested_address
)
    nested table prev_address store as nested_prev_address return as locator
;
```

Although a nested table appears as a part of the master table, internally, it is a separate table. Hence, we see the *store as* clause to allow the DBA to give the nested table a specific name. In this example, the *nested_prev_address* subordinate table can be indexed just like any other Oracle table. Also note the use of the "return as locator" SQL syntax. In many cases, returning the entire nested table at query time can be time-consuming. The use of the locator enables Oracle to use the pointer structures to dereference the location of the nested rows. As you may know from programming, a pointer dereference happens when you take a pointer to an object and ask the program to display the data that the pointer is pointing to. In other words, if we have a pointer to a customer row, we can dereference the object ID and see the data for that customer. The link to the nested tables uses an Oracle object ID (OID) instead of a traditional foreign key value.

Performance of SQL Object Extensions

Since this book is focused on SQL tuning, we need to take a look at the SQL performance ramifications of using object extensions. Overall, the performance of ADT tables is the same as that of any other Oracle table, but we do see significant performance differences when implementing *varray* tables and nested tables. Here is a summary of the significant features of the Oracle SQL object extensions.

- **Tables with Abstract Data Types**   Creating user-defined datatypes can greatly simplify the design of an Oracle database while also providing uniform data definitions for common data items. There is no downside for SQL performance, and the only downside for SQL syntax is the requirements that all references to ADTs be fully qualified.

- *Varray* **tables**   *Varray* tables have the benefit of avoiding costly SQL joins, and the ability to maintain the order of the *varray* items, based upon the sequence when they were stored. However, the longer row length of *varray* tables causes full-table scans to run longer, and the items inside the *varray* cannot be indexed. More important, *varrays* cannot be used when the number of repeating items is unknown or very large.

- **Nested tables**   Nested tables have the advantage of being indexed, and the repeating groups are separated into another table so as not to degrade the performance of full-table scans. Nested tables also allow for an infinite number of repeating groups. However, it sometimes takes longer to dereference the OID to get to the nested table entries than in ordinary SQL tables join operations, and most Oracle experts see no compelling benefit to choosing nested tables over traditional table joins.

Conclusion

Oracle has provided a wealth of extensions to SQL in order to improve the productivity of the language and improve the ability to model complex objects. The main point of this chapter is that these extensions can often change the execution plan for a SQL statement and special care must be taken to index Oracle tables so that SQL with BIFs and other extensions will be able to quickly access the table rows.

Next, we are going to go deeper into Oracle SQL internals and investigate the workings of the SQL optimizer. It is only with an in-depth knowledge of the SQL optimizer that you will be able to successfully tune a SQL statement.

CHAPTER
3

Understanding SQL
Execution

his chapter will focus on the internal processes that occur when Oracle receives and executes a SQL statement. We will examine the process of parsing the SQL statement, generating the execution plan, and executing the SQL statement. The four phases in SQL are parsing, binding, executing, and fetching the result set. Let's take a closer look at how an Oracle SQL statement is transformed within the library cache.

1. **Parse the SQL**   During the parse phase, the Oracle software searches for the SQL statement in the shared pool, checks the syntax and semantics, and in some cases, rewrites the query.

   - **Check security**   This phase validates the security rules to ensure that the requestor is authorized to view the data. This involves comparing the privileges of the user against the names of the tables in the SQL.

   - **Check SQL syntax**   This phase checks the syntax of the SQL statement to ensure that the statement is properly formatted.

   - **Optional query rewrite**   In certain cases Oracle will rewrite the query, changing table names or replacing literals with host variables before passing the SQL to the optimizer.

2. **Execute the SQL**   This phase involves the creation of the execution plan and the actual fetching of the table data.

   - **Generate the execution plan**   The generator accepts the parsed SQL and passes it to the SQL optimizer. The optimizer examines the SQL and the data dictionary and generates the internal execution plan. This plan is machine-level code that makes the required API calls to retrieve the data from disk. Oracle has numerous access methods to choose from when deciding how to service a query, and the optimizer is programmed to choose the access method that will either maximize speed or minimize computing resources.

   - **Bind the execution plan**   The bind process scans the SQL statement for bind variables and then assigns a value to each variable.

   - **Execute the execution plan**   The Oracle database applies the parse tree to the data buffers and performs all necessary disk I/O.

   - **Fetch the result rows**   This step retrieves rows for a SELECT statement during the fetch phase. Each fetch retrieves multiple rows, using an array fetch.

3. **Present the result set**   This phase performs all required sorting and translates and reformats all column data.

   ■ **Sort the result set**   This phase involves satisfying all *order by* or *group by* conditions in the SQL statement.

4. **Translate column data**   This phase involves reformatting and translating any column data that has been transformed with a BIF. We will go into greater detail on some of these steps as we move through this chapter, but our focus will be on SQL parsing and the generation of the execution plan. Let's begin by examining the parsing phase.

Parsing the SQL Statement

When a request is made by a program to retrieve data columns, Oracle receives the SQL statement and places it into the library cache areas of the shared pool. Once the statement is in the shared pool, Oracle invokes the parser to validate the SQL syntax. The basic purpose of the SQL parse is to validate the structure of the SQL syntax, verify that the user is authorized to view the data, and in some cases, reformulate the query to make it more efficient for the optimizer.

The process of parsing the SQL statement is illustrated in Figure 3-1.

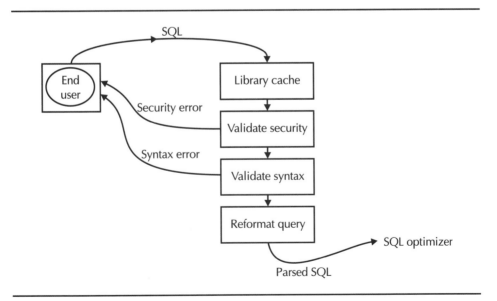

FIGURE 3-1.   *The parsing of a SQL statement*

While the basic process of parsing SQL is very straightforward, there are several optimal processes that will rewrite a SQL statement to make a faster execution plan.

- **Query_rewrite_enabled** This initialization parameter directs Oracle to rewrite data warehouse queries to prevent re-summarization of large volumes of data.

- **Cursor_sharing** When set to FORCE, this initialization parameter directs Oracle to replace literal values in SQL statements with host variables.

Oracle has recognized that SQL statements can sometimes be restructured to allow the optimizer to generate a more favorable execution plan. Let's take a closer look at these rewrite features.

Query Rewrite

Oracle has a special feature called *materialized views* that can greatly speed-up data warehouse queries. In a materialized view, a summary table is created from a base table, and all queries that perform a similar summation against the base table will be transparently rewritten to reference the pre-built summary table.

What follows is a simple example. We begin by creating a materialized view that sums sales data.

```
create materialized view
    sum_sales
build immediate
refresh complete
enable query rewrite
as
select
    product_nbr,
    sum(sales) sum_sales
from
    sales;
```

Now, when we have any query that summarizes sales, that query will be dynamically rewritten to reference the summary table.

```
alter session set query_rewrite_enabled=true;
set autotrace on

select
    sum(sales)
from
    sales
;
```

In the execution plan for this query we see that the *sum_sales* table is being referenced.

```
Execution Plan
----------------------------------------------------------
   0      SELECT STATEMENT Optimizer=CHOOSE (Cost=1 Card=1 Bytes=83)
   1    0   SORT (AGGREGATE)
   2    1     TABLE ACCESS (FULL) OF 'SUM_SALES' (Cost=1 Card=423
Bytes=5342)
```

NOTE
If you use bind variables in a query, the query will be not be rewritten to use materialized views even if you have enabled query rewrite.

Once the query rewrite feature is enabled, you can use standard SQL hints to force the SQL parser to rewrite the query.

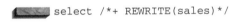
```
select /*+ REWRITE(sales)*/
...
```

As Oracle SQL evolves and becomes more sophisticated, there will be more cases where the SQL parser will rewrite queries into a more efficient form. Next, let's look at a method for making literal SQL reusable inside the library cache.

Using cursor_sharing in Oracle8*i* and Oracle9*i*

Cursor_sharing is a new initialization parameter in Oracle8*i* (8.1.6) that is designed to help manage the clutter problems with nonsharable SQL. *Cursor_sharing* can take the following values:

- **force**   The FORCE option forces statements that may differ in some literals but are otherwise identical to share a cursor, unless the literals affect the meaning of the statement. This is achieved by replacing literals with system-generated bind variables and causes increased sharing of literal SQL.

- **exact** (the default value)   The exact parameter causes only identical SQL statements to share a cursor. This is the standard pre-Oracle8*i* method.

When *cursor_sharing* is set to *force,* Oracle adds an extra layer of parsing that identifies statements as equivalent if they differ only in the values of literals, hashing them to identical library cache objects. You will see that under the right circumstances this setting can help solve the performance problems of literal SQL.

CAUTION
Oracle technical support states that cursor_sharing *should be set to* force *only when the risk of suboptimal plans is outweighed by the improvements in cursor sharing. Forcing cursor sharing among similar (but not identical) statements can have unexpected results in some DSS applications and in applications using stored outlines.*

Setting *cursor_sharing=force* may be worth considering if your system has these characteristics:

■ Are there a large number of statements in the shared pool that differ only in the values of their literals?

■ Is the response time low due to a very high number of library cache misses (i.e., hard parses and library cache latch contention)?

In cases where the DBA has added *cursor_sharing=force,* this directive has indeed made the SQL reusable, dramatically reducing the strain on the shared pool. The downside is Oracle's warning that some SQL can get suboptimal execution plans.

Oracle9*i* Enhancements to Cursor Sharing
A new feature in Oracle9*i* allows the CBO to change execution plans even when optimizer plan stability is used. This is called "peeking" and allows the CBO to change execution plans when the value of a bind variable would cause a significant change to the execution plan for the SQL.

To illustrate, consider a simple example of an index on a *region* column of a *customer* table. The region column has four values, *north, south, east* and *west.* The data values for the *region* column are highly skewed with 90% of the values in the south region. Hence, the CBO would be faster performing a full-table scan when *south* is specified, and an index range scan when *east, west,* or *north* is specified.

When using cursor sharing, the CBO changes any literal values in the SQL to bind variables. Hence, this statement would be changed as follows:

```
select
    customer_stuff
from
    customer
where
    region = 'west'
;
```

The transformation replaces the literal west with a host variable:

```
select
    customer_stuff
from
    customer
where
    region = ':var1'
;
```

In Oracle9*i*, the CBO "peeks" at the values of user-defined bind variables on the first invocation of a cursor. This lets the optimizer determine the selectivity of the *where* clause operator, and change the execution plan whenever the *south* value appears in the SQL.

This enhancement greatly improves the performance of cursor sharing when a bind variable is used against a highly skewed column.

Techniques to Reduce SQL Parsing

One of the goals of SQL tuning is to ensure that all preparsed SQL statements are reusable. Remember, to be reusable, an incoming SQL statement must exactly match a preparsed SQL statement in the library cache. Even small variations in SQL syntax will cause Oracle to reparse the SQL statement. The *v$sql.executions* column can be used to see the number of times a SQL statement has been reused. There are several techniques that can be used to ensure that all SQL is reusable.

■ **Place all SQL inside stored procedures**   When all SQL is encapsulated inside stored procedures, and the stored procedures are placed into packages, all SQL can be guaranteed to be identical.

■ **Avoid literal values in SQL**   Any SQL statement that contains embedded literal values is highly unlikely to be reused (e.g., *select * from sales where name = 'JONES';*). These non-reusable statements can fill the library cache with non-reusable SQL statements. The solution is to encourage all developers to use host variables in all SQL.

Next, let's look at the details on how Oracle generates the execution plan for a SQL statement.

Generating the Execution Plan

Because Oracle SQL is a declarative data access language, the SQL statement does not specify the navigation path to service the request. While using SQL as a purely declarative language is a great goal, in practice Oracle has found that hints are sometimes required to ensure that the optimizer generates an optimal execution plan. The job of the Oracle optimizer is to determine the fastest and most efficient way to service the query. When we talk about optimizing a query, you need to remember that Oracle makes a distinction between the speed of a query and the efficiency of a query. Oracle has two optimizer goals. Each of these goals reflects a general approach to satisfying SQL requests.

- **Maximize speed**   This goal focuses on returning the result set in the minimal amount of elapsed time. This goal is common for online transaction processing systems (OLTP), where fast response time is the primary goal. This goal is implemented with Oracle's *first_rows* optimizer mode.

- **Minimize resources**   This goal concentrates of servicing the query while using the minimum amount of machine and disk resources. This goal is most appropriate for batch-oriented Oracle databases where the speed of query completion is not a major concern. This goal is implemented with Oracle's *all_rows* optimizer mode.

While I will be going into greater detail about the optimizer mode in Chapter 4, suffice it to say that each Oracle optimizer mode uses a different set of goals for determining the optimal execution plan. The default optimizer mode for Oracle SQL is set by the initialization parameter called *optimizer_mode.*

When Oracle accepts the parsed SQL to generate the execution plan, it looks to the Oracle data dictionary for guidance. The setting of the Oracle initialization parameters and the presence of index and table statistics influence the decision of the SQL optimizers.

Oracle uses two types of SQL optimizers, the rule-based optimizer (RBO) and the cost-based optimizer (CBO). Although I will be discussing each of these modes in Chapters 14 and 15, you need to understand that Oracle relies on data dictionary information to determine the best method to retrieve the data. With the CBO, Oracle uses statistics that are created from running the *analyze* command, and with the RBO Oracle uses information about indexes in the data dictionary.

Oracle's default optimizer mode is called "choose." In the "choose" optimizer mode, Oracle will execute the rule-based optimizer if there are no statistics present for the table, or it will execute the cost-based optimizer if statistics are present. The danger with using the choose optimizer mode arises in cases where one Oracle table in a complex query has statistics and the other tables do not have statistics. When only some tables contain statistics, Oracle will use the cost-based optimization and estimate statistics (by sampling 5000 rows) for the other tables in the query at run time. This can cause significant slowdown in the performance of the individual query. Be careful when using the *choose* option.

When you give Oracle the ability to choose the optimizer mode, Oracle will favor the cost-based approach if *any* of the tables in the query have statistics. (Statistics are created with the *analyze table* command.) For example, if a three-table join is specified in *choose* mode and statistics exist for one of the three tables, Oracle will decide to use the cost-based optimizer. When this happens, the Oracle CBO will inspect the *num_rows* column of the *dba_tables* view. If *num_rows* is null, Oracle still estimate statistics based on a 5000-row sample. If the *num_rows* column is zero, Oracle will not perform a run-time table analysis. In short, if Oracle analyzes the table at run time, this action will dramatically slow down the query. Next, let's take a look at the different types of table access methods.

Table Access Methods

When fetching rows from a table, Oracle has several options. Each of these access methods obtains rows from a table, but they do it in very different ways:

- **Full-table scan**   This method reads every row in the table, sequentially accessing every data block up to the high water mark.

- **Hash retrieval**   A symbolic hash key is used to generate the ROWID for rows in a table with a matching hash value.

- **ROWID access**   This access selects a single row in a table by specifying its ROWID. The ROWID specifies the block number and the offset of the row in the data block. This is the fastest method for accessing a row, and it is commonly seen in execution plans where Oracle has retrieved a ROWID from an index and uses the ROWID to fetch the table row.

Let's take a closer look at these table access methods.

Full-Table Scan

In Oracle, a *full-table scan* is performed by reading all of the table rows, block by block, until the high-water mark for the table is reached (see Figure 3-2). As a general rule, full-table scans should be avoided unless the SQL query requires a majority of the data blocks in the table. However, this issue is clouded when you are using Oracle parallel query or when the *db_file_multiblock_read_count* is used on a database server with multiple CPUs. I will go into greater detail on this issue in Chapter 10, but for now let's just look at the situations where the SQL optimizer chooses a full-table scan.

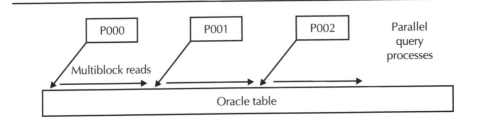

FIGURE 3-2. *A full-table scan with parallel query and multiblock reads*

Any one of the following conditions will cause Oracle to invoke a full-table scan:

- When no indexes exist for the table

- When a query does not contain a *where* clause

- When an indexed column reference is invalidated by placing it inside a BIF

- When a query uses the *like* operator, and it begins with a '%'

- With the cost-based optimizer, when a table contains a small number of rows

- When the *optimizer_mode=all_rows* in the initialization file

CAUTION
It is important to note that Oracle will always perform a full-table scan up to the high-water mark for the table. This behavior can cause excessive response times in cases where a significant number of rows have been deleted from a table. For example, in a table with 100 blocks of data that has had 90 blocks of rows deleted, full-table scans will continue to read 100 blocks. The remedy for this problem is to reorganize the table.

Next, let's look at hash access.

Hash Access
Oracle implements hash storage through single-table clusters and multiple table clusters. In a multiple table cluster, the hash is used to reduce I/O during join operations. When frequently joined tables are placed in a hash cluster, rows from both tables are placed in the same data block, such that a SQL join will need to

fetch fewer rows. Access with a hash is based on a symbolic key. The symbolic key is fed into the hashing algorithm that is programmed to quickly generate a hash value that is used to determine the data block where the row will reside, as shown in Figure 3-3. Because of the risk of relocating rows, hash access should only be used in static tables.

Hash row access should not be confused with a hash join in SQL. In a hash join, one table is accessed via a full-table scan, and a hash table is built in-memory from the result set. This hash table is then used to access the rows in the second table.

ROWID Access

Access by ROWID is the fastest way to get a single row. As you may already know, the ROWID for a row contains the data block number and the offset of the row in the block. Since all of the information required to fetch the data block is contained in the ROWID, the ROWID method can very quickly retrieve a row, as shown in Figure 3-4. In practice, select by ROWID is generally done when a ROWID is gathered from an index, and the ROWID is used to fetch the row. You may also see ROWID access when the row is re-retrieved inside an application program since the program acquired and stored the ROWID.

Next, let's take a quick look at index access methods. As you know, Oracle often uses indexes to gather row information.

Index Access Methods

As you may know, Oracle offers a variety of indexing methods including B-tree, bitmapped, and function-based indexes. Regardless of the index structure, an Oracle index can be thought of as a pair bond of a symbolic key and a ROWID. The goal of

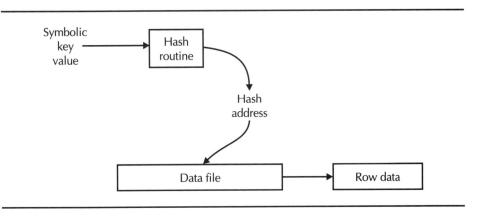

FIGURE 3-3. *Access with a hash*

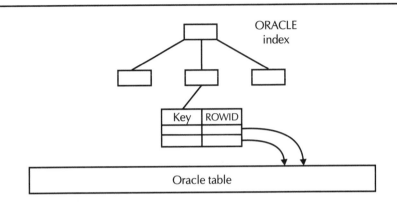

FIGURE 3-4. *Access by ROWID*

index access is to gather the ROWIDs required to quickly retrieve the desired table rows. Within Oracle, we see the following types of index access.

- **Index range scan**   This is the retrieval of one or more ROWIDs from an index. Indexed values are generally scanned in ascending order.

- **Index unique scan**   This is the retrieval of a single ROWID from an index.

- **Descending index range scan**   This is the retrieval of one or more ROWIDs from an index. Indexed values are returned in descending order.

- **And-equal filter**   This is an operation that gathers multiple sets of ROWIDs from the *where* clause of a query (e.g., *select customer_name from customer where status = 'OPEN' and age > 35;*). The *and-equal* operation compares the sets of ROWIDs and returns the intersection of these sets, thereby eliminating duplicates and satisfying the *and* conditions in the *where* clause.

Index Range Scan

The index range scan is one of the most common access methods. During an index range scan, Oracle accesses adjacent index entries and then uses the ROWID values in the index to retrieve the table rows (see Figure 3-5).

An example of an index range scan would be the following query.

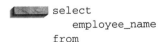
```
select
    employee_name
from
```

```
    employee
where
    home_city = 'Rocky Ford';
```

TIP
Because an index range scan fetches the ROWID list from the index, each ROWID will most likely point to a different data block causing a disk I/O for each block in the index range scan. In practice, many Oracle SQL tuning professionals will resequence the table rows into the same physical order as the primary index. This technique can reduce disk I/O on index range scans by several orders of magnitude. For details, see "Turning the Tables on Disk I/O" by Don Burleson in the January/February 2000 issue of Oracle Magazine *online.*

Oracle provides a column called *clustering_factor* in the *dba_indexes* view that tells you how synchronized the table rows are with your index. When the clustering factor is close to the number of data blocks, the table rows are synchronized with the index. As the *clustering_factor* approaches the number of rows in the table, the rows are out of sync with the index.

Fast Full-index Scan

Index full scans are sometimes called fast full-index scans, which were introduced in Oracle 7.3. There are some SQL queries that can be resolved by reading the

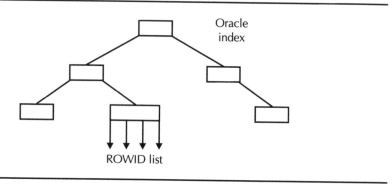

FIGURE 3-5. *An index range scan*

index without touching the table data. For example, the following query does not need to access the table rows, and the index alone can satisfy the query.

```
select distinct
    color,
    count(*)
from
    automobiles
group by
    color;
```

While some queries have always been able to return the desired result without touching the table data, Oracle enhanced the fast full-index scan to make it behave similar to a full-table scan. Just as Oracle has implemented the initialization parameter *db_file_multiblock_read_count* for full-table scans, Oracle allows this parameter to take effect when retrieving rows for a fast full-index scan. Since the whole index is accessed, Oracle allows multiblock reads. Also, a fast full-index scan is capable of using Oracle parallel query to further speed up the response time.

There is a huge benefit to not reading the table rows, but there are some requirements for Oracle to invoke the fast full-index scan.

- All of the columns required must be specified in the index. That is, all columns in the *select* and *where* clauses must exist in the index.

- The query returns more than 10 percent of the rows within the index. This 10 percent figure depends on the degree of multiblock reads and the degree of parallelism.

- You are counting the number of rows in a table that meet a specific criterion. The fast full-index scan is almost always used for *count(*)* operations.

The cost-based optimizer will make the decision about whether to invoke the fast full-index scan in accordance with the table and index statistics. You can also force a fast full-index scan by specifying the *index_ffs* hint, and this is commonly combined with the *parallel_index* hint to improve performance. For example, the following query forces the use of a fast full-index scan with parallelism:

```
select distinct /*+ index_ffs(c,pk_auto) parallel_index(automobile, pk_auto)
    color,
    count(*)
from
    automobiles
group by
    color;
```

It is not always intuitive whether a fast full-index scan is the fastest way to service a query because of all of the variables involved. Hence, most expert SQL tuners will time any query that meets the fast full-index scan criteria and see if the response time improves. Again, this is almost always fastest with *count(*)* operations. For counting operations, the fast full-index scans with *parallel_index* is clearly the fastest access method (see Figure 3-6).

Next, let's examine a very important SQL operation, the SQL join. It is through the join that Oracle navigates through the database and presents information from different tables based on a common column value.

Join Operations

While we will be exploring SQL tuning with joins in Chapter 14, we should have a brief review so that you understand how the type of join operation affects the execution plan for the SQL. While we will investigate each of these join techniques in detail in Chapter 16, let's take a quick survey of the most common join techniques.

Nested Loops Join

A *nested loop join* is an operation that has two tables, a smaller inner table and an outer table. Oracle compares each row of the inner set with each row of the outer

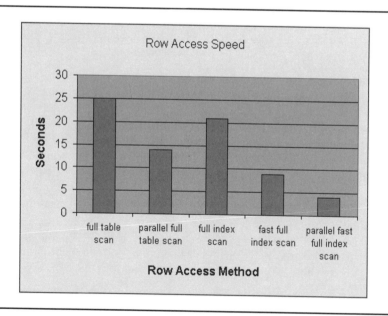

FIGURE 3-6. *Speed of* count(*) *operations*

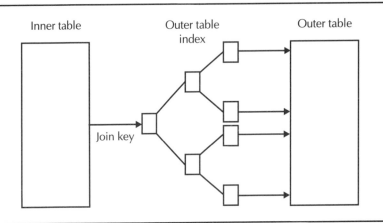

FIGURE 3-7. *A nested loop join*

set and returns those rows that satisfy a condition (see Figure 3-7). A nested loop join is commonly seen in conditions where an index exists on the inner table. If we use nested loop joins, we need to make sure that the proper driving table and the proper driving set are used by the query.

The nested loop join has the fastest response time in many cases (especially with small intermediate result row sets), but the hash join often offers the best overall throughput and faster performance where the intermediate row set is very large.

Hash Join

A *hash join* is an operation that performs a full-table scan on the smaller of the two tables (the driving table) and then builds a hash table in RAM memory. The hash table is then used to retrieve the rows in the larger table (see Figure 3-8). There are several types of hash joins, including the hash anti-join for cases of SQL that contains a *not in* clause followed by a subquery, and a hash semi-join. A hash join is a special case of a join that joins the table in RAM memory. In a hash join, both tables are read via a full-table scan (normally using multiblock reads and parallel query), and the result set is joined in RAM. This procedure can sometimes be faster than a traditional join operation.

Oracle provides the *hash_multiblock_io_count* initialization parameter to determine the number of multiblock reads that are performed by hash joins. We also have the hash anti-join. In the case of a hash anti-join, the SQL optimizer uses

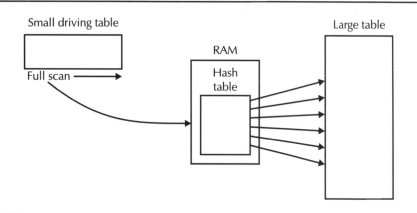

FIGURE 3-8.   *A hash join operation*

a nested loops algorithm for *not in* subqueries by default, unless the initialization parameter *always_anti_join* is set to *merge* or *hash* and various required conditions are met that allow the transformation of the *not in* subquery into a sort-merge or hash anti-join. You can place a *merge_aj* or *hash_aj* hint in the *not in* subquery to specify which algorithm the optimizer should use.

Sort Merge Join

A *sort merge* join is an operation that retrieves two sets of rows from the target tables and then sorts each row set by the join column. The merge phase combines each row from one set with the matching rows from the other, returning the intersection of the row sets (see Figure 3-9).

There are several permutations of the sort merge join, an outer merge join, an anti-merge join, and a semi-merge join. These permutations alter the merge phase from the goal of finding the intersections of the row sets to finding only those rows that meet the conditions of the SQL *where* clause.

STAR Query Join

With this new join method, data warehouse queries can run at blistering speeds, in some cases dozens of times faster than the original query. The STAR schema design involves creating a main fact table that contains all of the primary keys in the related data warehouse tables. This massive denormalization of the database structure means

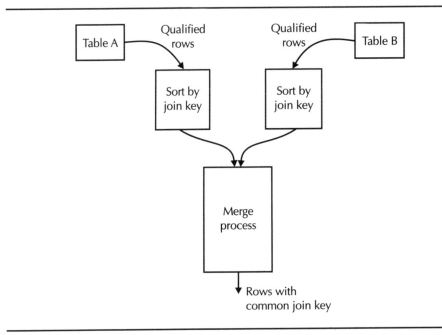

FIGURE 3-9. *A SQL sort merge join*

that just about any query against the STAR schema is going to involve the joining of many large tables, including a large fact table and many smaller reference tables. To invoke the STAR query path, the following characteristics must be present:

- There must be at least three tables being joined, with one large fact table and several smaller dimension tables.

- Prior to Oracle 8*i*, there must be a concatenated index on the fact table with at least three columns, one for each of the table join keys. After Oracle 8*i*, bitmap indexes are required.

- You must verify with an explain plan that the **NESTED LOOPS** operation is being used to perform the join.

Oracle follows a different procedure for processing STAR queries, depending on the Oracle version. Oracle will first service the queries against the smaller dimension tables, combining the result set into a Cartesian product table that is held in Oracle memory. This virtual table will contain all of the columns from all of the participating dimension tables. The primary key for this virtual table will be a composite of all of the keys for the dimension tables. If this key matches the composite index on the fact table, then the query will be able to process very quickly.

Once the sum of the reference tables has been addressed, Oracle will perform a nested loop join of the intermediate table against the fact table. This approach is far faster than the traditional method of joining the smallest reference table against the fact table and then joining each of the other reference tables against the intermediate table. The speed is a result of reducing the physical I/O. The indexes are read to gather the virtual table in memory, and the fact table will not be accessed until the virtual index has everything it requires to go directly to the requested rows via the index on the fact table.

Connect by Join

A *connect by* join is an operation for the retrieval of rows in a hierarchical order for a SQL query that contains a *connect by* clause. The *connect by* clause is seldom used in SQL statements. To see an example of the *connect by* clause, please see the *plan.sql* code that we use in this book to display SQL execution plans.

A Comparison of Join Speeds   The reason that Oracle offers several methods for joining tables is their experience that the nature of the tables greatly impacts the efficiency of the joining. By far, the three most popular join methods are the nested loop join, the sort merge join, and the hash join, in that order.

The sort merge join and the hash join are very similar in terms of function, while the nested loop join is quite different from the other join techniques. Table 3-1 summarizes the relative advantages of each join technique.

In sum, the nested loop join provides a faster response time for SQL queries that return small row subsets from each table. For large row subsets, the sort merge and hash join may result in faster execution time. Again, we will return to these join methods in detail in Chapter 16.

Now that you have a basic understanding of the Oracle join methods, let's explore the methods used by Oracle to sort a result set.

Join Type	Advantages	Sorting	Large Row Subsets	Index Required?
Sort merge join Hash join	Faster throughput	Yes	Fast	No
Nested loop join	Faster response time	No	Slow	Yes

TABLE 3-1.   *Relative Advantages of Join Types*

Sorting of the SQL Result Set

Oracle SQL does far more than simply extract the row information from the tables. By using Oracle SQL in conjunction with SQL*Plus, row information can be sorted, transformed, formatted, and displayed in a report format. In fact, SQL*Plus allows for sophisticated reports to be generated.

However, the execution plan for Oracle SQL will often change when the data is sorted and transformed. To fully understand how Oracle SQL execution is affected, let's explore the different methods for sorting data. Oracle provides several SQL directives that cause sorting of row data.

- **Order by** An operation that sorts a set of rows for a query with an *order by* clause

- **Join** An operation that sorts a set of rows before a merge join

- **Group by** An operation that sorts a set of rows into groups for a query with the *group by* clause

- **Aggregate** A retrieval of a single row that is the result of applying a group function to a group of selected rows

- **Select unique** An operation that sorts a set of rows to eliminate duplicates

- **Select distinct** An operation that forces duplicate rows to be eliminated from the result set and requires sorting to identify the duplicate rows

- **Create Index** The creation of an index always invokes a sort of the symbolic keys and ROWID values

As a small but very important component of SQL syntax, sorting is a frequently overlooked aspect of Oracle tuning. In general, an Oracle database will automatically perform sorting operations, and the SQL tuning expert must understand the SQL directives that invoke Oracle sorting.

At the time a session is established with Oracle, a private sort area is allocated in RAM memory for use by the session for sorting. If the connection is via a non-MTS dedicated connection, a program global area (PGA) is allocated according to the *sort_area_size init.ora* parameter. For connections via the multithreaded server, sort space is allocated in the *large_pool*. Unfortunately, the amount of memory used in sorting must be the same for all sessions, and it is not possible to add additional sort areas for tasks that require large sort operations. Therefore, the designer must strike a balance between allocating enough sort area to avoid disk sorts for the large sorting tasks and keeping in mind that the extra sort area will be allocated and not used by tasks that do not require intensive sorting. Of course, sorts that cannot fit into the *sort_area_size* will be paged out into the TEMP tablespaces for a disk sort. Disk sorts are about 14,000 times slower than memory sorts.

As I noted, the size of the private sort area is determined by the *sort_area_size init.ora* parameter. The size for each individual sort is specified by the *sort_area_retained_size init.ora* parameter. Whenever a sort cannot be completed within the assigned space, a disk sort is invoked using the temporary tablespace for the Oracle instance.

Disk sorts are expensive for several reasons. First, they are extremely slow when compared to in-memory sorts. Also, a disk sort consumes resources in the temporary tablespace. Oracle must also allocate buffer pool blocks to hold the blocks in the temporary tablespace. In-memory sorts are always preferable to disk sorts, and disk sorts will surely slow down an individual task, as well as impact concurrent tasks on the Oracle instance. Also, excessive disk sorting will cause a high value for free buffer waits, paging other tasks' data blocks out of the buffer.

From the perspective of tuning Oracle SQL, we must always be conscious of SQL statements that may invoke disk sorts. Because disk sorts are a matter of the volume of rows, we cannot tell from the execution plan if the sort is being performed in RAM or in the TEMP tablespace. As a general rule, sorts may often be avoided by forcing the use of an index. For example, let's consider the following simple SQL statement:

```
select
    department,
    employee_name
from
    employee
order by
    department,
    employee_name;
```

If this database has a high *db_file_multiblock_read_count* and Oracle parallel query is implemented for this table, the Oracle optimizer may be tempted to perform a full-table scan and sort the result set in the TEMP tablespace. However, the query may run faster with a fast full-index scan, provided that a concatenated index exists on the *department* and *employee_name* columns.

Again, an empirical test (with the SQL*Plus *set timing on* command) can be conducted to see if the speed of the fast full-table scan outweighs the speed of a full-table scan and a disk sort.

```
select /*+ index(employee,dept_name_idx) */
    department,
    employee_name
from
    employee
```

```
order by
    department,
    employee_name;
```

Conclusion

This chapter has explored the steps involved in parsing the SQL, the creation of the execution plan, and the actual execution of the SQL. I have noted that Oracle provides a complex set of SQL directives and hints that can be used to alter the execution plan. It is the goal of the SQL tuner to understand these methods of effecting the execution plan and ensuring that the optimal execution plan is generated for the SQL statement.

In the next chapter, we will take a close look at the Oracle SQL optimizers and see how the rule-based optimizer (RBO) differs from the cost-based optimizer (CBO). We will also explore how the Oracle SQL tuning professional can manipulate the optimizer to ensure maximum execution speed.

CHAPTER
4

Overview of the SQL
Optimizers

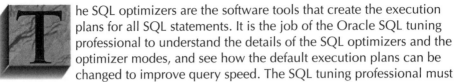he SQL optimizers are the software tools that create the execution plans for all SQL statements. It is the job of the Oracle SQL tuning professional to understand the details of the SQL optimizers and the optimizer modes, and see how the default execution plans can be changed to improve query speed. The SQL tuning professional must understand the relative advantages and disadvantages of each optimizer, and be able to set the default optimizer mode for an Oracle database to minimize the amount of manual SQL tuning. The main topics in this chapter include:

- Basic optimizer techniques

- The optimizer modes

- Tuning with the rule-based optimizer

- Tuning with the cost-based optimizer

- Setting the default optimizer mode

- Migrating to the cost-based optimizer

Let's begin with a discussion of the basic optimizer techniques.

Basic Optimizer Techniques

The purpose of SQL optimizers is to generate the fastest and least resource-intensive execution plan for a SQL statement. As discussed in Chapter 3, the goal of an optimizer may be to produce the fastest response time (*first_rows*) or the execution plan with the best overall throughput (*all_rows*). While these conflicting goals are noble, we need to understand how the Oracle SQL optimizers evolved and have a clear understanding of the strengths and shortcomings of each optimizer.

Oracle provides two optimizers, the rule-based optimizer (RBO) and the cost-based optimizer (CBO) as shown in Figure 4-1. Within these optimizers, we see several optimizer modes. Within Oracle, the term "optimizer mode" is synonymous with "optimizer goal," and both terms are used interchangeably within the Oracle documentation. This is because the Oracle initialization parameter *optimizer_mode* is used to set the database-wide default, while individual sessions can change the optimizer mode by using the *alter session set optimizer_goal* command.

While we will be discussing the optimizer goals in detail later in this chapter, it is important to note that the *optimizer_goal* can invoke either the RBO or the CBO. Table 4-1 summarizes the relationships between hints, optimizer goals, the optimizer mode, and the actual mode for the SQL statement. For example, we note that the use of any hint (except the RULE hint) causes Oracle to invoke the ALL_ROWS mode, even when the *optimizer_mode=rule.*

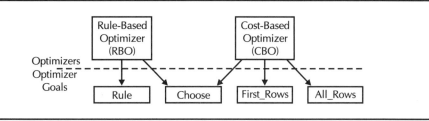

FIGURE 4-1. *The Optimizers and the optimizer goals*

Hint	Optimizer_goal	Optimizer_mode	Actual Mode
RULE	——	——	RULE
ALL_ROWS	——	——	ALL_ROWS
FIRST_ROWS	——	——	FIRST_ROWS
——	RULE	——	RULE
Any (except rule)	RULE	——	ALL_ROWS
——	ALL_ROWS	——	ALL_ROWS
Any	ALL_ROWS	——	ALL_ROWS
——	FIRST_ROWS	——	FIRST_ROWS
Any	FIRST_ROWS	——	FIRST_ROWS
——	Not set	RULE	RULE
Any	Not set	RULE	ALL_ROWS
——	Not set	ALL_ROWS	ALL_ROWS
Any	Not set	ALL_ROWS	ALL_ROWS
——	Not Set	FIRST_ROWS	FIRST_ROWS
Any	Not Set	FIRST_ROWS	FIRST_ROWS

TABLE 4-1. *The Relationship Between the SQL Optimizers and the Optimizer Mode*

Referring to Table 4-1, it is important to see how hints, optimizer goals, and *optimizer_mode* affect the actual mode. The most important point in this table is the fact that when a hint is used in a query, and the *optimizer_mode=rule*, then the actual mode used will be *all_rows*. This is a very common (and embarrassing) mistake usually made by junior DBAs when attempting to tune SQL with hints while using the rule-based default. It is important to recognize that hints (except the *rule* hint) will always change the actual optimizer mode to use the CBO.

Now that you see the structure of the optimizers, let's begin our discussion with an in-depth look at the rule-based optimizer.

The Rule-Based Optimizer

The rule-based optimizer (RBO) was the first Oracle optimizer and is nearly ten years old. The rule-based optimizer does not use any table or index statistics. Instead, the RBO uses heuristics to figure out the best access path to the data. Depending on the structure of the SQL statement, the RBO generates a list of possible execution plans.

The RBO uses an iterative process to generate an execution plan, examining each table in the *from* clause and all possible ways to join that table with other tables in the query. Each possible path is ranked for its relative cost, and the path with the lowest cost is chosen. Here are the steps:

For each table in the *where* clause:

■ A list of candidate execution plans is generated in terms of all possible access paths for the table.

■ A ranking value is then assigned to each candidate execution plan.

■ The RBO chooses the plan with the lowest rank.

For each remaining table in the *where* clause:

■ The RBO evaluates all possible join techniques that can be used to join the table with the result set from the third bulleted item above.

■ The technique with the lowest rank is chosen.

The rankings for the RBO are quite simple and rely on relative cost rankings for different operations. While it is not necessary to memorize these costs, it is important to note that this costing approach relies exclusively on metadata from the Oracle data dictionary.

Rule-Based Optimizer Ranks and SQL Operations
The following ranks show the relative costs of each type of SQL operation. These ranks are used by the RBO to determine the most efficient execution plan.

1. ROWID fetch

2. Single row by cluster join

3. Single row by hash cluster key

4. Single row by primary key

5. Cluster join

6. Hash cluster key

7. Indexed cluster key

8. Composite key

9. Single-column index

10. Bounded range search on indexed columns

11. Unbounded range search on indexed columns

12. Sort merge join

13. *Max* or *min* on an indexed column

14. *Order by* on an indexed column

15. Full-table scan

The rule-based optimizer is very elegant for its simplicity and often makes faster execution choices than the CBO. In fact, Oracle Applications products used the RBO until 2001 when the Oracle Applications 11*i* product was introduced. It is only with the release of Oracle8*i* (8.1.6) that the CBO has become faster than the RBO in many cases.

While it is very tempting to go into the relative advantages of the RBO and CBO within each successive release of Oracle, we can make some general observations about the characteristics of the rule-based optimizer:

■ **Always use the index**   If an index can be used to access a table, choose the index. Indexes are always preferred over a full-table scan or a sort merge join (a sort merge join does not require an index).

■ **Always starts with the driving table**   The last table in the *from* clause will be the driving table. For the RBO, this should be the table that chooses the fewest rows. The RBO uses this driving table as the first table when performing nested loop join operations.

■ **Full-table scans as a last resort**   The RBO is not aware of Oracle parallel query and multiblock reads, and it does not consider the size of the table. Hence, the RBO dislikes full-table scans and will use them only when no index exists.

■ **Any index will do**   The RBO will sometimes choose a less than ideal index to service a query. This is because the RBO does not have access to statistics that show the selectivity of indexed columns.

■ **Simple is sometimes better**   Prior to Oracle8*i*, the RBO often provided a better overall execution plan for some databases.

The Cost-Based Optimizer

Oracle's cost-based optimizer was created to provide a more sophisticated alternative to rule-based optimization because Oracle recognized that SQL optimization could be more effective if the optimizer was aware of details about the data in the tables and indexes. This data includes:

■ **Table data**

   ■ The number of rows

   ■ The number of physical data blocks

■ **Index data**

   ■ The number of unique values in the index

   ■ The distribution of values within the index

   ■ The selectivity of the index

   ■ The index clustering factor

While the goal of adding statistical information was noble, Oracle underestimated the complexity of creating an optimizer that would always choose the fastest execution plan. The early releases of the CBO in Oracle7 often made less than optimal execution decisions, and while the official policy of Oracle was for customers to use the CBO, Oracle continued to utilize the RBO for their own Oracle Application products.

The CBO and Statistics

The introduction of the CBO also brought forth a very important change in SQL theory. Prior to the CBO, the premise of Oracle was that a single execution plan could be derived that would always find the optimal execution plan.

When the CBO was introduced, Oracle provided a new SQL utility called *analyze* that would compute or estimate the statistics for an Oracle table or index. Oracle also recommended that tables and indexes be reanalyzed whenever important characteristics of the table or index have changed. Hence, Oracle professionals were quite upset to find that the execution plans for their SQL changed whenever they reanalyzed their database objects. By tying the execution plans to the characteristics of the data, a SQL statement might have a different execution plan every time new statistics were generated. This made SQL tuning quite difficult.

Gathering Statistics for the CBO

Oracle offers two method for collecting table and index statistics, the compute and estimate methods. Here is an example of the syntax:

```
analyze table customer compute statistics;
analyze table customer estimate statistics sample 5000 rows;
```

There has been a great deal of debate about whether it is better to compute or estimate statistics. Note that there are documented problems when taking less than a 25–30 percent sample of the rows in a table. This is due to the way Oracle calculates row counts. Contrary to early documentation, row counts are done by calculating average row size verses total occupied blocks and not a full count. In tables of several million rows, the row counts can be off by as much as 15 percent if a sample of less than 25 percent was used for the analysis.

The downside to running *compute statistics* is that it is very time consuming and resource intensive. The downside to running *estimate statistics* is that you need to be careful to get a statistically valid sample. In experiments using estimate statistics it has been found that a sample as low as 50 rows will generate a valid value for *num_rows* in the *dba_tables* view. However, most professional Oracle DBAs will estimate statistics based on a sample of 5,000 rows. This does not take much execution time but generates valid statistics.

The CBO and Column Histogram Data   The CBO also allows you to generate special statistics in cases where a data column contains highly skewed data. The syntax example appears here:

```
analyze table
    customer
estimate statistics
    sample 500 rows
for all indexed columns;
```

Column histogram information is only useful in cases of low-cardinality columns (e.g., bitmap indexes) where the data is highly skewed. For example, suppose we have a bitmapped index of U.S. state abbreviations. This index will only have 50 distinct values, and we would not need column histograms unless the data were not evenly distributed.

Let's take a simple example. Suppose that we have a *state_abbr_idx* on our customer table, with customers in all 50 states. The following query is used to fetch the customer list by state:

```
select
    customer_full_name,
    customer_full_address
from
    customer
where
    customer_full_address.state_abbr = ':var1:';
```

However, this query should not have a stable execution plan if the data is skewed. Let's assume that we have a disproportional amount of customers in North Carolina, with more than 60 percent of the rows for customers in North Carolina. To be effective, the CBO should invoke a full-table scan when the *where* clause of the query asks for customers in North Carolina. However, the CBO should invoke an index range scan in cases where the identical query asks for customers in Nevada. The use of column histograms will tell the CBO to consider the distribution of data when formulating the execution plan.

Also note that the *state_abbr* is coded by using a host variable. Prior to Oracle 9*i*, a query with a host variable could not use column histograms. Starting with Oracle 9*i*, the presence of the column histograms will cause the Oracle optimizer to insert the column values and reevaluate the query against the histogram data. This is called *peeking* and this may add significant overhead to this query because it must be reparsed every time that it is executed.

CAUTION
Column histograms should only be calculated for columns with a small number of distinct values where some column values represent a disproportional number of rows. Histograms are time consuming to calculate and may cause excessive reparsing of the SQL in the library cache. Because all indexed columns on a table will never be skewed, be careful to never use the all indexed columns *clause when computing histograms.*

The CBO and Hints

Because of the shortcomings of the CBO, Oracle began to offer hints that could be placed within a SQL statement to change the default CBO execution plan. The existence of hints confirms that the CBO does not always make the best choice of the execution plan, and we would expect the number of hints to decrease as the CBO became more sophisticated. Up to Oracle8*i*, however, the CBO continued to add new hints, and the list of hints now contains dozens of hints. When the CBO finally becomes sophisticated enough to always make the best execution plan, we can expect hints to become obsolete with the CBO.

Execution Plan Persistence

Oracle eventually recognized that execution plans should be static, especially after a SQL tuning professional has found the optimal execution plan. Until Oracle8*i*, the SQL tuning professional has to tune the SQL, locate the SQL source code, and add hints to ensure that the same execution plan was always generated.

With the introduction of Oracle8*i*, an exciting new feature was introduced called *optimizer plan stability*. Optimizer plan stability allows the SQL tuning professional to store an outline for the execution of a SQL statement. This stored outline has the dual purpose of reducing the parsing time required to generate the execution plan and ensuring that the same execution plan is always generated. This topic is so important to SQL tuning that I have dedicated Chapter 13 to this topic.

The Optimizer Modes

Within these two optimizers, Oracle provides several optimizer modes. An optimizer mode may be set for the entire database, or it may be set for a specific Oracle session. The optimizer modes include *rule, first_rows, all_rows,* and *choose.* Let's take a closer look at each of these goals.

rule mode

The rule hint will ignore the CBO and the statistics and generate an execution plan based solely on the basic data dictionary information. It is always a good idea to try tuning a specific SQL statement by using the RBO by using a *rule* hint or by issuing the *alter session set optimizer_goal=rule.* However, always remember that the RBO may choose a less than ideal index to service a query.

choose mode

The choose optimizer mode allows Oracle to choose the most appropriate optimizer goal. This is the default optimizer mode within Oracle, and it generally uses the presence of statistics to determine which optimizer to invoke. If no statistics exist, Oracle will use the *rule* goal. If statistics exist, Oracle will choose *first_rows* or *all_rows,* depending on the presence of indexes and the setting for parallelism and *db_file_multiblock_read_count.*

CAUTION
Having incomplete statistics with the choose optimizer mode can cause huge slowdowns. If Oracle detects a single table in a query with statistics, it will use the cost-based optimizer and estimate statistics for the other tables at run time. This can cause a huge slowdown of SQL execution. This problem is very common with Oracle DBA beginners because the default mode is choose, and because beginner DBAs sometimes selectively issue the analyze command, not realizing that they are affecting SQL execution times.

first_rows mode

This is a cost-based optimizer mode that will return rows as soon as possible, even if the overall query runs longer or consumes more resources. The *first_rows* optimizer mode usually involves choosing a full-index scan over a parallel full-table scan. Because the *first_rows* mode favors index scans over full-table scans, the *first_rows* mode is most appropriate for online systems where the end user wants to see some results as quickly as possible.

all_rows mode

This is a cost-based optimizer mode that ensures that the overall query time is minimized, even if it takes longer to receive the first row. This usually involves choosing a parallel full-table scan over a full-index scan. Because the *all_rows* mode favors full-table scans, the *all_rows* mode is best suited for batch-oriented queries where intermediate rows are not required for viewing.

Which Is "Better"? Fast Execution Versus Minimal Resource Usage

To understand Oracle's philosophy regarding fast execution and minimal resource consumption, you need to look at a simple example. To illustrate the difference between *all_rows* and *first_rows* with an overly simplistic example, consider the following query:

```
select
    last_name
from
    customer
order by
    last_name;
```

This query can be serviced in two ways:

- **Full-table scan**   Here we perform a full-table scan in parallel and sort the rows in the TEMP tablespace. For the sake of illustration, let's assume that this execution plan produces the fastest overall execution time and minimal use of resources (see Figure 4-2).

- **Full-index scan**   Here we retrieve the rows in *last_name* order by using a *last_name_index*. This technique results in more physical reads but begins to return sorted rows almost immediately (see Figure 4-3).

Again, assuming that we accept that the full-table scan and sort are less I/O intensive than the full-index scan, then we can clearly see the difference in the optimizer goals. The full-index scan will begin to return rows almost immediately at the expense of extra I/O, while the full-table scan will require less resources, but the result set will not be available until the end of the query.

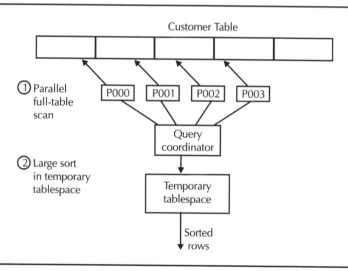

FIGURE 4-2.   *Perform a full-table scan and a sort* (all_rows)

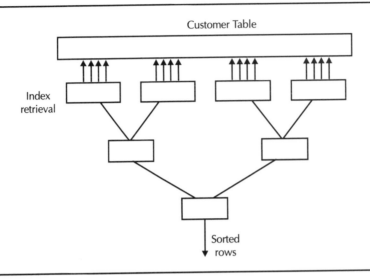

FIGURE 4-3. *Perform an index retrieval* (first_rows)

Tuning with Rule-Based Optimization

As we noted, the rule-based optimizer is the oldest and most stable of the optimizers. The rule-based optimizer is very simple and uses basic information in the data dictionary to make decisions about how to generate an optimal execution plan. Also, unlike with the cost-based optimizer, the order of tables in the *from* clause and the order of Booleans in the *where* clause affect the execution plan for the query.

If you are using any release of Oracle prior to Oracle8*i*, you may want to consider trying the RBO as your default optimizer. Before Oracle8*i*, the CBO had an erroneous propensity to invoke a full-table scan instead of using available indexes. Again, while the RBO is quite old, it can sometimes result in faster SQL execution. When tuning a SQL statement, the *rule* hint should be the first thing to try.

Since the RBO is still widely used, let's take a look at the rules for formulating a query.

Changing the Rule-Based Driving Table

In Oracle's rule-based optimizer, the ordering of the table names in the *from* clause determines the driving table. The driving table is important because it is retrieved first, and the rows from the second table are then merged into the result set from the first table. Therefore, it is essential that the second table return the fewest rows in terms of the *where* clause.

NOTE
The driving table is not always the table with the fewest rows. The Boolean conditions in the SQL where *clause must be evaluated, and the driving table should be the table that returns the smallest number of rows.*

With the rule-based optimizer, the table names are read from right to left. Hence, the LAST table in the *from* clause should be the table that returns the smallest number of rows. For setting the driving table for the rule-based optimizer, consider the following query, where the order table has 100,000 rows and the customer table has 50,000 rows.

```
Select
    customer_name,
    customer_phone
from
    customer,
    order
where
    customer_region = 'EAST'
and
    order_status = 'BACKORDER';
```

In this query, you see that the last table in the *from* clause is the order table, and the order table will be the driving table. This might make sense, since we know that this table has half the rows of the customer table. However, we must first evaluate the *where* clause, to see what table returns the smallest number of rows.

Let's assume that there are 10,000 customers in the WEST region and 30,000 backordered status columns. Given this information, we know that the customer table should be last in the *from* clause because it returns fewer rows.

When the Rule-Base Optimizer Fails to Use the Correct Index

The rule-based optimizer's greatest shortcoming is its failure to use the best index. There are cases where the rule-based optimizer fails to choose the best index to service a query because it is not aware of the number of distinct values in an index (the selectivity of the index). This is especially a problem when values within an index are highly skewed.

For example, let's assume in this example that there are 100,000 retired employees, 20,000 employees in the personnel department, and 500 employees who are both retired and belong to the personnel department. Let's also assume that we have a nonunique index on both the status and the department columns of our employee table.

We would expect that the most efficient way to service this query would be to scan the most selective index, in this case the department index, scanning the 20,000 retired employees to get the 500 in the personnel department. It would be far less efficient to scan the status index, reading through 100,000 retired employees to find those who work in the personnel department.

```
select
    count(*)
from
    employee
where
    department = 'PERSONNEL'
and
    status = 'RETIRED';
```

With the rule-based optimizer, we see the following execution plan:

```
SELECT STATEMENT
    SORT AGGREGATE
        SELECT BY ROWID EMPLOYEE
            NON-UNIQUE INDEX NON-SELECTIVE RANGE SCAN status_ix(status)
```

Even reversing the order of the items in the *where* clause does not change the fact that the rule-based optimizer is choosing to scan through all 100,000 retired employees looking for the 500 that belong to the personnel department. With the cost-based optimizer, we see that the selectivity of the indexes is known and that the most efficient index is used to service the request:

```
SELECT STATEMENT
    SORT AGGREGATE
        SELECT BY ROWID EMPLOYEE
            NON-UNIQUE INDEX NON-SELECTIVE RANGE SCAN
            dept_ix(department)
```

In sum, we need to pay careful attention to the indexes that are chosen by the rule-based optimizer, and either disable the indexes that we do not want to be used in the query or force the use of the index that we want. If we want to use the RBO for this type of query, the best indexes can be explicitly specified with an *index* hint, or unwanted indexes can be disabled by mixing data type on the index (i.e., *WHERE numeric_column_value = 123||' ')*.

Now let's move on and take a close look at tuning with the cost-based optimizer.

Tuning with Cost-Based Optimization (CBO)

The cost-based optimizer uses statistics that are collected from the table using the *analyze table* and *analyze index* commands. Oracle uses these metrics about the tables in order to intelligently determine the most efficient way to service the SQL query. It is important to recognize that in many cases the cost-based optimizer may not always make the proper decision in terms of the speed of the query, and Oracle has provided numerous hints to allow the DBA and developer to tune the execution plan.

The cost-based optimizer is constantly being improved, but there are still many cases in which the rule-based optimizer will result in faster Oracle queries. As I stated before, one of the first things a seasoned Oracle DBA does when tuning a SQL statement is to add a *rule* hint, or use the *alter session set optimizer goal = rule* statement in order to change the default optimizer mode from cost-based to rule-based optimization. Here is a list of common hints that are used to change the execution plan in the cost-based optimizer:

- **all_rows**   This is the cost-based approach designed to provide the best overall throughput and minimum resource consumption.

- **and_equal(table_name index_name1)**   This hint causes merge scans of two to five single-column indexes.

- **cluster(table_name)**   This hint requests a cluster scan of the table_name.

- **first_rows**   This is the cost-based approach designed to provide the best response time.

- **full**   This hint requests the bypassing of indexes, doing a full-table scan.

- **hash(table_name)**   This hint causes a hash scan of table_name.

- **hash_aj**   This hint is placed in a *not in* subquery to perform a hash anti-join.

- **index(table_name index_name)**   This hint requests the use of the specified index against the table. If no index is specified, Oracle will choose the best index.

- **index_asc(table_name index_name)**   This hint requests to use the ascending index on a range scan operation.

- **index_combine(table_name index_name)**   This hint requests that the specified bitmapped index be used.

- **index_desc(table_name index_name)**   This hint requests to use the descending index on a range scan operation.

- **merge_aj**   This hint is placed in a *not in* subquery to perform an anti-join.

- **no_expand**   The NO_EXPAND hint prevents the cost-based optimizer from considering OR-expansion for queries having OR conditions or IN-lists in the *where* clause. Usually, the optimizer considers using OR expansion and uses this method if it decides the cost is lower than not using it. This OR expansion is related to optimizer internals and does not mean that the logic itself will be changed and return a different result set.

- **no_merge**   This hint is used in a view to prevent it from being merged into a parent query.

- **nocache**   This hint causes the table cache option to be bypassed.

- **noparallel**   This hint turns off the parallel query option.

- **ordered**   This hint requests that the tables should be joined in the order that they are specified (left to right).

- **parallel(table_name degree)**   For full table scans, this hint requests that the table_name query be executed in parallel mode with "degree" processes servicing the table access.

- **push_subq**   This hint causes all subqueries in the query block to be executed at the earliest possible time.

- **rowid**   This hint requests a ROWID scan of the specified table.

- **rule**   This hint indicates that the rule-based optimizer should be invoked (sometimes due to the absence of table statistics).

- **star**   This hint forces the use of a star query plan, provided that there are at least three tables in the query and a concatenated index exists on the fact table.

- **use_concat**   This hint requests that a *union all* operation be used for all OR conditions.

- **use_hash(table_name1 table_name2)**   This hint requests a hash join against the specified tables.

- **use_merge**   This hint requests a sort merge operation.

- **use_nl(table_name)**   This hint requests a nested loop operation with the specified table as the driving table.

It is beyond the scope of this chapter to go into all of these hints, so for now, just consider hints to be the tools you use to tune cost-based execution plans. We will look at these in detail in later chapters.

Invoking the Cost-Based Optimizer

Before retrieving any rows, the cost-based optimizer must create an execution plan that determines the fastest method to access the desired table and indexes. Just like the RBO, the cost-based optimizer works by weighing the relative "costs" for different access paths to the data, and choosing the path with the smallest relative cost. Once the statistics have been collected, there are three ways to invoke the cost-based optimizer:

- Setting the *init.ora* parameter *optimizer_mode = all_rows, first_rows* or *choose*

- *alter session set optimizer_goal=all_rows* or *first_rows*

- Cost-based hints   */*+ all_rows */* or *--+ all_rows*

These "costs" for a query are determined with the aid of table and index statistics that are computed with the *analyze table* and *analyze index* commands in Oracle.

Gathering Statistics for the CBO

There is a debate raging in the Oracle community about how frequently to reanalyze statistics. Some Oracle DBAs feel that it is important that the statistics be refreshed periodically, especially when the distribution of data changes frequently, while other feel that there is only one optimal way to service a query and the execution plan should never change.

TIP
Oracle DBAs needs to choose their SQL tuning philosophy. If they feel that they want their execution plans to change, then they should reanalyze statistics frequently. If they feel that there is only one optimal execution plan for any query, then they will tune the SQL and use optimizer plan stability and stop refreshing statistics.

There are two approaches for reanalyzing statistics: custom scripts and the dbms_stats utility. Many DBAs write a quick SQL*Plus script to gather optimizer statistics. The following script will generate the proper SQL syntax.

analyze.ksh

```ksh
#!/bin/ksh

# First, we must set the environment . . . .
ORACLE_SID=xxx
export ORACLE_SID
ORACLE_HOME=`cat /var/opt/oracle/oratab|grep ^$ORACLE_SID:|cut -f2 -d':'`
export ORACLE_HOME
PATH=$ORACLE_HOME/bin:$PATH
export PATH

$ORACLE_HOME/bin/sqlplus /<<!

set pages 999
set heading off
set echo off
set feedback off

connect internal;

spool /export/home/oracle/analyze.sql;

select
'analyze table '||owner||'.'||table_name||' estimate statistics sample 5000
rows;'
from
   dba_tables
where
   owner not in ('SYS','SYSTEM','PERFSTAT');

select
'analyze index '||owner||'.'||index_name||' compute statistics;'
from
   dba_indexes
where
   owner not in ('SYS','SYSTEM','PERFSTAT');

spool off;

set echo on
set feedback on

@/export/home/oracle/analyze
exit
!
```

Most shops schedule a script like this to run weekly, or whenever there have been significant changes to the table data. However, it is not necessary to reanalyze tables and indexes that remain relatively constant. For example, a database where the tables have a constant number of rows and indexes where the distribution of values remains constant will not benefit from frequent analysis.

Another option is to use the dbms_stats utility. This utility has the following options:

- **gather_database_stats**   This gathers statistics for the entire instance.

- **gather_schema_stats**   This gathers statistics for a schema within an instance.

- **gather_index_stats**   This gathers statistics for indexes in a schema.

- **gather_table_stats**   This gathers statistics for tables in a schema.

The only real advantage of this package is that you can also use parallelism to analyze statistics. Let's take a quick look at how the dbms_stats package is invoked. The following query will analyze table statistics for a huge table, using 35 parallel query slaves.

```
BEGIN
    dbms_stats.gather_table_stats
(
        ownname=SCOTT,
        tabname=huge_table,
        estimate_rows=5000,
        degree=35
);
```

Next, let's examine the rules for determining the default optimizer mode.

Determining the Default Optimizer Mode

As I have noted, there are some shortcomings in the CBO and the RBO, and you must make a decision about the appropriate optimizer_mode default for your database. If your database has many thousands of SQL statements to tune, choosing the best overall optimizer mode can save you hundreds of hours of SQL tuning effort. Every database is different, both in the types of queries and the structures of the data. However, there are some general rules that can be applied:

- Prior to Oracle 8.1.6, queries that join three or more large tables will generally benefit from the rule-based optimizer or the *first_rows* hint.

- Queries that access bitmap or function-based indexes will benefit from the cost-based optimizer.

- Queries that will benefit from hash joins will similarly benefit.

- Queries that use STAR query hints need the cost-based optimizer.

- Databases at Oracle8*i* and beyond may benefit from the cost-based optimizer default.

The choice of default optimizers depends on the version of Oracle. Oracle recommends that all Oracle7 databases use rule-based optimization, and by Oracle8*i*, the cost-based optimizer has improved to the point where it can be considered for a default optimizer mode. Given that any Oracle environment would benefit from both optimizers, there are several choices. The DBA could make the cost-based optimizer the default and use rule hints when required or make rule-based the default and use cost hints and statistics when desired.

Many DBAs conduct a study where they bounce the *init.ora optimizer_mode* and then run the application for a day in each mode and collect statistics. From these overall comparisons, the proper default *optimizer_mode* becomes readily apparent. Here is the procedure:

1. Notify your end users that you are changing important parameters and ask them to call you if they notice any significant changes in performance. Also tell the end users that you can quickly put the system back into its original state.

2. Change the initialization file to change *optimizer_mode*.

3. Bounce the database.

4. Use tools to measure end-to-end response time for the most important transactions.

Again, the first step in any Oracle SQL tuning endeavor is to set the appropriate default for the whole database. This may save hundreds of hours of manual tuning.

Migrating to the Cost-Based Optimizer

As you know, the rule-based optimizer has remained essentially unchanged since Oracle6, while the cost-based optimizer is being constantly enhanced. Starting with Oracle8*i*, the CBO has been enhanced to the point where it provides better overall execution plans, and many shops are planning to migrate their SQL to the CBO after installing Oracle8*i*. This migration is very worthwhile, but there are pitfalls that must be considered.

Retraining the Development Staff

Seasoned Oracle developers who have been using the RBO for many years will find the CBO to be very foreign. Unlike the RBO, the CBO uses opposite sets of rules to determine the driving table, the wealth of CBO hints can be intimidating, and the query transformation techniques employed by the CBO can be aggravating to the novice. To ensure a successful migration to the Oracle8*i* CBO, the DBA and development staff should attend the appropriate training to ensure that they fully understand the CBO features.

Choose Your Cost-Based Optimizer Philosophy

Once your company has migrated to Oracle8*i* and made a decision to use the cost-based SQL optimizer, you must make a very important decision. Especially important in undertaking a migration to the CBO is documenting your company's philosophy regarding the relationship between the CBO statistics and the use of optimizer plan stability. Before undertaking a migration to the CBO, the Oracle DBA must develop a philosophy regarding CBO statistics and his or her ability to dynamically change SQL execution plans. This choice is heavily dependent upon the nature of the Oracle database, and either choice may be optimal.

Remember, some Oracle professionals subscribe to the theory that for any SQL query, there exists one, and only one, optimal execution plan. Once this optimal execution plan is located, it should be made persistent with optimizer plan stability. In contrast, other shops want their SQL to change execution plans whenever there has been a significant change to the CBO statistics.

Stable shops where the table statistics rarely change will want to employ optimizer plan stability to make execution plans persistent, while shops where the CBO statistics frequently change will tune their queries without optimizer plan stability so that the run-time optimizer is free to choose the most appropriate execution plan, based on the CBO statistics.

The choice of SQL philosophy has a dramatic impact on the approach to SQL tuning and maintenance.

- **Table and index statistics**   The dynamic philosophy relies heavily on the table and index statistics, and these statistics must be recomputed each time that a table has a significant change, while the static philosophy does not rely on statistics.

- **Optimizer plan stability**   The dynamic shop does not use optimizer plan stability, because they want the freedom for the execution plan to change whenever there is a major change to the data inside the tables. Conversely, the static shop relies on optimizer plan stability to make their tuning changes permanent and to improve SQL execution time by avoiding reparsing of SQL statements.

■ **Cursor sharing**   The dynamic shop often has SQL that is generated by ad hoc query tools with hard-coded literal values embedded within the SQL. As you know, hard-coded literal values make the SQL statements nonreusable unless the Oracle8*i cursor_sharing=force* is set in the Oracle initialization file. Shops that are plagued with nonreusable SQL can adopt either the persistent or the dynamic philosophy. To use optimizer plan stability with nonreusable SQL, the DBA will set *cursor_sharing=force* and then extract the transformed SQL from the library cache and use optimizer plan stability to make the execution plan persistent.

Let's take a closer look at these competing philosophies so that you can see which philosophy best fits your organization.

The Persistent SQL Philosophy

If your shop has relatively static tables and indexes, you may want to adopt the *persistent* SQL philosophy that states that there exists one, and only one, optimal execution plan for any SQL statement. Shops that subscribe to this philosophy are characterized by stable applications that have been tuned to use host variables (instead of literal values) in all SQL queries.

Persistent shops also have tables and indexes whose statistics rarely change the execution plan for their SQL queries, regardless of how often the statistics are recomputed. Many persistent shops have all of their SQL embedded inside PL/SQL packages, and the applications call their SQL using a standard PL/SQL function or stored procedure call. This insulates the SQL from the application programs, ensuring that all applications execute identical SQL, and also ensuring that all of the SQL has been properly tuned.

Choosing this approach means that all tuned SQL will utilize optimizer plan stability, and that the CBO statistics are only used for ad hoc queries and those new queries that have not yet been tuned. Of course, there is also a performance benefit to using optimizer plan stability because the SQL statements are preparsed and ready to run. This approach is generally used in shops where experience has shown that the execution plans for SQL rarely change after the CBO statistics have been reanalyzed.

The persistent SQL philosophy requires the DBA to write scripts to detect all SQL statements that do not possess stored outlines, and to tune these queries on behalf of the developers. I will discuss these techniques in detail in Chapter 13. The persistent SQL philosophy also requires less reliance on CBO statistics, and the DBA generally only analyzes tables when they are first migrated into the production environment. Since optimizer plan stability does not rely on statistics, the server overhead of periodically recomputing statistics for the CBO is avoided.

The Dynamic SQL Philosophy

The *dynamic* SQL philosophy entails the belief that a shop's Oracle SQL will change execution plans in accordance with the changes to the CBO statistics. Shops that subscribe to the dynamic SQL philosophy are characterized by highly volatile environments where tables and indexes change radically and frequently. These shops frequently reanalyze their CBO statistics and allow the CBO to choose the execution plan in accordance with the current status of their CBO statistics.

A good example of a shop that uses the dynamic SQL philosophy would be one where tables grow over a specified period of time and then are purged, and new data is reloaded. In these types of environments, the *num_rows* and *avg_row_len* for the tables are frequently changing, as are the distributions of index values. Decision support environments and scientific databases often adopt this philosophy because entirely new subsets of data are loaded into tables, the data is analyzed, the tables truncated, and a wholly different set of data is loaded into the table structures.

Other common characteristics of dynamic shops are those where the SQL cannot be easily tuned. Oracle databases that are accessed by casual users via ODBC, and third-party tools such as Crystal Report or Microsoft Access are often forced into the dynamic philosophy because the incoming SQL is always different. However, it is very important to note that the use of third-party application suites such as SAP and PeopleSoft does not always require the adoption of the dynamic philosophy. The SQL from these types of application suites can be captured in the library cache,
and optimizer plan stability can be used to make the execution plan persistent.

These shops require a very different approach to SQL tuning than persistent SQL shops. Each time new data is loaded or the data changes, the affected tables and indexes must be reanalyzed, and these shops often incorporate the dbms_stats package directly into their load routines. In Oracle8*i,* the DBA for dynamic shops must be always vigilant for changes to the distribution of index column values. When column values for any index become skewed, the DBA must create column histograms for the index so that the optimizer can choose between a full-table scan and an index range scan to service queries. Of course, these shops will benefit greatly with the use of Oracle9*i,* where the database will automatically create column histograms for index columns with skewed distributions.

Many companies adopt one of these philosophies without completely realizing the ramifications of their chosen approach. In practice, most shops begin with a dynamic philosophy and then undertake to migrate to the static approach after experience indicates that their execution plans rarely change after a reanalysis of the tables and indexes.

Remember, the Oracle8*i* features of *cursor_sharing* and optimizer plan stability are a godsend to many Oracle developers and offer a proven method to improve the tuning and persistence of SQL execution plans.

Conclusion

Before any Oracle professionals undertake serious Oracle SQL tuning, they must first master the basic optimizer modes and understand how they function. The major points of this chapter include these:

- The DBA must decide which default optimizer mode offers the best overall response time, and then tune the remaining queries.

- The DBA must decide whether to reanalyze statistics or to use optimizer plan stability.

- The DBA must understand the philosophical differences between *first_rows* and *all_rows*, and set the defaults accordingly.

Next, let's move on and take a closer look at SQL Internal processing. Getting into the bowels of the SQL optimizers will greatly aid you in your SQL tuning endeavors.

CHAPTER
5

SQL Internal Processing

his chapter is concerned with providing a detailed understanding of how SQL is processed within the Oracle database instance. We will be exploring the Oracle library cache, and you will see how you can write queries to see exactly what is happening to your SQL statements. We will also explore techniques for investigating SQL sort activity and see how you can quickly find SQL statements that are invoking disk sorts. Best of all, I will show you how to get the execution plan for all SQL statements in the library cache and create reports that show you exactly what your SQL is doing. This chapter will include the following sections:

- Oracle shared SQL and private SQL areas

- SGA statistics for SQL

- Inside the library cache

- Monitoring and tuning Oracle sorting

- Identifying high-impact SQL in the library cache

- Reporting on SQL in the library cache

Let's begin with an in-depth overview of the SQL areas.

Shared and Private SQL Areas

Within the library cache, Oracle stores the source for your SQL statement as well as the execution plan for the SQL. Within an individual SQL statement, Oracle partitions the SQL into several areas, a shared area and a private area (see Figure 5-1). In order to make all SQL statements reusable, Oracle segments the parts of the SQL statement that are generic into the shared area, specifically the original parse tree for the SQL and the execution plan. The private SQL area, which includes SQL information that is user-specific, is divided into a persistent area and a run-time area. The persistent area remains in memory unless the corresponding cursor has been closed. Hence, you should always close all open cursors that will not be used again for better memory utilization within the private SQL area because the run-time area is freed after the statement is executed.

The private area includes binding data, run-time buffers, cursors, host variables, and other control structures that are specific to the user. The separation of the SQL areas allows Oracle SQL to remain fully reentrant and reusable while allowing simultaneous execution of any SQL statement.

Next, let's look at some system-wide SGA statistics that can give us insight into our SQL behavior.

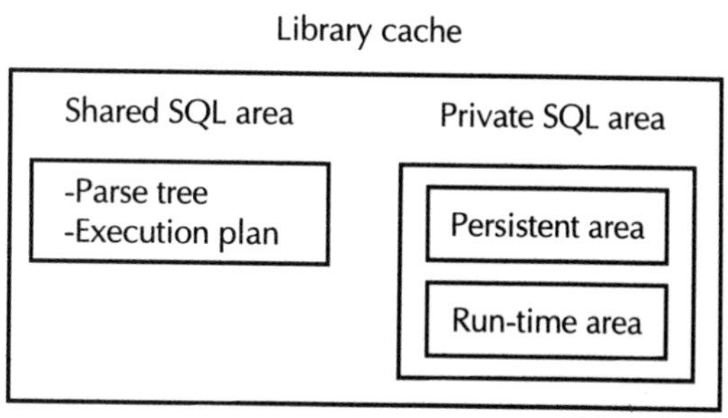

Library cache

Shared SQL area	Private SQL area
-Parse tree -Execution plan	Persistent area Run-time area

FIGURE 5-1.   *The SQL shared and private areas*

SGA Statistics for SQL

There are many ways to get an idea of the amount of SQL activity against a specific table. The easiest and fastest method is to run a query against the *v$systat* view and see the accumulated values since instance start-up time. The following script gives interesting information on the execution of SQL statements on tables.

stat.sql

```
column value format 999,999,999

select
    name,
    value
from
    v$sysstat
where
    name like 'table%';
```

Here is the output from this simple script. Next we see the accumulated totals since database start time:

```
NAME                                                             VALUE
----------------------------------------------------------- ------------
table scans (short tables)                                      71,718
table scans (long tables)                                        1,965
table scans (rowid ranges)                                          33
table scans (cache partitions)                                       0
table scans (direct read)                                            0
table scan rows gotten                                       4,544,406
table scan blocks gotten                                       131,723
```

```
table fetch by rowid                                          172,131
table fetch continued row                                       1,165
```

While these system-wide statistics do not provide the details about the individual SQL statements, they do provide some important insight into the SQL performance of the entire database. Let's look at these individual metrics.

- **Table Scans (short tables)**   This is the number of full-table scans performed on small tables. It is optimal to perform full-table scans on short tables rather than using indexes and to place these small tables in the KEEP buffer pool. Note that Table Scans (long tables) plus Table Scans (short tables) is equal to the number of full-table scans.

- **Table Scans (long tables)**   This is the total number of full-table scans performed on large tables. These should be carefully evaluated to see if the full-table scan can be removed by adding an index, or if the query speed might be improved by invoking Oracle parallel query (OPQ).

- **Table Scan Rows Gotten**   This is the number of rows scanned during all full-table scans.

- **Table Scan Blocks Gotten**   This is the number of blocks received via table scans.

- **Table Fetch by ROWID**   This is usually the number of rows that were accessed using an index, normally with nested loop joins.

- **Table Fetch by Continued Row**   This is the number of rows that are chained to another block. However, there are several anomalies in this metric, and a high value here may not necessarily indicate chained rows. Of course, this value will also be high if tables contain large objects with LOB, BLOB, or CLOB datatypes, since these rows will commonly exceed the database block size, thereby forcing the row to chain onto multiple blocks.

Again, this data will give you a general impression about the presence of offensive SQL statements within the library cache. Next, let's take a close look into the library cache and see how we can get details about individual SQL statements.

Inside the Library Cache

The library cache is arguably the most important area of the SGA. The shared SQL areas and the PL/SQL areas reside in the library cache, and this is the true center of activity within the Oracle database. As I mentioned, the activity of SQL within the library cache is critical to the performance of Oracle. I already discussed the use of *cursor_sharing* to make SQL reusable, but there are some other types of SQL statements that are always reparsed.

Reusable SQL Inside the Library Cache

One of the biggest problems with Oracle SQL prior to Oracle8*i* was that execution plans for SQL could not be stored. In Oracle8*i,* we have the ability to use the optimizer plan stability feature to create *stored outlines* to store the execution plan for a SQL statement, and I will discuss this new feature in Chapter 13. When Oracle recognizes an incoming SQL statement, it hashes the SQL syntax to the *dba_hints* view. If a stored outline exists, the execution plan is extracted from the *ol$hints* table, thereby bypassing the overhead of reparsing the SQL. However, Oracle still has problems recognizing "similar" SQL statements. For example, Oracle library cache will examine the following SQL statements and conclude that they are not identical:

```
SELECT * FROM customer;
Select * From Customer;
```

While capitalizing a single letter, adding an extra space between verbs, or using a different variable name might seem trivial, the Oracle software is not sufficiently intelligent to recognize that the statements are identical. Consequently, Oracle will reparse and execute the second SQL statement, even though it is functionally identical to the first SQL statement.

The best way to prevent SQL reloads is to encapsulate all SQL into stored procedures, and place these stored procedures into packages. This use of stored procedures removes all SQL from application programs and moves the SQL into Oracle's data dictionary. This method also has the nice side effect of making all calls to the Oracle database look like a logical function. For example, instead of having a complex SQL statement inside a program, you would have a single call to a stored procedure.

There are other ways to make storage reusable within the library cache. The *cursor_space_for_time init.ora* parameter can be used to speed executions within the library cache. Setting *cursor_space_for_time* to FALSE tells Oracle that a shared SQL area can be deallocated from the library cache to make room for a new SQL statement. Setting *cursor_space_for_time* to TRUE means that all shared SQL areas are pinned in the cache until all application cursors are closed. When this parameter is set to TRUE, Oracle will not bother to check the library cache on subsequent execution calls, because it has already pinned the SQL in the cache. This technique can improve the performance for some queries, but *cursor_space_for_time* should not be set to TRUE if there are cache misses on execution calls. Cache misses indicate that the *shared_pool_size* is already too small, and forcing the pinning of shared SQL areas will only aggravate the problem.

Another way to improve performance on the library cache is to use the *init.ora* *session_cached_cursors* parameter. As you probably know, Oracle checks the library cache for parsed SQL statements, but *session_cached_cursors* can be used to cache the cursors for a query. This is especially useful for tasks that repeatedly issue parse calls for the same SQL statement—for instance, where a SQL statement is repeatedly executed with a different variable value. An example would be the following SQL request that performs the same query 50 times, once for each state:

```
select
    sum(dollars_sold)
from
    sales_table
where
    region = :var1;
```

In Oracle8*i*, we can also reduce excessive SQL reparsing by setting *cursor_sharing=force.* This initialization parameter will dynamically rewrite all SQL that contains literal values and replace the literals with host variables. For applications that dynamically generate SQL with embedded literals, *cursor_sharing* is a godsend that can dramatically reduce library cache overhead and improve the performance of SQL.

Now that we have reviewed techniques for efficiently using library cache storage, let's look at a STATSPACK report that will show us what is happening inside Oracle. There are several metrics that address the inner workings of the library cache.

Monitoring the Library Cache Miss Ratio

The library cache miss ratio tells the DBA whether or not to add space to the shared pool, and it represents the ratio of the sum of library cache reloads to the sum of pins. In general, if the library cache ratio is over 1, you should consider adding to the *shared_pool_size.* Library cache misses occur during the parsing and preparation of the execution plans for SQL statements.

Library cache misses are an indication that the shared pool is not big enough to hold the shared SQL for all currently running programs. If you have no library cache misses (PINS = 0), you may get a small increase in performance by setting *cursor_space_for_time = true,* which prevents ORACLE from deallocating a shared SQL area while an application cursor associated with it is open. Library cache misses during the execute phase occur when the parsed representation exists in the library cache but has been bounced out of the shared pool.

The compilation of a SQL statement consists of two phases: the parse phase and the execute phase. When the time comes to parse a SQL statement, Oracle first checks to see if the parsed representation of the statement already exists in the library cache. If not, Oracle will allocate a shared SQL area within the library cache and then parse the SQL statement. At execution time, Oracle checks to see if a parsed representation of the SQL statement already exists in the library cache. If not, Oracle will reparse and execute the statement.

The following STATSPACK script will compute the library cache miss ratio. Note that the script sums all of the values for the individual components within the library cache and provides an instance-wide view of the health of the library cache.

rpt_lib_miss.sql

```
set lines 80;
set pages 999;

column mydate heading 'Yr.  Mo Dy  Hr.'              format a16
column c1      heading    "execs"                    format 9,999,999
column c2      heading    "Cache Misses|While Executing" format 9,999,999
column c3      heading    "Library Cache|Miss Ratio"  format 999.99999

break on mydate skip 2;

select
   to_char(snap_time,'yyyy-mm-dd HH24')  mydate,
   sum(new.pins-old.pins)                c1,
   sum(new.reloads-old.reloads)          c2,
   sum(new.reloads-old.reloads)/
   sum(new.pins-old.pins)                c3
from
   stats$librarycache old,
   stats$librarycache new,
   stats$snapshot     sn
where
   new.snap_id = sn.snap_id
and
   old.snap_id = new.snap_id-1
and
   old.namespace = new.namespace
group by
   to_char(snap_time,'yyyy-mm-dd HH24')
;
```

Here is the output. The preceding report can easily be customized to alert the DBA during times when there are excessive executions or library cache misses.

```
                         Cache Misses           Library Cache
Yr.  Mo Dy  Hr.    execs While Executing          Miss Ratio
--------------- ---------- --------------- -------------------------
2000-12-20 10       10,338               3                    .00029
2000-12-20 11      182,477             134                    .00073
```

2000-12-20 12	190,707	202	.00106
2000-12-20 13	2,803	11	.00392

Once this report identifies a time period where there may be a problem, STATSPACK provides the ability to run detailed reports to show the behavior of the objects within the library cache.

Monitoring Objects Within the Library Cache with STATSPACK

Within the library cache, hit ratios can be determined for all dictionary objects that are loaded into the RAM buffer. These objects include tables, procedures, triggers, indexes, package bodies, and clusters. None of these objects should be experiencing problems within the library cache. If any of the hit ratios fall below 75 percent, you can increase the size of the shared pool by adding to the *shared_pool_size init.ora* parameter.

The STATSPACK table *stats$librarycache* is the table that keeps information about library cache activity. The table has three relevant columns: namespace, pins, and reloads. The first column is the *namespace,* which indicates whether the measurement is for the SQL area, a table, a procedure, a package body, or a trigger. The second value in this table is *pins,* which counts the number of times an item in the library cache is executed. The *reloads* column counts the number of times the parsed representation did not exist in the library cache, forcing Oracle to allocate the private SQL areas in order to parse and execute the statement.

Let's look at the STATSPACK scripts that we can use to monitor these objects inside the library cache.

STATSPACK Reports for the Library Cache

The following script reports on the details within the objects inside the library cache. While it is often useful to see the specifics for each object, you must remember that the only objects that can be pinned into storage are PL/SQL packages. We will be covering the pinning of packages into the SGA later in this chapter.

rpt_lib.sql

```
set lines 80;
set pages 999;

column mydate heading 'Yr.  Mo Dy  Hr.' format a16
column reloads        format 999,999,999
column hit_ratio      format 999.99
column pin_hit_ratio format 999.99
```

```
break on mydate skip 2;

select
    to_char(snap_time,'yyyy-mm-dd HH24')  mydate,
    new.namespace,
    (new.gethits-old.gethits)/(new.gets-old.gets) hit_ratio,
    (new.pinhits-old.pinhits)/(new.pins-old.pins) pin_hit_ratio,
    new.reloads
from
    stats$librarycache old,
    stats$librarycache new,
    stats$snapshot       sn
where
    new.snap_id = sn.snap_id
and
    old.snap_id = new.snap_id-1
and
    old.namespace = new.namespace
and
    new.gets-old.gets > 0
and
    new.pins-old.pins > 0
;
```

Here is the output. One nice feature of this STATSPACK report is that it shows the activity within the library cache between each snapshot period.

Yr. Mo Dy Hr.	NAMESPACE	HIT_RATIO	PIN_HIT_RATIO	RELOADS
2000-12-20 10	BODY	1.00	1.00	5
	PIPE	1.00	1.00	0
	SQL AREA	.99	.96	2,957
	TABLE/PROCEDURE	1.00	.91	212
	TRIGGER	1.00	1.00	0
	BODY	1.00	1.00	5
	INDEX	1.00	1.00	0
2000-12-20 11	BODY	.99	.99	5
	CLUSTER	1.00	1.00	1
	INDEX	1.00	1.00	0
	PIPE	1.00	1.00	0
	SQL AREA	.98	.99	2,999
	TABLE/PROCEDURE	.99	1.00	221
	TRIGGER	1.00	1.00	0

From this report, the DBA can track the loading of each type of object and see the balance of the different object types inside the library cache.

Now let's look at the how to monitor the amount of SQL sorting within Oracle.

Tuning Oracle SQL Sorting

As a small but very important component of SQL syntax, sorting is a frequently overlooked aspect of Oracle tuning. In general, an Oracle database will automatically perform sorting operations on row data as requested by a *create index* or a SQL ORDER BY or GROUP BY statement. In general, Oracle sorting occurs under the following circumstances:

■ SQL using the *order by* clause

■ SQL using the *group by* clause

■ When an index is created

■ When a MERGE SORT is invoked by the SQL optimizer because inadequate indexes exist for a table join

At the time a session is established with Oracle, a private sort area is allocated in RAM memory for use by the session for sorting. If the connection is via a dedicated connection, a Program Global Area (PGA) is allocated according to the *sort_area_size init.ora* parameter. For connections via the multithreaded server, sort space is allocated in the *large_pool*. Unfortunately, the amount of memory used in sorting must be the same for all sessions, and it is not possible to add additional sort areas for tasks that require large sort operations. Therefore, the designer must strike a balance between allocating enough sort area to avoid disk sorts for the large sorting tasks, and not overwhelming the server RAM memory. We must also remember that the extra sort area will be allocated and not used by tasks that do not require intensive sorting. Of course, sorts that cannot fit into the *sort_area_size* will be paged out into the TEMP tablespaces for a disk sort. Disk sorts are about 14,000 times slower than memory sorts.

As I noted, the size of the private sort area is determined by the *sort_area_size init.ora* parameter. The size for each individual sort is specified by the *sort_area_retained_size init.ora* parameter. Whenever a sort cannot be completed within the assigned space, a disk sort is invoked using the temporary tablespace for the Oracle instance.

Disk sorts are expensive for several reasons. First, they are extremely slow when compared to an in-memory sort. Also, a disk sort consumes resources in the temporary tablespace. Oracle must also allocate buffer pool blocks to hold the blocks in the temporary tablespace. In-memory sorts are always preferable to disk sorts, and disk sorts will surely slow down an individual task as well as impact concurrent tasks on the Oracle instance. Also, excessive disk sorting will cause a high value for free buffer waits, paging other tasks' data blocks out of the buffer.

The following STATSPACK query uses the *stats$sysstat* table. From this table we can get an accurate picture of memory and disk sorts.

rpt_sorts_alert.sql

```
set pages 9999;

column mydate       heading 'Yr.  Mo Dy  Hr.' format a16
column sorts_memory  format 999,999,999
column sorts_disk    format 999,999,999
column ratio         format .99999

select
   to_char(snap_time,'yyyy-mm-dd HH24') mydate,
   newmem.value-oldmem.value sorts_memory,
   newdsk.value-olddsk.value sorts_disk,
   ((newdsk.value-olddsk.value)/(newmem.value-oldmem.value)) ratio
from
   perfstat.stats$sysstat oldmem,
   perfstat.stats$sysstat newmem,
   perfstat.stats$sysstat newdsk,
   perfstat.stats$sysstat olddsk,
   perfstat.stats$snapshot    sn
where
   newdsk.snap_id = sn.snap_id
and
   olddsk.snap_id = sn.snap_id-1
and
   newmem.snap_id = sn.snap_id
and
   oldmem.snap_id = sn.snap_id-1
and
   oldmem.name = 'sorts (memory)'
and
   newmem.name = 'sorts (memory)'
and
   olddsk.name = 'sorts (disk)'
and
   newdsk.name = 'sorts (disk)'
and
   newmem.value-oldmem.value > 0
   and
   newdsk.value-olddsk.value > 100
;
```

Here is the output from the script. Here, you can clearly see the number of memory sorts and disk sorts, and the ratio of disk to memory sorts.

Yr. Mo Dy Hr.	SORTS_MEMORY	SORTS_DISK	RATIO
2000-12-20 12	13,166	166	.01261
2000-12-20 16	25,694	223	.00868
2000-12-21 10	99,183	215	.00217
2000-12-21 15	13,662	130	.00952
2000-12-21 16	17,004	192	.01129
2000-12-22 10	18,900	141	.00746
2000-12-22 11	19,487	131	.00672
2000-12-26 12	12,502	147	.01176
2000-12-27 13	20,338	118	.00580
2000-12-27 18	11,032	119	.01079
2000-12-28 16	16,514	205	.01241
2000-12-29 10	17,327	242	.01397
2000-12-29 16	50,874	167	.00328
2001-01-02 08	15,574	108	.00693
2001-01-02 10	39,052	136	.00348
2001-01-03 11	13,193	153	.01160
2001-01-03 13	19,901	104	.00523
2001-01-03 15	19,929	130	.00652

This report can be changed to send an alert when the number of disk sorts exceeds a predefined threshold, and we can also modify it to plot average sorts by hour of the day and day of the week. The script that follows computes average sorts, ordered by hour of the day:

rpt_avg_sorts_hr.sql

```
set pages 9999;

column sorts_memory  format 999,999,999
column sorts_disk    format 999,999,999
column ratio         format .99999

select
   to_char(snap_time,'HH24'),
   avg(newmem.value-oldmem.value) sorts_memory,
   avg(newdsk.value-olddsk.value) sorts_disk
from
   perfstat.stats$sysstat oldmem,
   perfstat.stats$sysstat newmem,
   perfstat.stats$sysstat newdsk,
   perfstat.stats$sysstat olddsk,
   perfstat.stats$snapshot   sn
where
   newdsk.snap_id = sn.snap_id
and
   olddsk.snap_id = sn.snap_id-1
and
```

```
   newmem.snap_id = sn.snap_id
and
   oldmem.snap_id = sn.snap_id-1
and
   oldmem.name = 'sorts (memory)'
and
   newmem.name = 'sorts (memory)'
and
   olddsk.name = 'sorts (disk)'
and
   newdsk.name = 'sorts (disk)'
and
   newmem.value-oldmem.value > 0
group by
   to_char(snap_time,'HH24')
;
```

Here is the output from the script. We can now take this data and create a graph in a spreadsheet.

TO	SORTS_MEMORY	SORTS_DISK
00	18,855	11
01	19,546	15
02	10,128	5
03	6,503	8
04	10,410	4
05	8,920	5
06	8,302	7
07	9,124	27
08	13,492	71
09	19,449	55
10	19,812	106
11	17,332	78
12	20,566	76
13	17,130	46
14	19,071	61
15	19,494	68
16	20,701	79
17	19,478	44
18	23,364	29
19	13,626	20
20	11,937	17
21	8,467	7
22	8,432	10
23	11,587	10

Figure 5-2 shows the plot from the output. Here you see a typical increase in sort activity during the online period of the day. Sorts rise about 8:00 A.M. and then go down after 6:00 P.M.

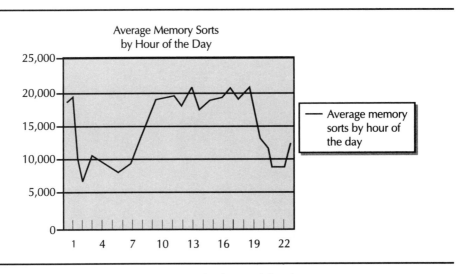

FIGURE 5-2. *Average memory sorts by hour of the day*

Now, let's run the script to compute the averages by the day of the week.

rpt_avg_sorts_dy.sql

```
set pages 9999;

column sorts_memory  format 999,999,999
column sorts_disk    format 999,999,999
column ratio         format .99999

select
   to_char(snap_time,'day')        DAY,
   avg(newmem.value-oldmem.value)  sorts_memory,
   avg(newdsk.value-olddsk.value)  sorts_disk
from
   perfstat.stats$sysstat oldmem,
   perfstat.stats$sysstat newmem,
   perfstat.stats$sysstat newdsk,
   perfstat.stats$sysstat olddsk,
   perfstat.stats$snapshot   sn
where
   newdsk.snap_id = sn.snap_id
```

```
and
   olddsk.snap_id = sn.snap_id-1
and
   newmem.snap_id = sn.snap_id
and
   oldmem.snap_id = sn.snap_id-1
and
   oldmem.name = 'sorts (memory)'
and
   newmem.name = 'sorts (memory)'
and
   olddsk.name = 'sorts (disk)'
and
   newdsk.name = 'sorts (disk)'
and
   newmem.value-oldmem.value > 0
group by
   to_char(snap_time,'day')
;
```

Again, we will take the result set and plot it in a chart. This time, let's plot the disk sorts.

DAY	SORTS_MEMORY	SORTS_DISK
friday	12,545	54
monday	14,352	29
saturday	12,430	2
sunday	13,807	4
thursday	17,042	47
tuesday	15,172	78
wednesday	14,650	43

Figure 5-3 shows the graph. In this database, the activity pattern on Tuesday shows a large number of disk sorts, with another smaller spike on Thursdays. For this database, the DBA may want to pay careful attention to the TEMP tablespaces on these days, and perhaps issue a *alter tablespace TEMP coalesce;* to create continuous extents in the TEMP tablespace.

At the risk of being redundant, I need to reemphasize that the single most important factor in the performance of any Oracle database is the minimization of disk I/O. Hence, the tuning of the Oracle sorting remains one of the most important considerations in the tuning of any Oracle database.

Now, let's turn our attention to the Oracle rollback segments and see how we can use STATSPACK to monitor, identify, and tune your high impact SQL statements.

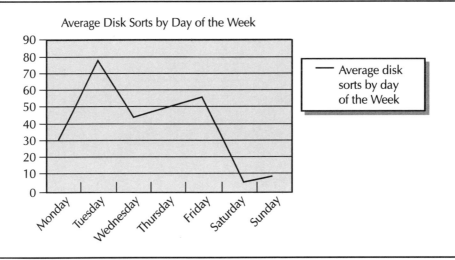

FIGURE 5-3. *Average disk sorts by day of the week*

Identifying High-Impact SQL in the Library Cache

We begin our investigation into Oracle SQL tuning by viewing the SQL that currently resides inside our library cache. Many people ask where they should start when tuning Oracle SQL. Tuning Oracle SQL is like a fishing expedition; you must first "fish" in the Oracle library cache to extract SQL statements, and then rank the statements by their amount of activity.

Oracle makes it quite easy to locate frequently executed SQL statements. The SQL statements in the *v$sqlarea* view are rank ordered by several values:

- **rows_processed** Queries that process a large number of rows will have high I/O and may also have an impact on the TEMP tablespace.

- **buffer_gets** High buffer gets may indicate a resource-intensive query.

- **disk_reads** High disk reads indicate a query that is causing excessive I/O.

- **sorts** Sorts can be a huge slowdown, especially if the sorts are being done on disk in the TEMP tablespace.

■ **executions** The more frequently executed SQL statements should be tuned first, since they will have the greatest impact on overall performance.

You can get lists of SQL statements from the *v$sqlarea* view or *stats$sql_summary* table in descending order on any of these variables.

The executions column of the *v$sqlarea* view and the *stats$sql_summary* table can be used to locate the most frequently used SQL. When fishing for SQL, you can use a tool to display the SQL in the library cache. The next section will cover two ways to extract high-impact SQL:

■ Extract SQL from *stats$sql_summary* with a STATSPACK SQL top-10 report.

■ Extract and analyze SQL from the library cache using *access.sql*.

Please note that either of these techniques can be used with either the historical STATSPACK *sql_summary* table or with the *v$sqlarea* view. The columns are identical.

A SQL Top-10 Report

What follows is an easy-to-use Korn shell script that can be run against your STATSPACK tables to identify high-use SQL statements. If you are not using STATSPACK, you can query the *v$sql* view to get the same information since instance start time.

rpt_sql.ksh

```ksh
#!/bin/ksh

# First, we must set the environment . . . .
ORACLE_SID=readtest
export ORACLE_SID
ORACLE_HOME=`cat /var/opt/oracle/oratab|grep ^$ORACLE_SID:|cut -f2 -d':'`
export ORACLE_HOME
PATH=$ORACLE_HOME/bin:$PATH
export PATH

echo "How many days back to search?"
read days_back

echo executions
echo loads
echo parse_calls
echo disk_reads
echo buffer_gets
echo rows_processed
```

```
echo sorts
echo
echo "Enter sort key:"
read sortkey

$ORACLE_HOME/bin/sqlplus perfstat/perfstat<<!


set array 1;
set lines 80;
set wrap on;
set pages 999;
set echo off;
set feedback off;

column mydate      format a8
column exec        format 9,999,999
column loads       format 999,999
column parse       format 999,999
column reads       format 9,999,999
column gets        format 9,999,999
column rows_proc   format 9,999,999
 column sorts       format 999,999

drop table temp1;
create table temp1 as
    select min(snap_id) min_snap
    from stats\$snapshot where snap_time > sysdate-$days_back;

drop table temp2;

create table temp2 as
select
    to_char(snap_time,'dd Mon HH24:mi:ss') mydate,
    executions                    exec,
    loads                         loads,
    parse_calls                   parse,
    disk_reads                    reads,
    buffer_gets                   gets,
    rows_processed                rows_proc,
    sorts                         sorts,
    sql_text
from
    perfstat.stats\$sql_summary sql,
    perfstat.stats\$snapshot      sn
where
    sql.snap_id >
    (select min_snap from temp1)
and
    sql.snap_id = sn.snap_id
order by $sortkey desc
;
```

```
spool off;

select * from temp2 where rownum < 11;

exit
!
```

Here is the listing from running this valuable script. Note that the DBA is prompted as to how many days back to search, and the sort key for extracting the SQL.

rpt_sql.ksh

```
How many days back to search?
7
executions
loads
parse_calls
disk_reads
buffer_gets
rows_processed
sorts

Enter sort key:
disk_reads

SQL*Plus: Release 8.1.6.0.0 - Production on Thu Dec 14 09:14:46 2000

(c) Copyright 1999 Oracle Corporation. All rights reserved.


Connected to:
Oracle8i Enterprise Edition Release 8.1.6.1.0 - 64bit Production
With the Partitioning option
JServer Release 8.1.6.1.0 - 64bit Production
```

MYDATE	EXEC	LOADS	PARSE	READS	GETS	ROWS_PROC	SORTS
SQL_TEXT							

```
-------------------------------------------------------------------11 Dec
1       866      1      866    246,877 2,795,211      865      4:00:09
DECLARE job BINARY_INTEGER := :job; next_date DATE := :mydate;  broken BOOLEAN :
= FALSE; BEGIN statspack.snap; :mydate := next_date; IF broken THEN :b := 1; ELSE
:b := 0; END IF; END;

11 Dec 1      863      1      863    245,768 2,784,834      862
1:00:29
DECLARE job BINARY_INTEGER := :job; next_date DATE := :mydate;  broken BOOLEAN :
= FALSE; BEGIN statspack.snap; :mydate := next_date; IF broken THEN :b := 1; ELS
E :b := 0; END IF; END;
```

```
11 Dec 1        866       1       866    245,325   597,647   129,993        866
4:00:09
INSERT INTO STATS$SQL_SUMMARY ( SNAP_ID,DBID,INSTANCE_NUMBER,SQL_TEXT,SHARABLE_M
EM,SORTS,MODULE,LOADED_VERSIONS,EXECUTIONS,LOADS,INVALIDATIONS,PARSE_CALLS,DISK_
READS,BUFFER_GETS,ROWS_PROCESSED,ADDRESS,HASH_VALUE,VERSION_COUNT )   SELECT MIN(
:b1),MIN(:b2),MIN(:b3),MIN(SQL_TEXT),SUM(SHARABLE_MEM),SUM(SORTS),MIN(MODULE),SU
M(LOADED_VERSIONS),SUM(EXECUTIONS),SUM(LOADS),SUM(INVALIDATIONS),SUM(PARSE_CALLS
),SUM(DISK_READS),SUM(BUFFER_GETS),SUM(ROWS_PROCESSED),ADDRESS,HASH_VALUE,COUNT(
1)   FROM V$SQL  GROUP BY ADDRESS,HASH_VALUE  HAVING (SUM(BUFFER_GETS) > :b4  OR
 SUM(DISK_READS) > :b5  OR SUM(PARSE_CALLS) > :b6  OR SUM(EXECUTIONS) > :b7 )

11 Dec 0        861       1       861    245,029  2,778,052        860          0
9:00:24
DECLARE job BINARY_INTEGER := :job; next_date DATE := :mydate;  broken BOOLEAN :
= FALSE; BEGIN statspack.snap; :mydate := next_date; IF broken THEN :b := 1; ELSE
E :b := 0; END IF; END;

11 Dec 1        864       1       864    244,587   595,861   129,605        864
2:00:02
INSERT INTO STATS$SQL_SUMMARY ( SNAP_ID,DBID,INSTANCE_NUMBER,SQL_TEXT,SHARABLE_M

EM,SORTS,MODULE,LOADED_VERSIONS,EXECUTIONS,LOADS,INVALIDATIONS,PARSE_CALLS,DISK_
READS,BUFFER_GETS,ROWS_PROCESSED,ADDRESS,HASH_VALUE,VERSION_COUNT )   SELECT MIN(
:b1),MIN(:b2),MIN(:b3),MIN(SQL_TEXT),SUM(SHARABLE_MEM),SUM(SORTS),MIN(MODULE),SU
M(LOADED_VERSIONS),SUM(EXECUTIONS),SUM(LOADS),SUM(INVALIDATIONS),SUM(PARSE_CALLS
),SUM(DISK_READS),SUM(BUFFER_GETS),SUM(ROWS_PROCESSED),ADDRESS,HASH_VALUE,COUNT(
1)   FROM V$SQL  GROUP BY ADDRESS,HASH_VALUE  HAVING (SUM(BUFFER_GETS) > :b4  OR
 SUM(DISK_READS) > :b5  OR SUM(PARSE_CALLS) > :b6  OR SUM(EXECUTIONS) > :b7 )
```

It is interesting to note in the preceding output that we see the STATSPACK
insert statement for the *stats$sql_summary* table.

Next, let's look at a technique that is probably the most valuable script in this book.

Reporting on SQL from the Library Cache

This section explores a technique that runs the Oracle8*i* *explain plan* statement on
all SQL statements in the library cache, analyzes all the execution plans, and
provides reports on all table and index access methods.

This tool will be used extensively throughout this text, so it is important that you
understand how this tool can be used to aid you in pursuit of suboptimal SQL
statements.

At first glance, it may be hard to fully appreciate the value of this technique and
the information produced by the reports. But if your database has a large library

cache, you can get some great insights into the internal behavior of the tables and indexes. The information also offers some great clues about what database objects you need to adjust. The reports are invaluable for the following database activities:

- **Identifying high-use tables and indexes**   See what tables the database accesses most frequently.

- **Identifying tables for caching**   You can quickly find small, frequently accessed tables for placement in the KEEP pool (Oracle8) or for use with the CACHE option (Oracle7). You can enhance the technique to automatically cache tables when they meet certain criteria for the number of blocks and the number of accesses. (I automatically cache all tables with fewer than 200 blocks when a table has experienced more than 100 full-table scans.)

- **Identifying tables for row resequencing**   To reduce I/O, you can locate large tables that have frequent index range scans in order to resequence the rows.

- **Dropping unused indexes**   You can reclaim space occupied by unused indexes. Studies have found that an Oracle database never uses more than a quarter of all indexes available or doesn't use them in the way for which they were intended.

- **Stopping full-table scans by adding new indexes**   Quickly find the full-table scans that you can speed up by adding a new index to a table.

The script is too long to reproduce in this book, but the source code for the scripts in this book can be found at **http://www.osborne.com/oracle/ code_archive.html**. Here are the steps to execute this script:

1. Download the *access.sql* and *access_report.sql* scripts.

2. Issue the following statements for the schema owner of your tables:

   ```
   grant select on v_$sqltext to schem_owner;
   grant select on v_$sqlarea to schem_owner;
   grant select on v_$session to schem_owner;
   grant select on v_$mystat to schem_owner;
   ```

3. Go into SQL*Plus, connect as the schema owner, and run *access.sql*.

You must be signed on as the schema owner in order to explain SQL statements with unqualified table names. Also, remember that you will get statistics only for the SQL statements that currently reside in your library cache. For very active databases, you may want to run this report script several times—it takes less than ten minutes for most Oracle databases.

Using the access.sql Script with STATSPACK

The *access.sql* script can be easily modified to use the *stats$sql_summary* tables to extract and explain historical SQL statements. All you need to do is change the reference to *v$sqlarea* to *stats_sql_summary,* and add the following to the *where* clause:

```
FROM
    stats$sql_summary s,
    stats$snapshot sn
WHERE
    s.snapshot_id = sn.snapshot_id
AND
    sn,snapshot_id = (select max(snapshot_id) from stats$snapshot;
```

Of course, you can modify the *access.sql* script to extract, explain, and report on any SQL in the *stats$sql_summary* table. Remember, though, that the SQL stored in the *stats$sql_summary* table is filtered by the thresholds stored in the *stats$statspack_parameter* table:

- **executions_th**   This is the number of executions of the SQL statement (default is 100).

- **disk_reads_th**   This is the number of disk reads performed by the SQL statement (default is 1,000).

- **parse_calls_th**   This is the number of parse calls performed by the SQL statement (default is 1,000).

- **buffer_gets_th**   This is the number of buffer gets performed by the SQL statement (default is 10,000).

Remember, a SQL statement will be included in the *stats$sql_summary* table if any *one* of the thresholds is exceeded.

Now, let's get back to *access.sql* and look at the valuable reports.

The access.sql Reports

As I noted, the *access.sql* script grabs all of the SQL in the library cache and stores it in a table called *sqltemp.* From this table, all of the SQL is explained in a single plan table. This plan table is then queried to produce the report that follows.

You should then see a report similar to the one listed here. Let's begin by looking at the output this technique provides, and then we'll examine the method for producing the reports. For the purpose of illustration, let's break up the report into several sections. The first section shows the total number of SQL statements in the library cache, and the total number that could not be explained. Some statements cannot be explained because they do not indicate the owner of the table. If your value for statements that cannot be explained is high, you are probably not connected as the proper schema owner when running the script.

Report from access.sql

```
PL/SQL procedure successfully completed.
```

```
Mon Jan 29                                                       page    1
                          Total SQL found in library cache

     23907

Mon Jan 29                                                       page    1
                      Total SQL that could not be explained

     65
```

The Full-table Scan Report

This is the most valuable report of all. Next we see all of the SQL statements that performed full-table scans, and the number of times that a full-table scan was performed. Also note the C and K columns. The C column indicates if an Oracle7 table is cached, and the K column indicates whether the Oracle8 table is assigned to the KEEP pool. As you will recall, small tables with full-table scans should be placed in the KEEP pool.

```
Mon Jan 29                                                       page    1
                          full table scans and counts
                Note that "C" indicates the table is cached.
```

OWNER	NAME	NUM_ROWS	C	K	BLOCKS	NBR_FTS
SYS	DUAL		N		2	97,237
SYSTEM	SQLPLUS_PRODUCT_PROFILE		N	K	2	16,178
DONALD	PAGE	3,450,209	N		932,120	9,999
DONALD	RWU_PAGE	434	N		8	7,355
DONALD	PAGE_IMAGE	18,067	N		1,104	5,368
DONALD	SUBSCRIPTION	476	N	K	192	2,087
DONALD	PRINT_PAGE_RANGE	10	N	K	32	874
ARSD	JANET_BOOKS	20	N		8	64
PERFSTAT	STATS$TAB_STATS		N		65	10

In the preceding report, you see several huge tables that are performing full-table scans. For tables that have less than 200 blocks and are doing legitimate full-table scans, we will want to place these in the KEEP pool. The larger table full-table scans should also be investigated, and the legitimate large-table full-table scans should be parallelized with the *alter table parallel degree nn* command.

An Oracle database invokes a large-table full-table scan when it cannot service a query through indexes. If you can identify large tables that experience excessive full-table scans, you can take appropriate action to add indexes. This is especially important when you migrate from Oracle7 to Oracle8, because Oracle8 offers indexes that have built-in functions. Another cause of a full-table scan is when the cost-based optimizer decides that a full-table scan will be faster than an index range scan. This occurs most commonly with small tables, which are ideal for caching in Oracle7 or placing in the KEEP pool in Oracle8. This full-table scan report is critical for two types of SQL tuning:

■ For a small-table full-table scan, cache the table by using the *alter table* xxx *cache* command (where xxx = table name), which will put the table rows at the most recently used end of the data buffer, thereby reducing disk I/O for the table. (Note that in Oracle8 you should place cached tables in the KEEP pool.)

■ For a large-table full-table scan, you can investigate the SQL statements to see if the use of indexes would eliminate the full-table scan. Again, the original source for all the SQL statements is in the SQLTEMP table. I will talk about the process of finding and explaining the individual SQL statements in the next section.

Next, we see the index usage reports. These index reports are critical for the following areas of Oracle tuning:

■ **Index usage** Ensuring that the application is actually using a new index. DBAs can now obtain empirical evidence that an index is actually being used after it has been created. All indexes will appear in this report, so it is easy to locate those indexes that are not being used.

■ **Row resequencing** Finding out which tables might benefit from row resequencing. Tables that have a large amount of index range scan activity will benefit from having the rows resequenced into the same order as the index. Resequencing can result in a tenfold performance improvement, depending on the row length. For details on row resequencing techniques, see Chapter 10.

Next, let's look at the index range scan report.

The Index Range Scan Report

Next we see the report for index range scans. The most common method of index access in Oracle is the index range scan. An index range scan is used when the SQL statement contains a restrictive clause that requires a sequential range of values that are indexes for the table.

Mon Jan 29   page   1
                            Index range scans and counts

OWNER	TABLE_NAME	INDEX_NAME	TBL_BLOCKS	NBR_SCANS
DONALD	ANNO_HIGHLIGHT	HL_PAGE_USER_IN_IDX	16	7,975
DONALD	ANNO_STICKY	ST_PAGE_USER_IN_IDX	8	7,296
DONALD	PAGE	ISBN_SEQ_IDX	120	3,859
DONALD	TOC_ENTRY	ISBN_TOC_SEQ_IDX	40	2,830
DONALD	PRINT_HISTORY	PH_KEY_IDX	32	1,836
DONALD	SUBSCRIPTION	SUBSC_ISBN_USER_IDX	192	210
ARSD	JANET_BOOK_RANGES	ROV_BK_RNG_BOOK_ID_	8	170
PERFSTAT	STATS$SYSSTAT	STATS$SYSSTAT_PK	845	32

The Index Unique Scan Report

Here is a report that lists index unique scans, which occur when the Oracle database engine uses an index to retrieve a specific row from a table. The Oracle database commonly uses these types of "probe" accesses when it performs a JOIN and probes another table for the JOIN key from the driving table. This report is also useful for finding out those indexes that are used to identify distinct table rows as opposed to indexes that are used to fetch a range of rows.

Mon Jan 29   page   1
                            Index unique scans and counts

OWNER	TABLE_NAME	INDEX_NAME	NBR_SCANS
DONALD	BOOK	BOOK_ISBN	44,606
DONALD	PAGE	ISBN_SEQ_IDX	39,973
DONALD	BOOK	BOOK_UNIQUE_ID	6,450
DONALD	ANNO_DOG_EAR	DE_PAGE_USER_IDX	5,339
DONALD	TOC_ENTRY	ISBN_TOC_SEQ_IDX	5,186
DONALD	PRINT_PERMISSIONS	PP_KEY_IDX	1,836
DONALD	RDRUSER	USER_UNIQUE_ID_IDX	1,065
DONALD	CURRENT_LOGONS	USER_LOGONS_UNIQUE_I	637
ARSD	JANET_BOOKS	BOOKS_BOOK_ID_PK	54
DONALD	ERROR_MESSAGE	ERROR_MSG_IDX	48

The Full-index Scan Report

The next report shows all index full scans. As you will recall, the Oracle optimizer will sometimes perform an index full scan in lieu of a large sort in the TEMP tablespace. You will commonly see full-index scans in SQL that have the ORDER BY clause.

```
Mon Jan 29                                             page    1
                         Index full scans and counts

OWNER       TABLE_NAME           INDEX_NAME             NBR_SCANS
---------   --------------------   ------------------   ------------
DONALD      BOOK                 BOOK_ISBN                  2,295
DONALD      PAGE                 ISBN_SEQ_IDX                 744
```

Although index full scans are usually faster than disk sorts, you can use one of several *init.ora* parameters to make index full scans even faster. These are the *V77_plans_enabled* parameters in Oracle7, which were renamed to *fast_full_scan_enabled* in Oracle8. You can use a fast full scan as an alternative to a full-table scan when an index contains all the columns needed for a query. A fast index full scan is faster than a regular index full scan because it uses multi-block I/O as defined by the *db_file_multiblock_read_count* parameter. It can also accept a parallel hint in order to invoke a parallel query, in the same fashion as a full-table scan. The Oracle database engine commonly uses index full scans to avoid sorting. Say you have a customer table with an index on the *cust_nbr* column. The database could service the SQL command *select * from customer order by cust_nbr;* in two ways:

- It could perform a full-table scan and then sort the result set. The full-table scan could be performed very quickly with *db_file_muiltiblock_read_count init.ora* parameter set, or the table access could be parallelized by using a *parallel* hint. However, the result set must then be sorted in the TEMP tablespace.

- It could obtain the rows in customer number order by reading the rows via the index, thus avoiding a sort.

Limitations of the access.sql Reports

The technique for generating these reports is not as flawless as it may appear. Because the "raw" SQL statements must be explained in order to obtain the execution plans, you may not know the owner of the tables. One problem with native SQL is that the table names are not always qualified with the table owner. To ensure that all the SQL statements are completely explained, many DBAs sign on to Oracle and run the reports as the schema owner.

A future enhancement would be to issue the following undocumented command immediately before each SQL statement is explained so that any Oracle database user could run the reports:

```
ALTER SESSION SET current_schema = 'tableowner';
```

This would change the schema owner immediately before explaining the SQL statement.

Now that we have covered the SQL reporting, let's move on to look at how the individual SQL statements are extracted and explained.

Conclusion

The material presented in this chapter will be referenced through the body of this book because we must be able to detect SQL with problems before we attempt to tune the statements.

Next, let's look at one of the most important areas of this book, the tuning of SQL table access.

CHAPTER
6

Tuning SQL
Table Access

his chapter deals with the low-level table access methods that are displayed from running the execution plan for the SQL statement. As you know from Chapter 3, any SQL statement may have several execution plans depending on the CBO statistics, the presence and types of indexes, and the *optimizer_mode*. At a lower level, each execution plan translates into table access methods. These low-level table access methods determine the overall response time for the SQL statement, so it is imperative that you understand the table access methods and how you can improve the throughput for table access.

When discussing Oracle table access methods, we must always remember that Oracle has only a few ways to access any Oracle table, and that the physical access is always performed by reading a database block. There are several ways to access Oracle data blocks from SQL:

- **Full-table scan** This can invoke multi-block reads and parallelism to improve access speed.

- **Index access** When using an index to retrieve a row, the index provides Oracle with the ROWID, which results in a request for a specific Oracle data block. We also see index range scans, where a range of values is retrieved from a table, and these accesses are based on a range of ROWIDs that are collected while reading the index nodes.

- **Fast full-index scan** This is a form of index where Oracle reads all of the data blocks within an index using multiblock reads and parallelism. It is the index equivalent of a full-table scan.

To fully understand Oracle table access methods, you must begin by carefully examining full-table scans. The SQL optimizer manages index access within Oracle automatically, but we will examine tricks for improving SQL index access in Chapter 20. Within an individual table, we can perform numerous administrative functions to improve the speed of SQL, including row resequencing and changing the table storage parameters. This chapter will cover the following table access issues:

- SQL tuning and full-table scans

- Table access via indexes

- Changing table access methods

- Resequencing table rows for reducing disk I/O

- Oracle storage parameters and table access performance
- Freelist management and table access performance

When you look at tuning any Oracle SQL statement, you must first understand the ways that an Oracle table can be accessed, and the internal block access techniques. Let's begin by examining the full-table scan.

SQL Tuning and Full-Table Scans

There are some important rules for when a SQL query should perform a full-table scan. Unnecessary large-table full-table scans cause a huge amount of unnecessary I/O and can drag down an entire database. The tuning expert first evaluates the SQL in terms of the number of rows returned by the query. If the query returns less than 40 percent of the table rows in an ordered table, or 7 percent of the rows in an unordered table, the query may be tuned to use an index in lieu of the full-table scan. The most common tuning for unnecessary full-table scans is adding indexes. Standard B-tree indexes can be added to tables, and bitmapped and function-based indexes can also eliminate full-table scans. The decision about removing a full-table scan should be based on a careful examination of the I/O costs of the index scan versus the costs of the full-table scan, factoring in the multi-block reads and possible parallel execution. In some cases an unnecessary full-table scan can be forced to use an index by adding an index hint to the SQL statement.

In cases where a small-table full-table scan is the fastest access method, the tuning professional should ensure that a dedicated data buffer is available for the rows. In Oracle7, you can issue *alter table xxx cache*. In Oracle8 and beyond, the small table can be cached by forcing the table into the KEEP pool.

Determining the Threshold for a Full-Table Scan

When making the decision to change a full-table scan to an index range scan, the primary concern is the speed of the query. In some cases, the full-table scan may have more physical disk I/Os, but the full-table scan will be faster because of a high degree of parallelism.

In other cases, you need to consider the number of rows retrieved as a function of the clustering of the rows in the table. For example, if your table is clustered or you have manually resequenced the rows into primary-key order, a great many adjacent rows can be read in a single I/O and an index range scan will be faster than a full-table scan for up to 40 percent of the table rows. On the other hand, if your table is totally unordered, a request for 10 percent of the table rows may cause the majority of the table data blocks to be read. Of course, you also need to consider the degree of parallelism on the table and the setting for *db_file_multi_block_read_count init.ora* parameter. Hence, the general guideline for replacing an index range scan is:

- **For row-sequenced tables**   Queries that retrieve less than 40 percent of the table rows should use an index range scan. Conversely, queries that read more than 40 percent of the rows should use a full-table scan.

- **For unordered tables**   Queries that retrieve less than 7 percent of the table should use an index range scan. Conversely, queries that read more than 7 percent of the table rows will probably be faster will a full-table scan.

Your mileage may vary, so it is always a good idea to test the execution speed in SQL*Plus by issuing the *set timing on* command.

Finding Full-Table Scans

The easiest way to find full-table scans in your database is to use the *access.sql* script from www.oraclepress.com. This script grabs all of the SQL in the library cache and stores it in a table called *sqltemp*. From this table, all of the SQL is explained into a single plan table. This plan table is then queried to produce the report that follows.

Here we see a list of all the tables that performed full-table scans, and the number of times that a full-table scan was performed. Also note the C and K columns. The C column indicates if an Oracle7 table is cached, and the K column indicates whether the Oracle8 table is assigned to the KEEP pool. As you will recall, small tables with full-table scans should be placed in the KEEP pool.

 Mon Jan 29   page   1
                              full table scans and counts
                   Note that "C" indicates the table is cached.

OWNER	NAME	NUM_ROWS	C	K	BLOCKS	NBR_FTS
SYS	DUAL		N		2	97,237
SYSTEM	SQLPLUS_PRODUCT_PRO		N	K	2	16,178
DONALD	PAGE	3,450,209	N		932,120	9,999
DONALD	RWU_PAGE	434	N		8	7,355
DONALD	PAGE_IMAGE	18,067	N		1,104	5,368
DONALD	SUBSCRIPTION	476	N	K	192	2,087
DONALD	PRINT_PAGE_RANGE	10	N	K	32	874
ARSD	JANET_BOOKS	20	N		8	64
PERFSTAT	STATS$TAB_STATS		N		65	10

In the preceding report, you see several huge tables that are performing full-table scans. If tables have less than 200 blocks and are doing legitimate full-table scans, we will want to place them in the KEEP pool. The larger table full-table scans should also be investigated, and the legitimate large-table full-table scans should be parallelized with the *alter table parallel degree nn* command.

An Oracle database invokes a large-table full-table scan when it cannot service a query through indexes. If you can identify large tables that experience excessive full-table scans, you can take appropriate action to add indexes. This is especially important when you migrate from Oracle7 to Oracle8, because Oracle8 offers indexes that have built-in functions. Another cause of a full-table scan is when the cost-based optimizer decides that a full-table scan will be faster than an index range scan. This occurs most commonly with small tables, which are ideal for caching in Oracle7 or placing in the KEEP pool in Oracle8. This full-table scan report is critical for two types of SQL tuning:

- For a small-table full-table scan, cache the table by using the *alter table xxx cache* command (where *xxx* = table name), which will put the table rows at the most recently used end of the data buffer, thereby reducing disk I/O for the table. (Note that in Oracle8, you should place cached tables in the KEEP pool.)

- For a large-table full-table scan, you can investigate the SQL statements to see if the use of indexes would eliminate the full-table scan. I will talk about the process of finding and explaining the individual SQL statements in the next section.

How the Optimizer Chooses a Full-Table Scan

There are several factors that influence the behavior of Oracle SQL with respect to invoking a full-table scan. These factors center around the choice of *optimizer_mode* and the state of dictionary statistics when using the CBO.

Rule-based Optimizer Mode

The rule-based Oracle optimizer is less sophisticated than the cost-based optimizer and does not have any information about the internal characteristics of the data inside the tables specified in the query. Hence, the RBO will always use an index if it detects that an index is available.

The Cost-Based Optimizer Modes

The cost-based optimizer modes, FIRST_ROWS and ALL_ROWS, have information about the data inside the tables. When the CBO estimates that the cost of a full-table scan is less than that of an index access, it may sometimes choose to perform a full-table scan even if indexes are present. The CBO uses the following factors to determine whether to perform a full-table scan:

- **The db_block_size**   Larger blocks will allow for the access of more rows in a single disk I/O.

- **Multiblock I/O**   The number of blocks that can be read in a multiblock I/O depends on the setting of the *db_file_multiblock_read_count* initialization parameter.

- **Index statistics**   The CBO evaluates the selectivity of the index and the depth of the index tree. It then computes the number of I/O operations that are required to service the query via the index.

- **The high-water mark for the table**   The high-water mark for the table determines the amount of data that is stored in the table. In cases where a significant number of rows have been deleted from a table, the high-water mark remains at the original level, and a full-table scan will often read many "dead" blocks below the high-water mark.

While in Oracle7 and Oracle8 the CBO would often falsely favor a full-table scan, in Oracle8*i* the CBO has been improved to the point that it will make an intelligent choice. I must also note that there are differences in the CBO optimizer modes and the propensity to invoke a full-table scan. Let's look at each mode:

ALL_ROWS Optimizer Mode   This is a cost-based optimizer mode that ensures that the overall query time is minimized, even if it takes longer to receive the first row. This usually involves choosing a parallel full-table scan over a full-index scan. Because the ALL_ROWS mode favors full-table scans, the ALL_ROWS mode is best suited for batch-oriented queries where intermediate rows are not required for viewing.

FIRST_ROWS Optimizer Mode   The FIRST_ROWS optimizer mode is designed to return rows as quickly as possible and will only perform a full-table scan when no indexes are available to service access to the table.

When the CBO Chooses a False Full-Table Scan

As I noted, the CBO will sometimes make a false choice in favor of a full-table scan, especially in Oracle7 and Oracle8. This problem occurs when the following conditions are true:

- **High-water mark too high**   When a significant number of deletes have taken place within a table, the high-water mark may be far higher than the actual number of populated blocks. Hence, the CBO will often wrongly invoke a full-table scan, relying on the high-water mark.

- **Wrong *optimizer_mode*** If the *optimizer_mode* is set to ALL_ROWS or CHOOSE, the SQL optimizer may favor full-table scans. If you want fast OLTP optimization, be sure to set your *optimizer_mode* to FIRST_ROWS.

- **Multiple table joins** Prior to Oracle8*i*, when the CBO detected more than three tables being joined in a query, the CBO will perform a full- table scan on one of the tables, even when indexes are available for the join.

- **Skewed indexes** If a candidate index in a query has skewed values, then the CBO might wrongly choose a full-table scan. For example, consider a query that asks for rows *where region=southern*. You have an index on the region column, but only one percent of the entries are for the southern region. In the absence of column histograms, the CBO does not know that southern region has high selectivity, and so it chooses a full-table scan.

Now that you see why the CBO may make a poor decision, let's explore methods for ensuring that we do not have unwanted full-table scans.

Preventing Unwanted Full-Table Scans

There are several conditions that contribute to an unnecessary full-table scan, and it is the job of the SQL tuning professional to locate and correct these conditions. They include both system-wide dictionary issues and issues with individual SQL statements.

Dictionary Issues

There are several issues with regard to information in the Oracle data dictionary that can cause the SQL optimizers to invoke a full-table scan against a table.

Tables with a Too-High High-Water Mark These tables should be reorganized to lower the high-water mark to the appropriate level. When a substantial number of rows are deleted from a table, the high-water mark remains at the prior level, giving the CBO a false sense of the size of the table (see Figure 6-1).

No Column Histograms on Skewed Indexes An index with highly skewed values should be analyzed for column histograms so that the CBO will know when it is proper to use an index. For example, assume we have a bitmapped index on a region column, and that 90 percent of the values are for the Northern region (see Figure 6-2).

In this case, queries against the Southern, Eastern, and Western regions will be faster using the index, while queries that specify the Northern region will be better with a full-table scan. It should be noted that Oracle9*i* will offer additional enhancements to histogram functionality. Instead of the DBA needing to determine which indexes have skewed distributions, the Oracle9*i* DBMS_STATS package will identify and gather histogram statistics on columns that it has determined will benefit from those statistics.

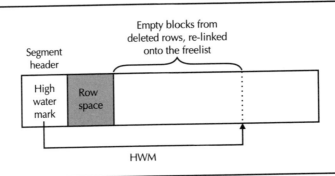

FIGURE 6-1. *A misleading high-water mark*

Using CHOOSE or ALL_ROWS as the optimizer_mode   These modes favor the full-table scan.

Setting Parallel Query   Setting a table to allow parallel query (for example, *alter table customer parallel 35;*) will often cause the CBO to invoke a false full-table scan. Be very careful when altering a table for parallelism because it can have disastrous effects on query performance.

SQL Syntax and Full-Table Scans

Within the scope of a SQL statement, there are many conditions that will cause the SQL optimizer to invoke a full-table scan. The Oracle SQL tuner should always be on the lookout for these types of conditions.

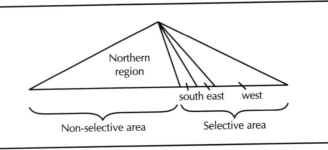

FIGURE 6-2. *A skewed index distribution*

Queries with NULL Conditions   Oracle cannot use an index to select NULL column values because the NULLs are not stored in the index. The example that follows would invoke a full-table scan:

```
select
    emp_name
from
    emp
where
    middle_name IS NULL;
```

Some developers get around the issue by replacing all NULL values with a literal "N/A" and then searching for N/A values. The following actions would prevent a full-table scan:

```
update
    emp
set
    middle_name to 'N/A'
where
    middle_name IS NULL;

select
    emp_name
from
    emp
where
    middle_name = 'N/A';
```

Queries Against Unindexed Columns   It is not uncommon to see queries in the library cache that specify columns in the *where* clause that do not have indexes. Finding these types of SQL statements is especially pleasant because an index can be quickly created to dramatically improve the performance of the query.

Queries with Like Conditions   Queries that use the *like* clause will invoke a full-table scan if the percent sign mask is used in the leading side of the query. For example, the following clause would not cause a full-table scan, because the *like* mask begins with characters and the existing index will be able to service the query.

```
select
    ename
    job,
    hiredate
```

```
from
    emp
where
    ename like 'BURLE%';
```

Here we see that the *ename_idx* can be used for this *like* condition.

```
OPERATION
------------------------------------------------------------------
OPTIONS                          OBJECT_NAME                POSITION
-----------------------------    -------------------------  ----------
SELECT STATEMENT
                                                                1


  INDEX
RANGE SCAN                       ENAME_IDX                       1
```

However, we run into full-table scans when the *like* mask has the percent sign in the beginning of the mask:

```
select
    ename
    job,
    hiredate
from
    emp
where
    ename like '%SON';
```

Here we see that a full-table scan is invoked and the index cannot be used.

```
OPERATION
------------------------------------------------------------------
OPTIONS                          OBJECT_NAME                POSITION
-----------------------------    -------------------------  ----------
SELECT STATEMENT
                                                               26


  INDEX
FULL SCAN                        ENAME_IDX                       1
```

If we have a lot of queries that use the *like* mask with a beginning percent sign and trailing character values, we can create a function-based index using the *reverse* BIF:

```
create index
    ename_reverse_idx
on emp
( reverse(ename) );
```

Next, we slightly alter our query to use the reverse operator:

```
select
    ename
    job,
    hiredate
from
    emp
where
    reverse(ename) like 'NOS%';
```

Here we see that our function-based index can be used for the trailing *like* operator:

```
OPERATION
----------------------------------------------------------------------
OPTIONS                             OBJECT_NAME                POSITION
-----------------------------   ----------------------------  ----------
SELECT STATEMENT
                                                                   1
  TABLE ACCESS
BY INDEX ROWID                      EMP
                                                                   1
    INDEX
RANGE SCAN                          ENAME_REVERSE_IDX
                                                                   1
```

Queries with a Not Equals Condition   You can specify a *not equals* condition in three ways in Oracle SQL. The following statements are identical:

```
select ename from emp where job <> 'MANAGER';
select ename from emp where job != 'MANAGER';
select ename from emp where job not in ('MANAGER');
```

The *not equals* condition or a *not in* condition will always use a full-table scan unless the column values are skewed and column histograms indicate that the index scan is faster. To illustrate, consider a region index where 90 percent of the values are for the Northern region. The following query would rightly choose a full-table scan because the index is very nonselective.

```
select
    customer_name,
    customer_status
from
```

```
    customer
where
    region<>'Southern'.
```

However, the following query would be better served by performing an index range scan because only a minority of the values are not in the Northern region.

```
select
    customer_name,
    customer_status
from
    customer
where
    region<>'Northern'.
```

Invalidating an Index with a BIF   When an index column is altered with a BIF in the *where* clause, the original index cannot be used. This problem is especially prevalent with DATE datatypes where the date is transformed to get a range of values. The following example will use the date index.

```
select
    customer_name,
    customer_status
from
    customer
where
    sales_date < sysdate-7;
```

However, a query for July 2001 sales would not be able to use the index because of the use of the *to_char* built-in function (BIF).

```
select
    customer_name,
    customer_status
from
    customer
where
    to_char(sales_date, 'YYYY-MM')='2001-06';
```

In cases where a function is commonly used against a column, function-based indexes can be created on the base table to remove the full-table scan. Function-based indexes are most commonly used with the following BIFS:

■ ***to_char*** These are commonly used when extracting date datatype values for a day of the week (*to_char(mydate,'day'*)), an hour of the day (*to_char(mydate,'HH24'*)), or a specific range of dates.

■ **substr**   The *substr* function is often used to query subsets of fixed-length character columns.

■ **decode**   The decode function is commonly used to translate abbreviated column identifiers into displayable characters.

The Oracle tuning professional should always be on the lookout for BIFs in SQL statements. The following SQL can be run against the *v$sqlarea* view to quickly identify SQL statements that might have a BIF in their *where* clause.

bif.sql

```
set lines 2000;

select
   sql_text,
   disk_reads,
   executions,
   parse_calls
from
   v$sqlarea
where
   lower(sql_text) like '% substr%'
or
   lower(sql_text) like '% to_char%'
or
   lower(sql_text) like '% decode%'
order by
   disk_reads desc
;
```

Again, it is very important that the Oracle professional constantly be on the lookout for BIFs that are causing a full-table scan. You can be the hero in these cases by quickly creating a function-based index to speed up the query.

Using an ALL_ROWS hint   Developers often add ALL-ROWS hints after reading that they will improve throughput, not realizing that response time will suffer. The ALL_ROWS optimizer goal is designed to improve throughput and tends to favor full-table scans. For any database that requires SQL queries to return some of the result set quickly, the *optimizer_mode* is set to FIRST_ROWS.

Using a Parallel Hint   Setting a parallel hint in a query will always cause the CBO to invoke a full-table scan. This is because all Oracle parallel queries must perform full-table scans in order to dedicate multiple query slaves. Many beginners will add a parallel hint to a SQL query, without testing to ensure that the parallel full-table scan is faster than using the index.

Now that we have covered full-table scans, let's take a look at methods for improving the performance of index range scans. Once we have tuned our SQL queries to use the index, there are several techniques that can be used to improve access speed, especially for queries that perform index range scans against a large number of rows.

Table Access via Indexes

Within Oracle, all indexes are accessed in a transparent fashion and there is very little that we can do to alter the way that Oracle utilizes an index. However, there are numerous internal techniques that we can use to change index access. I will cover these in detail in Chapter 20.

In the meantime, let's turn our attention to methods that can be used to change the Oracle table structures to reduce the amount of disk I/O that occurs when Oracle accesses tables. We will examine how resequencing rows can improve the performance of index range scans and see how the table storage parameters can affect the performance of Oracle *insert, update,* and *delete* statements.

It is important to recognize that there is a hierarchical relationship between the SQL statement, the execution plan, and the table access method (see Figure 6-3).

The SQL source code is used to generate the execution plan. The execution plan, in turn, dictates the table access methods. This is a clear hierarchy because a single SQL statement may be represented by many execution plans, depending on the *optimizer_mode,* hints, and the nature of the CBO statistics. Each execution plan may generate several table access methods, including full-table scans, index scans, and ROWID index access.

As I noted, each execution plan may combine several table access methods, and you must understand the low-level table access methods because they determine the elapsed time for the query. Next, let's look at the ways that the table access method may be changed.

Changing Table Access Methods

Because there are many different ways to write a SQL statement that provides identical results, one of the goals of tuning table access is to be able to rewrite SQL statements to get the desired execution plan. We will cover this topic in greater detail in Chapter 19, but I need to introduce this important concept here because rewriting SQL can dramatically change the table access method.

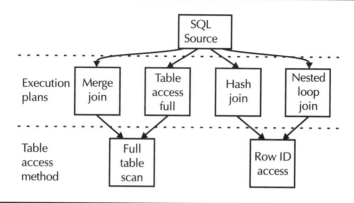

FIGURE 6-3. *The levels of SQL execution*

There are many things that can be done within Oracle to change the table access method for a SQL statement. These include:

- Changing an index from unique to nonunique

- Manually rewriting the SQL statement

- Adding or deleting an index

- Forcing a change with a hint

- Changing the *optimizer_goal* or *optimizer_mode*

In order to appreciate how these changes will affect the execution plan for a SQL statement, let's examine each of these scenarios.

Changing Indexes from Unique to Nonunique

Changing index structures to improve performance is most commonly seen in cases where subqueries are specified. The savvy Oracle SQL tuner is always on the lookout for both correlated and noncorrelated subqueries for several reasons. The foremost is to search for opportunities for replacing the subquery with a standard join, and the other is to examine the uniqueness of the indexes in the subquery to see if changing the index structure can change the table access method.

While we will examine the tuning of subqueries in detail in Chapter 19, for now, just note that subqueries can be specified in any of the following formats:

```
Where emp_name IN (subuery)
Where EXISTS (Subquery)
Where emp_name = (Subquery)
```

To see how changing an index can change the table access method, let's examine a simple example. The query that follows is intended to show all employees who received a bonus. In the Oracle demo database, bonuses are stored in a separate bonus table. To perform this query, we must specify the rows we want in the *emp* table and then look for matching rows in the bonus table:

```
select /*+ first_rows */
    ename,
    hiredate,
    comm
from
    emp
where
    ename IN (select ename from bonus)
;
```

Here is the execution plan, where nonunique indexes have been created on the *ename* columns in the *emp* and *bonus* tables:

```
OPERATION
-----------------------------------------------------------------------
OPTIONS                          OBJECT_NAME                  POSITION
-----------------------------    ---------------------------  ----------
SELECT STATEMENT
                                                                   331
    NESTED LOOPS
                                                                     1
      VIEW
                                 VW_NSO_1                            1
        SORT
UNIQUE                                                               1
          TABLE ACCESS
FULL                             BONUS                               1
        TABLE ACCESS
BY INDEX ROWID                   EMP                                 2
          INDEX
RANGE SCAN                       ENAME_IDX                           1
```

Why do we see the *view* in the execution plan when we know that both entities are tables? When the plan table OPERATION column contains the VIEW object with a *object_name* like VW_NSO_1, the operation represents a nested select operation.

Now, watch what happens when we replace the nonunique indexes with unique indexes on the *ename* column:

```
SQL> create unique index ename_idx on emp (ename);

Index created.

SQL> create unique index ename_bonus_idx on bonus (ename);

Index created.
```

Now we rerun the explain plan to see the execution plan for our query:

```
OPERATION
------------------------------------------------------------------------
OPTIONS                          OBJECT_NAME                    POSITION
-------------------------------  ----------------------------  ----------
SELECT STATEMENT
                                                                       1
  NESTED LOOPS
                                                                       1
    TABLE ACCESS
FULL                             EMP                                   1
    INDEX
UNIQUE SCAN                      ENAME_BONUS_IDX                       2
```

We now have changed the execution plan from a nested select to a standard nested index scan. Note how the presence of a unique rather than nonunique index radically changed the execution plan for the SQL statement.

Rewriting SQL Statements to Change the Table Access Method

There are many ways that a SQL statement can be changed to change the table access method. In the RBO, we can switch the table order in the *from* clause to change the driving table, and the order of the expressions in the *where* clause can change the table access method. Because of the many ways that a query can be rewritten, one of the common SQL tuning techniques is rewriting the SQL source. However, there are many hidden traps in query rewriting, and you must be very careful to ensure that your rewrite is equivalent to the original expression.

This is especially true when rewriting correlated and noncorrelated subqueries into standard joins to improve table access method. Whenever an Oracle SQL tuning professional sees a subquery in a SQL statement, his or her first inclination is to see if the query can be rewritten as a standard join. However, this can be very dangerous unless you know that the subquery is querying on unique values.

If a subquery is rewritten to specify the *Subquery* table in the *from* clause, the result set had better return only a single row, or otherwise the transformed query will return the wrong answer. Returning to our original example, let's try to count the number of employees who have ever received a bonus. This exercise assumes that the *ename* column is not unique.

```
select /*+ first_rows */
    count(*)
from
    emp
where
    ename IN (select ename from bonus)
;
```

Here is the output of the query and the execution plan:

```
    COUNT(*)
----------
         2
```

OPERATION			
OPTIONS		OBJECT_NAME	POSITION
SELECT STATEMENT			5
SORT			
AGGREGATE			1
MERGE JOIN			1
SORT			
JOIN			1
VIEW			
		VW_NSO_1	1
SORT			
UNIQUE			1
TABLE ACCESS			
FULL		BONUS	1
SORT			
JOIN			2
TABLE ACCESS			
FULL		EMP	1

Here we see a merge join, which translates into a full-table scan of both tables. As you know, a merge join does not rely on indexes and can be very time consuming because of the time required to perform the full-table scans.

It might be tempting to rewrite this query to replace the subquery with a standard join by moving the subquery table into the *from* clause and adding a condition to the *where* clause. This is a very common SQL tuning technique, and when done properly, it can result in huge performance gains.

```
select /*+ first_rows */
    count(*)
from
    emp,
    bonus
where
    emp.ename = bonus.ename
;
```

Can you see the problem with this query? Remember, the employee name is not unique, and we cannot guarantee that there will be only one bonus for each employee. If there are employees who have received multiple bonuses, the count will be incorrect. In this case, rewriting the query to replace the noncorrelated subquery with a standard join has not resulted in an equivalent query.

Here is the output and the execution plan. Note that it returns the wrong count, and instead of a count of the number of employees who have ever received a bonus, we see a Cartesian product of both tables!

```
    COUNT(*)
----------
         6
```

OPERATION			
OPTIONS		OBJECT_NAME	POSITION
SELECT STATEMENT			
SORT			
AGGREGATE			1
NESTED LOOPS			
			1
TABLE ACCESS			
FULL		BONUS	1
INDEX			
RANGE SCAN		ENAME_IDX	2

Here we see that the execution plan has changed favorably, and the full-table against the emp table has disappeared, but we have a real problem here because this query is not equivalent to the original subquery.

Why is a unique key required to transform a subquery into a join? The simple reason is that without the uniqueness guarantee, it is possible for the transformed query to produce a different result set. This is because when uniqueness is not guaranteed, multiple rows may be joined to the row in the surrounding query, thus producing a Cartesian product effect.

CAUTION
When rewriting subqueries to improve performance, always verify that there are unique indexes into both of the tables being joined. Otherwise, the reformulated query might return the incorrect result.

Again, we will go into great detail about this issue in Chapter 19, but for now you need to clearly understand that while rewriting subqueries can change the table access method and result in huge performance gains, it can be dangerous to attempt to rewrite subqueries unless you know that the reformulated query will return the identical result set.

Next, let's look at how table rows can be resequenced to improve the throughput of index range scans.

Resequencing Table Rows for Reducing I/O

Experienced Oracle DBAs know that I/O is the single greatest component of response time and regularly work to reduce I/O. Disk I/O is expensive because when Oracle retrieves a block from a data file on disk, the reading process must wait for the physical I/O operation to complete. Disk operations are 14,000 times slower than a row's access in the data buffers. Consequently, anything you can do to minimize I/O—or reduce bottlenecks caused by contention for files on disk—can greatly improve the performance of any Oracle database.

If response times are lagging in your high-transaction system, reducing disk I/O is the best way to bring about quick improvement. And when you access tables in a transaction system exclusively through range scans in primary-key indexes, reorganizing the tables with the CTAS (create table as select) method should be one of the first strategies you use to reduce I/O. By physically sequencing the rows in the same order as the primary-key index, this method can considerably speed up data retrieval.

Like disk load balancing, row resequencing is easy, inexpensive, and relatively quick. With both techniques in your DBA bag of tricks, you'll be well equipped to shorten response times—often dramatically—in high-I/O systems.

In high-volume online transaction processing (OLTP) environments in which data is accessed via a primary index, resequencing table rows so that contiguous blocks follow the same order as their primary index can reduce physical I/O and improve response time during index-driven table queries. This technique is useful only when the application selects multiple rows, when using index range scans, or if the application issues multiple requests for consecutive keys. Databases with random primary-key unique accesses won't benefit from row resequencing.

Most Oracle professionals will run the *access.sql* script from Chapter 5 to identify tables for possible row resequencing. This is done by examining the index range scan report to locate those tables whose table access is predominantly via index range scans. Remember, resequencing table rows will not adversely affect the performance of full-table scans or index unique scans. To get the most benefit, the candidate table should be heavily accessed using a single index key, and the index range scan report will clearly indicate these tables.

Let's explore how this works. Consider a SQL query that retrieves 100 rows using an index:

```
select
    salary
from
    employee
where
    last_name like 'B%';
```

This query will traverse the *last_name_index,* selecting each row to obtain the rows. As Figure 6-4 shows, this query will have at least 100 physical disk reads because the employee rows reside on different data blocks.

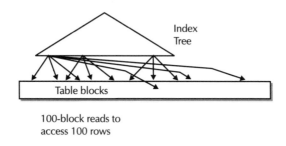

FIGURE 6-4. *An index query on unsequenced rows*

Now let's examine the same query where the rows are resequenced into the same order as the *last_name_index*. In Figure 6-5, you see that the query can read all 100 employees with only three disk I/Os (one for the index, and two for the data blocks), resulting in a saving of over 97 block reads.

The degree to which resequencing improves performance depends on how far out of sequence the rows are when you begin and how many rows you will be accessing in sequence. You can find out how well a table's rows match the index's sequence key by looking at the *dba_indexes* and *dba_tables* views in the data dictionary.

In the *dba_indexes* view, take a look at the *clustering_factor* column. If the clustering factor—an integer—roughly matches the number of blocks in the table, your table is in sequence with the index order. However, if the clustering factor is close to the number of rows in the table, it indicates that the rows in the table are out of sequence with the index.

The benefits of row resequencing cannot be underestimated. In large active tables with a large number of index scans, row resequencing can triple the performance of queries.

There are two ways to resequence Oracle table rows into a primary key order:

- Index cluster

- Manual resequencing of rows

Both of these methods will result in improved performance by reducing disk I/O, but they are implemented in very different ways. Let's take a look at each method.

Row Resequencing with Index Clusters

A popular method for row resequencing I mentioned earlier is the creation of an index cluster. The main advantage of an index cluster is that row data is stored in

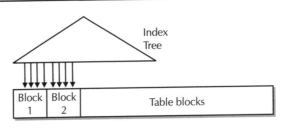

With resequenced rows
three block reads access
the 100 rows.

FIGURE 6-5. *An index query with sequenced rows*

data blocks in the same sequence as the index cluster key. Hence, index range scans that retrieve closely related key values will probably be able to fetch all of the rows in a single disk I/O. This is also popular in cases with a nonunique index whereby all rows with the same key values will be stored on adjacent data blocks.

Oracle provides a method for converting an existing table to a cluster table. As an example, consider the following table:

```
create table
customer (
    customer_key       number,
    customer_stuff     stuff_type
);
```

Let's assume that we have investigated the performance of SQL against this table, and virtually all index range scans are using the customer key. Here is how we can convert this table into a cluster table. First, we define the cluster and the index for the cluster:

```
create cluster
    cust_cluster
    (
        customer_key number
    );

create index
    cust_cluster_ind
on cluster
cust_cluster;
```

Next, we use CTAS to copy in the new table definition for the cluster. Note that we used the *where rownum < 1* clause to prevent the copying of the rows. This is because we will want to recopy the rows into the cluster in their proper order.

```
create table
    customer_new
cluster
    cust_cluster(customer_key)
as
    select *
    from
        customer
    where
    rownum < 1
;
```

Now, we have an empty cluster table and we are ready to populate it with the rows from our original customer table.

```
declare
customer     c1%rowtype;
placeholder number;
cursor
   c1
is
select
   customer_key
from
   customer;


begin
/*loop thru customer table*/
for customer in c1
loop
  /*Check if this cluster_key is already inserted in cluster*/
  begin
   select 1
   into
      placeholder
   from
      dual
   where
      exists (
         select 'X'
         from customer_new
         where customer_key=customer.customer_key);
   exception
     when NO_DATA_FOUND then
       /*Not in new table, so insert all rows with this cluster_key*/
       insert into
          customer_new
          (select * from customer
              where customer_key=customer.customer_key);
       commit;
  end;
end loop;
end;

rename customer     to customer_old;
rename customer_new to customer;

-- Finally, transfer Referential Integrity (RI) constraints
-- and non-cluster indexes
```

Row Resequencing with CTAS

Basically, the *create table as select* (CTAS) statement copies the selected portion of the table into a new table. If you select the entire table with an *order by* clause or an *index* hint, it will copy the rows in the same order as the primary index. In addition to resequencing the rows of the new table, the CTAS statement coalesces free space and chained rows and resets freelists, thereby providing additional performance benefits. You can also alter table parameters, such as initial extents and the number of freelists, as you create the new table, thereby preventing future chaining. The steps in a CTAS reorganization include:

1. Define a separate tablespace to hold the reorganized table.

2. Disable all referential integrity constraints.

3. Copy the table with CTAS.

4. Reenable all referential integrity constraints.

5. Rebuild all indexes on the new table.

The main benefit of CTAS over the other methods is speed. It is far faster to use CTAS to copy the table into a new tablespace (and then re-create all RI and indexes) than it is to use the export/import method. Using CTAS also has the added benefit of allowing the rows to be resequenced into the same order as the primary index, thereby greatly reducing I/O. Within CTAS, there are two general reorganization methods.

Two Alternatives for Using CTAS

It is always recommended that you resequence the table rows when performing a table reorganization with CTAS because of the huge I/O benefits. You can use the CTAS statement in one of two ways. Each of these achieves the same result, but they do it in very different ways:

■ Use CTAS in conjunction with the *order by* clause.

■ Use CTAS in conjunction with a "hint" that identifies the index to use.

The approach you choose depends on the size of the table involved, the overall processing power of your environment, and how quickly you must complete the reorganization.

The details of each CTAS approach are discussed more fully in the sections that follow, but in either case, when you create the new table, you can speed the process by using the Oracle *nologging* option (this was called *unrecoverable* in Oracle7). This skips the added overhead of writing to the redo log file. Of course, you cannot use the redo logs to roll forward through a *nologging* operation, and most DBAs take a full backup prior to using CTAS with *nologging.* Let's examine the two methods and see their respective differences.

Using CTAS with the *order by* Clause

When using CTAS with the *order by* clause, you are directing Oracle to perform the following operations, as shown in Figure 6-6.

As you can see, the full-table scan can be used with parallel query to speed the execution, but we still have a large disk sort following the collection of the rows. Because of the size of most tables, this sort will be done in the TEMP tablespace.

Here is an example of the SQL syntax to perform a CTAS with *order by:*

```
create table new_customer
    tablespace customer_flip
        storage (initial        500m
                 next            50m
                 maxextents      unlimited)
    parallel (degree 11)
    as select * from customer
    order by customer_number;
```

Using CTAS with *order by* can be very slow without the *parallel* clause. A parallel full-table scan reads the original table quickly (in nonindex order).

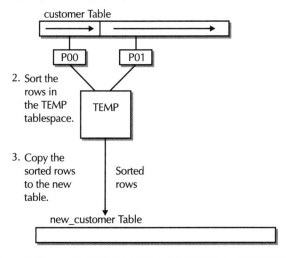

1. Perform a full table scan.

customer Table

POO   PO1

2. Sort the rows in the TEMP tablespace.

TEMP

3. Copy the sorted rows to the new table.

Sorted rows

new_customer Table

FIGURE 6-6.   *Using CTAS with order by*

As you know from Oracle parallel query, the CTAS operation will cause Oracle to spawn to multiple background processes to service the full-table scan. This often makes the *order by* approach faster than using the index-hint approach to CTAS. The choice to use *parallel* depends on the database server. If your hardware has multiple CPUs and many (perhaps hundreds of) processes, using *parallel* is likely to be significantly faster. However, if your hardware configuration has a relatively modest number of processes (such as the four specified in the example), the index-hint approach is likely to be faster.

Using CTAS with an Index Hint

The CTAS with an index hint executes quite differently than CTAS with *order by*. When using an index hint, the CTAS begins by retrieving the table rows from the original table using the existing index. Since the rows are initially retrieved in the proper order, there is no need to sort the result set, and the data is used immediately to create the new table, as shown in Figure 6-7.

The syntax for CTAS with an index hint appears here:

```
create table new_customer
    tablespace customer_flip
        storage  (initial              500m
                  next                 50m
                  maxextents           unlimited)
    as select /*+ index(customer customer_primary_key_idx) */  *
    from customer;
```

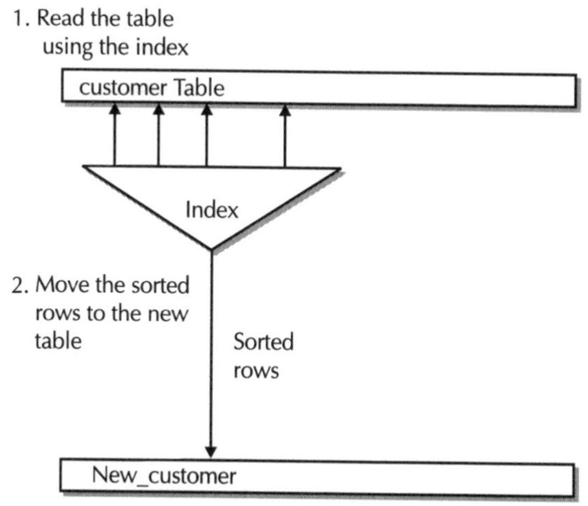

FIGURE 6-7.   *Using CTAS with an index hint*

When this statement executes, the database traverses the existing primary-key index to access the rows for the new table, bypassing the sorting operation. Most Oracle DBAs choose this method over the *order by* approach because the run time performance of traversing an index is generally faster than using the PARALLEL clause and then sorting the entire result set.

Next, let's take a look at the Oracle table storage parameters and see how they affect the performance of SQL statements.

Oracle Storage Parameters and Table Access Performance

Let's begin this section by introducing the relationship between object storage parameters and performance. Poor object performance within Oracle is experienced in several areas:

- **Slow inserts** Insert operations run slowly and have excessive I/O. This happens when blocks on the freelist only have room for a few rows before Oracle is forced to grab another free block.

- **Slow selects** Select statements have excessive I/O because of chained rows. This occurs when rows "chain" and fragment onto several data blocks, causing additional I/O to fetch the blocks.

- **Slow updates** Update statements run very slowly with double the amount of I/O. This happens when *update* operations expand a VARCHAR or BLOB column and Oracle is forced to chain the row contents onto additional data blocks.

- **Slow deletes** Large *delete* statements can run slowly and cause segment header contention. This happens when rows are deleted and Oracle must relink the data block onto the freelist for the table.

As you see, the storage parameters for Oracle tables and indexes can have an important effect on the performance of the database. Let's begin our discussion of object tuning by reviewing the common storage parameters that affect Oracle performance.

The pctfree Storage Parameter

The purpose of *pctfree* is to tell Oracle when to remove a block from the object's freelist. Since the Oracle default is *pctfree* = 10, blocks remain on the freelist while

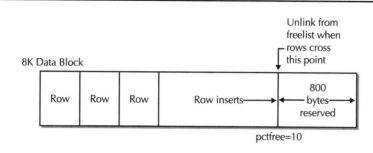

FIGURE 6-8. *The* pctfree *threshold*

they are less than 90 percent full. As shown in Figure 6-8, once an insert makes the block grow beyond 90 percent full, it is removed from the freelist, leaving 10 percent of the block for row expansion. Furthermore, the data block will remain off the freelist even after the space drops below 90 percent. Only *after* subsequent *delete* operations cause the space to fall below the *pctused* threshold of 40 percent will Oracle put the block back onto the freelist.

The pctused Storage Parameter

The *pctused* parameter tells Oracle when to add a previously full block onto the freelist. As rows are deleted from a table, the database blocks become eligible to accept new rows. This happens when the amount of space in a database block falls below *pctused,* and a freelist relink operation is triggered, as shown in Figure 6-9.

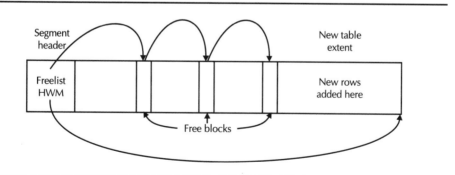

FIGURE 6-9. *The* pctused *threshold*

For example, with *pctused* = 60, all database blocks that have less than 60 percent will be on the freelist, as well as other blocks that dropped below *pctused* and have not yet grown to *pctfree*. Once a block deletes a row and becomes less than 60 percent full, the block goes back on the freelist. When rows are deleted, data blocks become available when a block's free space drops below the value of *pctused* for the table, and Oracle relinks the data block onto the freelist chain. As the table has rows inserted into it, it will grow until the space on the block exceeds the threshold *pctfree*, at which time the block is unlinked from the freelist.

The freelists Storage Parameter

The *freelists* parameter tells Oracle how many segment header blocks to create for a table or index. Multiple freelists are used to prevent segment header contention when several tasks compete to *insert, update,* or *delete* from the table. The *freelists* parameter should be set to the maximum number of concurrent update operations.

Prior to Oracle8*i,* you must reorganize the table to change the *freelists* storage parameter. In Oracle8*i,* you can dynamically add freelists to any table or index with the *alter table* command. In Oracle8i, adding a freelist reserves a new block in the table to hold the control structures.

The freelist Groups Storage Parameter for OPS

The *freelist groups* parameter is used in Oracle Parallel Server (Real Application Clusters). When multiple instances access a table, separate freelist groups are allocated in the segment header. The *freelist groups* parameter should be set to the number of instances that access the table. For details on segment internals with multiple freelist groups, see Chapter 13.

NOTE
The variables are called pctfree *and* pctused *in the* create table *and* alter table *syntax, but they are called* PCT_FREE *and* PCT_USED *in the* dba_tables *view in the Oracle dictionary.*

Summary of Storage Parameter Rules

The following rules govern the settings for the storage parameters *freelists, freelist groups, pctfree,* and *pctused.* As you know, the value of *pctused* and *pctfree* can easily be changed at any time with the *alter table* command, and the observant DBA should be able to develop a methodology for deciding the optimal settings for these parameters. For now, accept these rules, and I will discuss them in detail later in this chapter.

There is a direct trade-off between effective space utilization and high performance, and the table storage parameters control this trade-off:

- **For efficient space reuse** A high value for *pctused* will effectively reuse space on data blocks, but at the expense of additional I/O. A high *pctused* means that relatively full blocks are placed on the freelist. Hence, these blocks will be able to accept only a few rows before becoming full again, leading to more I/O.

- **For high performance** A low value for *pctused* means that Oracle will not place a data block onto the freelist until it is nearly empty. The block will be able to accept many rows until it becomes full, thereby reducing I/O at insert time. Remember that it is always faster for Oracle to extend into new blocks than to reuse existing blocks. It takes fewer resources for Oracle to extend a table than to manage freelists.

While I will go into the justification for these rules later in this chapter, let's review the general guidelines for setting of object storage parameters:

- Always set *pctused* to allow enough room to accept a new row. We never want to have free blocks that do not have enough room to accept a row. If we do, this will cause a slowdown, since Oracle will attempt to read five "dead" free blocks before extending the table to get an empty block.

- The presence of chained rows in a table means that *pctfree* is too low or that *db_block_size* is too small. In most cases within Oracle, RAW and LONG RAW columns make huge rows that exceed the maximum block size for Oracle, making chained rows unavoidable.

- If a table has simultaneous *insert* SQL processes, it needs to have simultaneous *delete* processes. Running a single purge job will place all of the free blocks on only one freelist, and none of the other freelists will contain any free blocks from the purge.

- The *freelist* parameter should be set to the high-water mark of updates to a table. For example, if the customer table has up to 20 end users performing *insert* operations at any time, the customer table should have *freelists* = 20.

- The *freelist groups* parameter should be set to the number of Oracle Parallel Server instances that access the table.

Freelist Management and Table Access Performance

One of the benefits of having Oracle is that it manages all of the free space within each tablespace. Oracle handles table and index space management for us and insulates humans from the inner workings of the Oracle tables and indexes. However, experienced Oracle tuning professionals need to understand how Oracle manages table extents and free data blocks.

Knowing the internal Oracle table management strategies will help you become successful in managing high-volume performance within Oracle. To be proficient at object tuning, you need to understand the behavior of freelists and freelist groups, and their relationship to the values of the *pctfree* and *pctused* parameters. This knowledge is especially imperative for enterprise resource planning (ERP) applications, where poor table performance is often directly related to improper table settings.

The most common mistake for the beginner is assuming that the default Oracle parameters are optimal for all objects. Unless disk consumption is not a concern, you must consider the average row length and database block size when setting *pctfree* and *pctused* for a table such that empty blocks are efficiently placed back onto the freelists. When these settings are wrong, Oracle may populate freelists with "dead" blocks that do not have enough room to store a row, causing significant processing delays.

This dead block problem occurs when the setting for *pctused* allows a block to relink onto the freelist when it does not have enough free space to accept a new row. I will explain the relationship between average row length and freelist behavior later in this chapter.

Freelists are critical to the effective reuse of space within the Oracle tablespaces and are directly related to the *pctfree* and *pctused* storage parameters. When the database is directed to make blocks available as soon as possible (with a high setting of *pctused*), the reuse of free space is maximized. However, there is a direct trade-off between high performance and efficient reuse of table blocks. When tuning Oracle tables and indexes, you need to consciously decide if you desire high performance or efficient space reuse, and set the table parameters accordingly. Let's take a close look at how these freelists affect the performance of Oracle.

Whenever a request is made to insert a row into a table, Oracle goes to a freelist to find a block with enough space to accept a row. As you may know, the freelist chain is kept in the first block of the table or index, and this block is known as the segment header. The sole purpose of the *pctfree* and *pctused* table allocation parameters is to control the movement of blocks to and from the freelists. While the freelist link and unlink operations are simple Oracle functions, the settings for freelist link *(pctused)* and unlink *(pctfree)* operations can have a dramatic impact on the performance of Oracle.

The default settings for all Oracle objects are *pctused* = 40 and *pctfree* = 10. As you may know from DBA basics, the *pctfree* parameter governs freelist unlinks. Setting *pctfree* = 10 means that every block reserves 10 percent of the space for row expansion. The *pctused* parameter governs freelist relinks. Setting *pctused* = 40 means that a block must become less than 40 percent full before being relinked on the table freelist.

Let's take a closer look at how freelist management works, and how it affects the performance of Oracle. Many neophytes misunderstand what happens when a block is readded to the freelist. Once a block is relinked onto the freelist after a delete, it will remain on the freelist even when the space exceeds 60 percent. Only reaching *pctfree* will take the database block off of the freelist.

Linking and Unlinking from the Freelists

As you now know, the *pctfree* and *pctused* table parameters are used to govern the movement of database blocks to and from the table freelists. In general, there is a direct trade-off between performance and efficient table utilization because efficient block reuse requires some overhead when linking and unlinking blocks with the freelist. As you may know, linking and unlinking a block requires two writes: one to the segment header for the freelist head node, and the other to the new block to make it participate in the freelist chain. The following general rules apply to freelists:

- **insert**   An *insert* may trigger the *pctfree* threshold, causing a freelist unlink. Since *insert* operations always use the free block at the head of the freelist chain, there will be minimal overhead when unlinking this block.

- **update**   An *update* that expands row length is affected by *pctfree,* but it will *not* cause a freelist unlink, since the target block would not be at the head of the freelist chain.

- **delete**   A *delete* of rows may trigger the *pctused* threshold and cause a freelist link.

You also need to understand how new free blocks are added to the freelist chain. At table extension time, the high-water mark for the table is increased, and new blocks are moved onto the master freelist, where they are, in turn, moved to process freelists. For tables that do not contain multiple freelists, the transfer is done five blocks at a time. For tables with multiple freelists, the transfer is done in sizes (5 * (number of freelists + 1)). For example, in a table with 20 freelists, 105 blocks will be moved onto the master freelist each time that a table increases its high-water mark.

To see how this works, let's review the mechanisms associated with freelist links and unlinks (see Figure 6-10).

The segment header contains a space to hold a pointer to the first free block in the table. Inside Oracle, a pointer to a block is called a *data block address,* or *DBA* for short. The first block on the freelist chain also has a space in the block header to contain the DBA for the next free block, and so on.

Let's explore what happens internally during row operations.

Freelist Unlinks with Insert Operations

As new rows are inserted, the block may be removed from the freelist if the free space becomes less than the bytes specified by *pctfree*. Since the block being inserted is always at the head of the freelist chain, only two blocks will be affected. In our example, let's assume that the *insert* has caused block 106 to be removed from the freelist chain:

1. Oracle detects that free space is less than *pctfree* for block 20 and invokes the unlink operation. Since block 20 is the first block on the freelist chain, Oracle reads the data block address (DBA) inside the block header and sees that the next free block is block 60.

2. Oracle next adjusts the freelist header node and moves the DBA for block 60 to the head of the freelist in the segment header. Block 20 no longer participates in the freelist chain, and the first entry in the freelist is now block 60, as shown in Figure 6-11.

Freelist Relinks with Update Statements

As updates to existing rows cause the row to expand, the block may be unlinked from the freelist if the free space in the block becomes less than *pctfree*. Of course,

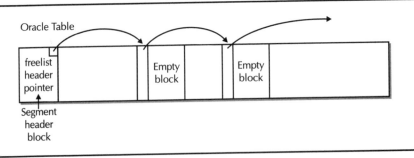

FIGURE 6-10. *A sample freelist chain*

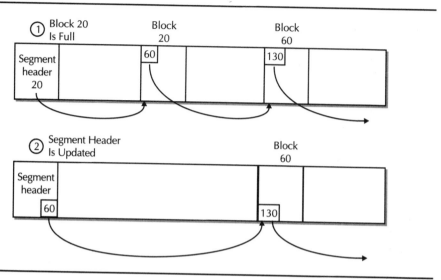

FIGURE 6-11. *A freelist unlink operation*

this will only happen if the row contains VARCHAR, RAW, or LONG RAW column datatypes, since these are the only datatypes that could expand upon *update*. Because the updated block is not at the head of the freelist chain, the prior block's freelist pointer cannot be adjusted to omit the block. Note that the dead block remains on the freelist even though it does not have room to accept a row.

The dead block remaining on the list will cause additional Oracle overhead, especially if there are a large number of "unavailable" blocks on the freelist. At run time, Oracle will incur additional I/Os when reading these freelists, and it will try the freelist as many as five times attempting to find a block with enough room to store the new row. After five attempts, Oracle will raise the high-water mark for the table.

Reducing Freelist Relinks

Either of these techniques will cause the freelists to be populated largely from new extents. Of course, this approach requires lots of extra disk space, and the table must be reorganized periodically to reclaim the wasted storage. Freelist relinks can be reduced in two ways:

- Freelist relinks can be "turned down" by setting *pctused* to 1. Setting *pctused* to a low value means that data blocks are not relinked onto the freelist chain unless they are completely empty.

■ Use the APPEND hint when adding rows. By using APPEND with inserts, you tell Oracle to bypass the freelists and raise the high-water mark for the table to grab a fresh, unused data block.

TIP
Remember the cardinal rule of object tuning. There is a direct trade-off between efficient space reuse and fast performance of insert statements. If high performance is more important than space reuse, you can use an Oracle8 SQL hint that will bypass freelist usage. By placing /+ append */ immediately after the INSERT keyword, you direct Oracle to increase the high-water mark for the table and place the row into a fresh empty block (see Figure 6-12). This hint ensures that all inserts are made into empty blocks, thereby improving the speed.*

Next, let's wrap up this chapter with a review of the major points.

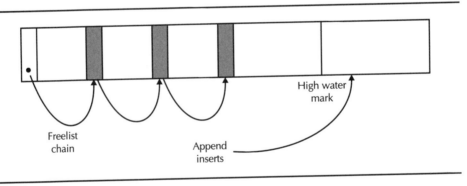

FIGURE 6-12.   *Using the APPEND option with SQL inserts*

Conclusion

When considering table access methods, you must remember that the number one goal of Oracle tuning is to carefully examine all large-table full-table scans and determine if the query will be better served by using an index. To fully investigate a SQL query, you must understand the creation of the execution plan and the relationship between the execution plan and the table access method. You must also remember that there are many reorganization and indexing techniques that will improve the ability of Oracle to perform an optimal table access. Remember, for any SQL statement there exists only one optimal table access method, and it is your job to locate that method and make it persistent.

Next we will take a closer look at the steps and goals of Oracle SQL tuning and provide a methodology for ensuring that all SQL statements are tuned and stay performing at optimal levels.

PART
II

Basic SQL Tuning

CHAPTER
7

The Steps to Oracle
SQL Tuning

uning individual SQL statements is one of the most time consuming and challenging areas of Oracle tuning. SQL tuning can also be quite tedious because of the complexity of some SQL statements, and a complex SQL statement can often take many hours to tune. If your database has thousands of complex SQL statements, this tuning can take many months. At a high level, Oracle SQL tuning involves the following activities:

1. Ensure that all prerequisite tuning has been done on the server, disk, network, instance, and tables.

2. Rank the SQL statements in your library cache to identify the statements that will result in the most benefit from SQL tuning (i.e., those with the highest number of executions).

3. Tune the SQL statement by adding hints, rewriting the query, or adding or changing indexes.

4. Make the SQL execution plan persistent by updating the SQL source code, or by using optimizer plan stability.

5. Repeat steps 2 through 4 until all SQL has been located and tuned.

There is some debate about when SQL tuning should be performed. Some experts believe that SQL tuning can be conducted first, before the server, disk, network, instance, and objects are tuned. In fact, this sequence is tested in the Oracle Certified Professional (OCP) exam. However, you must remember that there are dependencies between a SQL statement and its environment. With regards to the external environment, bottlenecks at the server disk or network level can skew the performance of SQL executions, thereby making it very difficult to tune the statement. The same issue applies to instance tuning. If we have not tuned the instance, resetting Oracle initialization parameters could undo the execution plans for SQL that has already been tuned. For example, changing the value of *db_file_multiblock_read_count* could change the behavior of the CBO, causing hundreds of SQL statements to change their execution plans.

Goals of SQL Tuning

Oracle SQL tuning is a phenomenally complex subject, and entire books have been devoted to the nuances of Oracle SQL tuning. However there are some general guidelines that every Oracle DBA follows in order to improve the performance of their systems. The goals of SQL tuning are simple:

■ **Remove unnecessary large-table full-table scans** Unnecessary full-table scans cause a huge amount of unnecessary I/O and can drag down an entire database. The tuning expert first evaluates the SQL in terms of the number of rows returned by the query. If the query returns less than 40 percent of the table rows in a row-resequenced table, or 7 percent of the rows in an unordered table, the query can be tuned to use an index in lieu of the full-table scan. The most common tuning for unnecessary full-table scans is adding indexes. Standard B-tree indexes can be added to tables, and bitmapped and function-based indexes can also eliminate full-table scans. The decision about removing a full-table scan should be based on a careful examination of the I/O costs of the index scan versus the costs of the full-table scan, factoring in the multiblock reads and possible parallel execution. In some cases an unnecessary full-table scan can be forced to use an index by adding an index hint to the SQL statement.

- **Cache small-table full-table scans**   In cases where a full-table scan is the fastest access method, the tuning professional should ensure that a dedicated data buffer is available for the rows. In Oracle7, you can issue cache commands, and in Oracle8 and beyond, the small table can be cached by forcing it into the KEEP pool.

```
alter table xxx cache; -- Oracle7
alter table xxx storage (buffer_pool keep); -- Oracle8
```

- **Verify optimal index usage**   This is especially important for improving the speed of queries. Oracle sometimes has a choice of indexes, and the tuning professional must examine each index and ensure that Oracle is using the proper index. This also includes the use of bitmapped and function-based indexes.

- **Verify optimal JOIN techniques**   Some queries will perform faster with NESTED LOOP joins, others with HASH joins, and others with MERGE or STAR joins.

- **Review Subqueries**   Every correlated and noncorrelated subquery should be examined to determine if the SQL query could be rewritten as a simple table join.

These goals may seem deceptively simple, but these tasks compose 90 percent of SQL tuning, and they don't require a thorough understanding of the internals of Oracle SQL.

Now that you understand the goals of SQL tuning, let's take a look at the steps of tuning. We will revisit many of these steps in detail in later chapters, but for now you need to understand the basic steps.

The SQL Tuning Process

The process of tuning Oracle SQL is both iterative and time-consuming. We begin by locating offensive SQL statements either by "fishing" them from the library cache or by extracting them from the *stats$sql_summary* table.

Next, we explain the SQL, tune each statement, and make the changes permanent.

NOTE
If you tune your SQL by adding an index, you can go backward in time and reexplain historical SQL in the stats$sql_summary *table. This technique will verify that the new indexes have improved the execution plans of historical SQL.*

There are several steps that are repeated until all major SQL is tuned:

1. **Locate**   Here we locate offensive and high-impact SQL statements using STATSPACK tables, the library cache, or the application source code.

2. **Extract**   Next we extract the offensive SQL syntax.

3. **Explain**   The extracted SQL from step 2 is then passed to the Explain Plan utility to get the execution plan.

4. **Tune**   We then tune the SQL with indexes, hints, and query rewrites. For each change, we reevaluate the new execution plan and test the execution time using the SQL*Plus *set timing on* command.

5. **Finalize**   Make the tuning permanent by changing the SQL source program or by creating a stored outline with the optimizer plan stability utility.

Of course, this is a highly simplified outline, since each step can be quite complicated. Let's take a closer look at each of these steps.

Step 1: Identify High-Impact SQL

We begin our investigation into Oracle SQL tuning by viewing the SQL that currently resides inside our library cache. Many people ask where they should start when tuning Oracle SQL. Tuning Oracle SQL is like a fishing expedition; you must first "fish" in the Oracle library cache to extract SQL statements, and rank the statements by their amounts of activity.

Oracle makes it quite easy to locate frequently executed SQL statements. The SQL statements in the *v$sqlarea* view are rank-ordered by several values. These are presented in order, with the most important first.

- **executions**   The more frequently executed SQL statements should be tuned first, since they will have the greatest impact on overall performance.

- **disk_reads**   High disk reads indicates a query that is causing lots of disk I/O.

- **rows_processed**   Queries that process a large number of rows will have high I/O and may also have an impact on the TEMP tablespace if sorting occurs.

- **buffer_gets**   High buffer gets may indicate a resource-intensive query.

- **sorts**   Sorts can be a huge slowdown, especially if the sorts are being done on disk in the TEMP tablespace.

You can get lists of your SQL statements from the *v$sqlarea* view or *stats$sql_summary* table in descending order of any of these variables.

The executions column of the *v$sqlarea* view and the *stats$sql_summary* table can be used to locate the most frequently used SQL. When fishing for SQL, you can use a third-party tool to display the SQL in the library cache or write your own extraction script. The next section will cover three ways to extract high-impact SQL:

- Extract SQL from *stats$sql_summary* with the STATSPACK SQL top-10 report *(rpt_sql_STATSPACK.ksh)*.

- Extract SQL from the *v$sqlarea* view using the *rpt_sql_cache.ksh* script.

- Extract and analyze SQL from the library cache using *access.sql*.

Please note that either of these techniques can be used with either the historical STATSPACK *stats$sql_summary* table or with the *v$sqlarea* view. The columns in *v$sqlarea* and *stats$sql_summary* are identical.

Ranking SQL Statements

When ranking SQL statements, we recognize that it is more important to tune a frequently executed SQL statement for a small performance gain than it is to tune a seldom-executed SQL statement for a huge performance gain.

In many cases, the Oracle professional does not have the time to locate and tune all of the SQL statements. It is also important to get an immediate measurable result, so that management will continue to fund the tuning effort. Hence, you must quickly locate those statements that are frequently executed and tune these statements first.

At some point, you will encounter diminishing marginal returns for your tuning effort (Figure 7-1). After you have tuned the frequently executed SQL and moved on to the less frequently executed SQL, you may find that the time and effort for tuning will not result in a cost-effective benefit.

Identifying High-Use SQL Statements

There are many ways to locate SQL statements. At the highest level, you have the choice of locating the SQL source code in several places:

- **Application programs**   Some Oracle professionals know the location of their SQL source code and interrogate the source code libraries to extract the SQL source code.

- **Library cache**   The library cache within the SGA will store the SQL source code and also provide statistics about the number of executions. Most SQL tuning professionals will use the *rpt_sql_cache.ksh* and the *access.sql* script for this purpose.

- **The stats$sql_summary table**   The STATSPACK *stats$sql_summary* table stores the source for all SQL statements that exceed the threshold values as defined in the *stats$statspack_parameter* table. The STATSPACK tables are useful because they keep a historical record of all of the important SQL. Most SQL tuning professionals will use the SQL top-10 script *(rpt_sql_STATSPACK.ksh)* for this purpose.

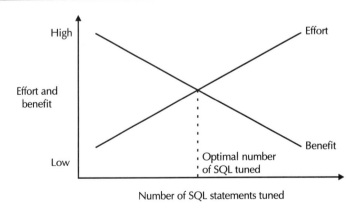

FIGURE 7-1.   *The diminishing marginal returns for SQL tuning*

■ Since the goal is to locate high-use SQL statements, the library cache and the *stats$sql_summary* table are excellent places to begin your quest for offensive SQL. For details on using STATSPACK for SQL tuning, see Donald Keith Burleson, *Oracle High-Performance Tuning with STATSPACK* (McGraw-Hill Professional Publishing, 2001).

Let's take a look at some tools that are used to identify high-impact SQL statements.

Using STATSPACK to Identify High-Impact SQL

Here is an easy-to-use Korn shell script that can be run against the STATSPACK tables to identify high-use SQL statements.

rpt_sql_STATSPACK.ksh

```ksh
#!/bin/ksh

# First, we must set the environment . . . .
ORACLE_SID=$ORACLE_SID
export ORACLE_SID
ORACLE_HOME=`cat /var/opt/oracle/oratab|\
   grep ^$ORACLE_SID:|cut -f2 -d':'`
export ORACLE_HOME
PATH=$ORACLE_HOME/bin:$PATH
export PATH

echo "How many days back to search?"
read days_back

echo executions
echo loads
echo parse_calls
echo disk_reads
echo buffer_gets
echo rows_processed
echo sorts
echo
echo "Enter sort key:"
read sortkey

$ORACLE_HOME/bin/sqlplus perfstat/perfstat<<!

set array 1;
set lines 80;
set wrap on;
```

```
set pages 999;
set echo off;
set feedback off;

column mydate        format a8
column exec          format 9,999,999
column loads         format 999,999
column parse         format 999,999
column reads         format 9,999,999
column gets          format 9,999,999
column rows_proc     format 9,999,999
column sorts         format 999,999

drop table temp1;
create table temp1 as
    select min(snap_id) min_snap
    from stats\$snapshot where snap_time > sysdate-$days_back;

drop table temp2;

create table temp2 as
select
    to_char(snap_time,'dd Mon HH24:mi:ss') mydate,
    executions                             exec,
    loads                                  loads,
    parse_calls                            parse,
    disk_reads                             reads,
    buffer_gets                            gets,
    rows_processed                         rows_proc,
    sorts                                  sorts,
    sql_text
from
    perfstat.stats\$sql_summary sql,
    perfstat.stats\$snapshot       sn
where
    sql.snap_id >
    (select min_snap from temp1)
and
    sql.snap_id = sn.snap_id
order by $sortkey desc
;
spool off;

select * from temp2 where rownum < 11;

exit
!
```

Here is the listing from running this valuable script. Note that the DBA is prompted as to how many days back to search, and for the sort key for extracting the SQL.

rpt_sql_STATSPACK.ksh Execution Listing

```
How many days back to search?
7
executions
loads
parse_calls
disk_reads
buffer_gets
rows_processed
sorts

Enter sort key:
disk_reads

SQL*Plus: Release 8.1.6.0.0 - Production on Thu Dec 14 09:14:46 2000

(c) Copyright 1999 Oracle Corporation. All rights reserved.


Connected to:
Oracle8i Enterprise Edition Release 8.1.6.1.0 - 64bit Production
With the Partitioning option
JServer Release 8.1.6.1.0 - 64bit Production

MYDATE         EXEC   LOADS   PARSE      READS       GETS  ROWS_PROC   SORTS
--------  ---------- -------- -------- ---------- ---------- ---------- -------
SQL_TEXT
----------------------------------------------------------------------11 Dec
1        866        1      866    246,877  2,795,211        865     4:00:09
DECLARE job BINARY_INTEGER := :job; next_date DATE := :mydate;  broken BOOLEAN :
= FALSE; BEGIN statspack.snap; :mydate := next_date; IF broken THEN :b := 1; ELSE
:b := 0; END IF; END;

11 Dec 1      863        1      863    245,768  2,784,834        862
1:00:29
DECLARE job BINARY_INTEGER := :job; next_date DATE := :mydate;  broken BOOLEAN :
= FALSE; BEGIN statspack.snap; :mydate := next_date; IF broken THEN :b := 1; ELS
E :b := 0; END IF; END;

11 Dec 1      866        1      866    245,325    597,647    129,993      866
4:00:09
INSERT INTO STATS$SQL_SUMMARY ( SNAP_ID,DBID,INSTANCE_NUMBER,SQL_TEXT,SHARABLE_M
EM,SORTS,MODULE,LOADED_VERSIONS,EXECUTIONS,LOADS,INVALIDATIONS,PARSE_CALLS,DISK_
READS,BUFFER_GETS,ROWS_PROCESSED,ADDRESS,HASH_VALUE,VERSION_COUNT )   SELECT MIN(
:b1),MIN(:b2),MIN(:b3),MIN(SQL_TEXT),SUM(SHARABLE_MEM),SUM(SORTS),MIN(MODULE),SU
```

```
M(LOADED_VERSIONS),SUM(EXECUTIONS),SUM(LOADS),SUM(INVALIDATIONS),SUM(PARSE_CALLS
),SUM(DISK_READS),SUM(BUFFER_GETS),SUM(ROWS_PROCESSED),ADDRESS,HASH_VALUE,COUNT(
1)    FROM V$SQL  GROUP BY ADDRESS,HASH_VALUE  HAVING (SUM(BUFFER_GETS) > :b4  OR
 SUM(DISK_READS) > :b5  OR SUM(PARSE_CALLS) > :b6  OR SUM(EXECUTIONS) > :b7 )


11 Dec 0      861        1      861    245,029 2,778,052        860         0
9:00:24
DECLARE job BINARY_INTEGER := :job; next_date DATE := :mydate;  broken BOOLEAN :
= FALSE; BEGIN statspack.snap; :mydate := next_date; IF broken THEN :b := 1; ELSE
E :b := 0; END IF; END;


11 Dec 1      864        1      864    244,587    595,861    129,605       864
2:00:02
INSERT INTO STATS$SQL_SUMMARY ( SNAP_ID,DBID,INSTANCE_NUMBER,SQL_TEXT,SHARABLE_M

EM,SORTS,MODULE,LOADED_VERSIONS,EXECUTIONS,LOADS,INVALIDATIONS,PARSE_CALLS,DISK_
READS,BUFFER_GETS,ROWS_PROCESSED,ADDRESS,HASH_VALUE,VERSION_COUNT )   SELECT MIN(
:b1),MIN(:b2),MIN(:b3),MIN(SQL_TEXT),SUM(SHARABLE_MEM),SUM(SORTS),MIN(MODULE),SU
M(LOADED_VERSIONS),SUM(EXECUTIONS),SUM(LOADS),SUM(INVALIDATIONS),SUM(PARSE_CALLS
),SUM(DISK_READS),SUM(BUFFER_GETS),SUM(ROWS_PROCESSED),ADDRESS,HASH_VALUE,COUNT(
1)    FROM V$SQL  GROUP BY ADDRESS,HASH_VALUE  HAVING (SUM(BUFFER_GETS) > :b4  OR
 SUM(DISK_READS) > :b5  OR SUM(PARSE_CALLS) > :b6  OR SUM(EXECUTIONS) > :b7 )
```

It is interesting to note in the preceding output that we see the STATSPACK *insert* statement for the *stats$sql_summary* table.

Next, let's look at a technique that is probably the most valuable script in this book.

Reporting on SQL from the Library Cache

There are two scripts that are commonly used to extract SQL from the library cache. Both utilize the *v$sqlarea* view to locate, display, and explain SQL statements in the library cache. We will begin with the simple script to display the top SQL and then look at a more sophisticated script that extracts and explains all of the SQL in the library cache.

Extracting SQL Source from the Library Cache

This script is substantially similar to the STATSPACK extraction script except that the SQL is extracted directly from the *v$sqlarea* view. This report will rank and display all SQL that currently resides in the library cache, and it is a good starting point for investigating SQL when you do not have a STATSPACK database.

rpt_sql_cache.ksh

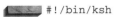

```
#!/bin/ksh

# First, we must set the environment . . . .
ORACLE_SID=$ORACLE_SID
```

```
export ORACLE_SID
ORACLE_HOME=`cat /var/opt/oracle/oratab|\
   grep ^$ORACLE_SID:|cut -f2 -d':'`
export ORACLE_HOME
PATH=$ORACLE_HOME/bin:$PATH
export PATH


echo executions
echo loads
echo parse_calls
echo disk_reads
echo buffer_gets
echo rows_processed
echo sorts
echo
echo "Enter sort key:"
read sortkey

$ORACLE_HOME/bin/sqlplus perfstat/perfstat<<!


set array 1;
set lines 80;
set wrap on;
set pages 999;
set echo off;
set feedback off;

column exec        format 9,999,999
column loads       format 999,999
column parse       format 999,999
column reads       format 9,999,999
column gets        format 9,999,999
column rows_proc   format 9,999,999
 column sorts       format 999,999


drop table temp2;

create table temp2 as
select
   executions                          exec,
   loads                               loads,
   parse_calls                         parse,
   disk_reads                          reads,
   buffer_gets                         gets,
   rows_processed                      rows_proc,
```

```
    sorts                                   sorts,
    sql_text
from
    v\$sqlarea
order by
    $sortkey desc
;
spool off;

select * from temp2 where rownum < 11;

exit
!
```

The output from this script is exactly the same as the output from the *rpt_sql_STATSPACK.ksh* script except that there is no display for the date. Next, let's look at a method for extracting and explaining all of the SQL in your library cache.

Explaining all SQL in the Library Cache

One step that is commonly used to locate SQL is using a script to extract and explain all of the SQL that currently reside in the library cache. I introduced these reports in Chapter 5, and I will explain this procedure in detail in Chapter 8.

At first glance, it may be hard to fully appreciate the value of this technique and the information produced by the reports. But if your database has a large library cache, you can get some great insights into the internal behavior of the tables and indexes.

The output from the *access.sql* script from Chapter 5 has several extremely useful reports. I will address them briefly here and go into greater detail in Chapter 8.

The Full-Table Scan Report   This is the most valuable report of all. Here you see all of the SQL statements that performed full-table scans, and the number of times that a full-table scan was performed. Also note the C and K columns. The C column indicates if an Oracle7 table is cached, and the K column indicates whether the Oracle8 table is assigned to the KEEP pool. As you will recall, small tables with full-table scans should be placed in the KEEP pool.

Mon Feb 29   page   1
```
                    full table scans and counts
              Note that "C" indicates the table is cached.
              "K" indicates the table is in the KEEP Pool
```

OWNER	NAME	NUM_ROWS	C	K	BLOCKS	NBR_FTS
SYS	DUAL		N		2	97,237
SYSTEM	SQLPLUS_PRODUCT		N	K	2	16,178
DONALD	PAGE	3,450,209	N		932,120	9,999
DONALD	RWU_PAGE	434	N		8	7,355
DONALD	PAGE_IMAGE	18,067	N		1,104	5,368
DONALD	SUBSCRIPTION	476	N	K	192	2,087
DONALD	PRINT_PAGE_RANGE	10	N	K	32	874
ARSD	JANET_BOOKS	20	N		8	64
PERFSTAT	STATS$TAB_STATS		N		65	10

In the preceding report, you see several huge tables that are performing full-table scans. For tables that have less than 200 blocks and are doing legitimate full-table scans, we will want to place these in the KEEP pool. The larger table full-table scans should also be investigated, and the legitimate large-table full-table scans should be parallelized with the *alter table parallel degree nn* command.

An Oracle database invokes a large-table full-table scan when it cannot service a query through indexes. If you can identify large tables that experience excessive full-table scans, you can take appropriate action to add indexes. This is especially important when you migrate from Oracle7 to Oracle8, because Oracle8 offers indexes that have built-in functions. Another cause of a full-table scan is when the cost-based optimizer decides that a full-table scan will be faster than an index range scan. This occurs most commonly with small tables, which are ideal for caching in Oracle7 or placing in the KEEP pool in Oracle8. This full-table scan report is critical for two types of SQL tuning:

- For a small-table full-table scan, in Oracle7 you can cache the table by using the *alter table xxx cache* command (where xxx = table name), which will put the table rows at the most recently used end of the data buffer, thereby reducing disk I/O for the table. In Oracle8, you should place cached tables in the KEEP pool with the *alter table xxx storage (buffer_pool keep)* command.

- For a large-table full-table scan, you can investigate the SQL statements to see if the use of indexes would eliminate the full-table scan. Again, the original source for all the SQL statements is in the SQLTEMP table. I will talk about the process of finding and explaining the individual SQL statements in the next section.

Next, we see the index usage reports. These index reports are critical for the following areas of Oracle tuning.

■ **Index usage** Ensuring that the application is actually using a new index. Using this report, DBAs can now obtain empirical evidence that an index is actually being used after it has been created.

■ **Row resequencing** Finding out which tables might benefit from row resequencing. Tables that have a large amount of index range scan activity will benefit from having the rows resequenced into the same order as the index. Resequencing can result in a tenfold performance improvement, depending on the row length.

Next, let's look at the index range scan report.

The Index Range Scan Report The most common method of index access in Oracle is the index range scan. This report is useful for telling you if a new index is being used by Oracle. An index range scan is used when the SQL statement contains a restrictive clause that requires a sequential range of values that are indexes for the table.

```
Mon Feb 29                                                        page    1
                          Index range scans and counts

  OWNER      TABLE_NAME            INDEX_NAME       TBL_BLOCKS    NBR_SCANS
  ---------  -------------------   -------------    ----------    ----------
  DONALD     ANNO_HIGHLIGHT        HL_PAGE_USER_I          16        7,975
  DONALD     ANNO_STICKY           ST_PAGE_USER_I           8        7,296
  DONALD     PAGE                  ISBN_SEQ_IDX           120        3,859
  DONALD     TOC_ENTRY             ISBN_TOC_SEQ_I          40        2,830
  DONALD     PRINT_HISTORY         PH_KEY_IDX              32        1,836
  DONALD     SUBSCRIPTION          SUBSC_ISBN_USE         192          210
  ARSD       JANET_BOOK_RANGES     ROV_BK_RNG_BOO           8          170
  PERFSTAT   STATS$SYSSTAT         STATS$SYSSTAT          845           32
  12 rows selected.
```

The Index Unique Scan Report Here is a report that lists index unique scans, which occur when the Oracle database engine uses an index to retrieve a specific row from a table. The Oracle database commonly uses these types of "probe" accesses when it performs a JOIN and probes another table for the JOIN key from the driving table. This report is also useful for finding out those indexes that are used to identify distinct table rows, as opposed to indexes that are used to fetch a range of rows.

```
Mon Feb 29                                                        page    1
                         Index unique scans and counts
```

OWNER	TABLE_NAME	INDEX_NAME	NBR_SCANS
DONALD	BOOK	BOOK_ISBN	44,606
DONALD	PAGE	ISBN_SEQ_IDX	39,973
DONALD	BOOK	BOOK_UNIQUE_ID	6,450
DONALD	ANNO_DOG_EAR	DE_PAGE_USER_IDX	5,339
DONALD	TOC_ENTRY	ISBN_TOC_SEQ_IDX	5,186
DONALD	PRINT_PERMISSIONS	PP_KEY_IDX	1,836
DONALD	RDRUSER	USER_UNIQUE_ID_IDX	1,065
DONALD	CURRENT_LOGONS	USER_LOGONS_UNIQUE_I	637
ARSD	JANET_BOOKS	BOOKS_BOOK_ID_PK	54
DONALD	ERROR_MESSAGE	ERROR_MSG_IDX	48

The Full-Index Scan Report   The next report shows all full index scans. As you
will recall, the Oracle optimizer will sometimes perform a full index scan in lieu
of a large sort in the TEMP tablespace. You will commonly see full-index scans in
blocks of SQL code that have the ORDER BY clause.

 Mon Feb 29   page   1
                          Index full scans and counts

OWNER	TABLE_NAME	INDEX_NAME	NBR_SCANS
DONALD	BOOK	BOOK_ISBN	2,295
DONALD	PAGE	ISBN_SEQ_IDX	744

 CAUTION
*Do not confuse the index full scan execution plan
with the fast full-index scan. The index full scan
reads each index node in SORTED order, while the
fast full-index scan is used to retrieve table rows
from the index in UNSORTED order (see Table 7-1).*

Execution Plan	Index Access Method	Values Returned
Index full scan	Sorted	Node by node
Fast full-index scan	Unsorted	Multiblock reads

TABLE 7-1.   *The Types of Full-Index Execution Plans*

Let's make sure you know the differences between an index full scan and a fast full-index scan:

- **Index full scan**   Oracle will choose an index full scan when the CBO statistics indicate that a full-index scan is going to be more efficient than a full-table scan and a sort of the result set. The full-index scan is normally invoked when the CBO determines that a query will return numerous rows in index order, and a full-table scan and sort option may cause a disk sort to the TEMP tablespace.

- **Fast full-index scan**   This execution plan is invoked when a index contains all of the values required to satisfy the query and table access is not required. The fast full-index scan execution plan will read the entire index with multiblock reads (using *db_file_multiblock_read_count*) and return the rows in unsorted order. In Oracle8*i*, fast full-index scans are available by default in the CBO, while in Oracle8 you must set the *fast_full_scan_enabled* initialization parameter. In Oracle7, you must set the *v733_plans_enabled* initialization parameter. You can force a fast full-index scan with the *index_fss* hint.

To see how the CBO evaluates a query for a full-index scan, let's take a simple example. The database could service the SQL command *select * from customer order by cust_nbr;* in two ways:

- It could perform a full-table scan and then sort the result set. The full-table scan could be performed very quickly with *db_ file_multiblock_read_count* initialization parameter set, or the table access could be parallelized by using a parallel hint. However, the result set must then be sorted in the TEMP tablespace.

- It could obtain the rows in index order by invoking the full-index scan by reading the rows via the index, thus avoiding a sort.

Now that we have reviewed the use of extraction tools for the library cache, let's take a look at using third-party GUI tools to locate SQL statements for tuning.

Using Third-Party Tools to Locate Offensive SQL

There are several third-party tools that can be used to quickly identify and tune suspect SQL statements. In a busy environment where the DBA must tune many SQL statements each day, the GUI interfaces of many third-party tools greatly speed up the tuning process. Another nice feature of the tools is their ability to allow push-button hints. This eliminates the problem of syntax errors within hints that sometimes happen with the manual method.

CAUTION
Remember that adding an index to tune one query may cause the execution plan for other queries to change. It is always a good idea to make your execution plans permanent (using optimizer plan stability or hints) to ensure that a new index does not inadvertently un-tune existing queries.

The following examples are from the Q Diagnostic Center software by Precise Software. This product, which does a very good job at quickly identifying suspect SQL, was written by John Beresniewicz, one of the best Oracle internals gurus in the world.

The following example shows the Q Diagnostic Center displaying all of the SQL from *v$sqlarea*. The GUI tools allow the DBA to re-sort the list of SQL statements by any parameter. In the example that follows, the DBA sorts the list of SQL by *rows_processed* (see Figure 7-2).

With a click of the Sorts button, the entire list can be redisplayed in descending order of the number of sorts (see Figure 7-3).

By clicking the sorting bar at the top of the list of SQL statements, the DBA can quickly identify those SQL statements that are frequently executed and place a processing burden on the database.

Let's move on to look at how to extract and explain suspect SQL statements.

Step 2: Extract and Explain the SQL Statement

As each SQL statement is identified, it will be "explained" to determine its existing execution plan and then tuned to see if the execution plan can be improved.

Explaining a SQL Statement

To see the output of an explain plan, you must first create a plan table in your schema. While we will review this in detail in Chapter 8, let's take a quick tour. Oracle provides the syntax to create a plan table in *$ORACLE_HOME/rdbms/admin/utlxplan.sql*. The listing that follows executes *utlxplan.sql* to create a plan table and then creates a public synonym for the plan table.

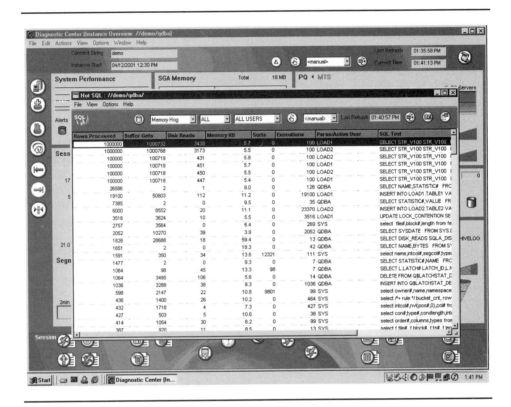

FIGURE 7-2. *Sorting SQL by* rows_processed

```
sql> @$ORACLE_HOME/rdbms/admin/utlxplan
Table created.

sql> create public synonym plan_table for sys.plan_table;
Synonym created.
```

Once the plan table is created, you are ready to populate the plan table with the execution plan for SQL statements.

We start by lifting a SQL statement from the *stats$sql_summary* table or from the library cache. I will show you the details for extracting the SQL in the next section. Here is a sample SQL statement that we have changed to add the explain plan statement:

```
delete from plan_table;

select ename from emp
where
reverse(ename) like 'GNI%';

explain plan
   set statement_id = 'test3'
for
select ename from emp
where
reverse(ename) like 'GNI%';

@plan
```

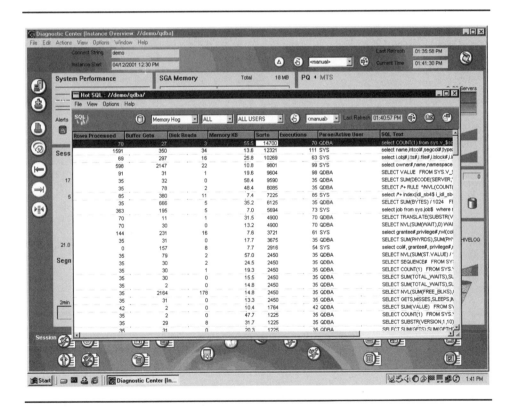

FIGURE 7-3. *Re-sorting the SQL list by number of sorts*

Note that we use the *plan.sql* script to display the execution plan.

plan.sql

```
rem plan.sql - displays contents of the explain plan table
set pages 9999;
select  lpad(' ',2*(level-1))||operation operation,
                options,
                object_name,
                position,
                other_tag
from plan_table
start with id=0
and
statement_id = 'test3'
connect by prior id = parent_id
and
statement_id = 'test3';
```

Now, let's see what happens when we execute *plan.sql*:

```
SQL> @exp
2 rows deleted.


ENAME
----------
KING


Explained.

    1   explain plan
    2      set statement_id = 'test3'
    3   for
    4   select ename from emp
    5   where
    6*  reverse(ename) like 'GNI%'

OPERATION
-----------------------------------------------------------------------
OPTIONS                        OBJECT_NAME                  POSITION
------------------------------ ---------------------------- ----------
SELECT STATEMENT
                                                                     1

    TABLE ACCESS
```

```
BY INDEX ROWID                    EMP                                1

    INDEX
RANGE SCAN                        ENAME_REVERSE_IDX                  1
```

Now that you see how the execution plan will change, let's turn our attention to the process of tuning a SQL statement.

Step 3: Tune the SQL Statement

For those SQL statements that possess a suboptimal execution plan, the SQL will be tuned by one of the following methods:

- **Hints**   Adding SQL hints will modify the execution plan.

- **Index**   Adding B-tree indexes can remove full-table scans.

- **Re-write**   Rewriting the SQL can change the execution plan, especially when changing the table order in the from clause with the RBO.

- **Bitmap Indexes**   Adding bitmap indexes allows you to index all low-cardinality columns that are mentioned in the *where* clause of the query.

- **PL/SQL**   Rewriting the SQL in PL/SQL can often improve performance. For certain queries, this can result in more than a twenty-fold performance improvement. The SQL would be replaced with a call to a PL/SQL package that contained a stored procedure to perform the query.

By far the most common approach is to add indexes and hints to the query. While we can instantly see the execution plan change as we add indexes and change hints, it is not always immediately evident which execution plan will result in the best performance.

Hence, the DBA will normally take the three most promising execution plans and actually execute the statement in SQL*Plus, noting the total elapsed time for the query by using the SQL*Plus *set timing on* command.

The details of all of the SQL hints are way beyond the scope of this book, but you can get details on all of the hints in the forthcoming Oracle Press book *Oracle High-Performance SQL Tuning* (October 2001), by Don Burleson.

An Actual Case-Study in SQL Tuning

The first activity of most SQL tuning sessions is to identify and remove unnecessary full-table scans. This SQL tuning activity can make a huge difference in SQL performance, since unnecessary full-table scans can take 20 times longer than using an index to service the query. Again, here are the basic steps in locating and fixing full-table scans:

1. Run the full-table scan report to locate SQL statements that produce full-table scans.

2. Query the *v$sqltext* or *v$sqlarea* view to locate the individual SQL statements.

3. Explain the statement to see the execution plan.

4. Add indexes or hints to remove the full-table scan.

5. Change the SQL source or store the outline to make the change permanent.

Let's quickly step through these activities and see how easy it is to improve the performance of SQL statements.

Get the Full-Table Scan Report

First, we run the *access.sql* script to extract and explain all of the SQL in the library cache. Here is a sample from an actual report:

 Mon Jan 29   page   1
```
                            full table scans and counts
                    Note that "C" indicates the table is cached.
                 "K" indicates that the table is in the KEEP pool


OWNER           NAME                 NUM_ROWS C K   BLOCKS   NBR_FTS
-------------   -------------------- ------------ - - -------- --------
SYS             DUAL                          N           2   97,237
SYSTEM          SQLPLUS_PRODUCT_PR            N  K        2   16,178
DONALD          PAGE                3,450,209 N     932,120    9,999
DONALD          RWU_PAGE                  434 N           8    7,355
DONALD          PAGE_IMAGE             18,067 N       1,104    5,368
DONALD          SUBSCRIPTION             476 N  K      192    2,087
DONALD          PRINT_PAGE_RANGE          10 N  K       32      874
ARSD            JANET_BOOKS               20 N           8       64
PERFSTAT        STATS$TAB_STATS              N          65       10
```

Here we see a clear problem with large-table full-table scans against the *page_image* table. The *page_image* table has 18,067 rows and consumes 1,104 blocks. The report shows 5,368 full-table scans against this table. Next, we can run a quick query to display the SQL source from v$sqlarea for the *page_image* table, looking for a SQL statement that has been executed about 5,000 times:

get_sql.sql

```
set lines 2000;

select
   sql_text,
   disk_reads,
   executions,
   parse_calls
from
   v$sqlarea
where
   lower(sql_text) like '%page_image%'
and
   executions > 5000
order by
   disk_reads desc
;
```

In the result from this query, we will look for SQL statements whose values for executions (5,201) approximate the value in the full-table scan report (5,368). From the output, you can clearly see the offensive SQL statement:

```
SELECT IMAGE_BLOB   FROM PAGE_IMAGE  WHERE (UPPER(BOOK_UNIQUE_ID) =
:b1   AND PAGE_SEQ_NBR = :b2   AND IMAGE_KEY = :b3 )

833        5201          148
```

Now that we have the SQL, we can quickly explain it and verify the full-table scan:

```
delete from plan_table where statement_id = 'test1';

explain plan set statement_id = 'test1'
for
SELECT IMAGE_BLOB   FROM PAGE_IMAGE
WHERE
   (UPPER(BOOK_UNIQUE_ID) = :b1
AND
   PAGE_SEQ_NBR = :b2   AND IMAGE_KEY = :b3 )
;
```

Here we run the execution plan showing our full-table scan:

```
OPERATION
---------------------------------------------------------------------
```

```
OPTIONS                           OBJECT_NAME                   POSITION
---------------------------       ---------------------------   ----------
SELECT STATEMENT
                                                                  168

   TABLE ACCESS
FULL                              PAGE_IMAGE                        1
```

Since this is a very simple query against a single table, we can look directly at the *where* clause to see the problem. The only condition in the *where* clause references *upper(book_unique_id),* and the Oracle optimizer has not detected a usable index on this column. Since we are on Oracle8, we can create a function-based index using the *upper* function:

```
create unique index book_seq_image_idx
   on page_image
     (upper(book_unique_id),
      page_seq_nbr,
      image_key)
   tablespace bookx
   pctfree 10
   storage (initial 128k next 128k maxextents 2147483645 pctincrease 0);
```

Now we rerun the execution plan and see that the full-table scan is replaced by an index scan:

```
OPERATION
--------------------------------------------------------------------
OPTIONS                           OBJECT_NAME                   POSITION
---------------------------       ---------------------------   ----------
SELECT STATEMENT


   TABLE ACCESS
BY INDEX ROWID                    PAGE_IMAGE                        1

      INDEX
UNIQUE SCAN                       BOOK_SEQ_IMAGE_IDX                1
```

Problem solved! The query went from an original execution time of 13 minutes to less than 10 seconds.

Now that you've seen the iterative process of locating and tuning SQL statements, let's look at how third-party GUI tools can speed up the process. This can be very important when the DBA must tune hundreds of SQL statements.

Fast SQL Tuning with Third-Party Tools

Now that you've seen how to tune SQL statements, let's look at how GUI tools can aid in quickly extracting and tuning SQL statements. In these examples, we will use the Q Diagnostic Center by Precise Software. With Q, the DBA is presented with the list of SQL from *v$sqlarea*, and the DBA just double-clicks the SQL statement to move the SQL into the Tuning window, as shown in Figure 7-4.

From this screen, you can double-click again and see details about the execution plan for the query. This display is especially handy because the screen also shows us the data dictionary details for each table in the query, as shown in Figure 7-5.

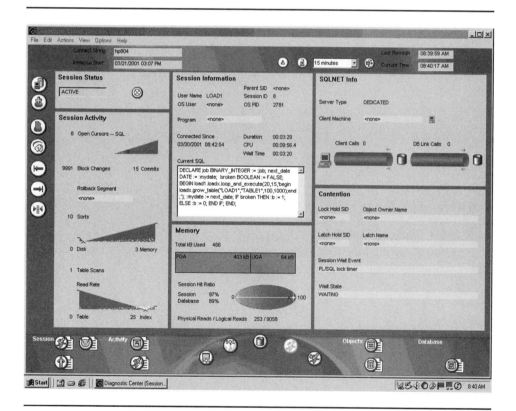

FIGURE 7-4.   *The Q Diagnostic Center Tuning window*

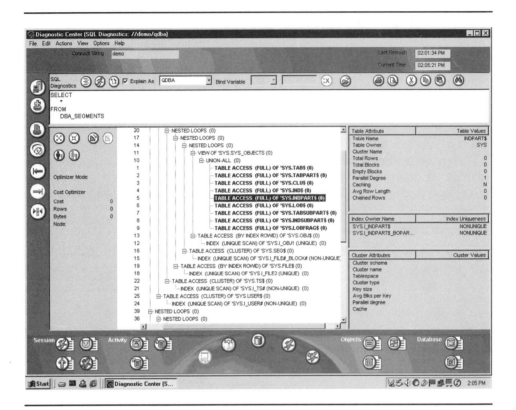

FIGURE 7-5. *The Execution Plan screen*

With this screen, the DBA can instantly see everything he or she needs to know about the tables and indexes, including the numbers of rows, blocks, and parallel options for each table in the query.

Conclusion

The purpose of this chapter is to provide a overall outline of the goals and steps of SQL tuning. While many experienced DBAs and developers are already well versed in these tools, it is often appropriate to apply a well-structured approach to SQL tuning.

Next, let's turn to one of the most useful chapters in this book. Chapter 8 will show you how to easily determine the execution plan to see how SQL is executed, and we will also examine the TKPROF utility.

CHAPTER
8

Understanding
Oracle SQL Utilities

his chapter is dedicated to looking at the tools that are used to extract the execution details for a SQL statement. While almost a dozen third-party tools can be used to deliver SQL execution information, Oracle provides a wealth of free tools and utilities for this purpose. The topics in this chapter will include:

- The explain plan utility

- Running a fast SQL trace

- Running TKPROF to get a SQL trace report

- Oracle's Center of Expertise (COE) SQL execution report

- Reporting on all SQL in the library cache

These reports provide a common basis for all SQL tuning activities, since they are all free of charge and readily available. Let's begin with the most basic tool of SQL tuning, the explain plan utility.

Explaining a SQL Statement

As I briefly mentioned in Chapter 7, to see the explain plan for a SQL statement, you must first create a plan table in your schema. Oracle provides the syntax to create a plan table in *$ORACLE_HOME/rdbms/admin/utlxplan.sql*. The listing that follows executes *utlxplan.sql* to create a plan table and then creates a public synonym for the *plan_table:*

```
sql> @$ORACLE_HOME/rdbms/admin/utlxplan
Table created.

sql> create public synonym plan_table for sys.plan_table;
Synonym created.
```

Once the plan table is created, you are ready to populate the plan table with the execution plan for SQL statements. The syntax for the explain plan utility is as follows:

```
explain plan
    set statement_id = '<your ID>'
    Into table <table name>
for
    <SQL statement>
;
```

To run an explain plan, we start by lifting a SQL statement from the *stats$sql_summary* table. I will show you the details for extracting the SQL in the next section. Here is the statement that we suspect is not optimized because it takes more than 11 minutes to execute. It is not important that we understand the purpose of this SQL, only that we note the basic structure of the statement.

```
SELECT
    B.ISBN,B.BOOK_TITLE,B.EDITION_NBR,B.AUTHOR_NAME,B.THUMBNAIL_TYPE,
    B.GLOSSARY_NBR,B.TABLE_CONTENTS_NBR,B.INDEX_NBR,B.PUBLIC_DOMAIN_FLAG,
    B.NBR_OF_REVIEWS,B.TOTAL_REVIEW_RATING,S.START_VISUAL_PAGE_NBR,
    S.END_VISUAL_PAGE_NBR,S.START_PAGE_SEQ_NBR,S.END_PAGE_SEQ_NBR,
    TO_CHAR(S.START_DATE,'DD-MON-YYYY HH24:MI:SS'),
    TO_CHAR(S.END_DATE,'DD-MON-YYYYHH24:MI:SS'),
    S.LAST_VIEWED_PAGE_SEQ_NBR,P.VISUAL_PAGE_NBR,
    TO_CHAR(S.TIME_LAST_VIEWED,'DD-MON-YYYYHH24:MI:SS'),
    S.PROFESSOR_USER_UNIQUE_ID,S.RETURNED_FLAG,
    S.TRIAL_SUBSC_FLAG
FROM
    BOOK B,
    SUBSCRIPTION S,
    PAGE P
WHERE
(S.USER_UNIQUE_ID = :b1  AND S.ISBN = B.ISBN  AND S.BOOK_UNIQUE_ID =
P.BOOK_UNIQUE_ID  AND S.LAST_VIEWED_PAGE_SEQ_NBR = P.PAGE_SEQ_NBR )
ORDER BY B.BOOK_TITLE;
```

It is always a good idea to get a visual "pattern" for the SQL statement before you get the execution plan. The preceding statement can be simplified into the following structure:

```
select
    stuff
from
    book,
    subscription,
    page
where
    user = :var
and
    subscription isbn = book isbn
and
    subscription book_id - page book_id
and
    subscription last_page_nbr_viewed = page page_nbr
```

Here we see a simple three-way table *join* where the result set is limited for a single user. Now that you understand the basic structure of the query, we can get the execution plan for this SQL statement by inserting the SQL into the following snippet:

```
delete from plan_table where statement_id = 'test1';

explain plan set statement_id = 'test1'
for
SELECT
B.ISBN,B.BOOK_TITLE,B.EDITION_NBR,B.AUTHOR_NAME,B.THUMBNAIL_TYPE,
B.GLOSSARY_NBR,B.TABLE_CONTENTS_NBR,B.INDEX_NBR,B.PUBLIC_DOMAIN_FLAG,
B.NBR_OF_REVIEWS,B.TOTAL_REVIEW_RATING,S.START_VISUAL_PAGE_NBR,
S.END_VISUAL_PAGE_NBR,S.START_PAGE_SEQ_NBR,S.END_PAGE_SEQ_NBR,
TO_CHAR(S.START_DATE,'DD-MON-YYYY HH24:MI:SS'),
TO_CHAR(S.END_DATE,'DD-MON-YYYYHH24:MI:SS'),
S.LAST_VIEWED_PAGE_SEQ_NBR,P.VISUAL_PAGE_NBR,
TO_CHAR(S.TIME_LAST_VIEWED,'DD-MON-YYYYH24:MI:SS'),
S.PROFESSOR_USER_UNIQUE_ID,S.RETURNED_FLAG,S.TRIAL_SUBSC_FLAG
FROM
    BOOK B,
    SUBSCRIPTION S,
    PAGE P
WHERE
(S.USER_UNIQUE_ID = :b1  AND S.ISBN = B.ISBN  AND S.BOOK_UNIQUE_ID =
P.BOOK_UNIQUE_ID  AND S.LAST_VIEWED_PAGE_SEQ_NBR = P.PAGE_SEQ_NBR )
ORDER BY B.BOOK_TITLE;
```

When you execute this code, you instruct Oracle to display the execution plan inside the plan table. To display the data inside the plan table, you can use the following script.

plan.sql

```
SET PAGES 9999;
SELECT  lpad(' ',2*(level-1))||operation operation,
        options,
        object_name,
        position
FROM plan_table
START WITH id=0
AND
statement_id = 'test1'
CONNECT BY prior id = parent_id
AND
statement_id = 'test1';
```

Here is the output from *plan.sql*. This display is known as the *execution plan* for the SQL statement. It describes in detail all of the access steps that are used to retrieve the requested rows.

OPTIONS	OBJECT_NAME	POSITION
SELECT STATEMENT		
SORT		
ORDER BY		1
NESTED LOOPS		
NESTED LOOPS		1
		1
TABLE ACCESS		
FULL	**PAGE**	**1**
TABLE ACCESS		
BY INDEX ROWID	SUBSCRIPTION	2
INDEX		
RANGE SCAN	SUBSC_ISBN_USER_IDX	1
TABLE ACCESS		
BY INDEX ROWID	BOOK	2
INDEX		
UNIQUE SCAN	BOOK_ISBN	1

In this listing, we see the TABLE ACCESS FULL PAGE. This is the dreaded full-table scan that causes excessive overhead for Oracle. The next question is whether this query needs to access all of the rows in the *page* table. To find out, let's look at the *where* clause for the query:

```
WHERE
    S.USER_UNIQUE_ID = :b1
AND
    S.ISBN = B.ISBN
AND
    S.BOOK_UNIQUE_ID = P.BOOK_UNIQUE_ID
AND
    S.LAST_VIEWED_PAGE_SEQ_NBR = P.PAGE_SEQ_NBR
```

Here we see that the only WHERE condition that applies to the page table is:

```
S.LAST_VIEWED_PAGE_SEQ_NBR = P.PAGE_SEQ_NBR
```

It then follows that Oracle should be able to retrieve the page rows by using an index on the *page_seq_nbr* column of the page table and there is no need to perform a time-consuming full-table scan.

This statement was extracted from a database where *optimizer_mode*=RULE, so the first thing we can try is to analyze all of the tables and indexes in the query and reexplain the query with a FIRST_ROWS hint:

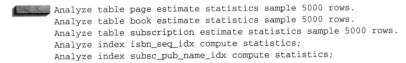

```
Analyze table page estimate statistics sample 5000 rows.
Analyze table book estimate statistics sample 5000 rows.
Analyze table subscription estimate statistics sample 5000 rows.
Analyze index isbn_seq_idx compute statistics;
Analyze index subsc_pub_name_idx compute statistics;
```

Here is the original explain with the FIRST_ROWS hint:

```
delete from plan_table where statement_id = 'test1';

explain plan set statement_id = 'test1'
for
SELECT /*+ first_rows */
B.ISBN,B.BOOK_TITLE,B.EDITION_NBR,B.AUTHOR_NAME,B.THUMBNAIL_TYPE,B.GLOSSARY_NBR,B.
TABLE_CONTENTS_NBR,B.INDEX_NBR,B.PUBLIC_DOMAIN_FLAG,B.NBR_OF_REVIEWS,B.TOTAL_REVIE
W_RATING,S.START_VISUAL_PAGE_NBR,S.END_VISUAL_PAGE_NBR,S.START_PAGE_SEQ_NBR,S.END_
PAGE_SEQ_NBR,TO_CHAR(S.START_DATE,'DD-MON-YYYY
HH24:MI:SS'),TO_CHAR(S.END_DATE,'DD-MON-YYYY
HH24:MI:SS'),S.LAST_VIEWED_PAGE_SEQ_NBR,P.VISUAL_PAGE_NBR,TO_CHAR(S.TIME_LAST_VIEW
ED,'DD-MON-YYYY
HH24:MI:SS'),S.PROFESSOR_USER_UNIQUE_ID,S.RETURNED_FLAG,S.TRIAL_SUBSC_FLAG    FROM
BOOK B,SUBSCRIPTION S,PAGE P  WHERE (S.USER_UNIQUE_ID = :b1  AND S.ISBN = B.ISBN
AND S.BOOK_UNIQUE_ID = P.BOOK_UNIQUE_ID  AND S.LAST_VIEWED_PAGE_SEQ_NBR =
P.PAGE_SEQ_NBR )ORDER BY B.BOOK_TITLE;

@plan
```

Now, when we run *plan.sql,* we see a totally different execution plan without any full-table scans:

```
OPERATION
------------------------------------------------------------------
OPTIONS                         OBJECT_NAME              POSITION
------------------------------  -----------------------  ----------
SELECT STATEMENT
                                                              27
  SORT
ORDER BY                                                       1
    NESTED LOOPS
                                                              1
      NESTED LOOPS
                                                              1
        TABLE ACCESS
BY INDEX ROWID                  SUBSCRIPTION                  1
          BITMAP CONVERSION
TO ROWIDS                                                     1
            BITMAP INDEX
FULL SCAN                       SUBSC_PUB_NAME_IDX            1
          TABLE ACCESS
BY INDEX ROWID                  BOOK                          2
            INDEX
UNIQUE SCAN                     BOOK_ISBN                     1
```

```
        TABLE ACCESS
BY INDEX ROWID          PAGE                    2
        INDEX
UNIQUE SCAN             ISBN_SEQ_IDX            1
```

When we reexecute the SQL in SQL*Plus with *set timing on,* the whole query executes in 18 seconds, for a savings of more than 10 minutes! This is just a simple example of the dramatic improvements you can make by tuning your SQL statements. Also note the use of the bitmap index in this execution plan.

NOTE
A host of third-party tools in the market show the execution plan for SQL statements. The most common way of determining the execution plan for a SQL statement is by using Oracle's explain plan utility. By using explain plan, the Oracle DBA can ask Oracle to parse the statement and display the execution class path without actually executing the SQL statement.

Now that we have covered the extraction and explaining of the SQL statement, let's go into more detail on getting execution details for SQL statements.

Reading an Execution Plan

Execution plans are often very difficult to interpret. While the beginner can scan the execution plan looking for TABLE ACCESS FULL, the more sophisticated experts closely examine the order of execution within an execution plan. In general, execution plans are read inside-out, starting with the most indented operation. Here are some general rules for reading an explain plan.

1. The first statement is the one that has the most indentation.

2. If two statements appear at the same level of indentation, the top statement is executed first.

To see how this works, let's reformat the execution plan from before to make the steps easier to see. Before you read on, see if you can place the steps in the actual order of execution.

```
SELECT STATEMENT
  SORT ORDER BY
    NESTED LOOPS
      NESTED LOOPS
        TABLE ACCESS BY INDEX ROWID        SUBSCRIPTION
          BITMAP CONVERSION TO ROWIDS
```

```
      BITMAP INDEX FULL SCAN        SUBSC_PUB_NAME_IDX
   TABLE ACCESS BY INDEX ROWID      BOOK
      INDEX UNIQUE SCAN             BOOK_ISBN
   TABLE ACCESS BY INDEX ROWID      PAGE
      INDEX UNIQUE SCAN             ISBN_SEQ_IDX
```

The indentation is clear, so we can work from inside-out, top-down and arrive at the following sequence of steps:

1. Bitmap index full scan on the *subsc_pub_name_idx* index

2. Bitmap conversion to ROWIDs

3. Index unique scan on the *book_isbn* index

4. Table access by ROWID on the *subscription* table

5. Table access by ROWID on the *book* table

6. Index unique scan on the *isbn_seq_idx* index

7. Nested loops scan of the result set

8. Table access by ROWID on the *page* table

9. Nested loop scan of the result set

10. Sorting the final result set

Hopefully, this will give you enough understanding to accurately know the order of the execution of steps in a SQL execution plan.

Also, please be aware that the execution plan output from explain plan is very different than the execution plan as stored in the *ol$hints* table. As you may know, in Oracle8*i* we have optimizer plan stability that is implemented via the Oracle *create outline* command. To see the difference, refer to Chapter 13, or execute the *outline.sql* script from the Oracle Press Web site.

For now, do not be concerned if you do not understand all of the different types of table access methods. I will be covering these access methods on an as-needed basis when we delve into the tuning details in subsequent chapters.

Running a Fast SQL Trace

Many developers are not aware how easy it is to use the autotrace facility to see the execution plan of a SQL statement. In addition to the execution plan, the autotrace facility gives the statistics for the SQL statement, and this can be very useful for debugging a SQL statement.

The execution plan shows the access path to the data and can be invaluable for Oracle SQL tuning. The statistics reveal the amount of Oracle resources that are allocated to servicing the SQL. Here is the procedure:

1. Run the *plustrce.sql* script while connected as the SYS database user. This script is located in the *$ORACLE_HOME/sqlplus/admin* directory.

```
SQL> connect internal;
Connected.
SQL> $ORACLE_HOME/sqlplus/admin/@plustrce
```

2. Run *utlxplan.sql* from the *$ORACLE_HOME/rdbms/admin* directory. This will create a plan table to hold the SQL execution plan.

```
SQL> @utlxplan
```

3. Now, you can issue the *set autotrace on* command in SQL*Plus to trace SQL execution and provide SQL statistics.

```
SQL>set autotrace on;

SELECT PAGE_SEQ_NBR    FROM reader.PAGE   WHERE (BOOK_UNIQUE_ID = 001 ) ;

PAGE_SEQ_NBR
------------
           1
           2
           3
           4
           5
         302
         303
         304

304 rows selected.


Execution Plan
----------------------------------------------------------
   0       SELECT STATEMENT Optimizer=FIRST_ROWS (Cost=2 Card=208 Bytes
           =5408)

   1    0    INDEX (RANGE SCAN) OF 'PAGE_U1_IDX' (UNIQUE) (Cost=2 Card=
           208 Bytes=5408)


Statistics
----------------------------------------------------------
```

```
  18  recursive calls
   0  db block gets
  27  consistent gets
   0  physical reads
   0  redo size
5245  bytes sent via SQL*Net to client
1982  bytes received via SQL*Net from client
  22  SQL*Net roundtrips to/from client
   3  sorts (memory)
   0  sorts (disk)
 304  rows processed
```

The trace facility is very useful when you want to know the details about the execution of a SQL query. Next let's look at a tool that provides even more detail about SQL execution.

The TKPROF Utility

The TKPROF utility is also known as the SQL trace facility. In addition to the execution plan, TKPROF provides a detailed report that shows the execution details for the SQL statement. Let's take a look at how TKPROF works.

Set the Environment for SQL Tracing

To enable TKPROF, you must set several Oracle initialization parameters and then turn on tracing with the *alter session set sql_trace=true* command. The following parameters need to be set up to get a SQL trace file.

- **sql_trace**   This parameter can be set at the instance level or at the session level. To set SQL trace for whole instances, add the following to your initialization file. This can create a huge amount of data in the Oracle *user_dump_dest* directory, and the system-wide option is rarely used because of the large amount of data generated.

  ```
  sql_trace=true
  ```

  To enable SQL trace at the session level, the following command can be entered from SQL*Plus:

  ```
  alter session set sql_trace=true;
  ```

- **timed_statistics**   The timed statistics parameter allows for the computation of SQL statistics such as CPU usage and elapsed time. This can be set in three ways. For instance-wide statistics, the following initialization parameter can be set:

  ```
  timed_statistics=true
  ```

For database-wide statistics after the instance is started, you can use the *alter system* command to turn on timed statistics:

```
alter system set timed_statistics=true;
```

At the session level, timed statistics can be set in SQL*Plus with the following command:

```
alter session set timed_statistics=true;
```

■ **user_dump_dest**   This initialization parameter specifies the location of the trace files. You will need to know the location of the trace files to create your TKPROF report

■ **max_dump_file_size**   This parameter must be set high enough to allow the complete trace file for a complex SQL statement.

NOTE
You must ensure that the ORACLE account that runs the query has a plan table by running utlxplan.sql when connected as the schema owner. You must also be connected as the schema owner user ID when running access.sql.

Generating the SQL Trace File

Once the *sql_trace=true* command is set with the *alter session* command, you will get a trace file for all SQL commands issued by your session. This trace file is known as a level-1 trace. You can also issue commands to cause Oracle to create a super-detailed level-4 trace file where additional detail is required.

Oracle will generate trace files for every session where the value of *sql_trace=true* and write them to the *user_dump_dest* destination. These file are stored in the form *$ORACLE_SID_ora_nnn.trc* in the trace directory, where *nnn* is a sequential number. Note that if you are not in the UNIX dba group, the generated files may not be accessible. If this is the case, you need to go to the DBA to change the UNIX permissions on the trace files before you can use TKPROF to format them. It is a good idea to note the date/time you create the trace file in case others are also creating trace files, since the identification is by a number in the filename.

Advanced SQL Trace File Generation
Oracle also provides a facility for getting a super-detailed trace file called a level-4 trace. This is generally only done at the request of Oracle Technical Support, but advanced SQL tuning professionals can sometimes find useful information in a level-4 trace file.

Generating a level-4 trace file requires that you know the SID and SERIAL# for the session to trace. You can use the following query to get the SID and SERIAL# for the session you wish to trace. To do this, we start by running *session.sql*:

session.sql

```
rem session.sql - displays all connected sessions
set echo off;
set termout on;
set linesize 80;
set pagesize 60;
set newpage 0;
ttitle "dbname Database|UNIX/Oracle Sessions";

set heading off;
select 'Sessions on database '||substr(name,1,8) from v$database;
set heading on;
select
        substr(a.spid,1,9) pid,
        substr(b.sid,1,5) sid,
        substr(b.serial#,1,5) ser#,
        substr(b.machine,1,6) box,
        substr(b.username,1,10) username,
        substr(b.osuser,1,8) os_user,
        substr(b.program,1,30) program
from v$session b, v$process a
 where
b.paddr = a.addr
and type='USER'
order by spid;

spool off;
```

Here is a sample of the output from *session.sql*. Note that it shows the OS PID, the SID, the SERIAL#, and the originating client:

```
SQL> @session
```

```
Sun Apr 01                                              page    1
                            UNIX/Oracle Sessions


PID    SID SER#  BOX    USERNAME    OS_USER  PROGRAM
----   --- ----- ------ ----------  -------- ------------------------------
7330   13 11967 sting  OPS$ORACLE  oracle   sqlplus@sting (TNS V1-V3)
8214   10 1261  taz    READER      root     rdbqry_ora@taz (TNS V1-V3)
```

Once you know the SID, you can issue the following command to get a level-4 trace file for a user. In this example, we will trace the session for SPID 10:

```
Connect system as sysdba;
ORADEBUG SETOSPID 10;
ORADEBUG EVENT 10046 TRACE NAME CONTEXT FOREVER, LEVEL 4
```

You can also use the *dbms_support* package to generate a level-4 trace file. To use the *dbms_support* package, you must specify the SID and SERIAL#:

```
EXEC DBMS_SUPPORT.START_TRACE_IN_SESSION(10,1261,waits=>false, binds=>true)
```

The *dbms_support* package also has a 'stop' command to turn off the level-4 trace.

```
EXEC DBMS_SUPPORT.STOP_TRACE_IN_SESSION(<SID>, <SERIAL#>)
```

Remember, these trace files are internal dumps, and they will not be readable until they are formatted for visual display. This is where we use the TKPROF utility.

Formatting the Trace File

Once you have generated the trace files, the next step is to format the trace file. This utilizes the TKPROF utility to format and make the trace file readable.

```
TKPROF <input-tracefile> <output-file> EXPLAIN=user/password
```

You can find the location of your input-tracefile with the following SQL*Plus command:

```
select
    name,
    value
from
    v$parameter
where
    name = 'user_dump_dest'
;
```

Here is the output that show that the trace files are written to /u01/app/oracle/admin/udump:

```
NAME
-------------------------------------------------------------
VALUE
-------------------------------------------------------------
user_dump_dest
/u01/app/oracle/admin/prodsys1/udump
```

The TKPROF utility has a wealth of command line options. You can type the TKPROF command from the UNIX prompt with no command line arguments to get a usage and parameter listing. As you can see, there are dozens of formatting options that can be applied to a trace file.

```
root>tkprof
Usage: tkprof tracefile outputfile [explain= ] [table= ]
               [print= ] [insert= ] [sys= ] [sort= ]
  table=schema.tablename   Use 'schema.tablename' with 'explain=' option.
  explain=user/password    Connect to ORACLE and issue EXPLAIN PLAIN.
  print=integer    List only the first 'integer' SQL statements.
  aggregate=yes|no
  insert=filename  List SQL statements and data inside INSERT statements.
  sys=no           TKPROF does not list SQL statements run as user SYS.
  record=filename  Record non-recursive statements found in the trace file.
  sort=option      Set of zero or more of the following sort options:
    prscnt  number of times parse was called
    prscpu  cpu time parsing
    prsela  elapsed time parsing
    prsdsk  number of disk reads during parse
    prsqry  number of buffers for consistent read during parse
    prscu   number of buffers for current read during parse
    prsmis  number of misses in library cache during parse
    execnt  number of execute was called
    execpu  cpu time spent executing
    exeela  elapsed time executing
    exedsk  number of disk reads during execute
    exeqry  number of buffers for consistent read during execute
    execu   number of buffers for current read during execute
    exerow  number of rows processed during execute
    exemis  number of library cache misses during execute
    fchcnt  number of times fetch was called
    fchcpu  cpu time spent fetching
    fchela  elapsed time fetching
    fchdsk  number of disk reads during fetch
    fchqry  number of buffers for consistent read during fetch
    fchcu   number of buffers for current read during fetch
    fchrow  number of rows fetched
    userid  userid of user that parsed the cursor
```

The first step in running TKPROF is to go to the *user_dump_dest* directory and find our trace file:

```
sting*prodsid1-/u01/app/oracle/admin/prodsid1/udump
>ls -alt|head
total 128
-rw-r-----   1 oracle   dba       5083 Apr  1 11:16 prodsid1_ora_7330.trc
```

Now, we can issue the TKPROF command from the UNIX prompt, directing the listing to a file called *mytrace.lst.* Note that we also use the sort options, sorting first by number of disk reads during execute followed by the number of reads during fetch.

```
root>tkprof testb1_ora_7330.trc mytrace.lst \
     explain=applsys/manager sort='(exedsk, fchdsk)'

TKPROF: Release 8.1.6.1.0 - Production on Sun Apr 1 11:19:18 2001

(c) Copyright 1999 Oracle Corporation.  All rights reserved.
```

Next, we can display the *mytrace.lst* file and see the details about the execution of our SQL statement. Let's take a look at the contents of a standard TKPROF report.

The TKPROF Report

The output file is a report laid out with the SQL statement given first, then the timed statistics for PARSE, EXECUTE, and FETCH, followed by the execution plan if the EXPLAIN option was used.

```
UPDATE mrp_relief_interface
     SET request_id = :sql_req_id,
     process_status = 3
     WHERE   inventory_item_id  IN
        (SELECT inventory_item_id
          FROM   mrp_relief_interface rel2
          WHERE  rel2.request_id IS NULL
          AND    rel2.error_message IS NULL
          AND    rel2.relief_type = 1
          AND    rel2.process_status = 2
          AND    rownum <= :batch_size
          AND    NOT EXISTS
            (SELECT 'x'
              FROM   mrp_form_query
              WHERE  query_id = :in_process_items
                 AND    number1  = rel2.inventory_item_id))
     AND request_id IS NULL
     AND error_message IS NULL
     AND relief_type = 1
     AND process_status = 2
```

call	count	cpu	elapsed	disk	query	current	rows
Parse	2	0.02	0.02	0	0	0	0
Execute	2	239.39	1003.16	274981	3792129	534	242
Fetch	0	0.00	0.00	0	0	0	0

```
total        4    239.41    1003.18     274981    3792129       534       242

Misses in library cache during parse: 1
Optimizer goal: RULE
Parsing user id: 41   (APPS)

Rows      Execution Plan
-------   --------------------------------------------------
      0   UPDATE STATEMENT    GOAL: RULE
      0    UPDATE OF 'MRP_RELIEF_INTERFACE'
    242     NESTED LOOPS
    234      VIEW
    242       SORT (UNIQUE)
    242        COUNT (STOPKEY)
    242         FILTER
1886651          TABLE ACCESS (BY INDEX ROWID) OF
                    'MRP_RELIEF_INTERFACE'
1886652           INDEX (RANGE SCAN) OF 'MRP_RELIEF_INTERFACE_N2'
                     (NON-UNIQUE)
    234           INDEX   GOAL: ANALYZED (RANGE SCAN) OF
                     'MRP_FORM_QUERY_N89' (NON-UNIQUE)
   3597      TABLE ACCESS (BY INDEX ROWID) OF 'MRP_RELIEF_INTERFACE'
   3831       INDEX (RANGE SCAN) OF 'MRP_RELIEF_INTERFACE_N2'
                 (NON-UNIQUE)
```

The best part of this report is the details showing all activity within the parse, execute, and fetch phases of SQL execution. For each of these phases, TKPROF reports timing and other statistical information as follows (bolded names that follow do *not* match the column headings in the listing—count, cpu, elapsed, disk, query, current, rows):

- **COUNT** This is the number of times that the SQL statement was parsed, executed, or fetched.

- **CPU** This is the total number of CPU seconds (in hundredths of a second) taken to perform each phase of the given SQL statement.

- **ELAPSED** This is the total amount of time (in hundredths of a second) from start to finish for each phase to be performed. This statistic can be viewed as "wall clock" time, but it does not include Net8 transmission time to a remote client.

- **DISK** This is the number of Oracle blocks read from disk for each phase. If *fetch* has high values, you should check for possible full-table scans in the execution plan.

- **QUERY** This is the total number of blocks fetched for consistent reads. If there are lots of *insert, update,* and *delete* transactions occurring when this trace file was generated, then this value can be high.

■ **CURRENT** This is the number of blocks acquired for modifying transactions such as *inserts, updates,* and *deletes.*

■ **ROWS** This is the number of rows operated on by either the *execute* or *fetch* phase.

Next, let's look at another great script provided by Oracle's Center of Expertise (COE). This script expands on the SQL Trace facility and also includes detailed information about the table and indexes that participate in the query.

Oracle's Center of Expertise (COE) SQL Analysis Report

Oracle Corporate Technical Support provides a great supplement to the standard explain plan utility in the form of a SQL*Plus script called *coe_xplain.sql.* This script enhances the SQL analysis by providing additional details about the database and all tables and indexes in the query.

You can download this script from the Oracle Web site at the following URL:

http://www.osborne.com/oracle/code_archive.html

The purpose of this script is to supplement the standard explain plan output with additional information about the status of the tables and indexes in your database. Let's take a look at how this script is used:

1. First, you download the script from Oracle Press Web site.

2. Next, you transfer the script to your server.

3. To add your SQL statement, go to section III and paste the SQL statement into the script, making sure that the SQL ends with a semicolon.

4. Finally, you enter SQL*Plus as the schema owner and execute *coe_xplain.*

This script begins by asking you what details you would like in addition to the standard explain plan. Following the data collection, this script generates two files:

■ *coe_statement.lst* This is a display of the SQL you inserted into section III of the script.

■ *coe_explain.lst* This file contain the detailed execution plan for the SQL and lots of other useful information.

Let's take a look at the output from this script. When executed, this script prompts the user about the amount of additional detail they need. When analyzing a SQL statement, it is a good idea to request all of the ancillary information.

```
>sqlplus system/manager

SQL*Plus: Release 9.0.3.0.0 - Production on Wed Feb 7 06:38:22 2001
(c) Copyright 2001 Oracle Corporation.  All rights reserved.
Connected to:
Oracle9i Enterprise Edition Release 8.1.6.1.0 - 64bit Production
With the Partitioning option
JServer Release 9.0.3.0.0 - 64bit Production

SQL> @coe_xplain
Unless otherwise instructed by Support, hit <Enter> for each parameter
1. Include count(*) of Tables in SQL Statement? <n/y> y
2. Include Table and Index Storage Parameters? <n/y/d> y
3. Include all Table Columns? <n/y> y
4. Include all Column Histograms? <n/y> y
5. Include relevant INIT.ORA DB parameters? <n/y> y
```

Now that the script has gathered our requirements, it displays the SQL statement and the execution plan for the SQL:

```
Generating...

explain plan set statement_id = 'COE_XPLAIN' into COE_PLAN_TABLE_&&initials for
/*=====================================================================
  Generate Explain Plan for SQL statement below (ending with a semicolon ';')
  ===================================================================== */
SELECT /*+ first_rows */
B.ISBN,B.BOOK_TITLE,B.EDITION_NBR,B.AUTHOR_NAME,B.THUMBNAIL_TYPE,B.GLOSSARY_NBR,B.
TABLE_CONTENTS_NBR,B.INDEX_NBR,B.PUBLIC_DOMAIN_FLAG,B.NBR_OF_REVIEWS,B.TOTAL_REVIE
W_RATING,S.START_VISUAL_PAGE_NBR,S.END_VISUAL_PAGE_NBR,S.START_PAGE_SEQ_NBR,S.END_
PAGE_SEQ_NBR,TO_CHAR(S.START_DATE,'DD-MON-YYYY H24:MI:SS'),TO_CHAR(S.END_DATE,'DD-
MON-YYYY HH24:MI:SS'), S.LAST_VIEWED_PAGE_SEQ_NBR, P.VISUAL_PAGE_NBR,
TO_CHAR(S.TIME_LAST_VIEWED,'DD-MON-YYYY HH24:MI:SS'), S.PROFESSOR_USER_UNIQUE_ID,
S.RETURNED_FLAG,S.TRIAL_SUBSC_FLAG   FROM BOOK B,SUBSCRIPTION S,PAGE P  WHERE
(S.USER_UNIQUE_ID = :b1  AND S.ISBN = B.ISBN  AND S.BOOK_UNIQUE_ID =
P.BOOK_UNIQUE_ID  AND S.LAST_VIEWED_PAGE_SEQ_NBR = P.PAGE_SEQ_NBR )ORDER BY
B.BOOK_TITLE;

Explained.

Ope  Exec


Typ Order Explain Plan (coe_xplain.sql 8.1/11.5 20010115)

--- ----- ---------------------------------------------------------------------
------------------------------------------------------------------------
ROW    12 SELECT STATEMENT Opt_Mode:RULE (RBO has been used)
```

```
SET    11 SORT (ORDER BY)

ROW    10 . NESTED LOOPS (OUTER)

ROW    7 .. NESTED LOOPS

ROW    4 ... NESTED LOOPS

ROW    2 .... TABLE ACCESS (BY INDEX ROWID) OF 'MRP.MRP_FORECAST_DESIGNATORS'

ROW    1 ....| INDEX (UNIQUE SCAN) OF 'MRP.MRP_FORECAST_DESIGNATORS_U1' (UNIQUE
)
ROW    3 .... INDEX (RANGE SCAN) OF 'MRP.MRP_FORECAST_ITEMS_U1' (UNIQUE)

ROW    6 ... TABLE ACCESS (BY INDEX ROWID) OF 'MRP.MRP_FORECAST_DATES'

ROW    5 .... INDEX (RANGE SCAN) OF 'MRP.MRP_FORECAST_DATES_N1' (NON-UNIQUE)

ROW    9 .. TABLE ACCESS (BY INDEX ROWID) OF 'MRP.MRP_FORECAST_UPDATES'

ROW    8 ... INDEX (RANGE SCAN) OF 'MRP.MRP_FORECAST_UPDATES_N2' (NON-UNIQUE)


Note: Card=Computed or Default Object Cardinality
```

Next, the report will be created and spooled to *coe_statement.lst* and *coe_explain.lst*. The *coe_statement.lst* shows the input SQL statement, but the valuable information is in *coe_explain.lst*. From this listing, we get far more detail than just the execution plan for the SQL. This report contains all of the information for any Oracle object that participates in the query.

First, we see additional information about the internal structure of Oracle tables and indexes:

- **Section I: Table information**   This section of the report shows all details for the table involved in the query, including the number of rows in the table, the parallel degree, a note if the table is partitioned, the chain count, and the number of freelists for the table.

- **Section I.a: Table statistics**   Next we see details on each table from the data dictionary, including the high-water mark, used blocks, empty blocks, and free space per allocated block. This information can be quite useful for detecting tables where the high-water mark is far above the table's row space.

- **Section I.b: Table storage parameters**   This section displays the PCTFREE, PCTUSED, and extent sizes for each table in the query.

- **Section II: Index parameters**   This includes everything you would want to know about the index, including the index type, index status parallelism, partitioning, and freelists.

- **Section II.a: Index statistics**   In this section, the report provides details on the cardinality of the index and the number of distinct keys.

- **Section II.b: Index storage parameters**   This section shows all of the indexes and the index column detail.

- **Section III: Table columns**   The next section displays all of the available information about each table column that participates in the query.

- **Section III.a: Index column statistics**   This section examines all of the available statistics for each column in the query. This includes the column size, cardinality, number of distinct values, and index selectivity.

- **Section III.b: Table column statistics**   This section of the report shows the individual characteristics of each column that is referenced in the SQL query. It shows all of the CBO statistics that have been collected abut each column.

- **Section IV: Histograms**   The histograms section is useful in cases where you may have a table column with a highly skewed distribution of values. As you may know, it is not a good idea to analyze column histograms unless you identify columns where the distribution of values is not uniform.

- **Section V: Oracle initialization parameters**   This section dumps the *init.ora* parameters from the *v$parameter* view. This completes the overall package, so the analyst will have access to every possible factor that influences the execution plan for the SQL statement.

This output listing should provide everything that is needed to properly tune the SQL statement, and most professional DBAs make frequent use of this script.

Reporting on SQL from the Library Cache

As was introduced in Chapter 7, it is often useful to execute the Oracle8*i explain plan* statement on all SQL statements in the library cache, analyzing all the execution plans, and providing reports on all table and index access methods.

At first glance, it may be hard to fully appreciate the value of this technique and the information produced by the reports. But if your database has a large library cache, you can get some great insights into the internal behavior of the tables and indexes. The information also offers some great clues about what database objects you need to adjust. The reports are invaluable for the following database activities:

- **Identifying high-use tables and indexes**   See what tables and indexes the database accesses the most frequently.

- **Identifying tables for caching**   You can quickly find small, frequently accessed tables for placement in the KEEP pool (Oracle8) or for use with the CACHE option (Oracle7). You can enhance the technique to automatically cache tables when they meet certain criteria for the number of blocks and the number of accesses. (I automatically cache all tables with fewer than 200 blocks when a table has experienced more than 100 full-table scans.)

- **Identifying tables for row resequencing**   You can locate large tables that have frequent index range scans in order to resequence the rows, to reduce I/O.

- **Dropping unused indexes**   You can reclaim space occupied by unused indexes. Studies have found that an Oracle database never uses more than a quarter of all indexes available or doesn't use them in the way for which they were intended.

- **Stopping full-table scans by adding new indexes**   Quickly find the full-table scans that you can speed up by adding a new index to a table.

The script is too long to reproduce in this book, but the source code for the scripts in this book can be found at www.osborne.com. Here are the steps to execute this script:

1. Download the *access.sql* and *access_report.sql* scripts.

2. Issue the following statements for the schema owner of your tables:
   ```
   grant select on v_$sqltext to schema_owner;
   grant select on v_$sqlarea to schema_owner;
   grant select on v_$session to schema_owner;
   grant select on v_$mystat to schema_owner;
   ```
3. Go into SQL*Plus, connect as the schema owner, and run *access.sql.*

You must be signed on as the schema owner in order to explain SQL statements with unqualified table names. Also, remember that you will get statistics only for the SQL statements that currently reside in your library cache. For very active databases, you may want to run this report script several times—it takes less than ten minutes for most Oracle databases.

Using the access.sql Script with STATSPACK

The *access.sql* script can be easily modified to use the *stats$sql_summary* tables to extract and explain historical SQL statements. All you need to do is change the reference to *v$sqlarea* to *stats_sql_summary,* and add the following to the *where* clause:

```
FROM
    stats$sql_summary s,
    stats$snapshot sn
WHERE
    s.snapshot_id = sn.snapshot_id
AND
    sn,snapshot_id = (select max(snapshot_id) from stats$snapshot;
```

Of course, you can modify the *access.sql* script to extract, explain, and report on any SQL in the *stats$sql_summary* table. Remember, though, that the SQL stored in the *stats$sql_summary* table is filtered by the thresholds stored in the *stats$statspack_parameter* table:

- **executions_th**   This is the number of executions of the SQL statement (default is 100).

- **disk_reads_th**   This is the number of disk reads performed by the SQL statement (default is 1000).

- **parse_calls_th**   This is the number of parse calls performed by the SQL statement (default is 1000).

- **buffer_gets_th**   This is the number of buffer gets performed by the SQL statement (default is 10,000).

Remember, a SQL statement will be included in the *stats$sql_summary* table if any *one* of the thresholds is exceeded. Now, let's get back to *access.sql* and look at the valuable reports.

The access.sql Reports

As I noted in Chapter 7, the *access.sql* script grabs all of the SQL in the library cache and stores it in a table called *sqltemp.* From this table, all of the SQL is explained into a single plan table. This plan table is then queried to produce the report that follows.

Let's begin by looking at the output this technique provides, and then we'll examine the method for producing the reports. For the purpose of illustration, let's break up the report into several sections. The first section shows the total number of

SQL statements in the library cache, and the total number that could not be explained. Some statements cannot be explained because they do not indicate the owner of the table. If the number of statements that cannot be explained is high, you are probably not connected as the proper schema owner when running the script.

Report from access.sql

PL/SQL procedure successfully completed.

```
Mon Jan 29                                              page    1
                      Total SQL found in library cache
     23907


                      Total SQL that could not be explained
        65
```

The Full-Table Scan Report

As I noted in Chapter 6, this is one of the most valuable SQL tuning reports. Here we see all of the SQL statements that performed full-table scans, and the number of times that a full-table scan was performed. We also see the number of rows and blocks in each table, and a flag that indicates whether the table is cached or in the KEEP pool.

We will go into greater detail on checking full-table scans on Chapter 10, but the main focus of this report is to ensure that the small tables are in the KEEP pool, and that the queries against the large tables are not "false" full-table scans that could be changed into an index range scan.

```
Mon Jan 29                                                page    1
                      full table scans and counts
              Note that "C" indicates the table is cached.
              "K" indicates the table is in the KEEP Pool


OWNER           NAME                   NUM_ROWS C K    BLOCKS   NBR_FTS
--------------- ---------------------- -------------- - - -------- --------
SYS             DUAL                            N          2   97,237
SYSTEM          SQLPLUS_PRODUCT_PRO             N  K       2   16,178
DONALD          PAGER                 3,450,209 N       932,120    9,999
DONALD          RWU_PAGE                    434 N          8    7,355
DONALD          PAGER_IMAGE              18,067 N      1,104    5,368
DONALD          SUBSTANT                    476 N  K     192    2,087
DONALD          PRINT_PAGER_RANGE            10 N  K      32      874
ARSD            JANET_BOOKS                  20 N          8       64
PERFSTAT        STATS$TAB_STATS                 N         65       10
```

The *access_report.sql* script also provides some great statistics on index usage. Next, let's look at the index range scan report.

The Index Range Scan Report

Next we see the report for index range scans. The most common method of index access in Oracle is the index range scan. An index range scan is used when the SQL statement contains a restrictive clause that requires a sequential range of values that are indexes for the table. Tables with a high number of index range scans may benefit from row-resequencing to reduce the amount of physical disk I/O.

```
Mon Jan 29                                                    page    1
                          Index range scans and counts

OWNER      TABLE_NAME            INDEX_NAME        TBL_BLOCKS    NBR_SCANS
---------  --------------------  --------------    ----------    ---------
DONALD     ANNO_HIGHLIGHT        HL_PAGE_USER_IX          16        7,975
DONALD     ANNO_STICKY           ST_PAGE_USER_IX           8        7,296
DONALD     PAGE                  ISBN_SEQ_IDX            120        3,859
DONALD     TOC_ENTRY             ISBN_TOC_SEQ_I           40        2,830
DONALD     PRINT_HISTORY         PH_KEY_IDX               32        1,836
DONALD     SUBSCRIPTION          SUBSC_ISBN_USEX         192          210
ARSD       JANET_BOOK_RANGES     ROV_BK_RNG_BOO            8          170
PERFSTAT   STATS$SYSSTAT         STATS$SYSSTAT_P         845           32
```

These index reports are critical for several areas of Oracle SQL tuning.

- **Index usage**   Ensuring that the application is actually using a new index. DBAs can now obtain empirical evidence that an index is actually being used after it has been created. Indexes that are not being used cause additional overhead for SQL *insert* and *update* statements and also waste valuable disk space.

- **Row resequencing**   The index range scan report is great for finding out which tables might benefit from row resequencing. Tables that have a large amount of index range scan activity will benefit from having the rows resequenced into the same order as the index. Resequencing can result in a tenfold performance improvement, depending on the average length of the rows in the table.

The Index Unique Scan Report

Here is a report that lists index unique scans, which occur when the Oracle database engine uses an index to retrieve a specific row from a table. The Oracle database commonly uses these types of "probe" accesses when it performs a JOIN and probes another table for the JOIN key from the driving table. This report is also useful for finding out those indexes that are used to identify distinct table rows as opposed to indexes that are used to fetch a range of rows.

```
Mon Jan 29                                              page     1
                        Index unique scans and counts

    OWNER       TABLE_NAME              INDEX_NAME              NBR_SCANS
    ---------   --------------------    --------------------    ------------
    DONALD      BOOK                    BOOK_ISBN                   44,606
    DONALD      PAGE                    ISBN_SEQ_IDX                39,973
    DONALD      BOOK                    BOOK_UNIQUE_ID               6,450
    DONALD      ANNO_DOG_EAR            DE_PAGE_USER_IDX             5,339
    DONALD      TOC_ENTRY               ISBN_TOC_SEQ_IDX             5,186
    DONALD      PRINT_PERMISSIONS       PP_KEY_IDX                   1,836
    DONALD      RDRUSER                 USER_UNIQUE_ID_IDX           1,065
    DONALD      CURRENT_LOGONS          USER_LOGONS_UNIQUE_I           637
    ARSD        JANET_BOOKS             BOOKS_BOOK_ID_PK                54
    DONALD      ERROR_MESSAGE           ERROR_MSG_IDX                   48
```

The Full-Index Scan Report

The next report shows all index full scans. As you will recall, the Oracle optimizer will sometimes perform an index full scan in lieu of a large sort in the TEMP tablespace. You will commonly see full-index scans in SQL that have the *order by* clause.

```
Mon Jan 29                                              page     1
                        Index full scans and counts

    OWNER       TABLE_NAME              INDEX_NAME              NBR_SCANS
    ---------   --------------------    --------------------    ------------
    DONALD      BOOK                    BOOK_ISBN                    2,295
    DONALD      PAGE                    ISBN_SEQ_IDX                   744
```

Limitations of the access.sql Reports

The technique for generating these reports is not as flawless as it may appear. Because the "raw" SQL statements must be explained in order to obtain the execution plans, you may not know the owner of the tables. One problem with native SQL is that the table names are not always qualified with the table owner. To ensure that all the SQL statements are completely explained, many DBAs sign on to Oracle and run the reports as the schema owner.

A future enhancement would be to issue the following undocumented command immediately before each SQL statement is explained so that any Oracle database user could run the reports:

```
ALTER SESSION SET current_schema = 'tableowner';
```

This would change the schema owner immediately before explaining the SQL statement.

Conclusion

Oracle provides a wealth of tools that quickly enable you to examine the run-time details of Oracle SQL execution. We can use the standard explain plan utility, TKPROF, or more advanced techniques such as Oracle's COE script and *access.sql* to give us detailed information about the physical access path to our table rows.

Next, let's turn our attention to tools that can be used for locating the most significant SQL statements.

CHAPTER
9

Locating Significant
SQL Statements

e have already discussed some of the methods for finding significant SQL statements in Chapter 7, but we need to go into additional detail about how to locate and tune those SQL statements that will have the most immediate benefit to the database. It is important to get an immediate and positive result from SQL tuning, and this chapter outlines the procedures for establishing a baseline optimizer mode and locating those SQL statements that will provide the most benefit for the least effort.

This chapter contains the following topics:

- Setting your instance-wide SQL baselines

- What constitutes a significant SQL statement?

- Techniques for extracting significant SQL for tuning

- Ongoing tuning of SQL statements

Let's begin our discussion by examining how to get a fast and immediate benefit from SQL tuning by adjusting the Oracle initialization parameters.

Establishing Your Instance-Wide SQL Baseline

When undertaking to tune all of the SQL in a database, it is unwise to leap headfirst into the task and begin to tune individual SQL statements.

Rather, most SQL tuning professionals begin by changing instance-wide parameters to establish a baseline for the tuning of individual SQL statements. This instance-wide tuning involves resetting some important initialization parameters, most notably the *optimizer_mode,* and ensuring that the optimal settings are in place for Oracle parallel query and multiblock reads.

Setting the Default Optimizer_Mode

This *optimizer_mode* is the most important of the initialization parameters for SQL tuning. Essentially, the choice for *optimizer_mode* is the rule-based mode (*rule*), or the cost-based optimizer modes (*first_rows* or *all_rows*). The *all_rows* cost-based optimizer mode is generally reserved for batch-oriented systems where throughput is more important than transaction response time. There are some general guidelines for the best optimizer mode for a given version of Oracle (Figure 9-1). The rule-based optimizer has not been changed since Oracle7, while the cost-based optimizer has been constantly improved for better performance. If we take Oracle's Applications

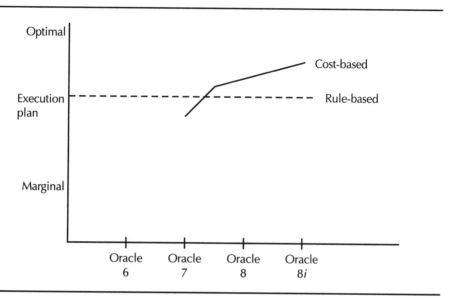

FIGURE 9-1.   *Optimizer mode and optimal execution plans*

software as a benchmark, we see that Oracle Applications used rule-based optimization until Oracle8*i* was introduced.

It is ironic that while Oracle's official posture was to recommend cost-based SQL optimization in Oracle7 and Oracle8, Oracle Corporation continued to use rule-based optimization for their own Oracle Applications software. Starting with Oracle8*i,* the cost-based optimizer has improved to the point where it can be considered as a default *optimizer_mode* for an entire database. If your database is using advanced features such as bitmapped or function-based indexes, you can still use a rule-based default and add statistics and *first_rows* or *all_rows* hints to invoke the CBO for those queries that require advanced indexes.

In addition to the version of the Oracle software, there are also some guidelines that can give you a hint about the best *optimizer_mode* for your system (Table 9-1).

The goal of establishing a baseline is to set the *optimizer_mode* such that the majority of SQL statements are optimized, thereby reducing the amount of individual SQL tuning. Let's illustrate this concept with a simple example. Assume that we have an OLTP database running Oracle 8.0.5, and the *optimizer_mode* has been defaulted to *choose,* and all of the tables and indexes have been analyzed. Since the *optimizer_mode=choose* will always use the CBO when statistics are present, we must first see if another default will result in faster overall performance. In this type of scenario, the choices are between the *rule* and *first_rows* optimizer mode defaults.

System Characteristic	Probable Default Optimizer Mode
Many n-way table joins	rule
Legacy systems from Oracle7	rule
Data warehouse	all_rows
Batch-oriented system	all_rows
OLTP with bitmapped indexes	first_rows
OLTP with function-based indexes	first_rows

TABLE 9-1. *System Characteristics and Probable Default Optimizer Mode*

Making the Default Optimizer Mode Permanent

To make sure that your SQL baseline remains permanent, it is a good idea to add the appropriate hint or stored outline to all of the SQL that uses the default optimizer mode. This can save hundreds of hours of work when you migrate to a later release of Oracle and you do not want the improved CBO to change SQL that you have already tuned.

For example, let's say that your evaluation showed that your best overall SQL performance is with *optimizer_mode=first_rows*. After seeing the initialization parameter, you should take the time to firm up all queries that benefit from the system-wide default.

This is done by adding the *first_rows* hint to the SQL source code, or by creating stored outlines for the SQL to ensure that they will always use the *first_rows* method. This will ensure that the default baseline remains, and it prevents changes to CBO statistics and upgrades from changing the execution plans.

Instance-Wide Parameters to Improve the Speed of Full-Table Scans

Once we have verified that a full-table scan is legitimate, based on the number of rows requested, we can look at improving the performance of the full-table scan. While I will be discussing this in detail in Chapter 10, we should review the initialization parameters that relate to the speed of full-table scans.

As a quick summary, we need to verify the following initialization parameters:

■ Multiblock read parameters are set according to the number of CPUs on your database server. These include *db_file_multiblock_read_count*, *hash_multiblock_io_count*, and *sort_multiblock_read_count*.

■ Oracle parallel query is properly configured for full-table scans. This includes setting the parameters *parallel_max_servers, optimizer_percent_parallel,* and *parallel_automatic_tuning.*

To enable parallel query, the DBA will locate those SQL statements that require full-table scans and then ensure that these queries utilize parallel query by adding the *full* and *parallel* hints to the SQL and making the change persistent with optimizer plan stability or by changing the SQL source code to include the hints.

CAUTION
It is very dangerous to enable parallel query for a table with the alter table *command. Once a table is marked for parallel query, the CBO may change the execution plan for existing queries to use parallel full-table scans instead of index scans. This well-intentioned mistake has crippled many databases.*

Other Initialization Parameters that Affect SQL Execution

There are also other initialization parameters that affect the speed of SQL queries, and these should be established prior to searching for high-impact SQL statements.

■ **db_block_buffers** Of course, the size of the Oracle data buffers will impact the performance of SQL statements. The data buffer hit ratio should always be checked, and the data buffer hit ratios for the *buffer_pool_keep* and *buffer_pool_recycle* should also be reviewed.

■ **hash_join_enabled** This defaults to TRUE in Oracle8 and is required to utilize hash joins.

■ **Hash_area_size** If this value is too small, the optimizer will often invoke a nested loop join instead of a hash join. A too-small *hash_area_size* is one of the most common reasons that a *use_hash* hint fails to invoke a hash join.

■ **hash_multiblock_io_count** Because a hash join often invokes a full-table scan, the *hash_multiblock_io_count* parameter determines the read-ahead capabilities for hash joins.

Once you have established the baseline *optimizer_mode,* you should already see a significant overall performance improvement for your SQL. This author has cut response time in half in Oracle7 databases, simply by changing the default *optimizer_mode=rule.* Of course, it gets trickier in Oracle8 and Oracle8*i* because of the improvements to the CBO.

Running the SQL Baseline Test

When performing a SQL baseline test, it is often a good idea to involve the end-user community. The SQL tuning professional generally meets with the end-user representatives and arranges to run the database on different days with different default optimizer modes. The end users are assured that the *optimizer_mode* can be changed back quickly by bouncing the database. Remember, for OLTP databases, the end users will have a very quick idea how effective the baseline change is on their system. You also ask the end users to note which transactions appear faster or slower, since this information will be invaluable to you when tuning the individual SQL statements.

By allowing the end-user community to determine the default *optimizer_mode* according to their perception of overall SQL response time, the DBA wins, and the end users win as well. The end users get an immediate improvement in SQL performance, and the DBA has less SQL statements to manually tune.

When measuring the overall performance of the database, you need to remember that the perception of the end users is far more important than internal Oracle statistics. By allowing your end users to determine the default *optimizer_mode,* you ensure their buy-in for your SQL tuning effort, and you also get some valuable tips on where to begin the manual tuning. If you request that your end users keep track of those transactions that run slower in each *optimizer_mode,* you can get right to work and immediately tune the SQL statements on your end users' lists.

Establishing the SQL baseline is only the first step in SQL tuning. Next, let's look at how to locate significant SQL statements for tuning.

What Constitutes a Significant SQL Statement?

There is some debate about which characteristic of a SQL statement makes it the best candidate for tuning. Some people always tune statements according to their values for *executions,* while others always tune SQL in order of *disk_reads,* tuning the statements with the highest *disk_reads* first. As a review, we can extract SQL statements from the library cache or the *stats$sql_summary* table, based on the following criteria:

- **executions**   The more frequently executed SQL statements should be tuned first, since they will have the greatest impact on overall performance.

- **disk_reads**   High disk reads indicates a query that is causing lots of disk I/O. While most SQL with high *disk_reads* consists of reports, online summaries and aggregations may have high *disk_reads* and should be carefully examined.

■ **rows_processed** Queries that process a large number of rows will have high I/O and may also have an impact on the TEMP tablespace if sorting occurs. Queries with high values for *rows_processed* may be reports or decision support queries that are not online transactions and may benefit from using the *all_rows* optimizer goal.

■ **buffer_gets** High buffer gets may indicate a resource-intensive query.

■ **memory_kb** This metric shows the memory used for each SQL statement. High *memory_kb* values are most often associated with large sorting operations.

■ **sorts** Sorts can be a huge slowdown, especially if the sorts are being done on disk in the TEMP tablespace.

As you now know, you can get lists of your SQL statements from the *v$sqlarea* view or STATSPACK *stats$sql_summary* table in descending order of any of these variables (see Figure 9-2). You can also use third-party tools such as the Q Diagnostic Center by Precise Software to quickly view SQL statements according to these characteristics. Of course, you do not need to buy expensive tools to perform this task. Let's take a quick look at some common methods for manually identifying high-impact SQL statements.

Techniques for Extracting Significant SQL for Tuning

Once we have tuned the initialization parameters and established a baseline *optimizer_mode,* we are ready to look into tuning individual SQL statements. Depending on our environment, we have choices about where to find this SQL, and once it is located, we have several options for observing the performance of the SQL inside the shared pool.

Identifying High-Use SQL Statements

There are many ways to locate SQL statements. At the highest level, you have the choice of locating the SQL source code in several places:

■ **Application programs** Some Oracle professionals know the location of their SQL source code and interrogate the source code libraries to extract the SQL source code.

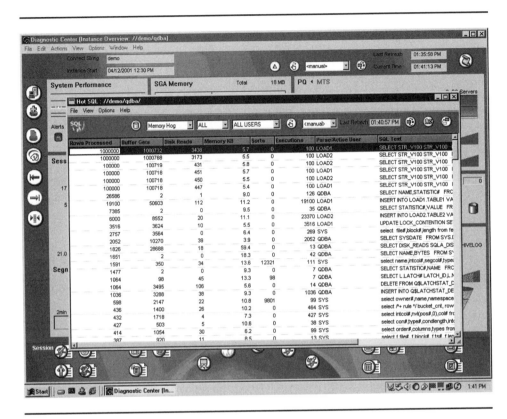

FIGURE 9-2. *Displaying SQL by* rows_processed *in the Q Diagnostic Center*

■ **The library cache** The library cache within the SGA will store the SQL source code, and it also provides statistics about the number of executions. Most SQL tuning professionals will use the *rpt_sql_cache.ksh* and *access.sql* scripts for this purpose.

■ **The *stats$sql_summary* table** The STATSPACK *stats$sql_summary* table stores the source for all SQL statements that exceed the threshold values as defined in the *stats$statspack_parameter* table. The STATSPACK tables are useful because they keep a historical record of all of the important SQL. Most SQL tuning professionals will use the SQL top-10 script *rpt_sql_STATSPACK.ksh* for this purpose.

The details about executing these scripts were covered in Chapter 7. Since the goal is to locate high-use SQL statements, the library cache and the *stats$sql_summary* table are excellent places to begin your quest for offensive SQL. For details on using STATSPACK for SQL tuning, see Donald Keith Burleson, *Oracle High-Performance Tuning with STATSPACK* (McGraw-Hill Professional Publishing, 2001). For details on using ranking tools for extracting SQL, see Chapter 7.

Extraction Scripts for SQL Statements

There are several techniques for extracting and ranking SQL. Many people use third-party tools, but there are several SQL*Plus scripts that can be used to locate important SQL statements. Here are some of the common techniques:

- Extract SQL from *stats$sql_summary* with the STATSPACK SQL top-10 report *(rpt_sql_STATSPACK.ksh)*.

- Extract SQL from the *v$sqlarea* view using *rpt_sql_cache.sql*.

- Extract and analyze SQL from the library cache using *access.sql*.

Please note that any of these techniques can be used with either the historical STATSPACK *stats$sql_summary* table or the *v$sqlarea* view. The columns in *v$sqlarea* and *stats$sql_summary* are identical, so it is very easy to write scripts that extract SQL from both locations.

When ranking SQL statements, we recognize that it is more important to tune a frequently executed SQL statement for a small performance gain than it is to tune a seldom-executed SQL statement for a huge performance gain. In many cases, the Oracle professional does not have the time to locate and tune all of the SQL statements. It is also important to get an immediate measurable result, so that management will continue to fund the tuning effort. Hence, you must quickly locate those statements that are frequently executed and tune these statements first.

At some point you will encounter diminishing marginal returns for your tuning effort (Figure 9-3). After you have tuned the frequently executed SQL and move on to the less frequently executed SQL, you may find that the time and effort for tuning will not result in a cost-effective benefit.

Ongoing Ranking of SQL Statements

Once you have established your baseline *optimizer_mode* and tuned the SQL, there is an ongoing process of rechecking your database for new SQL statements. The process of ongoing SQL extraction depends upon the method you used to make the tuning changes permanent. If you made your tuning changes permanent by adding hints to the source code, you need to check for SQL that does not possess hints. If you used stored outlines to make the tuning changes permanent, then you need to check for SQL that does not exist in the *DBA_OUTLINES* view.

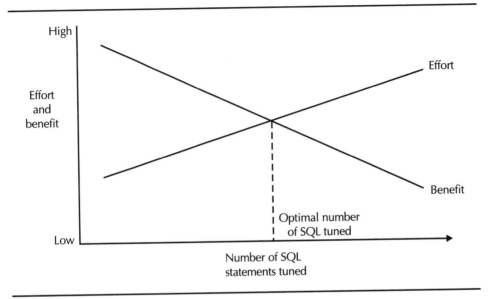

FIGURE 9-3. *The diminishing marginal returns for SQL tuning*

Let's look at two methods for identifying untuned SQL.

Finding New SQL Without Hints

If you are using hints to make your execution plan persistent, you can query the *v$sqlarea* view or *stats$sql_summary* table to extract SQL that does not have hints.

rpt_sql_nohint.ksh

```ksh
#!/bin/ksh

# First, we must set the environment . . . .
ORACLE_SID=$ORACLE_SID
export ORACLE_SID
ORACLE_HOME=`cat /var/opt/oracle/oratab|\
   grep ^$ORACLE_SID:|cut -f2 -d':'`
export ORACLE_HOME
PATH=$ORACLE_HOME/bin:$PATH
export PATH

echo "How many days back to search?"
read days_back
```

```
echo executions
echo loads
echo parse_calls
echo disk_reads
echo buffer_gets
echo rows_processed
echo sorts
echo
echo "Enter sort key:"
read sortkey

$ORACLE_HOME/bin/sqlplus perfstat/perfstat<<!


set array 1;
set lines 80;
set wrap on;
set pages 999;
set echo off;
set feedback off;

column mydate        format a8
column exec          format 9,999,999
column loads         format 999,999
column parse         format 999,999
column reads         format 9,999,999
column gets          format 9,999,999
column rows_proc     format 9,999,999
 column sorts         format 999,999

drop table temp1;
create table temp1 as
   select min(snap_id) min_snap
   from stats\$snapshot where snap_time > sysdate-$days_back;

drop table temp2;

create table temp2 as
select
   to_char(snap_time,'dd Mon HH24:mi:ss') mydate,
   executions                          exec,
   loads                               loads,
   parse_calls                         parse,
   disk_reads                          reads,
   buffer_gets                         gets,
   rows_processed                      rows_proc,
   sorts                               sorts,
   sql_text
```

```
from
   perfstat.stats\$sql_summary sql,
   perfstat.stats\$snapshot      sn
where
   sql.snap_id >
   (select min_snap from temp1)
and
   sql.snap_id = sn.snap_id
and
   sql.sql_text NOT LIKE '%/*+%'
order by $sortkey desc
;
spool off;

select * from temp2 where rownum < 11;

exit
!
```

Here is the output from this script. Simply put, it scans for SQL that does not have the /*+ string that delimits a hint. Of course, you should always use the /*+ syntax for hints and not the + method for denoting hints.

```
root>rpt_sql_nohint.ksh
How many days back to search?
55
executions
loads
parse_calls
disk_reads
buffer_gets
rows_processed
sorts

Enter sort key:
executions

SQL*Plus: Release 8.1.6.0.0 - Production on Mon Apr 2 13:51:50 2001

(c) Copyright 1999 Oracle Corporation. All rights reserved.


Connected to:
Oracle8i Enterprise Edition Release 8.1.6.1.0 - 64bit Production
With the Partitioning option
JServer Release 8.1.6.1.0 - 64bit Production
```

```
MYDATE                EXEC    LOADS    PARSE READS        GETS  ROWS_PROC
---------------  -------  --------  -------- -----  ----------  ----------
     SORTS
  --------
SQL_TEXT
-----------------------------------------------------------------------
07 Feb 11:00:38  97,244        9   14,220     0     224,685      97,244
         0
SELECT BOOK_UNIQUE_ID   FROM BOOK  WHERE (ISBN = :b1 )

07 Feb 09:00:42  96,368        9   14,217     0     222,933      96,368
         0
SELECT BOOK_UNIQUE_ID   FROM BOOK  WHERE (ISBN = :b1 )
```

Finding New SQL When Using Optimizer Plan Stability

The optimizer plan stability features of Oracle8*i* use stored outlines to alleviate the need to reparse a SQL statement each time it is called. While we will cover the use of optimizer plan stability in detail in Chapter 13, for now you need to know that Oracle will store the execution plan for any SQL statement in the *sql_text* column of the DBA_OUTLINES view.

Conclusion

This chapter has been concerned with the process of setting the SQL baseline parameters, finding significant SQL statements to tune, and periodically rechecking for new and untuned SQL statements. The major points in this chapter include:

- The baseline setting for optimizer_mode can make a huge positive impact of the performance of all SQL.

- The most benefit in tuning individual SQL statements is by locating those queries that are executed most frequently and those that consume the most resources.

Next, let's take a look at the evaluation and tuning of full-table scans. Full-table scans are very important to SQL tuning, and the Oracle SQL tuning professional must be able to evaluate and tune any query that invokes a full-table scan.

CHAPTER
10

Tuning Full-Table Scans
and Parallel Query

ne of the most important activities of SQL tuning is the evaluation and optimization of full-table scans. All full-table scans should be reviewed because the cost-based SQL optimizer often invokes an inappropriate full-table scan when it does not see a faster alternative to service the query, even though a faster execution plan exists. In Oracle8 and beyond, the propensity of the CBO to choose index range scans over full-table scans can be adjusted by lowering the value of the *optimizer_index_cost_adj* initialization parameter. See Chapter 14 for details on changing the default behavior of the CBO.

This chapter covers full-table scans and Oracle parallel queries because they are tightly coupled. You cannot use parallel query unless you have a full-table scan, and all legitimate full-table scans may benefit from parallel query, especially on Oracle servers with lots of CPUs.

Once a full-table scan has been reviewed and determined to be the optimal execution plan, the query can often be tuned by adding hints to invoke Oracle parallel query. Depending on the number of CPUs on the database server and the distribution of data files across disks, parallel full-table scans can process huge amounts of row data at blistering speeds.

This chapter contains the following topics:

- Evaluating the legitimacy of full-table scans

- Finding candidates for Oracle parallel query

- Introduction to Oracle parallel query

- Monitoring the use of Oracle parallel query

Let's begin with a brief overview of how to evaluate a query to see if a full-table scan is legitimate.

Evaluating the Legitimacy of a Full-Table Scan

When making the decision to change a full-table scan into an index range scan, the primary concern is the speed of the query. In some cases the full-table scan may have more physical disk I/Os, but the full-table scan will be faster because of a high degree of parallelism.

In other cases, you need to consider the number of rows retrieved as a function of the clustering of the rows in the table. For example, if your table is clustered or you have manually resequenced the rows into primary-key order, a great many adjacent rows can be read in a single I/O and an index range scan will be faster than a full-table scan for up to 40 percent of the table rows. On the other hand, if your table is totally unordered a request for 10 percent of the table rows may cause the majority of the table data blocks to be read. Of course, you also need to consider the *db_block_size,* the degree of parallelism on the table, and the setting for *db_file_multi_block_read_count init.ora* parameter. Hence, the general guideline for replacing a full-table scan with an index range scan is as follows:

- **For row-sequenced tables**   Queries that retrieve less than 40 percent of the table rows should use an index range scan. Conversely, queries that read more than 40 percent of the data blocks should use a full-table scan.

- **For un-ordered tables**   Queries that retrieve less than 7 percent of the table data blocks should use an index range scan. Conversely, queries that read more than 7 percent of the table data blocks will probably be faster with a full-table scan.

While these general guidelines help, it is always a good idea to test the execution speed in SQL*Plus by issuing the *set timing on* command. There is no substitute for experimentation. Even the most experienced SQL tuner must verify their execution plan by timing the query execution in SQL*Plus.

Remember to *always* make sure that the full table cannot be improved with index access. Each full-table scan SQL query should be evaluated, based upon the number of rows returned by the query. Full-table scans can be removed by the following methods:

- Adding a B-tree index

- Adding a bitmapped index

- Adding a function-based index

- Forcing the CBO to use an index with an *index* hint

Now that we have verified the legitimacy of a full-table scan, we are faced with invoking Oracle parallel query. To understand the issues, let's take a closer look at the internal operations of parallelism in Oracle.

Finding Candidate Tables for Oracle Parallel Query

To enable parallel query, the DBA will locate those SQL statements that participate in full-table scans and then ensure that these queries utilize parallel query. This is generally done by adding the full and parallel hints to the SQL and making the change persistent with optimizer plan stability or by changing the SQL source code to include the hints.

The first step in implementing parallelism for your database is to locate those large tables that experience frequent full-table scans. Using the *access.sql* script from Chapter 6, we can begin by observing the full-table scan report that was produced by analyzing all of the SQL that was in the library cache:

```
Mon Jan 29                                              page    1
                       full table scans and counts
             Note that "C" indicates that the table is cached.
             "K" indicates that the table is in the KEEP Pool.


OWNER           NAME                  NUM_ROWS C K   BLOCKS  NBR_FTS
-------------   --------------------  -------------- - - -------- --------
SYS             DUAL                           N          2   97,237
EMPDB1          PAGE                  3,450,209 N    932,120    9,999
EMPDB1          RWU_PAGE                    434 N          8    7,355
EMPDB1          PAGE_IMAGE               18,067 N      1,104    5,368
EMPDB1          SUBSCRIPTION                476 N K      192    2,087
EMPDB1          PRINT_PAGE_RANG              10 N K       32      874
ARSP            JANET_BOOKS                  20 N          8       64
PERFSTAT        STATS$TAB_STATS              N           65       10
```

In the preceding report, we see several large tables that are performing full-table scans. As we noted in Chapter 6, if we see legitimate small-table full-table scans, we will want to place these tables in the KEEP pool. The large-table full-table scans should also be investigated, and the legitimate large-table full-table scans should be parallelized by adding a *parallel* hint to the SQL statement.

CAUTION
The DBA should always investigate large-table full-table scans to ensure that they require more than 40 percent of sequenced table blocks or 7 percent of unsequenced table blocks before implementing parallel query on the tables.

Using the KEEP Pool

For all tables that are small (i.e., those where you have enough *db_block_buffers* to hold all of the blocks in the table), you should always use the KEEP pool to cache the table rows. The threshold for the number of blocks in the table depends upon the size of your *db_block_buffers,* since you must increase the size of *buffer_pool_keep* every time you add a table to the KEEP pool. For example, if you add a table with 400 blocks to the KEEP pool, you must increase *buffer_pool_keep* by 400. Of course, this increase will decrease the number of available blocks in the DEFAULT pool by 400 blocks, so you may also want to increase the *db_block_buffers.*

Placing small tables in the KEEP pool is analogous to the table caching option in Oracle7, and it can dramatically improve the speed of small table full-table scans because there will be no physical disk I/O. Of course, Oracle parallel query will not improve the speed of small table full-table scans, especially if all of the table blocks already reside in the KEEP pool.

Introduction to Oracle Parallel Query

Oracle has implemented parallel query features that allow a query to effectively parallelize queries with both symmetric multiprocessing (SMP) and massively parallel processing (MPP) architectures. Using these parallel features on a massively parallel machine, it is possible to read a one-gigabyte table with subsecond response time. Let's begin with a review of these architectures.

NOTE
Oracle parallel query works only with databases that perform full-table scans. A well-tuned online transaction database will seldom perform full-table scans and will not benefit from Oracle parallel query.

As I stated, Oracle parallel query will only work with queries that perform a full-table scan, and it is very important that the DBA understand that indexes are the enemy of parallel query. To invoke parallel query, you must also force the SQL optimizer to perform a full-table scan. Hence, it follows that Oracle parallel query will only improve queries that must read the majority of the data blocks in a table.

Oracle parallel query achieves improved speed because multiple processes can be directed to read a table. Parallel query works best on servers that have multiple CPUs because multiple CPUs allow for simultaneous queries. A later section in this chapter will show you how to see how many CPUs you have on your database server.

Starting with Oracle release 7.2, you can partition a SQL query into subqueries and dedicate separate processors to each one. Here's how it works: Instead of having a single query server to manage the I/O against the table, parallel query allows the Oracle query server to dedicate many processes to simultaneously access the whole table (see Figure 10-1).

Let's take a look at the techniques for invoking parallel query and determining the optimal degree of parallelism.

Invoking Oracle Parallel Query

There are several *init.ora* parameters to be set when using Oracle parallel query. Many of these are default values and are set by Oracle when your database is created. Oracle parallel query can be turned on in several ways. You can turn it on permanently for a table, or you can isolate the parallel query to a single table.

Permanent parallelism (Not recommended for cost-based optimization)

```
Alter table customer parallel degree 35;
```

Single query parallelism

```
select /*+ FULL(emp) PARALLEL(emp, 35) */
        emp_name
    from
        emp;
```

Note the use of the double hints in the preceding query. Most Oracle DBAs always use the *full* hint with the *parallel* hint because they are both required to use Oracle parallel query.

CAUTION
It is very dangerous to enable Oracle parallel query for a table with the alter table *command. Once a table is marked for parallel query, the CBO may change the execution plan for existing queries to use parallel full-table scans instead of index scans. This well-intentioned mistake has crippled many databases, since queries that used to run fast with indexes will now use a full-table scan.*

Most Oracle DBAs identify those tables that perform full-table scans and then add hints to specify the degree of parallelism for the query. This way, all full-table scans against the tables will invoke Oracle parallel query. It can be very dangerous to turn on parallelism with the *alter table* command because the CBO may change other queries' execution plans to perform full-table scans based on the new setting for parallelism. This could adversely affect hundreds of SQL statements.

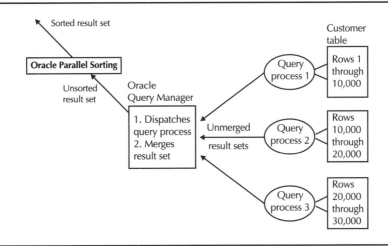

FIGURE 10-1. *An Oracle parallel query with full-table scan*

Oracle Parallel Query Initialization Parameters

There are several important *init.ora* parameters that have a direct impact on the behavior of Oracle parallel query. The values for these parameters are heavily dependent on the number of CPUs and the amount of RAM on your database server.

- *sort_area_size* The higher the value, the more memory is available for individual sorts on each parallel process. Note that the *sort_area_size* parameter allocates memory for every query on the system that invokes a sort. For example, if a single query needs more memory, and you increase the *sort_area_size, all* Oracle tasks will allocate the new amount of sort area, regardless of whether they will use all of the space. It is also possible to dynamically change the *sort_area_size* for a specific session with the *alter session* command. This technique can be used when a specific transaction requires a larger sort area than the default for the database.

- *parallel_min_servers* This value specifies the minimum number of query servers that will be active on the instance. There are system resources involved in starting a query server, and having the query server started and waiting for requests will accelerate processing. Note that if the actual number of required servers is less than the values of *parallel_min_servers,* the idle query servers will be consuming unnecessary overhead, and the value should be decreased.

- *parallel_max_servers* This value specifies the maximum number of query servers allowed on the instance. This parameter will prevent

Oracle from starting so many query servers that the instance cannot service all of them properly.

■ *optimizer_percent_parallel* This parameter defines the amount of parallelism that the optimizer uses in its cost functions. The default of 0 means that the optimizer chooses the best serial plan. A value of 100 means that the optimizer uses each object's degree of parallelism in computing the cost of a full-table scan operation.

NOTE
Cost-based optimization will always be used for any query that references an object with a nonzero degree of parallelism. Hence, you should be careful when setting parallelism if your default is optimizer_mode=RULE.

Setting the Optimal Degree of Parallelism

Determining the optimal degree of parallelism for Oracle tasks is not easy. Because of the highly volatile nature of most SMP systems, there is no general rule that will apply to all situations. As you may know, the degree of parallelism is the number of operating system processes that are created by Oracle to service the query.

Oracle states that the optimal degree of parallelism for a query is based on several factors. These factors are presented in their order of importance:

■ The number of CPUs on the server

■ The number of physical disks that the table resides upon

■ For parallelizing by partition, the number of partitions that will be accessed, based upon partition pruning (if appropriate)

■ For parallel DML operations with global index maintenance, the minimum number of transaction freelists among all the global indexes to be updated. The minimum number of transaction freelists for a partitioned global index is the minimum number across all index partitions. This is a requirement in order to prevent self-deadlock.

For example, if your system has 20 CPUs and you issue a parallel query on a table that is stored on 15 disk drives, the default degree of parallelism for your query is 15 query servers.

There has been a great deal of debate about what number of parallel processes results in the fastest response time. As a general rule, the optimal degree of parallelism can be safely set to N-1 where N is the number of processors in your SMP or MPP cluster. Remember, the proper degree of parallelism will always result in faster execution, provided you have a massively parallel server (Figure 10-2) with lots of CPUs.

In practice, the best method is a trial-and-error approach that is always verified by timing the query. When tuning a specific query, the DBA can set the query to force a full-table scan and then experiment with different degrees of parallelism until the fastest response time is achieved.

Finding the Number of CPUs on Your Database Server

Sometimes the Oracle DBA does not know the number of CPUs on the database server. The following UNIX commands can be issued to report on the number of CPUs on the database server. If your server supports them, you can also use the *top* or *glance* utilities to see the number of CPUs on the server.

Windows NT   If you are using Windows NT, you can find the number of CPUs by entering the Control Panel and choosing the System icon.

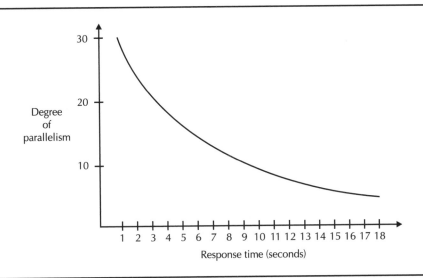

FIGURE 10-2. *Execution time as a function of parallel degree*

Linux   To see the number of CPUs on a Linux server, you can *cat* the */proc/cpuinfo* file. In this example, we see that our Linux server has four CPUs:

```
>cat /proc/cpuinfo|grep processor|wc -l
     4
```

Solaris   In Sun Solaris, the *prsinfo* command can be used to count the number of CPUs on the processor.

```
>psrinfo -v|grep "Status of processor"|wc -l
      24
```

IBM-AIX   The following example, taken from an AIX server, shows that the server has four CPUs:

```
>lsdev -C|grep Process|wc -l

     36
```

HP-UX   In HP UNIX, you can use the *ioscan* command to find the number of CPUs on your server.

```
>ioscan -C processor | grep processor | wc -l
6
```

NOTE
Parallel hints will often speed up index creation even on single-processor machines. This is not because there is more processing power available, but because there is less I/O wait contention with multiple processes. On the other end of the spectrum, we generally see diminishing elapsed time when the degree of parallelism exceeds the number of processors in the cluster.

There are several formulas for computing the optimal parallelism. Oracle provides a formula for computing the optimal parallelism *P* based on the number of CPUs and the number of disks that the file is striped onto. Assume that *D* is the number of devices that the table is striped across (either SQL*loader striping or OS striping). Assume that *C* is the number of CPUs available:

P = ceil(D/max(floor(D/C), 1))

Simply put, the degree of parallelism for a table should generally be the number of devices on which the table is loaded, scaled down so that it isn't too much greater than the number of CPUs. For example, with ten devices and eight CPUs, a good choice for the degree of parallelism is ten. With only four CPUs, a better choice of parallelism might be five.

However, this complex rule is not always suitable for the real world. A better rule for setting the degree of parallelism is to simply use the number of CPUs:

P = (number of CPUs)-1

As a general rule, you can set the degree of parallelism to the number of CPUs on your server, minus one. The minus one is used because one processor will be required to handle the parallel query coordinator.

Setting Automatic Parallelism

Oracle parallel query allows you to control the number of parallel query slave processes that service a table. Oracle parallel query processes can be seen on the server because background processes will start when the query is serviced. These factotum processes are generally numbered from P000 through P*nnn*. For example, if our server is on AIX, we can create a script to gather the optimal degree of parallelism and pass this argument to the SQL.

parallel_query.ksh

```
#!/bin/ksh
# Get the number of CPUs
num_cpu=`lsdev -C|grep mem|wc -1`
optimal_parallelism=`expr $num_cpu`-1

sqlplus system/manager<<!
select /*+ FULL(employee_table)
          PARALLEL(employee_table, $optimal_parallelism)*/
```

```
   employee_name
from
   employee_table;
exit
!
```

Resource Contention and Oracle Parallel Query

There are several sources of contention in Oracle parallel query. As already mentioned, Oracle parallel query works best on servers that have multiple CPUs, but we can often see disk contention when the whole table resides on the same physical disk. In short, the use of Oracle parallel query can precipitate several external bottlenecks. These include:

- **Overloaded processors** This is normally evidenced when the vmstat run queue values exceed the number of CPUs on the server.

- **Disk enqueues** When multiple processes compete for data blocks on the same disk, I/O-related slowdowns may occur on the disk I/O subsystem. Disk enqueues are evidenced by high activity from the UNIX iostat utility and from the wait (wa) column of the AIX vmstat utility.

- **Increased RAM usage** The parallel sorting feature of Oracle8 may increase the demands on the server RAM memory. This is because each parallel query process can allocate storage in the size *sort_area_size* in RAM to manage the sort.

Let's explore things that we can do to prevent contention-related slowdowns when using Oracle parallel query. To be most effective, the table should be partitioned onto separate disk devices, such that each process can do I/O against its segment of the table without interfering with the other simultaneous query processes. However, the client/server environments of the twenty-first century rely on RAID or a logical volume manager (LVM), which scrambles data files across disk packs in order to balance the I/O load. Consequently, full utilization of parallel query involves "striping" a table across numerous data files, each on a separate device. It is also important to note that large contiguous extents can help the query coordinator break up scan operations more efficiently for the query servers. Even if your system uses RAID or a logical volume manager (such as Veritas), you can still realize some performance gains from using parallel query. In addition to using multiple processes to retrieve the table, the query manager will also dedicate numerous processes to simultaneously sort the result set (see Figure 10-3).

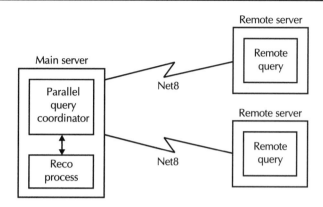

FIGURE 10-3. *Increased RAM memory demands with Oracle parallel query*

As you know, a RAM memory overload can cause swapping on the database server. Because of the parallel sorting feature, it is also a good idea to beef up the memory on the processor. We may also see the TEMP tablespace fall short on space when using parallel query and parallel DML. Here is an example of the error:

```
SQL> alter session enable parallel dml;

Session altered.

SQL> insert /*+ parallel(customer, 6) */ into customer;
2 select /*+ full(c) parallel(c, 6) */
3 from customer c;

ERROR at line 3:
ORA-12801: error signaled in parallel query server P000
ORA-01652: unable to extend temp segment by 128000 in tablespace
CUSTOMER_TS
```

Disk Contention with Oracle Parallel Query　　Many DBAs are surprised to note that Oracle parallel query does not always improve the speed of queries where the whole table resides on a single physical disk.

The data retrieval for a table on a single disk will not be particularly fast, since all of the parallel retrieval processes may be competing for a channel on the same disk. But each sort process has its own sort area (as determined by the *sort_area_size init.ora* parameter), so the sorting of the result set will progress very quickly. In addition to full-table scans and sorting, the parallel query option also allows for parallel processes for merge joins and nested loops.

Using parallel query Hints

Invoking the parallel query with hints has several prerequisites. The most important prerequisite is that the execution plan for the query specify a full-table scan. If the output of the execution plan does not indicate a full-table scan, the query can be forced to ignore the index by using the FULL hint.

The number of processors dedicated to servicing a SQL request is ultimately determined by Oracle query manager, but the programmer can specify the upper limit on the number of simultaneous processes.

When using the cost-based optimizer, the PARALLEL hint can be embedded into the SQL to specify the number of parallel query slave processes. For instance, in the query that follows we invoke 35 parallel query slaves because we are on a 36-CPU database server:

```
select /*+ FULL(employee_table) PARALLEL(employee_table, 35) */
    employee_name
from
    employee_table
where
    emp_type = 'SALARIED';
```

If you are using an SMP or MPP database server with many CPUs, you can issue a parallel request and leave it up to each Oracle instance to use its default degree of parallelism. For example:

```
select /*+ FULL(employee_table)
            PARALLEL(employee_table, DEFAULT, DEFAULT) */
    employee_name
from
    employee_table
where
    emp_type = 'SALARIED';
```

Oracle also provides the *parallel_automatic_tuning init.ora* parameter to assist in setting the best degree of parallelism. When setting *parallel_automatic_tuning,* you only need to specify parallelism for a table, and Oracle will dynamically change the *parallel_adaptive_multi_user* parameter to override the execution plan in favor of maintaining an acceptable overall load on the database. You should also note that setting *parallel_automatic_tuning* will cause extra storage in the large pool because Oracle will allocate message buffers from the large pool instead of the shared pool.

Parallel Queries and Table Joins

When joining multiple tables, you can specify that each table retrieve its rows using a full-table scan. When tuning SQL, if you make the determination that a full-table scan is appropriate, you must then determine how the tables can be joined using parallel query, and you can also experiment with different join techniques such as nested loop, hash, and sort merge joins.

TIP
When evaluating the performance of SQL parallel queries, there is no substitute for timing the query. There are so many factors involved in overall response time that it is easier to time the execution of the query with different parallel join plans and choose the one with the fastest response time.

Within the Oracle *plan_table*, we see that Oracle keeps the parallelism in a column called *other_tag*. The *other_tag* column will tell you the type of parallel operation that is being performed within your query.

For parallel queries, it is important to display the contents of the *other_tag* in the execution. Some SQL professionals keep a special version of *plan.sql* called *pq_plan.sql* for displaying details about parallel execution.

pq_plan.sql

```
set echo off
set long 2000
set pagesize 10000

column query       heading "Query Plan" format a80
column other       heading "PQO/Remote Query" format a60 word_wrap
column x           heading " " format a18

select distinct
   object_node "TQs / Remote DBs"
from
   plan_table
where
   object_node is not null
order by
   object_node;
```

```
select lpad(' ',2*(level-1))||operation||' '||options||' '
    ||object_name||' '
    ||decode(optimizer,'','','['||optimizer||'] ')
    ||decode(other_tag,'',decode(object_node,'','','['||object_node||']')
    ,'['||other_tag||' -> '||object_node||']')
    ||decode(id,0,'Cost = '||position) query
    ,null  x
    ,other
from
    plan_table
start with id = 0
connect by prior id = parent_id;
```

Here is a sample query with parallel full-table scans. Let's examine the different display formats for the execution plans for *plan.sql* and *pq_plan.sql*.

```
select /*+ use_merge(e,b) parallel(e, 4) parallel(b, 4) */
    e.ename,
    hiredate,
    b.comm
from
    emp e,
    bonus b
where
    e.ename = b.ename
;
```

Here is the standard output from *plan.sql:*

```
OPERATION
-----------------------------------------------------------------------
OPTIONS                      OBJECT_NAME                   POSITION
---------------------------- ----------------------------  ----------
OTHER_TAG
-----------------------------------------------------------------------
SELECT STATEMENT
                                                                  5
  MERGE JOIN
                                                                  1
PARALLEL_TO_SERIAL
    SORT
JOIN                                                              1
PARALLEL_COMBINED_WITH_PARENT
      TABLE ACCESS
FULL                         EMP                                  1
```

```
PARALLEL_TO_PARALLEL
     SORT
JOIN                                                                       2
PARALLEL_COMBINED_WITH_PARENT
       TABLE ACCESS
FULL                                  BONUS                                1
PARALLEL_TO_PARALLEL
```

Here is the same execution plan displayed with *pq_plan.sql*. Let's take a look at this
output and compare the display formats.

TQs / Remote DBs
```
------------------------------------------------------------------------
:Q36000
:Q36001
:Q36002
```


Query Plan
```
------------------------------------------------------------------------
                    PQO/Remote Query
------------------- ----------------------------------------------------
SELECT STATEMENT    [FIRST_ROWS] Cost = 5


   MERGE JOIN    [PARALLEL_TO_SERIAL -> :Q36002]
                    SELECT /*+ ORDERED NO_EXPAND USE_MERGE(A2) */
                    A1.C0,A1.C1,A2.C1 FROM :Q36000 A1,:Q36001 A2 WHERE
                    A1.C0=A2.C0

     SORT JOIN    [PARALLEL_COMBINED_WITH_PARENT -> :Q36002]


       TABLE ACCESS FULL EMP [PARALLEL_TO_PARALLEL -> :Q36000]
                    SELECT /*+ NO_EXPAND ROWID(A1) */ A1."ENAME"
                    C0,A1."HIREDATE" C1 FROM "EMP" A1
                    WHERE ROWID BETWEEN :B1
                    AND :B2

     SORT JOIN    [PARALLEL_COMBINED_WITH_PARENT -> :Q36002]


       TABLE ACCESS FULL BONUS [PARALLEL_TO_PARALLEL -> :Q36001]
                    SELECT /*+ NO_EXPAND ROWID(A1) */
                    A1."ENAME" C0,A1."COMM" C1
                    FROM "BONUS" A1 WHERE ROWID BETWEEN :B1 AND :B2
```

Here you see more detail about the internals of the execution plan, including details about the parallel query execution modes (*other_tag* in *plan_table*) and details about the tables that participate in the query.

In practice, most SQL tuning professionals keep two copies of scripts to display execution plan information. Let's take a closer look at the *other_tag* column in the *plan_table* and investigate the possible values and their meanings.

Values for the other_tag Column in plan_table

To fully understand a parallel execution plan, you must review the possible values for the *other_tag* column in the *plan_table*. This column is used by Oracle to provide additional detail about the type of parallel operation that is being performed during the execution of the query. Here are the possible values for *other_tag*:

- **Parallel_to_serial**   This is usually the first operation in the execution plan, and it is where a parallel full-table scan is passed to the query coordinator for merging.

- **Parallel_from_serial**   This is a condition where the parallel processes wait for a serial operation to complete. In many cases, this is a warning that your query may not be optimized, since the parallel processes are not allowed to begin immediately upon execution of the query.

- **Parallel_to_parallel**   This tag is seen in cases such as a sort merge join where a parallel full-table scan is immediately followed by a parallel disk sort in the TEMP tablespace.

- **Parallel_combined_with_parent**   This is a parallel full-table scan that is combined with an index lookup, as is the case with a nested loop join.

- **Parallel_combined_with_child**   This is a case where a parallel full-table scan is combined with a child operation.

- **Serial**   This is a linear operation such as an index scan.

CAUTION
Always investigate an other_tag *value of* parallel_from_serial. *This is because your query may have a bottleneck whereby the parallel query slaves are waiting unnecessarily for a serial operation, such as an index range scan.*

Now that you see the basics of parallel execution plans, let's explore some of the typical implementations of parallel join operations.

Nested Loop Joins with Parallel Query

In a nested loop join, Oracle normally uses indexes to join the tables. However, you can create an execution plan that will invoke a nested loop join that performs a parallel full-table scan against one of the tables in the join. In general, you should perform the parallel full-table scans on only one of the tables that are being joined, and this is normally the driving table for the query. As you will recall, in the CBO the driving table is the first table in the *from* clause.

Here is an example of a query execution plan that is forced to perform a nested loop join with a parallel query on the *emp* table. Note that we have invoked the *ordered* hint to direct the CBO to evaluate the tables in the order they are presented in the *where* clause.

```
select /*+ ordered use_nl(bonus) parallel(e, 4) */
    e.ename,
    hiredate,
    b.comm
from
    emp e,
    bonus b
where
    e.ename = b.ename
;
```

Here is the execution plan for this query. There we see the parallel operations on the *emp* table.

```
OPERATION
-----------------------------------------------------------------
OPTIONS                          OBJECT_NAME                 POSITION
-----------------------------    -----------------------   ----------
OTHER_TAG
-----------------------------------------------------------------
SELECT STATEMENT
                                                                 329
   NESTED LOOPS
                                                                   1
PARALLEL_TO_SERIAL
      TABLE ACCESS
FULL                             EMP                               1
PARALLEL_COMBINED_WITH_PARENT
      TABLE ACCESS
BY INDEX ROWID                   BONUS                             2
PARALLEL_COMBINED_WITH_PARENT
         INDEX
RANGE SCAN                       ENAME_BONUS_IDX                   1
```

Depending on the query, a parallel nested loop join will often provide excellent performance. However, depending upon the characteristics of the data in your tables, you may find that a parallel sort merge join or hash join will offer faster response time.

Sort Merge Joins and Parallel Query

The sort merge operation is the most ideal for parallel query because a merge join always performs full-table scans against the tables. Sort merge joins are generally best for queries that produce very large result sets such as daily reports and table detail summary queries. Here we see a simple query that has been formed to perform a sort merge using parallel query against both tables.

```
select /*+ use_merge(e,b) parallel(e, 4) parallel(b, 4) */
    e.ename,
    hiredate,
    b.comm
from
    emp e,
    bonus b
where
    e.ename = b.ename
;
```

Here is the output of the execution plan:

```
OPERATION
----------------------------------------------------------------------
OPTIONS                           OBJECT_NAME                 POSITION
---------------------------------  --------------------------  ----------
OTHER_TAG
----------------------------------------------------------------------
SELECT STATEMENT
                                                                     5
  MERGE JOIN
                                                                     1
PARALLEL_TO_SERIAL
    SORT
JOIN                                                                 1
PARALLEL_COMBINED_WITH_PARENT
      TABLE ACCESS
FULL                              EMP                                1
PARALLEL_TO_PARALLEL
    SORT
JOIN                                                                 2
PARALLEL_COMBINED_WITH_PARENT
      TABLE ACCESS
FULL                              BONUS                              1
PARALLEL_TO_PARALLEL
```

Again, please note that a sort merge join does not use indexes to join the tables. In most cases, index access is faster, but a sort merge join may be appropriate for a large table join without a *where* clause, or in queries that do not have available indexes to join the tables.

Hash Joins in Parallel

Oracle hash joins are notoriously hard to set up within Oracle, and the Oracle Metalink archives are full of problem reports regarding successful hash join invocation. I will discuss hash joins in detail in Chapter 16, but for now, just be aware that Oracle reads the driving table into a RAM array of *hash_area_size* and uses a special hashing technique to join the memory array with the larger table.

For equi-join operations, hash joins can outperform nested loop joins, especially in cases where the driving table is small enough to fit entirely into the *hash_area_size*. If the driving table is too large, the hash join will write temporary segments into the TEMP tablespace, slowing down the query. Since the reading of the table rows for a hash join is the most time-consuming operation in a hash join, setting parallelism on the table can dramatically improve the performance and throughput of the query.

Here is an example of a query that forces a parallel hash join. Note that the *emp* table is set as the driving table:

```
select /*+ use_hash(e,b) parallel(e, 4) parallel(b, 4) */
    e.ename,
    hiredate,
    b.comm
from
    emp e,
    bonus b
where
    e.ename = b.ename
;
```

Here is the execution plan for the hash join. Note that both tables in this join are using parallel query to obtain their rows:

```
OPERATION
--------------------------------------------------------------
OPTIONS                     OBJECT_NAME                  POSITION
--------------------------   --------------------------   ----------
OTHER_TAG
--------------------------------------------------------------
SELECT STATEMENT
                                                                3
  HASH JOIN
                                                                1
PARALLEL_TO_SERIAL
```

```
    TABLE ACCESS
FULL                            EMP                                    1
PARALLEL_TO_PARALLEL
    TABLE ACCESS
FULL                            BONUS                                  2
```

For equi-join SQL, hash joins are often faster than nested loop joins, especially in cases where the driving table is filtered into a small number of rows in the query's *where* clause. Here are some tips for ensuring that a hash join is enabled and optimized for your query.

- **Check initialization parameters**   Make sure that you have the proper settings for *optimizer_index_cost_adj, hash_multiblock_io_count, optimizer_max_permutations,* and *hash_area_size.* You can see Chapter 16 for details on setting these parameters.

- **Verify driving table**   Make sure that the smaller table is the driving table (the first table in the *from* clause). This is because a hash join builds the memory array using the driving table.

- **Analyze CBO statistics**   Check that tables and/or columns of the join tables are appropriately analyzed.

- **Check for skewed columns**   Column histogram statistics are recommended *only* for nonuniform column distributions in low-cardinality indexes. If needed, you can override the join order chosen by the cost-based optimizer using the ORDERED hint.

- **Check RAM region**   Ensure that *hash_area_size* is large enough to hold the smaller table in memory. Otherwise, Oracle must write to the TEMP tablespace, slowing down the hash join.

- **Monitor parallel query slave rows**   For parallel hash joins, make sure there is no skew in the slave processes' workloads by monitoring CPU usage, and reviewing the *v$pq_tqstat* view (see the *pq_server.sql* script in the following section). Monitoring parallel slave row statistics during the elapsed time of the hash join will show whether there is slave workload skew. Also note that skews could also occur because there are very few values in the column being equi-joined.

To summarize, Oracle parallel query will often improve the performance of large-table joins, and you must carefully experiment with the different join methods to determine the best join plan. Now let's move on to look at how the Oracle DBA can monitor the behavior of parallel query slave processes.

Monitoring the Use of Oracle Parallel Query

There are several STATSPACK tables and *v$* views that can be used to monitor the activity of the parallel query background processes. Unfortunately, parallel query activity is only measured at the database level, and you cannot find the specific tables that are the target of the parallel query. Let's begin by looking at the *v$pq_tqstat* view, and then we'll see the STATSPACK methods for measuring parallel query activity.

Monitoring Parallel Execution Activity

Oracle provides a *v$* view that can be used to show the behavior of individual parallel query processes. The *v$pq_tqstat* view shows the execution pattern for the parallel query and the use of parallel query slave processes for the query.

Here is the SQL statement to display the most recent parallel query execution details.

pq_server.sql

```
select
    tq_id,
    server_type,
    process,
    num_rows
from
    v$pq_tqstat
where
    dfo_number =
    (select max(dfo_number)
     from
        v$pq_tqstat)
order by
    tq_id,
    decode (substr(server_type,1,4),
      'Prod', 0, 'Cons', 1, 3)
;
```

Here is some sample output that was retrieved immediately following a parallel query:

```
     TQ_ID SERVER_TYP PROCESS     NUM_ROWS
---------- ---------- ---------- ----------
         0 Producer   P003              173
         0 Producer   P001              188
         0 Producer   P004              219
         0 Producer   P002              197
         0 Producer   P000              777
         0 Consumer   QC                796
```

This listing shows five parallel query "Producer" processes, which translate into parallel query slaves, with the OS process names P000 through P004. In this case, we know that the P000 process is the parallel query coordinator because it is labeled a "Consumer" and because it contains the sum of the rows retrieved by processes P001 through P004. The TQ_ID column refers to the parallel execution step. In the case of this query, we had a single full-table scan, so all values are zero. In a more complex query with a parallel full-table scan, we would see multiple steps in the TQ_ID column.

As a general rule, we look for an equal number of rows processed by each parallel query slave. If a single parallel query slave receives a disproportional amount of rows, then the entire query will take longer to complete. A disproportional distribution can sometimes occur when the CBO statistics are not current because the tables and indexes have changes since last being analyzed. You might also see an uneven distribution of rows when the target table is partitioned and the partitions are of unequal sizes.

The *v$pq_tqstat* view is most useful when you suspect that a parallelized query is not optimized, and it will provide sufficient detail to show the exact operations within the parallel row extraction process.

Monitoring Oracle Parallel Query with STATSPACK

In addition to monitoring parallel execution for individual queries, you can also monitor parallel query activity for your whole database. Using STATSPACK, you can query the *stats$sysstat* table to extract the number of parallelized queries that have been run during each time period between your STATSPACK snapshots.

Rpt_parallel.sql

```
set pages 9999;

column nbr_pq format 999,999,999
column mydate heading 'yr.  mo dy Hr.'

select
   to_char(snap_time,'yyyy-mm-dd HH24')       mydate,
   new.value  nbr_pq
from
   perfstat.stats$sysstat    old,
   perfstat.stats$sysstat    new,
   perfstat.stats$snapshot   sn
where
   new.name = old.name
and
   new.name = 'queries parallelized'
and
   new.snap_id = sn.snap_id
and
   old.snap_id = sn.snap_id-1
and
   new.value > 1
order by
   to_char(snap_time,'yyyy-mm-dd HH24')
;
```

Here is a sample of the output. This will quickly show the DBA the time periods when parallel full-table scans are being invoked:

```
SQL> @rpt_parallel

yr.  mo dy hr.        nbr_pq
-------------- --------------
2001-03-12 20         3,521
2001-03-12 21         2,082
2001-03-12 22         2,832
2001-03-13 20         5,152
2001-03-13 21         1,835
2001-03-13 22         2,623
2001-03-14 20         4,274
2001-03-14 21         1,429
2001-03-14 22         2,313
```

In this example, we see that there appears to be a period each day between 8:00 P.M. and 10:00 P.M. when tasks are executing parallel queries against tables.

In practice, you may want to run the STATSPACK report to identify periods of high parallel query activity and then go to the *stats$sql_summary* table to examine and tune the individual parallel queries. Of course, you can also examine parallel query summaries since database start-up time by using the *v$pq_sysstat* view.

Monitoring Oracle Parallel Query with V$ Views

To see how many parallel query servers are busy at any given time, the following query can be issued against the *v$pq_sysstat* view:

```
select
    statistic,
    value
from
    v$pq_sysstat
where
    statistic = 'Servers Busy';

STATISTIC          VALUE
---------          -----
Servers Busy       30
```

In this case, we see that 30 parallel servers are busy at this moment. Do not be misled by this number. Parallel query servers are constantly accepting work or returning to idle status, so it is a good idea to issue the query many times over a one-hour period to get an accurate reading of parallel query activity. Only then will you receive a realistic measure of how many parallel query servers are being used.

There is one other method for observing parallel query from inside Oracle. If you are running Oracle on UNIX, you can use the *ps* command to see the parallel query background processes in action:

```
ps -ef|grep "ora_p"
```

Parallel Queries and Distributed Tables

There is an alternative to parallelism for Oracle distributed queries. In a distributed environment, Oracle parallel query can be simulated when using Net8 to perform simultaneous remote queries on each remote Net8 server. Interestingly, double parallelism can be achieved if the remote server invokes parallel full-table scans. While each query is executing simultaneously on each remote server, each query can be using Oracle parallel query.

These types of parallel queries are most useful in distributed databases where a single logical table has been partitioned into smaller tables at each remote node.

This approach is very common in ERP applications where each remote Net8 server requires autonomy, while the corporate office requires a method to query each cloned table as if it were local. For example, a customer table that is ordered by customer name may be partitioned into a customer table at each remote database, such that we have a *new_york_employee* table, a *california_employee* table, and so on. This vertical table partitioning approach is very common with distributed databases where local autonomy of processing is important.

With the tables partitioned onto different databases at different geographical locations, how can we meet the needs of the corporate headquarters where a complete view is required? How can they query all of these remote tables as a single unit and treat the logical customer table as a single entity? For large queries that may span many logical tables, the isolated tables can then easily be reassembled to use Oracle's parallel query facility:

```
create view
    all_employee
as
    select *
    from
        new_york_employee@manhattan
UNION ALL
    select *
    from
        california_employee@los_angeles
UNION ALL
    select *
    from
        japan_employee@tokyo;
```

We can now query the *all_employee* view as if it were a single database table, and Oracle will automatically recognize the *union all* clause and fire off simultaneous queries against each of the three base tables. It is important to note that the distributed database manager will direct that each query be processed at the remote location, while the query manager waits until each remote node has returned its result set. For example, the following query will assemble the requested data from the three tables in parallel, with each query being separately optimized. The result set from each subquery is then merged by the query manager process and delivered to the front-end application.

```
select
    employee_name
from
    all_employee
where
    salary > 500000;
```

In a query like this, a large distributed transaction will invoke parallel queries at each remote database. Note that these parallel queries will not necessarily perform full-table scans, but the remote data requests will be issued and managed by the Oracle Distributed Recovery Manager (RECO) process (Figure 10-4).

Next, let's wrap up this chapter and cover the major points to consider when evaluating and tuning full-table scans.

Conclusion

This chapter has been concerned with identifying full-table scans, evaluating the legitimacy of the full-table scan, tuning full-table scans for optimal performance, and monitoring full-table scan activity in your database. The main points of this chapter include these:

- Oracle will often perform a full-table scan even if a faster way exists to access the table.

- All full-table scans should be evaluated to see if the full-table scan can be replaced by index access. Always question the legitimacy of a full-table scan.

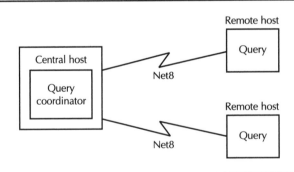

FIGURE 10-4. *A distributed parallel query*

■ Large-table full-table scans will run far faster with Oracle parallel query.

■ Small-table full-table scans will run faster by placing the table blocks in the KEEP pool.

■ Turning on parallelism with the *alter table* command is dangerous because it can change the behavior of the execution plans for all queries that involve the table.

■ The degree of parallelism depends on the number of CPUs and the distribution of a table across disks.

■ You can monitor the parallel query slave behavior by using the *v$pq_tqstat* view. You should always make sure that the parallel query slaves are accessing an equivalent number of rows.

■ You can monitor the historical instance-wide behavior of queries by using STATSPACK. When a period of high parallel query activity is identified, you can go to the STATSPACK *stats$sql_summary* table and extract and evaluate the individual SQL statements.

■ Parallelism can be used to improve the speed of table joins, including nested loop joins, hash joins, and sort merge joins.

■ Legitimate sort merge joins should always use parallel query because a sort merge join requires full-table scans against both tables.

Next, let's move on and take a look at optimizing sorting operations for Oracle SQL statements.

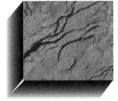

CHAPTER
11

Optimizing Sorting for
Oracle SQL Statements

s a small but very important component of SQL execution, sorting is a frequently overlooked aspect of Oracle SQL tuning. In general, an Oracle database will automatically perform sorting operations on row data as requested by an *order by* or *group by* clause, but there are other SQL clauses that also cause sorting. Oracle sorting happens transparently to the user and occurs under the following circumstances:

- When SQL contains an *order by* clause

- When SQL contains a *group by* clause

- When SQL contains a *select distinct* clause

- When an index is created

- When SQL contains a *union* or *minus* operation

- When a sort merge join is invoked by the SQL optimizer

At the time a session is established with Oracle, a private sort area is allocated in RAM for use by the session for sorting. If the connection is via a dedicated connection, a Program Global Area (PGA) is allocated according to the *sort_area_size init.ora* parameter. For connections via the multithreaded server, sort space is allocated in the region allocated by the *large_pool_size* initialization parameter.

Unfortunately, the amount of memory used in sorting must be the same for all sessions, and it is not possible to increase the *sort_area_size* with the *alter session* command. Therefore, the designer must strike a balance between allocating enough sort area to avoid disk sorts for the large sorting tasks while not overloading the RAM demands on the database server. You must also keep in mind that the extra sort area will be allocated and not used by tasks that do not require intensive sorting. Of course, sorts that cannot fit into the *sort_area_size* will be paged out into the TEMP tablespace for a disk sort.

Disk sorts are about 14,000 times slower than memory sorts. Also, a disk sort consumes resources in the TEMP tablespace and may impact the performance of other concurrent SQL sorts because Oracle must allocate buffer pool blocks to hold the blocks in the TEMP tablespace.

In-memory sorts are always preferable to disk sorts, and disk sorts will surely slow down an individual task and may also impact concurrent tasks on the Oracle instance. Also, excessive disk sorting will cause a high value for free buffer waits, paging other tasks' data blocks out of the Oracle block buffer. In short, our goal is to perform a sort only when it is required to service the query, and to ensure that the settings for in-memory sorts and disk sorts are optimal.

Let's begin with a review of the Oracle initialization parameters that affect sorting behavior.

Initialization Parameters Relating to Oracle Sorting

As I noted, the size of the private sort area is determined by the *sort_area_size* initialization parameter. In addition, there are several other parameters that affect the performance of disk sorts. To see your initialization parameters, just enter the following commands in SQL*Plus:

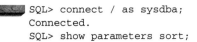

```
SQL> connect / as sysdba;
Connected.
SQL> show parameters sort;

NAME                              TYPE    VALUE
--------------------------------- ------- ------------------------------
nls_sort                          string
sort_area_retained_size           integer 0
sort_area_size                    integer 10000
sort_multiblock_read_count        integer 2
```

We will be looking at most of these parameters in this chapter. Let's begin with the most important, the *sort_area_size* parameter.

The sort_area_size Parameter

The proper value for the *sort_area_size* parameter is a delicate trade-off for the Oracle DBA. Unlike other initialization parameters, *sort_area_size* is allocated for each and every connected Oracle session (unless you are using the multithreaded server). Hence, for databases with a large number of users, an increase in *sort_area_size* can cause a RAM overload. If *sort_area_size* is set too low, then there will be excessive disk sorts. As *sort_area_size* increases, more and more sorts will be able to complete without going to disk.

However, there is a decreasing benefit to making *sort_area_size* too large. Because every connected session will allocate a memory region of *sort_area_size,* a large amount of RAM may be wasted just to improve the speed of a few queries.

In practice, the DBA will increase the value of *sort_area_size* over time, using STATSPACK to monitor the number of memory sorts and disk sorts each hour. When increasing *sort_area_size* results in only marginal reductions on disk sorts, then the proper size has been reached (Figure 11-1). Hence, setting the optimal *sort_area_size* is an ongoing activity, and the DBA will recheck the value every few months in case the sort activity of the queries has changed.

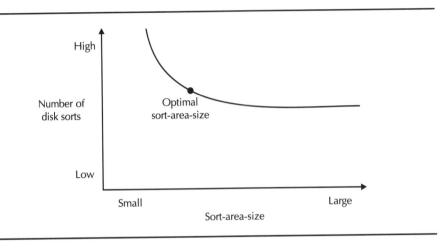

FIGURE 11-1. *Diminishing marginal reductions in disk sorts by increasing sort_area_size*

The sort_area_retained_size Parameter

The *sort_area_retained_size* initialization parameter governs the amount of memory to retain after a disk sort has completed. The purpose of this parameter is to remove the overhead of reissuing the OS memory allocation command (the *malloc* command in UNIX) whenever the Oracle session requires memory for another sort operation. The *sort_area_retained_size* defaults to zero.

On non-UNIX systems, when the process completes, the memory region is returned to the operating system (in case of a dedicated connection) or to the shared pool in cases of shared connections using the multithreaded server. On UNIX systems with dedicated listener connections, setting *sort_area_retained_size* will have little effect. This is because Oracle releases *malloc* memory with the *free* command, and the *free* command releases UNIX memory to the user global area, where it remains available for subsequent sorts by the session.

Hence, the *sort_area_retained_size* parameter is seldom useful for improving the performance of sorting.

The sort_multiblock_read_count Parameter

Under Oracle 8*i,* another way to improve sort performance using temporary tablespaces is to tune the parameter *sort_multiblock_read_count* for large disk sorts that require segments in the TEMP tablespace. The *sort_multiblock_read_count* parameter has the same effect as the parameter *db_file_multiblock_read_count* on full-table scans, except it applies to sort operations on blocks within the TEMP tablespace. The default value for *sort_multiblock_read_count* is 2.

If the sort space requirement is greater than *sort_area_size,* increasing the value of *sort_multiblock_read_count* forces the sort to read a larger section of each run into memory during the merge pass phase of the sort. Setting *sort_multiblock_read_count* also forces the sort process to reduce the merge width, or number of runs, that can be merged in one merge pass, thereby improving performance.

Obsolete Oracle8 Sort Parameters

There are several obsolete parameters in Oracle8*i* that may be of interest to SQL tuners who are still using Oracle8.

- **sort_direct_writes** This parameter was used to speed up disk sorts. In Oracle8, *sort_direct_writes* was found to be always useful, but starting with Oracle8*i* the database always uses direct writes and the parameter has disappeared. In prior releases of Oracle7 and Oracle8, *sort_direct_writes* could be set to TRUE.

- **sort_write_buffers** This parameter specified the number of buffers per sort process. For example, if *sort_write_buffers* is set to 2 and you have five slaves sorting, each slave process gets two buffers.

Optimizer Mode and Sort Activity

As you will recall from an earlier chapter, the *all_rows* optimizer mode favors disk sorts, while the *first_rows* mode prefers indexes. This is because of the differences between the goals of reducing overall machine resources *(all_rows)* and delivering the rows as quickly as possible *(first_rows).*

However, there are cases when an *order by* clause on a large result set causes a disk sort. In these cases, none of the rows will be available to the query even though we may be getting excellent response time from the I/O subsystem.

Removing Sorts by Adding Indexes

One of the best ways to remove full-table scans and unnecessary sorts is by adding indexes. When operating in *first_rows* mode, Oracle will always try to resolve an *order by* clause by using an index in lieu of a sort operation. However, you must always remember that while an index will retrieve the rows far faster than a sort, the index scan will have slower overall throughput than the sort operation. We will go into greater detail on this topic in Chapter 20.

Unnecessary Sorts

There are many cases when Oracle performs a sort operation even though a sort is not required. This generally happens when one of the following conditions is present:

- **Missing index**   Many DBAs are not aware that a column index is required for a query until they begin SQL tuning.

- **Sort merge join**   Anytime a sort merge join is requested, a sort will be performed to join the key values. In many cases, a nested loop join is a better choice because it is more efficient and does not require sorting or full-table scans.

- **Using the *distinct* clause**   Using the *distinct* clause on a query will always invoke a sort to remove the duplicate rows. There are many documented cases of erroneous SQL statements that have a *distinct* clause even though there can never be duplicate rows in the result set.

Once we have ensured that a sort is legitimate and cannot be removed with an index, we can then turn our attention to monitoring the overall sorting activity on our instance.

Monitoring Sorting Activity

The STATSPACK utility provides a great historical reference to sorting activity in Oracle. Upon increasing *sort_area_size,* you can track the reduction in disk sorts over time. We presented all of the sorting activity reports in Chapter 5, but this is an important topic and it warrants a closer review.

It is very important for the Oracle administrator to always keep a very close watch on both in-memory and sorts to disk. As we know, we can never control the activities of our end-user community and often we will see sorting activity coming along at different times when our Oracle database may not be prepared to handle the load.

An excellent example of this can be found on systems that have been monthly-cycle processing. During the month, online SQL transactions demand sort activity, which is purely confined to the RAM memory defined by the sort_area_size parameter. However, at the end of each month, we see very large reports being generated, each of which consumes a significant amount of sort activity in the TEMP tablespace. The resulting disk I/O associated with this activity in the TEMP tablespace can cripple the performance of any other SQL statements that require very large sorting.

Hence, it is very important for the Oracle administrator to keep a close on both the disk sorts and memory sorts on an hourly basis. Most DBAs use the Oracle STATSPACK utility for this purpose and create custom e-mail alerts to notify them when out-of-bounds sort activity is detected.

Here is the output from the script. Here you can clearly see the numbers of memory sorts and disk sorts as well as the ratio of disk to memory sorts:

Yr. Mo Dy Hr.	SORTS_MEMORY	SORTS_DISK	RATIO
2000-12-20 12	13,166	166	.01261
2000-12-20 16	25,694	223	.00868
2000-12-21 10	99,183	215	.00217
2000-12-21 15	13,662	130	.00952
2000-12-21 16	17,004	192	.01129
2000-12-22 10	18,900	141	.00746
2000-12-22 11	19,487	131	.00672
2000-12-26 12	12,502	147	.01176
2000-12-27 13	20,338	118	.00580
2000-12-27 18	11,032	119	.01079
2000-12-28 16	16,514	205	.01241
2000-12-29 10	17,327	242	.01397
2000-12-29 16	50,874	167	.00328
2001-01-02 08	15,574	108	.00693
2001-01-02 10	39,052	136	.00348
2001-01-03 11	13,193	153	.01160
2001-01-03 13	19,901	104	.00523
2001-01-03 15	19,929	130	.00652

This report can be changed to send an alert when the number of disk sorts exceeds a predefined threshold, and we can also modify it to plot average sorts by hour of the day and day of the week.

Some DBAs will locate periods of high sorting activity and then go to the *stats$sql_summary* table and extract the SQL for that snapshot for detailed analysis. Next, let's look at how we can locate repeating periods of high disk sorting activity.

Trend Reporting for Oracle Sorts

One important task for you is to develop a sort signature. All databases show repeating trends, both by day of the week and hour of the day. By tracking and plotting sort activity averages for hours of the day and day of the week, you will have a sorting signature that will direct you to the SQL statements that are causing the sorting activity.

Sort Signature by Hour of the Day

It is not a trivial job to the Oracle DBA to monitor the sort signatures for their individual databases. As we've already noted in Chapter 5, sorting activity can fluctuate by the hour of the day, the day of the week, and the individual day within monthly cycles. In order to prevent the Oracle DBA for having to constantly monitor sort activity, many DBAs take the STATSPACK reports (which are fully presented in chapter 5), and modify them with so that they can determine those times in which an inordinate account of disk sorting activity takes place.

For the detail scripts and output for developing sort signatures, please refer to chapter 5. The importance of creating sort signatures cannot be underestimated. In highly dynamic Oracle databases, it's not always evident which SQL statements are invoking sort operations and the times that the sort operations are invoked.

By correlating these STATSPACK sort reports with information in the *stats$sql_summary* table, the Oracle database administrator can retroactively identify those times in which his Oracle database is experiencing high sort activity and directly pair the sort activity to the individual SQL statements that requested the sorting.

Figure 11-2 shows the plot from the output of an average sort report. Here we see a typical increase in sort activity during the online period of the day. Sort activity rises about 8:00 A.M. and then goes down after 6:00 P.M.

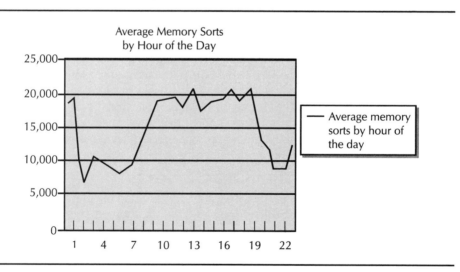

FIGURE 11-2. *Average memory sorts by hour of the day*

Again, we can use these graphs to impress management and also look for clues about where to find SQL statements that cause significant sort activity.

Sort Activity by Day of the Week

We can also get some great trend information by plotting the sort activity averages by the day of the week. This can tell us those days when the sort activity is highest, and if we bounce our database each night, we may want to adjust the *sort_area_size* according to the expected amount of sort activity for each day.

For the detail scripts for developing the I/O signature by the day of the week, please refer to the *rpt_avg_sorts_dy.sql* script in Chapter 5. From this script we can develop a sorting signature for all sort activities based on the day of the week. This monitoring off sort activity by day of the week is especially important for the Oracle administrator because they need to be able to tease out those days of the week that have excessive sort activity and take the appropriate tuning action for the Oracle instance.

For example, if you're using Oracle9*i*, you can use the *alter system* command to dynamically change the sort_area_size for your database on those days in which you experience a high degree in sorting activity. This can reduce the amount of sorts that go to your TEMP tablespace and improve the overall throughput of your Oracle database system.

The natural extension of this technique in Oracle9i is to provide a foundation by which trends in daily SQL activity can be identified, and the Oracle instance can be automatically reconfigured on those days in order to accommodate the changes in processing demanded by the SQL that is submitted on those days.

DAY	SORTS_MEMORY	SORTS_DISK
friday	12,545	54
monday	14,352	29
saturday	12,430	2
sunday	13,807	4
thursday	17,042	47
tuesday	15,172	78
wednesday	14,650	43

Figure 11-3 is the graph showing average sorts per day. In this database, the activity pattern on Tuesday shows a large number of disk sorts, with another, smaller, spike on Thursdays. For this database, you may want to pay careful attention to the TEMP tablespaces on these days and perhaps issue an *alter tablespace TEMP coalesce;* command to create continuous extents in the TEMP tablespace. If you bounce the database every night, you may want to increase the *sort_area_size* every

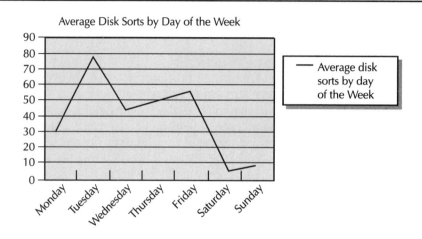

FIGURE 11-3. *Average disk sorts by day of the week*

Tuesday to reduce the number of disk sorts. In Oracle9*i*, the *sort_area_size* can be changed with an *alter system* command, so bouncing the database is not required.

At the risk of being redundant, I need to reemphasize that the single most important factor in the performance of any Oracle database is the minimization of disk I/O. Hence the tuning of the Oracle sorting remains one of the most important considerations in the tuning of any Oracle database.

Now let's wrap up this chapter by covering the main points and concepts about sorting.

Conclusion

This chapter recognizes that sorting is a time-consuming but necessary operation that is commonly performed for SQL result sets. The main points of this chapter include these:

■ Disk sorts are 14,000 times slower than in-memory sorts.

■ The *sort_area_size* parameter is the RAM region allocated for each connected session to perform sorting, except for users connecting into the multithreaded server.

■ Oracle will always try to resolve a sort in the memory region allocated by *sort_area_size*. Only after Oracle cannot continue the sort will Oracle invoke a disk sort and transfer the memory frames to the TEMP tablespace and continue the sort.

■ Some sorts will always be too big to sort in memory, and disk sorts for SQL in large batch reports cannot be avoided.

■ The STATSPACK utility is a great way to track the amount of disk sorting on your database and measure the results from increasing *sort_area_size*.

Next, let's take a look at how we can use Oracle hints to change the execution plans for Oracle SQL statements and how we can make permanent changes to the execution plan for SQL statements.

CHAPTER
12

Tuning with
Oracle Hints

his chapter covers the use of Oracle SQL hints and shows how hints can be used to alter the execution plan for a SQL statement and make sure that a SQL statement always uses the specified execution plan even when the table and index statistics change.

This chapter will cover the following topics:

- Introduction and history of hints

- Specifying hints in SQL queries

- Optimizer hints

- Table join hints (see also Chapter 16)

- Table anti-join hints

- Index hints (see also Chapter 20)

- Parallel hints

- Table access hints

- Hints in subqueries

Note that I will not cover the details about the use of specific hints for tuning SQL statements, because I will cover individual hints in the appropriate chapter.

Let's begin with a brief review of Oracle SQL hints and see how they are used to alter execution plans for SQL.

Introduction and History of Hints

Hints were first introduced in Oracle7 as a remedy for shortcomings in the newly developed cost-based optimizer. Oracle has always intended to eventually make hints obsolete as the cost-based optimizer improved, but SQL hints remain alive and well in Oracle8*i*. The idea of using hints is very controversial to the SQL purists who believe that the SQL optimizer should be intelligent enough to always choose the proper execution plan, but hints have become a useful necessity for SQL tuning.

In general, hints serve a dual purpose:

1. They are used to alter the execution plan for a SQL statement.

2. They can be used as an alternative to stored outlines to permanently change the execution plan for a SQL statement.

When a hint is added to a SQL statement during tuning, you are then faced with making your tuning change take effect. If you are on a release of Oracle prior to Oracle8*i*, you must locate the originating SQL statement in the source code and add the hint. If you are using Oracle8*i*, you can make the hint permanent without touching the SQL source code by using optimizer plan stability. This technique is fully covered in Chapter 13.

Specifying Hints in SQL Queries

Most Oracle beginners are quite confused when their hint fails to make a change to the execution plan. One problem with Oracle hints is that they are placed inside comments. Because Oracle hints are placed inside comments, a mistake in syntax will cause the hint to be ignored, without any kind of error message.

Let's review the cardinal rules for hints:

- **Carefully check the hint syntax** It is always a good idea to use the full-comment syntax for a hint. For example, the */+* *hint* */* syntax is generally preferred to the *– –+ hint* syntax.

- **Use the table alias** Whenever you have a query that specifies an alias for a table, you cannot use the table name. Instead, you must specify the table alias name. For example, the following query will invoke the *index* hint because the *emp* table is aliased with "e":

  ```
  select /*+ index(e,dept_idx) */ * from emp e;
  ```

- **Never reference the schema name in a hint** Hints will be ignored when the schema owner is specified in the hint. For example, the following hint will be ignored:

  ```
  select /*+ index(scott.emp,dept_idx) */ * from emp;
  ```

- **Validate the hint** A hint will be ignored if it assumes an access path that is not available. For example, specifying an index hint on a table that has no indexes, or specifying a parallel hint for an index range scan, will be ignored. You need to be especially careful with validation of hints because it is not always obvious that a hint is contradictory with the query. For example, consider the following query in the *emp* table with no index on the *ename* column.

  ```
  select /*+ first_rows */ * from emp order by ename;
  ```

  This hint is invalid because the *first_rows* optimizer mode is incompatible with the *order by* clause. The *order by* clause requires a sort, and no rows can be returned until the sort is complete. Table 12-1 shows incompatible hints and access methods.

Let's begin our discussion by reviewing the hints that change the optimizer mode for a specific SQL statement.

Optimizer Hints

Optimizer mode hints are used to redirect the overall optimizer goal. The most common mode for SQL tuning is the *rule* hint, which is used when you suspect that the CBO is using a suboptimal execution plan. It should be noted that the optimizer hints only cause Oracle to apply the optimizer to the SQL, and additional hints can still be added for further tuning.

Hint	When Ignored
cluster	When used with a noncluster table
hash	When used with a noncluster table
hash_aj	When no subquery exists
index	When the specified index does not exist
index_combine	When no bitmapped indexes exist
merge_aj	When no subquery exists
parallel	When a plan other than TABLE ACCESS FULL is invoked
push_subq	When no subquery exists
star	When improper indexes exists on the fact table
use_concat	When no multiple *or* conditions exist in the *where* clause
use_nl	When indexes do not exist on the tables

TABLE 12-1. *Conditions That Invalidate Hints*

The all_rows Hint

The *all_rows* hint represents the cost-based approach designed to provide the best overall throughput and minimum resource consumption. The *all_rows* mode favors full-table scans and is not suitable for OLTP databases. When adding this hint to a rule-based database, make sure that all tables and indexes that participate in the query have statistics with the *analyze* command.

The rule Hint

The *rule* hint directs Oracle to apply rule-based optimization to the query. This hint is generally the first one to try when tuning a SQL statement where you suspect that the CBO is generating a suboptimal execution plan.

The *rule* hint ignores the table and index statistics and uses basic heuristics to generate an execution plan. Up until the release of Oracle8*i*, the rule-based optimizer often generated a faster execution plan than cost-based optimization.

The first_rows Hint

This is the cost-based approach designed to provide the best response time. Just as with the guidelines for adding the *all_rows* hint, make sure that all tables and indexes that participate in the query have statistics with the *analyze* command. The *first_rows* hint is useful when testing the execution plan for a database with a questionable optimizer mode such as *choose.* By using the *first_rows* hint, you can tune your SQL for what the CBO considers to be the fastest response time. Generally, all SQL running under *optimizer_mode=choose* should be tested with the *first_rows* and *rule* hints to see if the performance will improve.

Next, let's look at how hints can be used to improve the efficiency of a table join.

Table Join Hints

Oracle provides a wealth of hints to direct the various types of table joins. As you will recall from an earlier chapter, Oracle can invoke a nested loop join, a sort merge join, a hash join, or a star join. Because table joins are the most time consuming of all Oracle SQL execution steps, the Oracle hints for table joins are frequently used to test the execution speed of various join techniques.

The use_hash Hint

The *use_hash* hint requests a hash join against the specified tables. Essentially, a hash join is a technique whereby Oracle loads the rows from the driving table (the smallest table, first after the *where* clause) into a RAM area defined by the *hash_area_size* initialization parameter (Figure 12-1).

Oracle then uses a hashing technique to locate the rows in the larger second table. As I mention in Chapter 10, a hash join is often combined with parallel query in cases where both tables are very large.

The following query is an example of a query that has been hinted to force a hash join with parallel query:

```
select /*+ use_hash(e,b) parallel(e, 4) parallel(b, 4) */
    e.ename,
    hiredate,
    b.comm
from
    emp e,
    bonus b
where
    e.ename = b.ename
;
```

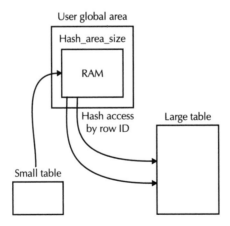

FIGURE 12-1. *A hash join and RAM usage*

Here is the execution plan for the hash join. Note that both tables in this join are using parallel query to obtain their rows:

```
OPERATION
-----------------------------------------------------------------------
OPTIONS                          OBJECT_NAME                  POSITION
----------------------------   ---------------------------   ----------
  SELECT STATEMENT
                                                                     3
    HASH JOIN
                                                                     1
PARALLEL_TO_SERIAL
      TABLE ACCESS
FULL                             EMP                                 1
PARALLEL_TO_PARALLEL
      TABLE ACCESS
FULL                             BONUS                               2
```

Hash joins are often faster than nested loop joins, especially in cases where the driving table is filtered into a small number of rows in the query's *where* clause.

Enabling Your Database to Accept the use_hash Hint

The *use_hash* hint is very finicky, and there are many conditions that must be satisfied. It is not uncommon to find that a *use_hash* hint is ignored and here are some common causes of this problem.

- **Check initialization parameters** Make sure that you have the proper settings for *optimizer_index_cost_adj, hash_multiblock_io_count, optimizer_max_permutations,* and *hash_area_size.* You can see Chapter 16 for details on setting these parameters.

- **Verify driving table** Make sure that the smaller table is the driving table (the first table in the *from* clause). This is because a hash join builds the memory array using the driving table.

- **Analyze CBO statistics** Check that tables and/or columns of the join tables are appropriately analyzed.

- **Check for skewed columns** Histograms are recommended only for nonuniform column distributions. If necessary, you can override the join order chosen by the cost-based optimizer using the *ordered* hint.

- **Check RAM region** Ensure that *hash_area_size* is large enough to hold the smaller table in memory. Otherwise, Oracle must write to the TEMP tablespace, slowing down the hash join.

The use_merge Hint

The *use_merge* hint forces a sort merge operation. The sort merge operation is often used in conjunction with parallel query because a sort merge join always performs full-table scans against the tables. Sort merge joins are generally best for queries that produce very large result sets such as daily reports and table detail summary queries, or tables that do not possess indexes on the join keys. Here we see a simple query that has been formed to perform a sort merge using parallel query against both tables.

```
select /*+ use_merge(e,b) parallel(e, 4) parallel(b, 4) */
    e.ename,
    hiredate,
    b.comm
from
    emp e,
    bonus b
where
    e.ename = b.ename
;
```

Here is the output of the execution plan for this query. Note the full-table scans and the sort merge operation:

```
OPERATION
-------------------------------------------------------------------
OPTIONS                             OBJECT_NAME                POSITION
-------------------------------  -------------------------  ----------
 SELECT STATEMENT
                                                                   5

  MERGE JOIN
                                                                   1
PARALLEL_TO_SERIAL
     SORT
JOIN                                                               1
PARALLEL_COMBINED_WITH_PARENT
       TABLE ACCESS
FULL                                EMP                            1
PARALLEL_TO_PARALLEL

     SORT
JOIN                                                               2
PARALLEL_COMBINED_WITH_PARENT
       TABLE ACCESS
FULL                                BONUS                          1
PARALLEL_TO_PARALLEL
```

It is important to note that a sort merge join does not use indexes to join the tables. In most cases, index access is faster, but a sort merge join may be appropriate for a large table join without a *where* clause, or in queries that do not have available indexes to join the tables.

The use_nl Hint

The *use_nl* hint forces a nested loop join against the target tables. Unlike the other join hints that specify both tables, the *use_nl* hint only requires the name of the driving table (the first table in the *from* clause when using the CBO). Nested loop joins are the oldest of the join techniques and are almost always used with rule-based optimization (i.e., the *rule* hint).

The *use_nl* hint is seldom used in SQL tuning because both the CBO and the RBO tend to favor nested loop joins over hash or merge joins. However, the *use_nl* hint is sometimes useful for changing the driving table without changing the order of the tables in the *from* clause. This is because it is not always evident which table should be the driving table. Sometimes both tables have a comparable distribution of rows, and you can often improve the performance of a nested loop join by changing the driving table for the join.

Here is an example of the use of the *use_nl* hint and the resulting execution plan:

```
select /*+ use_nl(e) */
    e.ename,
    hiredate,
    b.comm
from
    emp e,
    bonus b
where
    e.ename = b.ename
;
```

Here is the execution plan. It is interesting to note that this is the same execution generated by both the RBO and CBO without any hints:

```
OPERATION
-----------------------------------------------------------------------
OPTIONS                          OBJECT_NAME                   POSITION
-----------------------------   ---------------------------   ----------
    SELECT STATEMENT
                                                                    3281
      NESTED LOOPS
                                                                       1
        TABLE ACCESS
```

```
FULL                        EMP                                   1
     TABLE ACCESS
BY INDEX ROWID              BONUS                                 2
        INDEX
RANGE SCAN                  ENAME_BONUS_IDX                       1
```

The star Hint

The *star* hint forces the use of a star query plan, provided that there are at least three tables in the query and proper index exists on the fact table. The *star* hint is far faster than the traditional method of joining the smallest reference table against the fact table, and then joining each of the other reference tables against the intermediate table. However, there are several rules that must be met to invoke a *star* hint:

- There must be at least three tables being joined, with one large fact table and several smaller dimension tables.

- There must be an index on the fact table columns, one for each of the table join keys. Starting with Orable 8i, bitmap indexes are required instead of a concatenated index.

- You must verify with an explain plan that the nested loop join operation is being used to perform the join.

Let's take a close look at how a star join works. Oracle will first service the queries against the smaller dimension tables, combining the result set into a Cartesian product table that is held in Oracle memory. This virtual table will contain all of the columns from all of the participating dimension tables (Figure 12-2). The primary key for this virtual table will be a composite of all of the keys for the dimension tables. If this key matches the composite index on the fact table, then the query will be able to process very quickly. Once the sum of the reference tables has been addressed, Oracle will perform a nested-loop join of the intermediate table against the fact table.

This star join approach is far faster than the traditional method of joining the smallest reference table against the fact table and then joining each of the other reference tables against the intermediate table. The speed is a result of reducing the physical I/O. The indexes are read to gather the virtual table in memory, and the fact table will not be accessed until the virtual index has everything it requires to go directly to the requested rows via the composite index on the fact table.

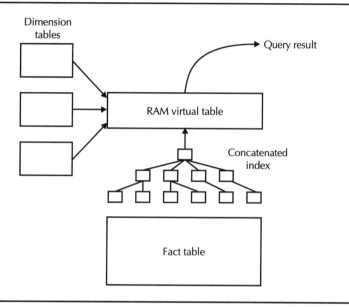

FIGURE 12-2. *A star table join*

Table Anti-Join Hints

Now that we have covered table joins, let's explore the SQL anti-join. An *anti-join* is an operation that is generally used when the SQL statement specifies a NOT IN or a NOT EXISTS clause. For example, the following query is used to locate customers who do not have bad credit.

```
select
    customer_name
from
    customer
where
    customer_number NOT IN
    (
     select
        customer_number
     from
        bad_credit_history
    )
;
```

As you can see, there are many legitimate times when you will need to filter rows from one table in terms of the nonexistence of rows in another table. Let's take a look at some useful Oracle hints that can aid you in your quest to make anti-joins efficient.

However, it is still a good idea to discourage general use of the NOT IN clause (which invokes a subquery) and to prefer NOT EXISTS (which invokes a correlated subquery), since the query returns no rows if *any* rows returned by the subquery contain null values.

The merge_aj Hint

The *merge_aj* hint is placed in a NOT IN subquery to perform an anti-join where full-table access is preferred over index access. As an example, consider this query, where we display the names of all departments that have no salesmen:

```
select
    dname
from
    dept
where
    deptno NOT IN
    (select
        deptno
    from
        emp
    where
        job = 'SALESMAN')
;
```

The performance of this type of query can be extremely poor when null values are allowed for the data column in the subquery. The subquery is reexecuted once for every row in the outer query block! Here is the execution plan:

OPERATION OPTIONS	OBJECT_NAME	POSITION
SELECT STATEMENT		1
FILTER		1
TABLE ACCESS FULL	DEPT	1
TABLE ACCESS BY INDEX ROWID	EMP	2
INDEX RANGE SCAN	JOB_IDX	1

There is an alternative method for evaluating NOT IN subqueries that does not reevaluate the subquery once for each row in the outer query block; it should be considered when the outer query block generates a large number of rows. This method can only be used when NOT NULL predicates exist on the subquery column and you have a hint in the subquery query block. The anti-join can be executed as either a *hash_aj* or *merge_aj* hint depending on the desired join type.

CAUTION
The anti-join hints merge_aj *and* hash_aj *will only work if the column requested in the* not in *clause has a NOT NULL constraint.*

Now, we add a *merge_aj* hint to the subquery, and also ensure that there is a NOT NULL constraint on the deptno column.

```
select
    dname
from
    dept
where
    deptno NOT IN
    (select /*+ merge_aj */
       deptno
     from
       emp
     where
       job = 'SALESMAN')
;
```

Here we see that the execution plan for the query has changed and the merge anti-join is invoked in place of the filter operation:

```
OPERATION
------------------------------------------------------------------
OPTIONS                         OBJECT_NAME                 POSITION
------------------------------  --------------------------  ----------
  SELECT STATEMENT
                                                                 5
    MERGE JOIN
ANTI                                                             1
      SORT
JOIN                                                             1
        TABLE ACCESS
FULL                            DEPT                            1
      SORT
```

UNIQUE			2
VIEW			1
		VW_NSO_1	
TABLE ACCESS			
BY INDEX ROWID		EMP	1
INDEX			
RANGE SCAN		JOB_IDX	1

The hash_aj Hint

The *hash_aj* hint is placed in a NOT IN subquery to perform a hash anti-join in cases where a hash join is desired. Here is an example of the *hash_aj* hint placed inside a subquery:

```
select
    dname
from
    dept
where
    deptno NOT IN
    (select /*+ hash_aj */
        deptno
     from
        emp
     where
        job = 'SALESMAN')
;
```

Here we see that the execution plan specifies a hash join, with a full-table scan on the department table.

```
OPERATION
-------------------------------------------------------------------
OPTIONS                          OBJECT_NAME              POSITION
----------------------------     ------------------------ ----------
```

OPERATION / OPTIONS	OBJECT_NAME	POSITION
SELECT STATEMENT		3
HASH JOIN		
ANTI		1
TABLE ACCESS		
FULL	DEPT	1
VIEW		
	VW_NSO_1	2
TABLE ACCESS		
BY INDEX ROWID	EMP	1
INDEX		
RANGE SCAN	JOB_IDX	1

In sum, the *merge_aj* and *hash_aj* hints may dramatically improve the performance of NOT IN subqueries, provided that the subquery column is NOT NULL. Next, let's take a look at how you can direct the Oracle optimizer to use a specific index.

Index Hints

While we will investigate tuning with indexes in detail in Chapter 20, let's make a quick review of using *index* hints. *Index* hints are quite useful when tuning SQL, especially in cases where the optimizer chooses the "wrong" index (e.g., not the most selective index). This happened most often when using the rule-based optimizer, but there are also cases where an *index* hint is appropriate for the CBO.

Index hints can also be placed inside subqueries. Oracle provides the *index* hint, the *and_equal* hint, the *index_asc* hint, the *index_combine* hint, the *index_desc* hint, and the *index_ffs* hint to redirect the optimizer's use of indexes to access table rows.

Let's begin our discussion with the most common hint, the *index* hint.

The Index Hint

The *index* hint is used to explicitly specify a table name, in which case the optimizer will use the best index on the table, or the table and index name, in which case the optimizer will use the specified index.

There are a number of rules that need to be followed to invoke an *index* hint:

- If table name or index name is spelled incorrectly, then the hint will not be used. Here we see a query with a misspelled table name:

  ```
  select /*+ index(erp, dept_idx) */ * from emp;
  ```

- The table name is mandatory in the hint. For example, the following hint will be ignored because the table name is not specified in the query:

  ```
  select /*+ index(dept_idx) */ * from emp;
  ```

- The table alias must be used if the table is aliased in the query. For example, the following query will ignore the *index* hint because the *emp* table is aliased with "e":

  ```
  select /*+ index(emp,dept_idx) */ * from emp e;
  ```

- The index name is optional. If not specified, the optimizer will use the "best" index on the table, but this is not recommended for permanent tuning. The following query will direct the optimizer to choose the best index for the *emp* table:

  ```
  select /*+ index(e) */ * from emp e;
  ```

The most important of these rules is to always specify both the table name and the index name in an *index* hint. There is always a small chance that a change in the CBO statistics might cause the optimizer to use a different index, and it is considered good practice to always specify both the table name and the index name.

CAUTION
In Oracle8i, the optimizer may have transformed or rewritten your query. This may cause the optimizer to choose an access path that makes the use of the index invalid, and this may result in the index *hint being ignored.*

The index_join Hint

The index_join hint explicitly instructs the optimizer to use an index join as an access path. For the hint to have a positive effect, a sufficiently small number of indexes must exist that contain all the columns required to resolve the query.

The and_equal Hint

The *and_equal* hint is used when a table has several nonunique single column indexes and you want multiple indexes to be used to service the query. The *and_equal* hint merges the indexes and makes the separate indexes behave as if they were a single concatenated index.

The *and_equal* hint requires the specification of the target table name and at least two index names, and no more than five index names. For example, assume that we have the following query to retrieve the names of all salesman that report to manager 7698. Let's also assume that there exists a nonunique index on *job* and another nonunique index on *mgr*.

```
select
    ename,
    job,
    deptno,
    mgr
from
    emp
where
    job = 'SALESMAN'
and
    mgr = 7698;
```

Here is the default CBO execution plan for the query. Pay careful attention to the row access method:

```
OPERATION
-------------------------------------------------------------------
OPTIONS                      OBJECT_NAME                 POSITION
-------------------------- ------------------------- ----------
  SELECT STATEMENT
                                                            1
  TABLE ACCESS
BY INDEX ROWID               EMP                           1
    INDEX
RANGE SCAN                    JOB_IDX                       1
```

From this execution plan, we see that the optimizer chooses to perform an index range scan on the *job_idx,* and then perform ROWID probes into the *emp* table to find those employees for manager 7698. If we can tell Oracle to merge *job_idx* and *mgr_idx,* then we can resolve the query without probing every *emp* row for manager 7698.

To do this, we add the *and_equal* hint, specifying the table name, and the nonunique indexes on *job* and *mgr.*

```
select /*+ and_equal(emp, job_idx, mgr_idx) */
    ename,
    job,
    deptno,
    mgr
from
    emp
where
    job = 'SALESMAN'
and
    mgr = 7698
;
```

Here is the execution plan:

```
OPERATION
-------------------------------------------------------------------
OPTIONS                      OBJECT_NAME                 POSITION
-------------------------- ------------------------- ----------
  SELECT STATEMENT
                                                           30
  TABLE ACCESS
BY INDEX ROWID               EMP                           1
    AND-EQUAL
```

```
           INDEX
RANGE  SCAN                    JOB_IDX                    1
           INDEX
RANGE  SCAN                    MGR_IDX                    2
```

Here we see a very different execution plan. As we see, instead of just using the *job_idx* and probing for all rows in that job, it treats the indexes as if they were a single, concatenated index (Figure 12-3).

Since the query performs index range scans on both indexes, a ROWID intersection operation will return only those ROWIDs that match both conditions in the *where* clause. The query only probes the *emp* table when it knows the rows needed, thereby saving unnecessary table I/O.

The index_asc Hint

The *index_asc* hint requests to use the ascending index on a range scan operation. Since this is the default behavior of the optimizers anyway, this hint has very limited use in SQL tuning.

The no_index Hint

The *no_index* hint forces the optimizer to ignore the presence of an index. The *no_index* hint is most commonly used in cases where you have determined that a parallel full-table scan will outperform an index range scan. This index is equivalent to the *full* hint and is rarely used in SQL tuning.

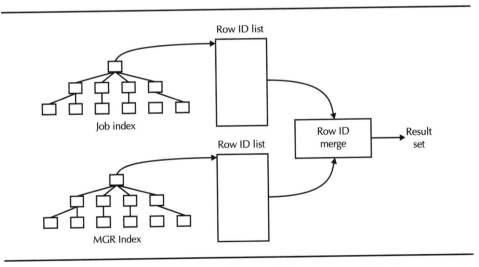

FIGURE 12-3. *Merging nonunique indexes with the* and_equal *hint*

The index_desc Hint

The *index_desc* hint requests to use the descending index on a range scan operation. The *index_desc* hint gives better performance in cases where you are calculating the maximum values of a column with the *max* built-in function.

```
select /*+ index_desc(emp, sal_idx) */
    ename,
    max(salary)
from
    emp
;
```

Here we see that the index access method has changed from ascending to descending.

The index_combine Hint

The *index_combine* hint is used to force a bitmap access path for the table. If no indexes are given as arguments for the *index_combine* hint, the optimizer will choose whatever Boolean combination of bitmap indexes has the best costing estimate for the table access. The *index_combine* hint directs the optimizer to perform a ROWID intersection operation from both bitmaps (Figure 12-4). In practice, it is always a good idea to specify the table name and both index names in the hint.

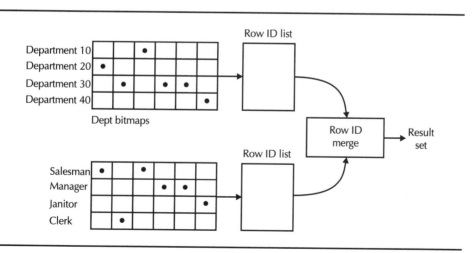

FIGURE 12-4. *A bitmap index merge execution*

For example, assume the following bitmap indexes on the *emp* table:

```
create bitmap index
    dept_bit
on
    emp
    (deptno);

create bitmap index
    job_bit
on
    emp
    (job);
```

Now, let's look at the query. Here we filter the result rows where *job=salesman* and *deptno=30*.

```
select
    ename,
    job,
    deptno,
    mgr
from
    emp
where
    job = 'SALESMAN'
and
    deptno = 30
;
```

Here is the execution plan. Please note that we are using a bitmap index on *deptno* and then filtering for the *job* rows:

```
OPERATION
-----------------------------------------------------------------
OPTIONS                              OBJECT_NAME              POSITION
------------------------------       ----------------------   ----------
  SELECT STATEMENT
                                                                 1

  TABLE ACCESS
BY INDEX ROWID                       EMP                         1
      BITMAP CONVERSION
TO ROWIDS                                                        1
      BITMAP INDEX
SINGLE VALUE                         DEPT_BIT                    1
```

Now, we add the *index_combine* hint to our query.

```
select /*+ index_combine(emp, dept_bit, job_bit) */
    ename,
    job,
    deptno,
    mgr
from
    emp
where
    job = 'SALESMAN'
and
    deptno = 30
;
```

Here is the new execution plan:

```
OPERATION
---------------------------------------------------------------------
OPTIONS                         OBJECT_NAME                 POSITION
-----------------------------   -------------------------   ----------
  SELECT STATEMENT
                                                                    2
   TABLE ACCESS
BY INDEX ROWID                  EMP                                 1
      BITMAP CONVERSION
TO ROWIDS                                                           1
        BITMAP AND
          BITMAP INDEX
SINGLE VALUE                    DEPT_BIT                            1
          BITMAP INDEX
SINGLE VALUE                    JOB_BIT                             2
```

Here we see that the bitmap indexes are merged together with a BITMAP
CONVERSION execution method. This bitmap merge method will dramatically
reduce the execution time of queries on large tables.

The index_ffs Hint

As I noted in earlier chapters, the index fast full scan is used in cases where a query
can be resolved without accessing any table rows. Remember not to confuse the
index fast full scan with a full-index scan.

When the *index_ffs* is invoked, the optimizer will scan all of the blocks in the
index using multiblock reads and access the index in nonsequence order. You can
also make an index fast full scan even faster by combining the *index_fss* hint with a
parallel hint.

The *index_ffs* hint can also be used to trick the SQL optimizer when you need to select on the values for the second column in a concatenated index. This is because the entire index is accessed, and, depending on the amount of parallelism, an index fast full scan may be faster than an index range scan. Using the *index_ffs* hint is especially useful for shops where the tables are huge and creating a new index would require gigabytes of extra disk space. In the case of very large tables where no high-level index key exists for the required search column, the fast full-index scan will always be faster than a full-table scan.

For example, consider the following concatenated index on two nonunique columns.

```
create index
   dept_job_idx
on
   emp
   (deptno, job);
```

Now, consider the following SQL, and assume that there is no index on the job column.

```
select
   ename,
   job,
   deptno,
   mgr
from
   emp
where
   job = 'SALESMAN'
;
```

Here is the execution plan. As we expect, we see a full-table scan on the *emp* table:

```
OPERATION
---------------------------------------------------------------------
OPTIONS                          OBJECT_NAME                POSITION
-------------------------------  -------------------------  ----------
   SELECT STATEMENT
                                                                  1
   TABLE ACCESS
   FULL                          EMP                             1
```

Now, we take the same query and add the *fast_ffs* hint, making sure to specify the table name and the index name.

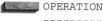

```
select  /*+ index_ffs(emp, dept_job_idx) */
    ename,
    job,
    deptno,
    mgr
from
    emp
where
    job = 'SALESMAN'
;
```

Here we see that the full-table scan is replaced by the faster fast full-index scan:

```
OPERATION
----------------------------------------------------------------------
OPTIONS                         OBJECT_NAME                 POSITION
--------------------------   --------------------------- ----------
  SELECT STATEMENT
                                                                34
    TABLE ACCESS
BY INDEX ROWID                  EMP                              1
      INDEX
FULL SCAN                       DEPT_JOB_IDX                     1
```

NOTE
The index fast full scan execution plan is the mechanism behind fast index create and re-create.

The use_concat Hint

The *use_concat* hint requests that a *union all* execution plan be used for all OR conditions in the query, rewriting the query into multiple queries. The *use_concat* hint is commonly invoked when a SQL query has a large amount of OR conditions in the *where* clause.

For example, consider the following query where a B-tree index exists on *job, deptno,* and *sal.* It is interesting to note that if the indexes were bitmap indexes, the execution would not perform a full-table scan. This is because Oracle automatically uses bitmap indexes where a query has multiple OR conditions on bitmap index columns.

```
select
    ename
from
    emp
```

```
where
   deptno = 10
or
   sal < 5000
or
   job = 'CLERK';
```

Here we have two choices. Because all of the index columns are low cardinality, we could create three bitmap indexes on *deptno, sal,* and *clerk,* causing a bitmap merge execution plan. Our other choice is to invoke *use_concat* hint to break the query into three separate B-tree index scans whose result sets will be combined with the *union* operator.

Here is the execution plan for this query with B-tree indexes. Note that we must perform a full-table scan to satisfy the multiple OR conditions in the *where* clause:

OPERATION		
OPTIONS	OBJECT_NAME	POSITION
SELECT STATEMENT		1
TABLE ACCESS **FULL**	**EMP**	**1**

If our indexes had been bitmap indexes, we would have seen a far faster execution plan:

OPERATION		
OPTIONS	OBJECT_NAME	POSITION
SELECT STATEMENT		4
TABLE ACCESS BY INDEX ROWID	EMP	1
BITMAP CONVERSION TO ROWIDS		1
BITMAP OR		1
BITMAP INDEX SINGLE VALUE	EMP_DEPTNO_BIT	1
BITMAP MERGE		2
BITMAP INDEX		

```
RANGE SCAN                        EMP_SAL_BIT                    1
        BITMAP INDEX
SINGLE VALUE                      EMP_JOB_BIT                    3
```

Now, returning to our example with three B-tree indexes, let's add the *use_concat* hint and see the change to the execution plan.

```
select /*+ use_concat */
    ename
from
    emp
where
    deptno = 10
or
    sal < 5000
or
    job = 'CLERK';
```

Here we see that the full-table scan has been replaced with a union of three queries, each using the B-tree index for the single columns and the CONCATENATION plan to *union* the result sets:

```
OPERATION
-------------------------------------------------------------------------
OPTIONS                         OBJECT_NAME                    POSITION
-------------------------------  --------------------------   ----------
  SELECT STATEMENT
                                                                  3
    CONCATENATION
      TABLE ACCESS
BY INDEX ROWID                    EMP                             1
        INDEX
RANGE SCAN                        EMP_JOB                         1
      TABLE ACCESS
BY INDEX ROWID                    EMP                             2
        INDEX
RANGE SCAN                        EMP_SAL                         1
      TABLE ACCESS
BY INDEX ROWID                    EMP                             3
        INDEX
RANGE SCAN                        EMP_DEPT                        1
```

For details on tuning queries with multiple OR conditions, please see Chapter 14. Next let's take a look at how parallel hints can be added to queries to improve the performance of full-table scans.

Parallel Hints

As I noted in Chapter 10, parallel hints can greatly improve the speed of queries that perform full-table scans. For details on using parallel query for tuning, see Chapter 10.

The parallel Hint

For full-table scans, the *parallel* hint requests that the table name query be executed in parallel mode with the number of parallel query slaves specified by the *degree* parameter. It is very important to always combine the *full* hint with the *parallel* hint to ensure that a full-table scan is invoked. This is because the *parallel* hint will be ignored if the optimizer does not choose a full-table scan to access the table rows.

The following example of a *parallel* hint is used on a database server with 36 CPUs:

```
select /*+ FULL(emp) PARALLEL(emp, 35) */
       ename
from
    emp;
```

The pq_distribute Hint

The *pq_distribute* hint is used in data warehouses to improve parallel join operation performance when using partitioned tables. The *pq_distribute* hint allows you to specify how rows of joined tables should be distributed among producer and consumer parallel query servers. The *pq_distribute* hint accepts three parameters: the table name, the outer distribution, and the inner distribution.

As I discussed in Chapter 10, we always want to avoid the PARALLEL_TO_PARALLEL execution plan when performing a parallel query join. Performing a PARALLEL_TO_PARALLEL operation means that the incoming and outgoing data streams are parallelized, resulting in slow join performance. On the other hand, invoking the PARALLEL_COMBINED_WITH_PARENT operation means that sort and merge operations are combined into one operation.

Prior to the use of the *pq_distribute* hint, Oracle DBAs would often fake out the SQL optimizer by deleting the CBO statistics on the inner table to force the PARALLEL_COMBINED_WITH_PARENT operation. This is because the SQL optimizer evaluates the size of candidate broadcast tables in terms of the CBO statistics. If a table is above a threshold value, the table will be joined via the PARALLEL_TO_PARALLEL execution mode, resulting in very slow execution times.

There are six acceptable combinations for table distribution with the *pq_distribute* hint. We use the *emp* table in these examples. Remember that the order of the parameters is outer distribution followed by inner distribution.

- **_pq_distribute(emp, hash, hash)_**   This maps the rows of each table to consumer parallel query servers using a hash function on the join keys. When mapping is complete, each query server performs the join between a pair of resulting partitions. This hint is recommended when the tables are comparable in size and the join operation is implemented by hash join or sort-merge join.

- **_pq_distribute(emp, broadcast, none)_**   This ensures that all rows of the outer table are broadcast to each parallel query server, while the inner table rows are randomly partitioned. This hint is recommended when the outer table is very small compared to the inner table. A rule of thumb is to use the _Broadcast/None_ hint if the size of the inner table times the number of parallel query servers is greater than the size of the outer table.

- **_pq_distribute(emp, none, broadcast)_**   This forces all rows of the inner table to be broadcast to each consumer parallel query server. The outer table rows are randomly partitioned. This hint is recommended when the inner table is very small compared to the outer table. A rule of thumb is to use the _None/Broadcast_ hint if the size of the inner table times the number of parallel query servers is less than the size of the outer table.

- **_pq_distribute(emp, partition, none)_**   Maps the rows of the outer table using the partitioning of the inner table. The inner table must be partitioned on the join keys. This hint is recommended when the number of partitions of the outer table is equal to, or nearly equal to, a multiple of the number of parallel query servers.

- **_pq_distribute(emp, none, partition)_**   This combination maps the rows of the inner table using the partitioning of the outer table. The outer table must be partitioned on the join keys. This hint is recommended when the number of partitions of the outer table is equal to, or nearly equal to, a multiple of the number of query servers.

- **_pq_distribute(emp, none, none)_**   Each parallel query server performs the join operation between a pair of matching partitions, one from each table. Remember, both tables must be equi-partitioned on the join keys.

The noparallel Hint

The _noparallel_ hint is used in cases where you do not want parallelism invoked against the full-table scan. This might be the case in queries that perform full-table scans against small tables. In the case of full-table scans against small tables, you should place the table in the KEEP pool, and turn off parallel query for the table.

Note that in most cases, the CBO will recognize that the table is small and will not use parallel query.

Table Access Hints

The following hints are used for specialized table access methods. In sophisticated queries, this class of hints can be used to direct each step in the access of multiple table accesses within a query.

The full Hint

The *full* hint requests the bypassing of indexes and invokes a full-table scan. This is often used in conjunction with a *parallel* hint. The most common use of the *full* hint is in cases where you have determined that an index range scan retrieves a significant number of table blocks and a parallel full-table scan will improve the speed of the query.

Cluster Table Hints

Oracle provides a specialized table storage mechanism as an alternative to row-sequenced tables. Oracle clusters are used in cases where two tables have a one-to-many relationship and the vast majority of queries access the tables from owner to member (Figure 12-5).

This table storage technique stores the owner and member table rows on adjacent blocks such that a single block I/O will retrieve rows from both tables. In order to improve the speed of table joins in a cluster, Oracle provides a *hash* hint and a *cluster* hint.

The hash Hint

The *hash* hint explicitly chooses a hash scan to access the specified cluster table.

```
select /*+ hash */
   emp.ename,
   deptno
from
   emp e,
   dept d
where
   e.deptno = d.deptno
and
   deptno = 20;
```

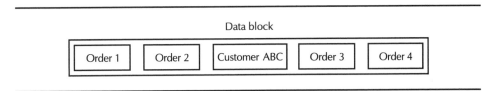

FIGURE 12-5.   *An Oracle cluster with multiple tables*

The cluster Hint
The *cluster* hint explicitly chooses a cluster scan to access the specified table.

```
select /*+ cluster */
    emp.ename,
    deptno
from
    emp e,
    dept d
where
    e.deptno = d.deptno
and
    deptno = 20;
```

The no_expand Hint
The *no_expand* hint prevents the cost-based optimizer from considering OR expansion for queries having OR conditions or IN lists in the *where* clause. Usually, the optimizer considers using OR expansion and uses the *no_expand* method if it decides the cost is lower than not using it. This OR expansion is related to optimizer internals and does not mean that the logic itself will be changed and return a different result set.

The nocache Hint
In Oracle7, the *nocache* hint overrides the *alter table xxx cache* syntax and specifies that the blocks for this table are placed at the least recently used end of the buffer cache when a small-table full-table scan is performed. In Oracle8, the *nocache* hint directs that table blocks specified for the KEEP pool be placed at the midpoint of the DEFAULT pool instead of the KEEP pool.

This hint is rarely used in SQL tuning because all of the small tables should properly be placed in the KEEP pool, and there is never a need to change this behavior.

The ordered Hint

In the cost-based optimizer, the *ordered* hint requests that the tables should be joined in the order that they are specified in the *from* clause, with the first table in the *from* clause specifying the driving table.

The *ordered* hint is commonly used in conjunction with other hints to ensure that multiple tables are joined in their proper order. For example, we may have a query that joins five tables together, and we want several of the joins to use a hash join and other tables to use a nested loop join. The *ordered* hint is very common in tuning data warehouse queries that join more than four tables together.

TIP
Large n-way table joins with seven or more tables can often take more than 30 minutes to parse the SQL. This is because Oracle must evaluate all possible table join orders. For example, with eight tables, Oracle must evaluate 8!, or 40,320, possible join combinations. Most people use the ordered *hint to bypass this very expensive and time-consuming SQL parsing operation.*

For example, the following query uses the *ordered* hint to join the tables in their specified order in the *from* clause *(emp, dept, sal, bonus).* We further refine the execution plan by specifying that the *emp* to *dept* join use a hash join and the *sal* to *bonus* join use a nested loop join.

```
select /*+ ordered use_hash (emp, dept) use_nl (sal, bonus) */
from
    emp,
    dept,
    sal,
    bonus
where . . .
```

The ordered_predicates Hint

The *ordered_predicates* hint is a specialized hint that is specified in the *where* clause of a query, and it directs the order in which the Boolean predicates in the *where* clause are evaluated. To see how this hints works, let's review the standard method used by the CBO to evaluate SQL predicates.

1. Subqueries are evaluated before the outer Boolean conditions in the *where* clause.

2. All Boolean conditions without built-in functions or subqueries are evaluated in their order in the *where* clause.

3. With Boolean predicates with built-in functions, the optimizer computes the cost of each predicate and evaluates them in increasing order of their costs.

These evaluation rules can be overridden by using the *ordered_predicates* hint. This hint is the equivalent of resequencing Booleans in the *where* clause for the RBO, where the *where* clause items are evaluated in the order that they appear in the query.

The push_subq Hint

The *push_subq* hint causes all subqueries in the query block to be executed at the earliest possible place in the execution plan. Normally, subqueries that are not merged are executed as the last step in the execution plan. If the subquery is relatively inexpensive and reduces the number of rows significantly, then it improves the overall performance to evaluate the subquery as soon as possible. The *push_subq* hint has no effect if the subquery is using a sort merge join, or when the subquery references a remote table. For more details on this hint for SQL tuning, see Chapter 19.

Hints in Subqueries

Many Oracle professionals are not aware that every subquery in a SQL statement can use hints to improve the execution plan of the subquery.

We need to note that a table-specific hint placed in the outer query will not be pushed through into the subquery. Remember, an *index* hint specifying only the table name alias ("a" in this case) means that the optimizer is directed to choose the most appropriate index.

```
select /*+ INDEX(a) */
    a.empno
from
    dept b,
    emp a,
    salgrade c
where
    EXISTS (
```

```
    select
        a.empno
    from
        dept b,
        emp a,
        salgrade c
    where
        a.deptno=b.deptno
    and
        a.job <> 'clerk'
    and
        a.sal between c.losal and c.hisal
    )
and
    a.deptno=b.deptno
and
    a.job <> 'clerk'
and
    a.sal between losal and hisal;
```

Here is one of the least efficient execution plans possible, the dreaded Cartesian merge scan. For each row in the outer query, the inner query will be reexecuted. This is an extremely inefficient way of performing this query, and we know that it would run far faster if we were able to tell it to utilize an index for the subquery.

CAUTION
Although the Oracle8i SQL optimizer will automatically try to rewrite SQL and will actually use a Cartesian product to accomplish some queries, seeing a Cartesian join in your execution plan is always a cause for concern. Whenever you see a CARTESIAN table access method, always check to ensure that all of your tables have the proper join clauses in your where *clause. For example, if you are joining eight tables, you should have seven equality conditions in the* where *clause to specify the join keys for the tables.*

```
OPERATION
-----------------------------------------------------------------------
OPTIONS                           OBJECT_NAME                  POSITION
-----------------------------   ---------------------------   ----------
  SELECT STATEMENT
                                                                 538344
    FILTER
```

```
        NESTED LOOPS
            MERGE JOIN
    CARTESIAN                                               1
            INDEX
    FULL SCAN                   DEPT_DEPT                   1
            SORT
    JOIN                                                    2
                TABLE ACCESS
    FULL                        SALGRADE                    1
            TABLE ACCESS
    BY INDEX ROWID              EMP                         2
            INDEX
    RANGE SCAN                  DEPT_EMP                    1
        NESTED LOOPS
            MERGE JOIN
    CARTESIAN                                               1
            INDEX
    FULL SCAN                   DEPT_DEPT                   1
            SORT
    JOIN                                                    2
                TABLE ACCESS
    FULL                        SALGRADE                    1
            TABLE ACCESS
    BY INDEX ROWID              EMP                         2
            INDEX
    RANGE SCAN                  DEPT_EMP                    1
```

Now, we move the hint from the outer query to the subquery. Note that the *index* hint is now specified inside the *exists* clause.

```
select
    a.empno
from
    dept b,
    emp a,
    salgrade c
where
    EXISTS (
        select /*+ INDEX(a) */
            a.empno
        from
            dept b,
            emp a,
            salgrade c
        where
            a.deptno=b.deptno
        and
```

```
            a.job <> 'clerk'
        and
            a.sal between c.losal and c.hisal
        )
and
    a.deptno=b.deptno
and
    a.job <> 'clerk'
and
    a.sal between losal and hisal;
```

Here we see that the execution plan has changed and the Cartesian merge join has disappeared:

OPERATION		
OPTIONS	OBJECT_NAME	POSITION
SELECT STATEMENT		
		108281
FILTER		
		1
NESTED LOOPS		
		1
NESTED LOOPS		
TABLE ACCESS		
FULL	SALGRADE	1
TABLE ACCESS		
BY INDEX ROWID	EMP	2
INDEX		
FULL SCAN	JOB_IDX	1
INDEX		
RANGE SCAN	DEPT_DEPT	2
NESTED LOOPS		
NESTED LOOPS		
TABLE ACCESS		
FULL	SALGRADE	1
TABLE ACCESS		
BY INDEX ROWID	EMP	2
INDEX		
FULL SCAN	JOB_IDX	1
INDEX		
RANGE SCAN	DEPT_DEPT	2

In summary, hints in a subquery are recognized and do affect the execution plan for that subquery. They do not, however, affect the execution plan of the outer query.

Now let's wrap up this chapter with a review of the major points about SQL query hints.

Conclusion

Oracle hints are the most common tools for tuning Oracle SQL. For hints to be effective, you must thoroughly understand the compatibility between hints and table access methods. The main points of this chapter include these:

- Because hints are placed inside comments, they will be ignored if the hint is incompatible with the existing execution plan or when the hint is formatted improperly.

- When using the RBO, hints can be used to change specific queries to use the CBO. Always remember to analyze all table and indexes that participate in the query.

- When using the CBO, you can start tuning a suspect SQL statement by adding the *rule* or *first_rows* hint.

- Hints can be applied to subqueries, but a hint in the outer query will not carry over into the subquery.

Next let's take a look at SQL tuning with the Oracle8*i* optimizer plan stability feature.

CHAPTER
13

Tuning with Optimizer
Plan Stability

his chapter discusses the use of optimizer plan stability in Oracle8*i* and shows how you can improve the run-time performance of SQL statements and also provide a easy method to permanently change the execution plans for SQL statements. This chapter will cover the following topics:

- Introduction to stored outlines

- Preparing Oracle for stored outlines

- How to create and modify a stored outline

- Managing a stored outline

Introduction to Stored Outlines

The optimizer plan stability feature of Oracle8*i* has been a long time coming. The earlier databases such as DB2 and IDMS have had the ability to store execution plans since the 1980s, and the concept of stored SQL outlines has had widespread acceptance in the non-Oracle world for decades.

The argument behind optimizer plan stability is that there exists only one optimal execution plan for any SQL statement, and once located, the execution plan should never change, even when the CBO statistics or initialization parameters are changed. Of course, this philosophy is contrary to the basic tenet of Oracle cost-based optimization, which expects SQL statements to change execution plans when the characteristics of the table and index statistics change, or when a change is made to an important initialization parameter such as *sort_area_size* or *db_file_multiblock_read_count.*

Regardless of philosophy, creating a stable execution plan for Oracle SQL has two major benefits:

- **Change execution plan without touching SQL source code**   Many databases have SQL that is dynamically generated (e.g., SAP) or SQL that resides in unreachable PC libraries. For these types of applications, stored outlines allow you to change the execution plan for the SQL without the need to change the SQL source code.

- **Permanent SQL tuning changes**   Once tuned, optimizer plan stability allows for SQL statements to always have the same execution plan. There will be no surprises when a change is made to an important initialization parameter such as *sort_area_size* or when the CBO statistics change.

TIP
Stored outlines are great for tuning SQL in database application suites where the SQL source is not available or cannot be changed. For example, SAP and PeopleSoft applications products can now have SQL tuning without touching the source code.

Now that we see the benefits of using stored outlines, let's take a look at how optimizer plan stability works. When a SQL statement enters Oracle8*i,* the database will perform the following actions (Figure 13-1).

1. **Check shared pool**   Hash the SQL statement and see if an identical statement is ready to go in the shared pool. If it is found, reexecute the SQL statement from the shared pool.

2. **Check stored outlines**   If the SQL is not found in the shared pool, check for a stored outline in DBA_OUTLINES view in the OUTLINE tablespace. If a stored outline is found, load it into the shared pool and begin execution.

3. **Start from scratch**   If nothing for the SQL statement is found in the shared pool or stored outlines, parse the SQL, develop an execution plan, and begin execution.

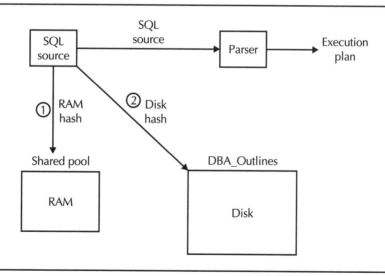

FIGURE 13-1.   *Executing a new SQL statement*

Optimizer plan stability can also aid us in our SQL tuning effort. Oracle provides a package called *outln_pkg* that allows you to manage your stored outlines and Oracle also provides an option for the ALTER SYSTEM and ALTER SESSION commands for the automatic collections of stored outlines for all of your SQL statements. However, it is not a good idea to turn-on the option to automatically store outlines unless you are prepared to examine each stored outline and ensure that the best execution plan is being used.

If you have already tuned your SQL, you can *alter system set_stored_outlines=true* and Oracle will define plans for all issued SQL statements in all sessions at the time they are executed; these stored plans will be reused until altered or dropped. If you have not tuned your SQL, you can create individual stored outlines for your session by entering the *alter session set_stored_outlines=true* command.

Just as the shared pool will not reuse a SQL statement unless it is identical to a previous statement, the effective use of stored outlines depends on the statement being reissued in an identical fashion each time it is used. If even one space is out of place, the stored outline is not reused. Whenever possible, all SQL should be stored in PL/SQL procedures, functions, or packages, and bind variables should always be used to ensure that the SQL is reusable. This allows reuse of the stored image of the SQL as well as reuse of your stored outlines.

The Philosophy Behind Optimizer Plan Stability

The use of stored outlines depends heavily upon the nature of the SQL that you have in your shop. If your system is characterized by dynamic tables where the number of rows may change daily from 1,000,000 to 100, then you would probably not want to use optimizer plan stability, because you would want the CBO to reevaluate the execution plan for each SQL statement based on the current CBO statistics.

On the other hand, if your tables are relatively stable, using stored outlines will greatly improve the performance of your SQL because the SQL parse phase is bypassed. You also have the peace of mind of knowing that a SQL statement will always use the same execution plan regardless of changes to Oracle initialization parameters and CBO statistics.

Remember, there are many DBAs who feel that for any SQL statement there exists only one optimal execution plan, and once located, it should never change. If you are one of these DBAs, then stored outlines can greatly aid your SQL tuning effort.

If you choose to implement stored outlines for all of your SQL, you must also remember that CBO statistics will only be used by new queries. Hence, you may want to reduce the frequency of your reanalysis of tables and indexes.

The use of stored outlines also aids you when you are migrating from rule-based to cost-based optimization. While you begin to tune SQL statements to use the CBO, you can use optimizer plan stability to ensure that your other SQL statements continue to use their rule-based execution plans. Let's take a look at how this works.

Using Optimizer Plan Stability When Migrating to the CBO

Because Oracle8*i* is the first release of Oracle where the CBO has comparable execution speeds to the RBO, many DBAs are looking at methods for safely migrating their SQL into a database with a cost-based optimizer default. If your application was developed using the rule-based optimizer, then you may have already invested a considerable amount of effort into manually tuning the SQL statements to optimize performance.

Most RBO applications use a rule-based default optimizer mode *(optimizer_mode=rule)* and then tune specific SQL queries with cost-based hints. While the tuned SQL has hints to ensure fast execution speeds, the majority of the SQL using the rule-based default may change execution plans when migrated into a database with a cost-based optimizer default *(optimizer_mode=first_rows)*. You can use optimizer plan stability to preserve your execution plans when upgrading from rule-based to cost-based optimization.

By creating stored outlines for every SQL statement before switching to cost-based optimization, you can use the plans generated by the rule-based optimizer, while statements generated by newly written applications developed after the switch use cost-based plans. To create and store outlines for your system before migrating to the CBO, use the *alter system set use_stored_outlines=true* command. This will create an execution plan for every SQL statement.

Later, when you are ready to see if your nonhinted rule-based SQL statements will run faster with the Oracle8*i* CBO, you can run a query against the DBA_OUTLINES to identify those SQL statements that do not contain hints and tune them individually using the procedures described later in this chapter.

Next, let's get started and see how to prepare your database to allow optimizer plan stability.

Preparing Oracle for Stored Outlines

Several steps need to be completed before Oracle will use stored outlines. These include:

- Setting the *use_stored_outlines* command
- Verifying important initialization parameters
- Creating the outline package
- Defining the tablespace for the stored outlines

Setting the use_stored_outlines Command

Oracle provides a parameter called *use_stored_outlines* to enable optimizer plan stability. The *use_stored_outlines* parameter is *not* an initialization parameter, although it probably will become an initialization parameter in Oracle9*i*. To enable the use of stored outlines for the whole database, you can issue the following command:

```
alter system set use_stored_outlines=true;
```

However, a new parameter called USE_PRIVATE_OUTLINES enables the use of a category of outlines strictly for the current session while other sessions may use a different set. In addition 9i OEM has a outline editor to facilitate changing the outlines.

Of course, this command must be reissued each time the database is restarted. Most Oracle DBAs add this command to the post-startup procedure that executes *dbms_shared_pool.keep* to pin Oracle packages into the shared pool.

You can also enable optimizer plan stability at the session level by issuing the *alter session set use_stored_outlines=true* command, but it is much more effective to enable stored outlines at the database level, provided that your system does not generate SQL with embedded literal values.

CAUTION
The outln *users default system tablespace can become exhausted if the* alter system set create_stored_outlines=true *and your application issues* lots *of nonreusable SQL with literal values. If this happens, set* cursor_sharing=force *in your initialization file and use the* drop_unused *function of the outline package to remove the unused outlines.*

Verifying Important Initialization Parameters

Oracle recommends several initialization parameters that must be set in order to use stored outlines. These parameters include:

- **cursor_sharing=force**   Set this parameter if your system uses SQL with embedded literal values. With *cursor_sharing* set, the SQL will be rewritten to replace the literals with host variables, making the stored outlines reusable.

- ***query_rewrite_enabled=true***   This enables materialized views.

- ***star_transformation_enabled=true***   This enables the star join.

- ***optimizer_features_enable=true***   This will enable the initialization parameters *b_tree_bitmap_plans, complex_view_merging, fast_full_scan_enabled,* and *push_join_predicate.*

Create the Outline Package

You will need to install the *outln_pkg* package to get the procedures available to maintain your stored outlines. Upon installation of the Oracle8*i* software, a user named *outln* is created with a password of *outln*. The script to create the *outn_pkg* packages is called *dbmsol.sql* in the $ORACLE_HOME/rdbms/admin directory. Here is a listing from the creation:

```
SQL> connect / as sysdba;
Connected.
SQL> @$ORACLE_HOME/rdbms/admin/dbmsol
```

Also, note that the catproc.sql script builds this using the following calls:

```
@@catol.sql
@@dbmsol.sql
@@prvtol.plb

rem - If catol.sql and prvtol.sql aren't run you won't get the catalog views or
the package body.
```

Note that this script creates the following synonyms and grants after installing the *sys.outln_pkg* package:

```
CREATE PUBLIC SYNONYM outln_pkg FOR sys.outln_pkg;
GRANT EXECUTE ON outln_pkg TO dba;
GRANT EXECUTE ON outln_pkg TO outln;

CREATE PUBLIC SYNONYM outline FOR sys.outln_pkg;
GRANT EXECUTE ON outline TO dba;
GRANT EXECUTE ON outline TO outln;
```

As we can see, you can reference the *outline* package by the name *outln_pkg* or *outline*. Now that the *outline* package is installed, you can now describe the *outline* procedure and see all of the available functions:

```
SQL> desc outline;
PROCEDURE DROP_BY_CAT
```

```
Argument Name                          Type                In/Out Default?
----------------------------           -----------------   ------ --------
CAT                                    VARCHAR2            IN
PROCEDURE DROP_COLLISION
FUNCTION DROP_COLLISION_EXPACT RETURNS VARCHAR2
PROCEDURE DROP_EXTRAS
FUNCTION DROP_EXTRAS_EXPACT RETURNS VARCHAR2
PROCEDURE DROP_UNREFD_HINTS
FUNCTION DROP_UNREFD_HINTS_EXPACT RETURNS VARCHAR2
PROCEDURE DROP_UNUSED
PROCEDURE UPDATE_BY_CAT
Argument Name                          Type                In/Out Default?
----------------------------           -----------------   ------ --------
OLDCAT                                 VARCHAR2            IN     DEFAULT
NEWCAT                                 VARCHAR2            IN     DEFAULT
```

Next let's look at how to create a tablespace for the *outln* user to hold the stored outlines.

Create the Stored Outline Tablespace

The *outln* user requires a separate tablespace because your database may store thousands of stored outlines and it is a good idea to segregate the outlines into a separate tablespace for improved manageability. Here is the syntax to create the tablespace:

```
create tablespace
    outline_ts
datafile
    '/u01/oradata/PROD/outline.dbf'
size
    10M
default storage
    (initial 10K next 20K minextents 1 maxextents unlimited)
online;

Tablespace created.
```

Next, we alter the *outln* user to use this tablespace by default.

```
alter user
    outln
default tablespace
    outline_ts;

User altered.
```

We are now ready to start capturing stored outlines. Let's take a look at how it works.

How to Create and Modify a Stored Outline

The best way to show how to use stored outlines to change the execution plan for a SQL statement is to illustrate the procedure with a simple example. Let's start with a simple query to display the sum of all salaries for each department.

```
select
    dname,
    loc,
    sum(sal)
from
    emp,
    dept
where
    emp.deptno(+) = dept.deptno
and
    dept.deptno = 10
group by
    dname,
    loc
;
```

Here is the output from this query:

```
DNAME           LOC             SUM(SAL)
--------------- --------------- ----------
ACCOUNTING      NEW YORK              8750
```

Find the Fastest Execution Plan

Now let's take a look at the execution plan for this query. Note that it uses *all_rows* optimization and does a full-table scan even though there is an index on the *emp* table:

```
OPERATION
----------------------------------------------------------------------
OPTIONS                         OBJECT_NAME                    POSITION
------------------------------- ------------------------------ ----------
SELECT STATEMENT
                                                                      5
  SORT
GROUP BY                                                               1
    NESTED LOOPS
OUTER                                                                  1
      TABLE ACCESS
```

```
BY INDEX ROWID                   DEPT                              1
        INDEX
RANGE SCAN                       DEPT_DEPT                         1
      TABLE ACCESS
FULL                             EMP                               2
```

Of course, this query will run faster if we direct the SQL to use the *emp* index to access the *emp* rows. When we reexecute the query with a *rule* hint, we see the full-table scan disappear.

```
select /*+ rule */
    dname,
    loc,
    sum(sal)
from
    emp,
    dept
where
    emp.deptno(+) = dept.deptno
and
    dept.deptno = 10
group by
    dname,
    loc
;
```

Let's assume that we have done a timing of this query, and it is faster with rule-based optimization because it uses the *dept_dept* index instead of a full-table scan.

```
OPERATION
----------------------------------------------------------------------
OPTIONS                          OBJECT_NAME              POSITION
----------------------------     -----------------------  ----------
SELECT STATEMENT
   SORT
GROUP BY                                                         1
     NESTED LOOPS
OUTER                                                           1
       TABLE ACCESS
BY INDEX ROWID                   DEPT                            1
       INDEX
RANGE SCAN                       DEPT_DEPT                       1
       TABLE ACCESS
BY INDEX ROWID                   EMP                             2
           INDEX
RANGE SCAN                       DEPT_EMP                        1
```

If we assume that the *emp* and *dept* tables are very large, then changing the SQL to use the index will improve the performance of the query. Of course, you should always verify your hint by reexecuting the SQL with the SQL*Plus *set timing on* command to ensure that the hint improves performance. Now let's create our first stored outline.

Create the Stored Outline for the Original Query

Outlines are created using the CREATE OUTLINE command. The syntax for this command is:

```
CREATE [OR REPLACE] OUTLINE
    outline_name
[FOR CATEGORY category_name]
ON
    sql_statement;
```

Where:

- **outline_name**   This is a unique name for the outline. Automatic outlines are stored as SYS_OUTLINE-*nnn,* where *nnn* is a large unique number.

- **[FOR CATEGORY category_name]**   This optional clause allows more than one outline to be associated with a single query by specifying multiple categories, each named uniquely.

- **ON sql_statement**   This specifies the SQL statement for which the outline is prepared.

To illustrate the syntax, here we create a stored outline for the original SQL.

```
create or replace outline
    cbo_sql
on
select
    dname,
    loc,
    sum(sal)
from
    emp,
    dept
where
    emp.deptno(+) = dept.deptno
and
    dept.deptno = 10
group by
    dname,
    loc
;
```

The query to display stored outline plans is very different in format than the explain plan utility. Here is the code to display the execution plan inside the *ol$hints* table.

outline.sql

```
set echo off;
set verify off;
set feedback off;

column hint format a40;

select
    sql_text
from
    dba_outlines
where
    name = upper('&1');

select distinct
    lpad(' ',2*(level-1))||hint_text hint,
    hint#,
    table_tin,
    stage#
from
    outln.ol$hints
start with
    hint#=1
connect by prior
    hint# = hint#-1
and
    ol_name = upper('&1')
order by
    stage#,
    hint#
;
```

Now when we query the stored outline, we see a very different form of the execution plan:

```
SQL> @outline cbo_sql

SQL_TEXT
-----------------------------------------------------------------
select
    dname,
```

```
    loc,
    sum(sal)
from
    emp,
    dept
where
    emp.deptno(+)
```

HINT	HINT#	TABLE_TIN	STAGE#
NOREWRITE	10	0	1
NOREWRITE	9	0	2
NO_EXPAND	1	0	3
PQ_DISTRIBUTE(EMP NONE NONE)	2	1	3
USE_NL(EMP)	3	1	3
ORDERED	4	0	3
NO_FACT(EMP)	5	1	3
NO_FACT(DEPT)	6	2	3
FULL(EMP)	7	1	3
FULL(DEPT)	8	2	3

Create a Stored Outline for the Hinted Query

In the next step, we create a new execution plan for the modified SQL statement. After creating this stored outline, we can then swap the stored outlines, replacing the original execution plan with our hinted execution plan.

```
create or replace outline
    rbo_sql
on
select /*+ rule */
    dname,
    loc,
    sum(sal)
from
    emp,
    dept
where
    emp.deptno(+) = dept.deptno
and
    dept.deptno = 10
group by
    dname,
    loc
;
```

Now, let's run *outline.sql* and see the new execution plan:

```
SQL> @outline rbo_sql

SQL_TEXT
------------------------------------------------------------------
select /*+ rule */
    dname,
    loc,
    sum(sal)
from
    emp,
    dept
where
    emp.deptno(+) = dept.deptno
and
    dept.deptno = 10
group by
    dname,
    loc
```

HINT	HINT#	TABLE_TIN	STAGE#
NOREWRITE	9	0	1
RULE	10	0	1
NOREWRITE	8	0	2
NO_EXPAND	1	0	3
USE_NL(EMP)	2	1	3
ORDERED	3	0	3
NO_FACT(EMP)	4	1	3
NO_FACT(DEPT)	5	2	3
INDEX(EMP DEPT_DEPT)	6	1	3
FULL(DEPT)	7	2	3

Here we see that we have the stored outline for the original query and another stored outline for our tuned query. We are now ready to swap the stored outlines for these two queries so that the original query will use the improved stored outline.

Swap the Stored Outlines

The final step in the tuning is to swap the desired *rbo_sql* outline with our original *cbo_sql* outline. We will do this by running the *swap_outlines.sql* script. It will prompt you for the name of the original stored outline and the name of the improved stored outline. It will then swap the outlines between the two statements, transferring our desired execution plan to the original SQL statement (Figure 13-2).

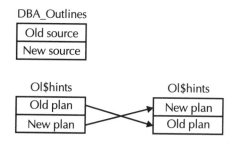

FIGURE 13-2. *Swapping a stored outline*

swap_outlines.sql

```
set echo off;
set feedback off;

prompt Enter the old outline name:
accept old

prompt Enter the new outline name:
accept new

update
    outln.ol$hints
set
    ol_name=decode(ol_name,upper('&new'),
             upper('&old'),upper('&old'),upper('&new'))
where
    ol_name IN (upper('&new'),upper('&old'));
commit;

prompt Here is the new outline for &old
@outline &old@outline &old
```

Here is the listing from *swap_outlines.sql*. Note that it displays the original SQL source, but with our improved execution plan:

```
SQL> @swap_outlines
Enter the old outline name:
cbo_sql
Enter the new outline name:
rbo_sql

Here is the new outline for cbo_sql
```

```
SQL_TEXT
------------------------------------------------------------------
select
   dname,
   loc,
   sum(sal)
from
   emp,
   dept
where
   emp.deptno(+)
```

HINT	HINT#	TABLE_TIN	STAGE#
NOREWRITE	9	0	1
RULE	10	0	1
NOREWRITE	8	0	2
NO_EXPAND	1	0	3
USE_NL(EMP)	2	1	3
ORDERED	3	0	3
NO_FACT(EMP)	4	1	3
NO_FACT(DEPT)	5	2	3
INDEX(EMP DEPT_DEPT)	6	1	3
FULL(DEPT)	7	2	3

Now that we understand how stored outlines are used to improve query performance, and how to tune a query using stored outlines, let's move to a higher level and examine how you can manage stored outlines for your whole database.

Managing Stored Outlines

Because the stored outline feature is new with Oracle8i, there are only a few rudimentary views and procedures to aid in the management of SQL stored outlines. As Oracle continues to enhance the functionality of optimizer plan stability, these tools will grow more robust.

Oracle provides two dictionary structures to aid in stored outline management, the DBA_OUTLINES view and the ol$hints table. Oracle also provides the outline package to aid in the categorization and management of stored outlines.

Using the Dictionary Views and Tables for Stored Outlines

Oracle provides several views to help display stored outlines, most notably the DBA_OUTLINES view and the ol$hints table. Together, these structures will tell you everything you need to know about the status of stored outlines in your database. Here are the columns in the DBA_OUTLINES view:

```
SQL> desc dba_outlines;
 Name                                      Null?    Type
 ----------------------------------------- -------- ----------------
 NAME                                               VARCHAR2(30)
 OWNER                                              VARCHAR2(30)
 CATEGORY                                           VARCHAR2(30)
 USED                                               VARCHAR2(9)
 TIMESTAMP                                          DATE
 VERSION                                            VARCHAR2(64)
 SQL_TEXT                                           LONG
```

We also have a DBA_OUTLINE_HINTS view, but it does not contain as much useful information as *ol$hints,* and it is seldom used because it lacks detail about the sequence of the stored outline steps.

```
SQL> desc dba_outline_hints;
 Name                                      Null?    Type
 ----------------------------------------- -------- ------------------
 NAME                                               VARCHAR2(30)
 OWNER                                              VARCHAR2(30)
 NODE                                               NUMBER
 STAGE                                              NUMBER
 JOIN_POS                                           NUMBER
 HINT                                               VARCHAR2(512)
```

To see the stored execution plans for a SQL statement, you must reference the *outln.ol$hints* view. Note that we created a public synonym for *ol$hints* to make it easily accessible by all users:

```
SQL> create public synonym ol$hints for outln.ol$hints;
Synonym created.

SQL> desc ol$hints;
 Name                                      Null?    Type
 ----------------------------------------- -------- ----------------
 OL_NAME                                            VARCHAR2(30)
 HINT#                                              NUMBER
 CATEGORY                                           VARCHAR2(30)
 HINT_TYPE                                          NUMBER
 HINT_TEXT                                          VARCHAR2(512)
 STAGE#                                             NUMBER
 NODE#                                              NUMBER
 TABLE_NAME                                         VARCHAR2(30)
 TABLE_TIN                                          NUMBER
 TABLE_POS                                          NUMBER
```

Once a stored outline is used, the used column in DBA_OUTLINES will change. Here we execute the original query and check to see if the stored outline was used:

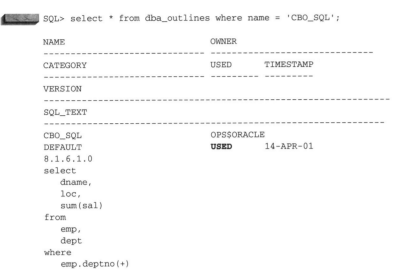

```
SQL> select * from dba_outlines where name = 'CBO_SQL';

NAME                               OWNER
---------------------------------  -----------------------------
CATEGORY                           USED      TIMESTAMP
---------------------------------  --------- ---------
VERSION
-----------------------------------------------------------------
SQL_TEXT
-----------------------------------------------------------------
CBO_SQL                            OPS$ORACLE
DEFAULT                            USED      14-APR-01
8.1.6.1.0
select
   dname,
   loc,
   sum(sal)
from
   emp,
   dept
where
   emp.deptno(+)
```

Here we can run a query to see our automatically generated outlines, as evidenced by their names in the SYS_OUTLINE-*nnn*.

```
SQL> select * from dba_outlines
  2  where name like 'SYS_OUTLINE%';

NAME                               OWNER
---------------------------------  -----------------------------
CATEGORY                           USED      TIMESTAMP
---------------------------------  --------- ---------
VERSION
-----------------------------------------------------------------
SQL_TEXT
-----------------------------------------------------------------
SYS_OUTLINE_0104142013050001       READER
DEFAULT                            UNUSED    14-APR-01
8.1.6.1.0
SELECT ATTRIBUTE,SCOPE,NUMERIC_VALUE,CHAR_VALUE,DATE_VALUE FROM SYSTEM.PRODUCT_P

SYS_OUTLINE_0104142013050002       READER
DEFAULT                            UNUSED    14-APR-01
8.1.6.1.0
SELECT CHAR_VALUE FROM SYSTEM.PRODUCT_PRIVS WHERE   (UPPER('SQL*Plus') LIKE UPPE
```

```
SYS_OUTLINE_0104142013050003    READER
DEFAULT                         UNUSED    14-APR-01
8.1.6.1.0
SELECT DECODE('A','A','1','2') FROM DUAL

SYS_OUTLINE_0104142013270004    READER
DEFAULT                         USED      14-APR-01
8.1.6.1.0
select nbr_pages from book
```

Next, let's look at how the outline package is used to help us manage our stored outlines.

Using the Outline Package

The *outline* package contains several procedures that can help us manage our stored outlines. These procedures allow us to drop, categorize, and manage all stored outlines. The *outline* package contains the following functions and stored procedures.

- **Procedures**   *drop_collision, drop_extras, drop_unrefd_hints, drop_unused, update_by_cat*

- **Functions**   *drop_collision_expact, drop_extras_expact, drop_unrefd_hints_expact*

Let's begin by looking at a procedure to identify and drop unused stored outlines.

Identify and Drop Unused Stored Outlines

One of the problems with systems that generate SQL with literal values is that there will be a huge number of nonreusable SQL statements. In these cases, *cursor_sharing=force* should be set to rewrite the SQL to replace the literals with host variables, thereby making the SQL reusable.

For example, *cursor_sharing* will transform this statement, removing the literal and replacing it with a host variable:

```
select * from customer where cust_name = 'JONES';
```

into a reusable form:

```
select * from customer where cust_name = :var1;
```

Oracle provides a procedure for dropping stored outlines that are not reused. Let's begin by running a query to see if our database has SQL statements that have never been reused.

```
SQL> set long 1000
SQL> select * from dba_outlines where used='UNUSED';

NAME          OWNER  CATEGORY USED     TIMESTAMP VERSION     SQL_TEXT
------------  ------ ---------- --------- ---------- -------------
TEST_OUTLINE SYSTEM TEST UNUSED 08-MAY-99 8.1.3.0.0
                                             select a.table_name,
                                               b.tablespace_name,
                                                c.file_name from
                                                    dba_tables a,
                                                dba_tablespaces b,
                                                  dba_data_files c
                                                    where
                                              a.tablespace_name =
                                                b.tablespace_name
                                            and b.tablespace_name
                                              = c.tablespace_name
                                                  and c.file_id =
                                                         (select
                                              min(d.file_id) from
                                                  dba_data_files d
                                                         where
                                              c.tablespace_name =
                                                d.tablespace_name)
```

Now, we are ready to drop any stored outlines that have not been used. We do this by running the *drop_unused* procedure in the *outline* package.

```
SQL> execute outline_pkg.drop_unused;

PL/SQL procedure successfully completed.

SQL> select * from dba_outlines where used='UNUSED';

no rows selected
```

Remember, there is no recovery for this procedure, so you should always make sure that you no longer want the unused stored outlines before running *drop_unused*.

Managing Categories with Stored Outlines

Oracle provides a method whereby specific categories of stored outlines may be created. The categories can be very useful when you want to segregate stored outlines for testing purposes or when you want to separate stored outlines.

However, the stored outlines in each category will always be used when a SQL statement enters the SQL parser, regardless of the category name, so it is important to remember that you cannot use stored outline categories to segregate stored outlines from execution. Categories are only used for the purpose of grouping related stored outlines. Let's take a quick look at these procedures in the stored outline category.

The drop_by_cat Procedure

The *drop_by_cat* procedure drops all outlines that belong to a specific category. The procedure *drop_by_cat* has one input variable, *cat*, a VARCHAR2 that corresponds to the name of the category you want to drop.

```
create or replace outline
    cbo_sql
for category
    my_test
on
select
    dname,
    loc,
    sum(sal)
from
    emp,
    dept
where
    emp.deptno(+) = dept.deptno
and
    dept.deptno = 10
group by
    dname,
    loc
;
```

Now, we can display all stored outlines in the *my_test* category:

```
SQL> set long 1000;
SQL> select * from dba_outlines where category='MY_TEST';

NAME                              OWNER
-------------------------------- --------------------------------
CATEGORY                          USED      TIMESTAMP
-------------------------------- --------- ---------
VERSION
-----------------------------------------------------------------
SQL_TEXT
-----------------------------------------------------------------
CBO_SQL                           OPS$ORACLE
MY_TEST                           UNUSED    15-APR-01
8.1.6.1.0
```

```
select
   dname,
   loc,
   sum(sal)
from
   emp,
   dept
where
   emp.deptno(+) = dept.deptno
and
   dept.deptno = 10
group by
   dname,
   loc
```

Now, to remove all stored outlines in the *my_test* category, we invoke the *drop_by_cat* procedure:

```
SQL> exec outline.drop_by_cat('MY_TEST');

PL/SQL procedure successfully completed.

SQL> select * from dba_outlines where category='MY_TEST';

no rows selected
```

Next, let's look at the *update_by_cat* procedure.

The update_by_cat Procedure

The *update_by_cat* procedure merges all of the outlines in one category to a new category. This procedure is tricky because if a SQL in a stored outline already has an outline in the target category, then it is *not* merged into the new category. In other words, duplicates are not merged into the new category. Let's illustrate this with a simple example.

Here we create three stored outlines. Please note that the SQL for *prod_sql1* is identical to the SQL in *test_sql1*.

```
create outline
   test_sql1
for category
   test
on
select * from dba_indexes;

create outline
   test_sql2
```

```
for category
   test
on
select * from dba_constraints;

create outline
  prod_sql1
for category
   prod
on
select * from dba_indexes;
```

Now we can select the names and categories and verify the placement of the SQL stored outlines in their categories:

```
SQL> select
   name,
   category
from
   dba_outlines
order by
   category;

NAME                                 CATEGORY
-------------------------------      -----------------------------
PROD_SQL1                            PROD
TEST_SQL1                            TEST
TEST_SQL2                            TEST
```

Next, we execute the *update_by_cat* procedure to merge the TEST stored outlines into the PROD category.

```
SQL> exec outline.update_by_cat('TEST','PROD');

PL/SQL procedure successfully completed.
```

As we mentioned, because *prod_sql1* is identical to *test_sql1,* we expect that the *test_sql1* will not have been merged into the PROD category. Let's check and see:

```
SQL> select name,category from dba_outlines order by category;

NAME                                 CATEGORY
-------------------------------      -----------------------------
TEST_SQL2                            PROD
PROD_SQL1                            PROD
TEST_SQL1                            TEST
```

To summarize, the *update_by_cat* is used to merge UNIQUE SQL statements from one stored outline category to another category. Duplicate stored outlines are *not* merged into the new category.

Conclusion

The optimizer plan stability feature of Oracle8*i* is an exciting new way to improve the speed of SQL and also provide a method for making tuning changes permanent. The major points of this chapter include these:

■ In future releases of Oracle, stored outlines promise to improve SQL performance because SQL statements with stored outlines do not have to reformulate an execution plan when they are invoked.

■ Stored outlines improve SQL tuning because an improved execution plan for a SQL statement can be stored without touching the original SQL source code.

■ Stored outlines are great for tuning databases where the SQL source is not available, such as SAP and PeopleSoft applications products.

■ Stored outlines can be turned on at the system level with the *alter system set use_stored_outlines=true* command. This will cause every SQL statement to store an outline with the name SYS_OUTLINE_*nnn*.

■ Stored outlines can be set at the session level with the *alter session set use_stored_outlines=true* command. This is the recommended method for tuning individual SQL statements.

■ You can change a stored outline for a SQL statement by creating and storing an improved stored outline and running the *swap_outlines.sql* script to swap in your improved stored outline.

■ Databases with lots of nonreusable SQL with embedded literal values may quickly fill the outline tablespace unless *cursor_sharing=force* is set in the initialization file.

■ Oracle provides a crude category management tool for creating and merging categories of stored outlines.

Next, let's take a look at SQL tuning with the cost-based optimizer and see how you can maximize your benefits from exploiting the new cost-based hints.

CHAPTER
14

Tuning with the
Cost-Based Optimizer

his chapter is devoted to techniques for getting the most out of the cost-based optimizer when tuning SQL. The material in this chapter is intended to provide a general framework for SQL tuning. The topics in this chapter include:

- Cost-based optimization and SQL tuning

- Cost-based initialization parameters

- Analyzing tables and indexes

- Using STATSPACK to monitor execution plans

Most Oracle databases have a hodgepodge of SQL statements that use hints and have queries that execute in both rule-based optimization and cost-based optimization. Hence, the focus of this chapter will be tuning your database when you have a cost-based default optimizer_mode, either all_rows or first_rows.

Statistics and Cost-Based Optimization

One of the requirements of cost-based optimization is the presence of statistics on tables and indexes. For tables, the statistics give a general idea of the number of rows in the table, the average row length within the table, and other statistics that are gathered by examining sample rows from the table. As you know, table statistics are generated using the *analyze table* command syntax. For indexes, the *analyze index* command is used in order to gather information about each index that participates in the cost-based query.

The statistics for indexes include information about the number of distinct values within the index, the number of entries in the index, and the physical storage characteristics of the index within the tablespace. In the case where an index has been analyzed for column histograms, we also see individual buckets that are created with statistics about the distribution of data within the index. As you know, column histograms are only useful in cases where an index has a highly skewed distribution of values, such that a query against one value in the index is faster with a full-table scan, whereas another query against the same index with a different column value would be better served by using an index range scan.

These statistics are used in conjunction with the cost-based optimizer to formulate a decision tree of different execution plans, each with an estimated cost for each plan (Figure 14-1).

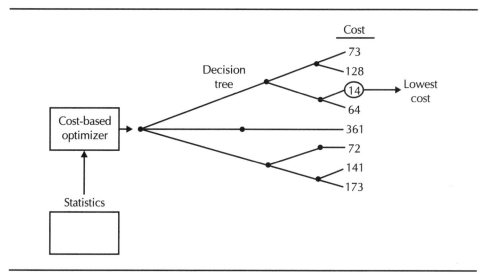

FIGURE 14-1.   *Using statistics with the cost-based optimizer*

The optimizer then evaluates the plan tree and chooses the execution plan with the lowest estimated cost.

Dynamic versus Static CBO Execution Plan Philosophy

While the basic concept of using the table and index characteristics in the formulation of the execution plan is quite good, there is a philosophical choice that needs to be made regarding the dynamic nature of SQL execution plans. The whole idea behind periodically reanalyzing tables and indexes is that the execution plans for your SQL may change as the characteristics of the data change. When adopting this dynamic approach, you must give full faith to the cost-based optimizer to choose the appropriate execution plan, and you cannot use optimizer plan stability (stored outlines) to make the SQL changes permanent. If you adopt the dynamic SQL execution philosophy, you may tune your SQL only by physically changing your SQL by adding hints to the source code. You must also ensure that any hints that you add are general enough (e.g., the *first_rows* hint) to allow the optimizer to evaluate several execution plans.

On the other hand, some SQL tuning professionals subscribe to the notion that there exists only one appropriate execution plan for any given SQL query, and they utilize stored outlines to ensure that once tuned, the same execution plan is always invoked. When adopting the static philosophy, the only exception to this rule is the case of skewed indexes, where the SQL tuning professional deliberately does not create stored outlines, allowing the optimizer to detect the most appropriate access plan given the skew of the index columns.

Frequency of Statistics Gathering

There's a great debate within the Oracle community about how frequently to reanalyze statistics, and the level of detail in the sample size for the statistics (Figure 14-2). Some DBAs subscribe to the notion that the SQL statistics should be reanalyzed very frequently to ensure optimal statistics and better CBO execution plans. Others subscribe to the notion that statistics should only be recomputed when the basic nature of the table data changes.

Along the other dimension, we see debate regarding the sample size that should be used when computing statistics. We have two options available within the *analyze table* command, the *computes statistics* option and the *estimate statistics* command syntax. When we issue a *computes statistics* command, the entire table is examined via a full-table scan, and very accurate statistics are then placed inside the data dictionary for use by the cost-based optimizer. By using the *estimate statistics* syntax, samples are taken from the table, and the samples are stored within the

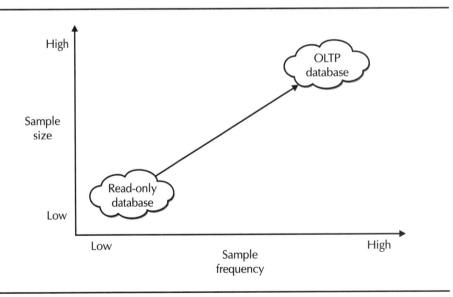

FIGURE 14-2. *Statistics gathering frequency versus sample size*

data dictionary. At the heart of this issue are the time and database resource consumption required to reanalyze all of the tables.

As you might remember from your college statistics classes, a sample size greater than 40 gives us averages that are within two standard deviations from the mean for the population that is being sampled. Within Oracle, however, there still exists a great deal of debate about the trade-offs between taking more detail row samples and the additional quality of the resulting statistics (Figure 14-3). Some people argue that a sample 50 rows from each and every table gives excellent statistics in order to drive their cost-based optimizers, while other DBAs insist that a sample of at least 5,000 rows is required for many tables in order to get accurate statistics. Remember, the decisions of the cost-based optimizer are only as good as the statistics that are being fed to it.

Essentially we see the debate regarding cost-based optimization falling along two dimensions, the frequency of analysis and the depth of the analysis. We also have to remember that if we plan to use optimizer plan stability on all our queries, the statistics are meaningless to the cost-based optimizer because the execution plan has been predetermined and saved in a stored outline.

Computing statistics for tables and indexes can be a very time-consuming operation, especially for data warehouses as systems that have many gigabytes or terabytes of information. In the real world, most Oracle professionals use the *estimate statistics* clause, sample a meaningful percentage of their data, and choose a

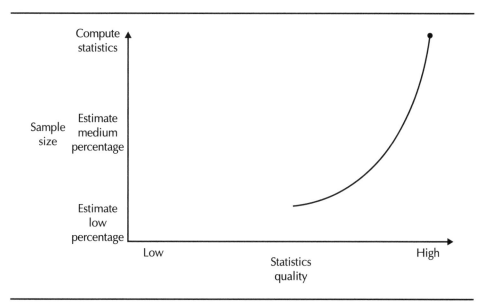

FIGURE 14-3. *The sample size as a function of the quality of the estimate*

reanalysis frequency that coincides with any scheduled changes to the database that might affect the distribution of values. For example, if a database runs purges from their transaction table each month, the period immediately following the purge would be a good time to reanalyze the CBO statistics.

Regardless of your philosophy, let's take a look at how you can automate the reanalysis of your CBO statistics.

Gathering Statistics for the CBO

It is important that the statistics are refreshed periodically, especially when the distribution of data changes frequently. For this reason, the following SQL may be used to run the analyze statements for all of the tables and indexes. It is not always a good idea to use Oracle's *dbms_utility.analyze_schema* or *dbms_ddl.analyze_object* package to perform this task, since a failure on one of the statements can affect the results of subsequent *analyze* statements. When working with databases that do not employ stored outlines, I use the following script to generate and execute the proper SQL *analyze* syntax.

analyze.ksh

```ksh
#!/bin/ksh

# First, we must set the environment . . . .
ORACLE_SID=$ORACLE_SID
export ORACLE_SID
# The line below is for Solaris databases.  Otherwise, use /etc/oratab
ORACLE_HOME=`cat /var/opt/oracle/oratab|grep ^$ORACLE_SID:|cut -f2 -d':'`
export ORACLE_HOME
PATH=$ORACLE_HOME/bin:$PATH
export PATH

$ORACLE_HOME/bin/sqlplus /<<!

set pages 999
set heading off
set echo off
set feedback off

connect internal;

spool /export/home/oracle/analyze.sql;
select
'analyze table '||owner||'.'||table_name||' estimate statistics sample
5000 rows;'
from dba_tables
```

```
where owner not in ('SYS','SYSTEM','PERFSTAT');

select
'analyze index reader.'||index_name||' compute statistics;'
from dba_indexes
where owner not in ('SYS','SYSTEM','PERFSTAT');

spool off;

set echo on
set feedback on

@/export/home/oracle/analyze

exit
!
```

Most shops schedule a script like this to run weekly, or whenever there have
been significant changes to the table data. However, it is not necessary to reanalyze
tables and indexes that remain relatively constant. For example, a database in which
the tables have a constant number of rows and indexes where the distribution of
values remains constant will not benefit from frequent reanalysis. Let's continue
with an overview of the important issues of SQL tuning with a cost-based
default optimizer.

Cost-Based Optimization
and SQL Tuning

Unless you have a brand-new system that was developed on Oracle8*i*, chances are
that you've already had some experience with running both cost-based optimization
and rule-based optimization together inside the same database. As the cost-based
optimizer continues to improve, more and more SQL statements can be moved from
rule-based optimization into cost-based optimization, and this is especially true in
Oracle8*i*. However, it is not immediately obvious which of your SQL statements
will benefit from a cost-based optimization approach, and there is no substitute for
manually tuning and evaluating the elapsed speed of each query to find the fastest
execution plan.

Prior to Oracle8*i*, most Oracle systems used the default *optimizer_mode=rule*
and tuned individual SQL statements with cost-based hints to take advantage of the
new Oracle8 features such as function-based and bitmap indexes. However, now
that Oracle8*i*'s cost-based optimizer has reached the point where it is compatible
with rule-based optimization, many SQL tuning professionals are experimenting

with using a cost-based default *optimizer_mode* and then individually tuning queries to achieve the fastest execution plans.

As I noted in our review of Oracle hints in Chapter 12, you have a huge number of options available to use to tune when using the cost-based optimizer. Some of the new features that we can take advantage of with cost-based optimization include bitmap indexes, function-based indexes, star query joins, materialized views, and a host of other new hints that are all designed to improve the response time of our Oracle SQL statements.

As I noted in Chapter 7, the first thing most SQL tuning professionals do when they encounter a suspect SQL program is to add a *rule* hint and see if the execution plan becomes more efficient. Even under cost-based optimization, this is still a very good approach to take because the rule-based optimizer in general will provide very good execution plans except when cost-based indexes are present. The RBO does not understand function-based or bitmap indexes and ignores them when developing an execution plan.

When running your database with a cost-based default, there are particular subsets of SQL queries that are the most important for your SQL tuning effort. Simple queries that select from a single table, or DML statements such as inserts and updates, are not as important as complex SQL queries. By complex, I mean those kinds of queries that join multiple tables together, including subqueries and queries that have very complicated Boolean predicates in the SQL *where* clause. These are the types of SQL statements that will benefit most from tuning.

While we have already covered the basic methods for tuning SQL statements in earlier chapters, it is helpful to categorize the cost-based SQL tuning options according to the type of access that is being performed. We generally see three classes of queries:

- Cost-based multiple table join techniques (see also Chapter 16)
- Cost-based subquery optimization techniques (see also Chapter 19)
- Queries with complex Boolean predicates in the *where* clause

Within each of these areas, there are sets of rules that direct us to possible hints that can be applied to these classes of queries in order to improve the overall execution speed. As I noted over and over again in earlier chapters, the only way to tell for sure if a hint is going to improve the execution speed of the query is to actually execute the query. Even with Oracle8*i*, costing estimates from the cost-based optimizer do not provide as accurate a measure of the real execution speed of the query as do actually running the query and timing the query elapsed time with the SQL*Plus *set timing on* command.

The cost-based optimizer uses "statistics" that are collected from the table using the *analyze table* and *analyze index* commands. Oracle uses these metrics about the tables in order to intelligently determine the most efficient way of servicing the SQL query. It is important to recognize that in many cases the cost-based optimizer may not always make the proper decision in terms of the speed of the query, and Oracle has provided numerous hints to allow the DBA and developer to tune the execution plan. The cost-based optimizer is constantly being improved, but there are still many cases where the rule-based optimizer will result in faster Oracle queries. One of the first things a seasoned Oracle DBA does when tuning a SQL statement is to add a *rule* hint, or use the *alter session set optimizer_goal = rule* statement in order to change the default optimizer mode from cost-based to rule-based optimization.

Before retrieving any rows, the cost-based optimizer must create an execution plan that tells Oracle the order in which to access the desired tables and indexes. The cost-based optimizer works by weighing the relative "costs" for the different execution paths to the data, and it chooses the path with the smallest relative cost. Once the statistics have been collected, there are three ways to invoke the cost-based optimizer:

■ Setting the *init.ora* parameter *optimizer_mode = all_rows, first_rows,* or *choose*

■ ALTER SESSION SET *optimizer_goal=all_rows* or *first_rows*

■ Cost-based hints /*+ all_rows */ or --+ all_rows

These "costs" for a query are determined with the aid of table and index statistics that are computed with the *analyze table* and *analyze index* commands in Oracle.

When we begin to tune a SQL statement with a cost-based optimizer default, the first step is to take a look at the suspect query and categorize the query according to the type of table access method. Once we've developed a pattern for each SQL statement, it becomes very easy to go to the select set of hints that may be able to improve the execution time for the query. To illustrate, the following sections will examine each one of the basic SQL models and explore the types of hints that can be used under cost-based optimization to improve the execution plan for the query.

Let's take a look at each of these three categories of queries: table joins, subqueries, and complex Boolean expressions.

Cost-Based Table Joins

If we have a query that joins multiple tables together, we want a look at the wealth of hint options available to us for changing the method by which the join takes place within Oracle. As you will remember from earlier chapters, Oracle provides three basic methods for joining tables together, the nested loop join *(use_nl)*, the sort merge join *(use_merge),* and the hash join *(use_hash).* In addition to these basic join techniques, we can also add parallelism to improve table join speeds for sort merge queries.

One of the shortcomings of the cost-based optimizer prior to Oracle8i was that when more than four tables were joined, the cost-based optimizer almost always invoked a full-table scan on one of the tables. It is still possible to see these suboptimal execution plans with the CBO in Oracle8i, depending upon the complexity of the table joins that you are performing.

As a general rule, nested loop joins and hash joins should always use indexes on all of the tables, and a full-table scan should never be invoked in order to service the table join, except in the case of a sort merge join. When tuning cost-based SQL statements that perform table joins, the following steps are commonly executed:

1. Search the existing execution plan for full-table scans. If you see that the execution plan invokes a full-table scan against one of the tables, one of the first things you might want to try is to use an *index* hint or a *rule* hint in order to force all of the tables to use indexes.

2. Try timing the execution of the query using different join techniques. For example, the *use_hash* hint may be used in cases where we are performing a *not in* subquery and we have enough RAM available to perform a hash join against the specified tables. If the query retrieves the majority of blocks in the table as determined by the Boolean conditions in the *where* clause, we might consider invoking a *use_merge* hint combined with a *parallel* hint in order to improve the speed of the query.

Once the optimal execution plan has been verified by using the SQL*Plus *set timing on* command, we make the change permanent by creating a stored outline for the SQL statement. The complete procedure for doing this is fully described in Chapter 13.

Next, let's take a look at tuning cost-based SQL statements that involve subqueries.

Tuning Cost-Based SQL Statements with Subqueries

When we see a SQL statement that specifies a subquery, we first need to carefully check the *where* clause and determine if the subquery is a noncorrelated subquery or a correlated subquery. A *correlated subquery* is a query whereby the key in the subquery is correlated (using the = operator) with a column that is selected in the outer query. On the other hand, a *noncorrelated subquery* is a query where the subquery executes independently of the outer query, passing a result set to the outer query at the end of its execution. Noncorrelated subqueries are commonly seen when using the IN, NOT IN, EXISTS, and NOT EXISTS SQL clauses.

TIP
The use_hash *hint was originally designed for equi-joins, such as NOT IN joins, anti-joins, and joins with equality conditions (such as where cust.cust_nbr = order.cust_nbr). You should always try the* use_hash *hint when tuning these types of queries.*

Rewriting Subqueries into Standard Joins

To understand sub-queries, let's examine three equivalent SQL queries that produce the same result with different syntax. In many cases, sub-queries can be structured to use either of the subquery types, and they can sometimes be replaced by a standard join. For example, consider a query to display all students who received an "A" in any class. This can be written as a standard join, a noncorrelated subquery, or a correlated subquery. The standard join will always run faster than a subquery, and individual SQL statements should be carefully evaluated to see if the subquery can be replaced with a standard join.

A Standard Join

```
select
    *
from
    student,
    registration
where
    student.student_id = registration.student_id
and
    registration.grade = 'A';
```

A Noncorrelated Subquery

```
select
    *
from
    student
where
    student_id =
    (select student_id
        from registration
        where
        grade = 'A'
    );
```

A Correlated Subquery

```
select
    *
from
    student
where
    0 <
    (select count(*)
        from registration
        where
        grade = 'A'
        and
        student_id = student.student_id
    );
```

Here we see the same query result, specified in three ways. This ability to specify the same query in many different forms is very important to those tuning SQL statements. Whenever possible, you want to replace subqueries with a standard join, and you must be familiar with all of the possible ways to manually rewrite a query to make the execution plan more efficient.

Tuning Complex Boolean Queries

It is not uncommon in a production environment to find very complex combinations of AND and OR logic in the *where* clause of your SQL statement. The order and combination of the Boolean values dictates to the SQL optimizer the execution plan that will be taken in order to service the query. For example, a SQL query with a lot of OR statements might invoke a CONCATENATION execution plan to determine the result set.

There are several types of complex Boolean constructs worth exploring, and this section will focus on queries with compound OR or compound AND conditions.

Compound OR Conditions in Boolean Predicates

There are cases in SQL statements where you may have a large chain of OR conditions that are ANDed together with other statements in the SQL query. This includes large in-lists (e.g., *where owner in ('SYS','SYSTEM','PERFSTAT')*). There are two flavors of compound OR statements in SQL syntax:

■ Where the same columns contain OR'ed values:

```
where
   status = 'retired'
or
   status = 'active
or
   status = 'apprentice'
or
   state_of_residence IN ('NY','NC','WA','HI','CO');
```

■ Where each OR condition refers to a different column:

```
where
   (
      status = 'retired'
    or
      state_of_residence = 'NC'
    or
      department = 'accounting'
   )
and
   (
      age > 65
    or
      department = 'marketing
    or
      state_of_residence = 'NY'
   );
```

For example, consider the following query for examples of OR expansion:

```
select /*+ first_rows */
   ename
from
   emp
where
   deptno in (10, 15, 20, 22, 26, 28, 31)
and
   (
      job = 'CLERK'
    or
```

```
      job = 'SALESMAN'
   or
      job = 'SECRETARY'
   )
;
```

For this type of OR where all columns are the same, the cost-based execution plan depends on the presence of indexes. Here is the execution plan with bitmap indexes on *job* and *deptno*:

```
OPERATION
----------------------------------------------------------------
OPTIONS                      OBJECT_NAME                 POSITION
--------------------------   --------------------------  ----------
  SELECT STATEMENT
                                                               1
    INLIST ITERATOR
                                                               1
      TABLE ACCESS
BY INDEX ROWID               EMP                               1
        INDEX
RANGE SCAN                   EMP_DEPTNO_BIT                    1
```

Next, let's explore the more onerous query where the OR columns do not reference the same column. For example, consider the following query where a B-tree index exists on *job, deptno,* and *sal.* It is interesting to note that if the indexes were bitmap indexes, the execution would not perform a full-table scan. This is because Oracle automatically uses bitmap indexes where a query has multiple OR conditions on bitmap index columns.

```
select
   ename
from
   emp
where
   deptno = 10
or
   sal < 5000
or
   job = 'CLERK';
```

Here we have two choices. Because all of the index columns are low cardinality, we could create a bitmap index on *deptno, sal,* and *clerk,* causing a bitmap merge execution plan. Our other choice is to invoke the *use_concat* hint to break the query into three separate B-tree index scans whose result sets will be combined with the *union* operator.

The *use_concat* hint requests that a UNION ALL execution plan be used for all OR conditions in the query, rewriting the query into multiple queries. The *use_concat* hint is commonly invoked when a SQL query has a large number of OR conditions in the *where* clause.

Here is the execution plan for this query. Note that we must perform a full-table scan to satisfy the multiple OR conditions in the *where* clause:

```
OPERATION
-----------------------------------------------------------------------
OPTIONS                         OBJECT_NAME                 POSITION
----------------------------    --------------------------  ----------
 SELECT STATEMENT
                                                                   1
 TABLE ACCESS
FULL                            EMP                                1
```

If our indexes had been bitmap indexes, we would have seen a far faster execution plan using the BITMAP CONVERSION TO ROWIDS method of intersecting the bitmap indexes:

```
OPERATION
-----------------------------------------------------------------------
OPTIONS                         OBJECT_NAME                 POSITION
----------------------------    --------------------------  ----------
 SELECT STATEMENT
                                                                   4
 TABLE ACCESS
BY INDEX ROWID                  EMP                                1
   BITMAP CONVERSION
TO ROWIDS                                                          1
     BITMAP OR
                                                                   1
       BITMAP INDEX
SINGLE VALUE                    EMP_DEPTNO_BIT                     1
       BITMAP MERGE
                                                                   2
       BITMAP INDEX
RANGE SCAN                      EMP_SAL_BIT                        1
       BITMAP INDEX
SINGLE VALUE                    EMP_JOB_BIT                        3
```

Now, let's add the *use_concat* hint and see the change to the execution plan.

```
select /*+ use_concat */
    ename
from
```

```
    emp
where
    deptno = 10
or
    sal < 5000
or
    job = 'CLERK';
```

Here we see that the full-table scan has been replaced with a union of three queries, each using the B-tree index for the single columns and the CONCATENATION plan to UNION together the result sets.

OPERATION		
OPTIONS	OBJECT_NAME	POSITION
SELECT STATEMENT		3
CONCATENATION		
TABLE ACCESS		
BY INDEX ROWID	EMP	1
INDEX		
RANGE SCAN	EMP_JOB	1
TABLE ACCESS		
BY INDEX ROWID	EMP	2
INDEX		
RANGE SCAN	EMP_SAL	1
TABLE ACCESS		
BY INDEX ROWID	EMP	3
INDEX		
RANGE SCAN	EMP_DEPT	1

Now, let's take a look at queries that contain compound AND predicates.

Compound AND Conditions in Boolean Predicates

We also see specialized cost-based tuning optimization techniques for compound AND conditions in a SQL query. Prior to the introduction of bitmap indexes, a concatenated index could be used when a query had multiple AND conditions.

For example, assume the following bitmap indexes on the *emp* table:

```
create bitmap index
    dept_bit
on
    emp
    (deptno);
```

```
create bitmap index
   job_bit
on
   emp
   (job);
```

Now, let's look at another query. Here we filter the result rows where *job=salesman* and *deptno=30* and *sal* > 1000:

```
select /*+ first_rows */
   ename,
   job,
   deptno,
   mgr
from
   emp
where
   job = 'SALESMAN'
and
   deptno = 30
and
   sal > 1000
;
```

Here is the execution plan when using B-tree indexes on the *job, dept,* and *sal* columns. Note that the CBO chooses the most selective of the three indexes and uses that index:

```
OPERATION
----------------------------------------------------------------------

OPTIONS                        OBJECT_NAME                  POSITION
----------------------------   --------------------------   ----------
  SELECT STATEMENT
                                                                  1
  TABLE ACCESS
BY INDEX ROWID                 EMP                                1
    INDEX
RANGE SCAN                     EMP_DEPTNO                         1
```

Now, we drop the B-tree indexes and replace them with three bitmap indexes.

It makes sense to have the *deptno* index as a bitmap index because there are only 10 distinct departments. It also makes sense to make the *job* column a bitmap index because there are only 15 distinct job titles. In the real world, it does not make sense to make *sal* a bitmapped index, because it is a scalar numeric value, but we have done it here purely for illustrative purposes. Note the change to the execution plan after changing the index structures. Next we see that the *dept* column is still used, but we invoke the BITMAP CONVERSION execution method.

```
OPERATION
---------------------------------------------------------------------
OPTIONS                          OBJECT_NAME               POSITION
---------------------------- -------------------------- ----------
  SELECT STATEMENT
                                                                1
  TABLE ACCESS
BY INDEX ROWID                   EMP                            1
    BITMAP CONVERSION
TO ROWIDS                                                       1
      BITMAP INDEX
SINGLE VALUE                     DEPT_BIT                       1
```

Now, because we have bitmap indexes, we can further improve the speed of this query by using the *index_combine* hint to our query. The *index_combine* hint is used to force a bitmap access path for the table. If no indexes are given as arguments for the *index_combine* hint, the optimizer will choose whatever Boolean combination of bitmap indexes has the best costing estimate for the table access.

The *index_combine* hint directs the optimizer to perform a ROWID intersection operation from both bitmaps. In practice, it is always a good idea to specify the table name and both index names in the hint. Here is the same query with the *index_combine* hint, specifying all three bitmap indexes. For this example, we created a *dept_bit* and *job_bit* index on *dept* and *job* columns.

```
select /*+ index_combine(emp, emp_deptno_bit, emp_job_bit, emp_sal_bit)  */
    ename,
    job,
    deptno,
    mgr
from
    emp
where
    job = 'SALESMAN'
and
    deptno = 30
and
    sal > 1000
;
```

Here is the new execution plan:

```
OPERATION
-----------------------------------------------------------------------
OPTIONS                          OBJECT_NAME                 POSITION
-----------------------------  ---------------------------  ----------
 SELECT STATEMENT
                                                                    4
  TABLE ACCESS
BY INDEX ROWID                   EMP                                1
    BITMAP CONVERSION
TO ROWIDS                                                           1
    BITMAP AND
1
        BITMAP INDEX
SINGLE VALUE                     EMP_DEPTNO_BIT                     1
        BITMAP INDEX
SINGLE VALUE                     EMP_JOB_BIT                       2
            BITMAP MERGE
                                                                    3

            BITMAP INDEX
RANGE SCAN                       EMP_SAL_BIT                        1
```

Here we see that the bitmap indexes are merged together with a BITMAP CONVERSION TO ROWIDS and the BITMAP AND execution method. This bitmap merge method will dramatically reduce the execution time of queries on large tables by merging the resulting ROWIDs from each bitmap index.

In summary, compound AND conditions can be serviced with an index by adding a concatenated index for B-tree values and bitmap indexes for columns values with low cardinality. When using bitmap indexes, you can invoke the *index_combine* hint to improve the performance of queries with compound AND predicates.

Next, let's take a look at initialization parameters that affect the behavior of the cost-based optimizer.

Initialization Parameters That Affect Cost-Based Optimizer Behavior

There are many initialization parameters that affect the behavior of the cost-based optimizer and SQL hints. Often, there are prerequisite initialization parameters that are required in order for a hint to be invoked. For example, the *star_transformation_enabled* initialization parameter must be set to TRUE or a *star* hint will have no effect on the execution plan for the SQL.

Other initialization parameters affect the threshold for invoking a hint. For example, the *hash_area_size* initialization parameter controls the threshold for the invocation of a *use_hash* hint. In any case, all of the following initialization parameters affect the costing that determines the execution plan for the CBO.

Initialization Parameters That Affect Table Joins

While we will be going into greater detail on tuning table joins in Chapter 16, you need to understand the relationship between the initialization parameters and table join behavior. The following initialization parameters can be used to direct the CBO to use different table join techniques.

Limiting the Number of SQL Query Permutations

Oracle provides initialization parameters to control the amount of work performed by the cost-based optimizer when evaluating a query. While parsing is quite fast for simple queries, complex queries with more than six tables can parse for many minutes while Oracle evaluates every possible table join combination.

Sometimes, data warehouse DBAs are perplexed when they find that a 15-way table join takes 30 minutes to parse! This is because there are 15 factorial possible permutations of the query and over one trillion (1,307,674,368,000) query permutations.

While the ultimate solution is to employ stored outlines to remove the parsing phase, Oracle has two important initialization parameters that work together to control the number of possible execution plans generated by the Oracle optimizer.

TIP

If you do not have complex SQL queries that join five or more tables together, you need not be concerned with the optimizer_search_limit *or* optimizer_max_permutations *parameters. These only apply when Oracle is computing possible table join combinations for queries with large numbers of tables.*

The optimizer_search_limit Parameter   The *optimizer_search_limit* parameter specifies the maximum number of table join combinations that will be evaluated by the CBO when deciding the best way to join multiple tables. The reason is to prevent the optimizer from spending an inordinate amount of time on every possible join ordering. The *optimizer_search_limit* parameter also controls the threshold for invoking a star join hint, and a star hint will be honored when the number of tables in the query is less than the *optimizer_search_limit*. The default value is 5.

TIP
Most SQL tuning experts always use the ordered
*hint for any query involving four or more tables.
This eliminates the time-consuming evaluation of
the SQL parses for table join orders, and it improves
the speed of the query. However, when tuning the
SQL to determine the best table join order, it is wise
to leave* optimizer_search_limit *to a high value so
that all possible table join orders are considered.*

If the number of tables in the query is less than *optimizer_search_limit,* the
optimizer examines all possible table join combinations. The number of join orders
is the factorial value of the number of tables in the query. For example, a query
joining five tables would have 5! = 5 * 4 * 3 * 2 * 1 = 120 possible combinations
of table join orders. The number of possible evaluations is the factorial of the
optimizer_search_limit, so with the default value for *optimizer_search_limit*
of five, the cost-based optimizer will evaluate up to 120 table join orders.

The *optimizer_search_limit* and *optimizer_max_permutations* parameters work
together, and the optimizer will generate possible table join permutations until the
value specified by *optimizer_search_limit* or *optimizer_max_permutations* is exceeded.
When the optimizer stops evaluating table join combinations, it will choose
the combination with the lowest cost. For example, queries joining nine tables
together will exceed the *optimizer_search_limit* but still may spend expensive time
attempting to evaluate all 362,880 possible table join orders (nine factorial) until
the *optimizer_max_permutations* parameter has exceeded its default limit of
80,000 table join orders.

However, when tuning a SQL statement when you plan to use optimizer plan
stability to make the execution plan permanent, it is acceptable to temporarily set
the *optimizer_search_limit* up to the number of tables in your query, tune the query
by reordering the table names in the *where* clause, and then use the ordered hint
with stored outlines to make the change permanent.

NOTE
The use of the ordered *hint overrides
the* optimizer_search_limit *and* optimizer_
max_permutations *parameters. This is because
the* ordered *hint requests that the tables be joined
in the order that they appear in the* from *clause of
the query. The* ordered *hint is the way most SQL
tuning professionals disable table join evaluation,
once the optimal join order has been determined.*

The optimizer_max_permutations Parameter   The *optimizer_ max_ permutations* initialization parameter defines the upper boundary for the maximum number of permutations considered by the cost-based optimizer. Unfortunately, with large numbers of tables, the time spent evaluating a single permutation can be significantly greater than with fewer tables. This means that 50,000 permutations with a 15-way table join can take significantly longer than a query with an 8-way table join. The *optimizer_max_permutations* parameter is dependent on the *optimizer_ search_limit* initialization parameter, and the default value for optimizer_ max_ permutations is 80,000.

When determining the upper boundary for the number of query permutations to evaluate, the CBO uses the following rule: If the number of non–single row tables in a query is less than *optimizer_search_limit*+1, then the maximum number of permutations is the larger of

$$\frac{optimizer\_max\_permutations}{(number\,of\,possible\,start\,tables + 1)}$$

and

$$\frac{optimizer\_search\_\lim it\,factorial}{(number\,of\,possible\,start\,tables + 1)}$$

For example, if we are joining five tables, we get the following values:

$$\frac{Maximum\,permutations = 80,000\,/\,6 = 13,333}{Search\,Limit = 5!/\,6 = 120\,/\,6 = 20}$$

The larger of these values is 13,333, and this is the maximum number of permutations that will be considered by the optimizer. It should be readily apparent at this point that the CBO will be quite slow if it must evaluate 13,333 possible query permutations.

TIP
In your large data warehouse environment with n-way table joins, make sure you use optimizer plan stability to avoid the time-consuming parse phase. For new production queries, try setting the optimizer_max_permutations to a low value such as 500. For queries with more than six tables, the parse phase can take up to 20 minutes to evaluate more than 100,000 possible query permutations. The best advice is always to use stored outlines with data warehouse SQL queries to bypass the long parse times.

Even with a very high value of 80,000 allowed permutation evaluations, there is still a chance that the optimizer may stop before it has located the optimal join order for a large data warehouse query. Consider a 15-way table join with 15! or over one trillion (1,307,674,368,000) possible query permutations. By cutting off the maximum permutations at 80,000, we leave open a good chance that the optimizer will give up too early.

The following list is intended to indicate total permutations and what percentage 80,000 is of this number. This may give an idea of how accurate or not the evaluation of a particular plan may or may not be.

Number of tables (n)	Total number of possible permutations (n!)	Proportion of total represented by 80,000 permutations (80,000 / n! * 100)
1	1	Not Relevant
2	2	Not Relevant
3	6	Not Relevant
4	24	Not Relevant
5	120	Not Relevant
6	720	Not Relevant
7	5040	Not Relevant
8	40320	Not Relevant
9	362880	22%
10	3628800	2.2%
11	39916800	0.2%
12	479001600	0.016%
13	6226020800	0.001284%
14	87178291200	0.000092%
15	1307674368000	0.000006%

Clearly, there is a problem when submitting queries where the parse phase must evaluate over 80,000 possible permutations.

In the real world, most DBAs size down *optimizer_max_permutations* in their production environment and *always* use optimizer plan stability (stored outlines) to prevent time-consuming reparsing of the large n-way table joins. Once the best table join order has been found, you can make it permanent by manuallyspecifying the join order for the tables by adding the *ordered* hint to the query and saving the stored outline for the hinted query. See Chapter 13 for details on this procedure.

Before Oracle8*i* (8.1.7), the optimizer often did not make enough permutations to find the optimal table join order. A fix is created in Oracle8*i* (8.1.7) to change the algorithm used to choose the initial join orders in an attempt to improve the chance of finding the best plan. To enable the fix in 8.1.7, a new hidden initialization parameter called *_new_initial_join_orders=true* must be added to your *init.ora* file.

The push_join_predicate Parameter

Prior to Oracle8*i*, the *push_join_predicate* parameter is used when views participate in a table join. This parameter is obsolete starting with Oracle8*i*. It controls whether the optimizer will attempt to push join predicates into a view. Predicates can only be pushed if *push_join_predicate=true* and the prerequisites conditions are met. The view must contain one of the following conditions:

- A *group by* clause

- An aggregation function such as sum or avg

- A *select distinct* clause

- A *join* hint

Note that prior to Oracle8*i*, this feature is automatically enabled by setting the *optimizer_features_enable* parameter. In Oracle8*i* and beyond, *push_join_predicate* is the default behavior.

The optimizer_index_caching Parameter

The *optimizer_index_caching* parameter is a percentage parameter with valid values between zero and 100. This parameter lets you adjust the behavior of the cost-based optimizer to select nested loop joins more often or less often. The cost of executing a nested loop join where an index is used to access the inner table is highly dependent on the caching of that index in the buffer cache. The amount of index caching depends on factors, such as the load on the system and the block access patterns of different users, that the optimizer cannot predict. Of course, you may cache an index by placing the data block in the KEEP pool, thereby ensuring that the blocks are always cached.

Setting *optimizer_index_caching* to a higher percentage makes nested loop joins look less expensive to the optimizer, which will be more likely to pick nested loop joins over hash or sort merge joins.

The default value for the *optimizer_index_caching* parameter is 0, which gives the highest preference to hash joins and sort merge joins. Resetting this parameter can be very dangerous if you are not using stored outlines because it could change the execution plans for thousands of SQL statements. Also, because the cost-based optimizer will generally only invoke sort merge joins when there are no indexes on the joined tables, this parameter has the most effect on the invocation of hash joins.

Initialization Parameters Affecting CBO Behavior for Hash Joins

The hash join is one of the trickiest to implement because of the dependencies with the Oracle initialization parameters. Here is a brief summary of the hash join parameters. For more information on hash join hints, see Chapter 12, and for details on tuning hash joins, see Chapter 16.

The hash_area_size Parameter   The *hash_area_size* parameter specifies the maximum amount of memory, in bytes, to be used for the hash join. If this parameter is not set, its value defaults to twice the value of the *sort_area_size* parameter. Unlike many other initialization parameters that you cannot change without bouncing the database, *hash_area_size* is changed with the *alter session set hash_area_size=nnn* command.

The RAM for *hash_area_size* is allocated from the User Global Area (UGA) of a user process. For dedicated server connections, this is part of process memory (PGA). For multithreaded servers, the UGA is allocated from either the Shared Pool or the *large_pool*, if the *large_pool* is configured.

The *hash_area_size* is allocated for a process that executes a hash join, and it does not cause increased RAM consumption for queries that are not executing hash joins. As a general rule, the *hash_area_size* should be set to the size of the smaller table in the query, because the contents of this table will be hashed into the RAM region.

The hash_join_enabled Parameter

In Oracle7 and Oracle8, the *hash_join_enabled* parameter must be set to TRUE to invoke a hash join. In Oracle8*i* *hash_joined_enabled=true* is the default value.

The hash_multiblock_io_count Parameter

Because hash joins often read sequential blocks from the TEMP tablespace, the *hash_multiblock_io_count* parameter allows multiblock reads against the TEMP tablespace. It is advisable to set the NEXT extent size to greater than the value for *hash_multiblock_io_count* to reduce disk I/O. This is the same behavior we see when setting the *db_file_multiblock_read_count* parameter for data tablespaces, except that this applies only to the multiblock access of segments in the TEMP tablespace.

The star_transformation_enabled Parameter

The *star_transformation_enabled* parameter determines whether a cost-based query transformation will be applied to star queries. If set to TRUE, the optimizer will consider performing a cost-based query transformation on the n-way table join.

This parameter also relates to the *optimizer_search_limit* parameter, as this parameter must be LESS THAN the number of tables in the n-way table join in order for the optimizer to consider a star join. With the default value of five, only queries that join six or more tables are eligible for star optimization.

Also, star optimization requires that a fully concatenated index exist on the fact table. In other words, if you have a fact table with 10 dimension tables, you must have a single index on the fact table with all 10 foreign keys into the dimension tables.

The optimizer_feature_enable Parameter

The *optimizer_feature_enable* parameter is a meta-parameter set to the defaults for other initialization parameters. Introduced in Oracle 8.0.4, it is a generic parameter that is set to the current version of your database.

The value for *optimizer_feature_enable* is set for your release of Oracle (*optimizer_feature_enable =8.1.6),* and it will default to your database version for Oracle releases greater than 8.0.4. The *optimizer_feature_enable* is a meta-parameter that set the values of many other initialization parameters. When *optimizer_feature_enable* is set, the following initialization parameters are set to TRUE.

- b_tree_bitmap_plans

- complex_view_merging

- fast_full_scan_enabled

- push_join_predicate

Of course, you will always want these features, so it is best to leave this parameter at the existing setting.

Initialization Parameters That Affect CBO Index Behavior

Several initialization parameters control the way that the cost-based optimizer treats indexes.

The fast_full_scan_enabled Parameter

The *fast_full_scan_enabled* parameter is obsolete in Oracle8*i*, where it is the default behavior, but in releases prior to Oracle8*i*, it controls whether the optimizer will consider an index fast full scan when deriving the execution plan for your query. It is important to note that the *fast_full_scan_enabled* parameter does *not* disable the *index_ffs* hint but instead controls whether CBO will consider index fast full scans in the absence of any cost-based hints.

If you want to force a range scan rather than a fast full scan at the SQL statement level, you can use the *index_asc* and *index_desc* hints.

The optimizer_index_cost_adj Parameter

The *optimizer_index_cost_adj* parameter is an initialization parameter that can be very useful for SQL tuning. It is a numeric parameter with values from zero to 1,000 and a default value of 1,000. It can also be enabled at the session level by using the *alter session set optimizer_index_caching = nn* syntax. This parameter lets you tune the optimizer behavior for access path selection to be more or less index friendly, and it is very useful when you feel that the default behavior for the CBO favors full-table scans over index scans.

The default value is 1,000, and any value less than 1,000 makes the CBO view indexes less expensive. If you do not like the propensity of the CBO first_rows mode to favor full-table scans, you can lower the value of *optimizer_index_cost_adj* to 10, thereby telling the CBO to always favor index scans over full-table scans.

TIP
If you are having slow performance because the CBO first_rows mode is favoring too many full-table scans, you can reset the optimizer_index_cost_adj *parameter to immediately tune all of the SQL in your database to favor index scans over full-table scans. This is a "silver bullet" that can improve the performance of an entire database in cases where the database is OLTP and you have verified that the full-table scan costing is too low.*

Even in Oracle 8.1.7, the CBO sometimes falsely determines that the cost of full-table scan is less than the cost of an index access. The *optimizer_index_cost_adj* parameter is a great approach to whole-system SQL tuning, but you will need to evaluate the overall effect by slowly resetting the value down from 1,000 and observing the percentage of full-tale scans. You can also slowly bump down the value of *optimizer_index_cost_adj* when you bounce the database and then either use the *access.sql* scripts (see Chapter 9) or reexamine SQL from the STATSPACK *stats$sql_summary* table to see the net effect of index scans on the whole database.

Conclusion

This chapter has been concerned with the default behavior of the cost-based optimizer and has explored how the CBO handles complex table joins, subqueries, and complex Boolean expressions. We also investigated some important initialization parameters and showed how they affect the costing estimates for cost-based optimization.

The major points in this chapter include these:

- When using the CBO, you must make a philosophical choice between dynamic execution plans and static execution plans. This decision affects your use of stored outlines and how often you reanalyze CBO statistics.

- Oracle provides several CBO hints that can improve the choice of join methods.

- For data warehouse queries that join more than five tables, the *optimizer_max_permutations* parameter can be used to ensure that a query evaluates all possible table join combinations. After tuning, it is critical that these queries use stored outlines to avoid SQL parse times that can often exceed 30 minutes.

- You can change the default behavior of the CBO by adjusting numerous initialization parameters. This approach often allows you to establish a very fast baseline before starting the individual tuning of SQL statements.

- The CBO sometimes falsely determines that the cost of a full-table scan is less than the cost of an index access. The *optimizer_index_cost_adj* parameter will change the costing for index scans, making them more attractive.

Next, let's take a look at tuning with the rule-based optimizer and see how it can be used to tune SQL queries.

CHAPTER
15

Tuning with the
Rule-Based Optimizer

ver since Oracle first introduced the cost-based optimizer in Oracle7, tuning professionals have been struggling with coping with dual optimizer modes. While Oracle Corporation continued to recommend the cost-based optimizer, many SQL tuning professionals found that the rule-based optimizer often created the most efficient execution plans. In this author's experience, over 80 percent of Oracle7 databases used rule-based optimization. In Oracle8, this number dropped to about 60 percent, and in Oracle8*i* we see that about 40 percent of databases still find faster overall execution plans for their systems using rule-based execution (Figure 15-1).

Today we must make a decision between a predictable and stable rule-based optimizer or the intelligent and often unpredictable cost-based optimization. Even in Oracle8*i*, there are still conditions (especially n-way table joins) where the CBO fails to use all of the available indexes and performs an unnecessary full-table scan on a table. This is a well-known shortcoming of cost-based optimization, and many SQL tuning professionals will add a *first_rows* hint and lower the value of *optimizer_index_cost_adj,* thereby telling the CBO to always favor index scans over full-table scans. Others will simply code a *rule* hint to ensure that the proper indexes are being used to join the tables.

Regardless of the approach, tuning SQL for the rule-based optimizer is very different from tuning SQL with cost-based optimization. This chapter will cover the following topics:

- Invoking rule-based optimization

- The problem of using *choose* as the default optimizer mode

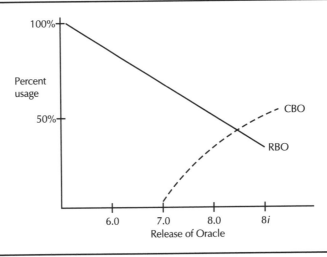

FIGURE 15-1.   *Relative use of default optimizer modes*

■ Using a rule-based optimizer mode as the database default

■ Tuning with the rule-based optimizer

Invoking Rule-Based Optimization

The RBO is very easy to invoke, and there are three ways to invoke the rule-based optimizer at the session or database level:

■ Setting the *init.ora* parameter *optimizer_mode=rule*

■ At the session level using *alter session set optimizer_goal=rule;*

■ Adding rule hints to cost-based SQL: */*+ rule */* or *--+ rule*

Of course, setting rule-based optimization is the easy part. The challenge is determining when to invoke rule-based optimization to improve the speed of your SQL query. Let's begin with a discussion of the *choose* optimizer mode and see how it flips between cost-based and rule-based optimization methods.

The Problem of Using Choose as the Default Mode

One of the most confounding problems with Oracle databases happens when they do not explicitly set their *optimizer_mode* parameter in their *init.ora* file. As you may know, when no *optimizer_mode* is specified, Oracle8*i* defaults to *optimizer_mode=choose.*

The *choose* default mode is very dangerous for several reasons. The choose mode evaluates whether to use the RBO or the CBO according to the presence or absence of CBO statistics. If statistics exist, then use the CBO; else use the RBO. The problem comes in when table and indexes are "accidentally" analyzed. For example, a DBA might want to know the average row length for a table and issue the analyze table command to populate the *avg_row_len* column in the DBA_TABLES view, not realizing that he or she has just changed the execution plans for dozens of SQL statements.

The real problem with the choose mode is that whenever *any* table or index contains statistics, the choose mode assumes that you want to use the CBO and uses internal statistics (such as the number of data blocks allocated to the tables) to estimate statistics for the other tables in the query. These estimates are quite poor and usually result in a suboptimal execution plan for the query. This statistics estimation is done during the parse phase of SQL execution, and the time required to gather statistics for the CBO can be very significant.

It is very common in shops that are new to Oracle and use the default *optimizer_mode=choose.* One of the first things that I look at when a shop complains of poor SQL response time is the default optimizer mode and the existence of complete statistics for the CBO. Most Oracle shops do not use *choose* as their default, and conduct a test of performance using each optimizer mode and settle upon a default of *rule, first_rows,* or *all_rows* as their default optimizer mode.

Using a Rule-Based Default Optimizer Mode

Some Oracle8*i* databases continue to use a rule-based default *(optimizer_mode=rule),* and the DBA tunes selected queries by adding cost-based hints and selectively analyzing tables and indexes. This allows the best of both worlds because the reliable and predictable rule-based optimizer is used for the simple SQL, while queries that required specialized access methods such as bitmap indexes or hash joins can still use cost-based optimization.

The choice about using a rule-based default is generally made by running the production database for one day in *rule* mode and another day in *first_rows* mode, and then choosing the appropriate default in accordance with performance feedback from end users and internal performance measurements from STATSPACK. The goal is to minimize the amount of manual SQL tuning by choosing a default optimizer mode with the best overall performance. This empirical approach ensures that a minimal number of SQL statements will have a sub-optimal execution plan.

One problem with the *first_rows* or *all_rows optimizer_mode* is that it forces all statements into CBO whether they have statistics or not. In the preceding scenario, the DBA should also make sure all indexes and tables are analyzed.

When using a rule-based default, you can still use all of the robust features of Oracle8*i*, including optimizer plan stability (stored outlines), cursor sharing, and the advanced cost-based hints. However, you always need to keep in mind the differences between cost-based and rule-based optimization. The driving table for cost-based optimization (when using the *ordered* hint) is the reverse of that for rule-based optimization, and rule-based queries are generally tuned by resequencing table names in the *from* clause and predicates in the *where* clause. Conversely, cost-based tuning relies on hints, CBO statistics, and the settings for numerous initialization parameters to determine the optimal table join order and overall execution plan.

The Driving Table Location Problem

It is a real problem in Oracle SQL that the driving table is reversed between the rule-based optimizer and the cost-based optimizer. In the RBO, the driving table is the *last* table in the *from* clause, while in the CBO the driving table is always determined by the CBO. In cases where the *ordered* hint is specified, Oracle will use the driving table as the *first* table in the *from* clause. As you will recall, the *ordered* hint is very useful for reducing the parse time of large n-way table joins by specifying the table join order.

This makes it very challenging for the SQL tuning professional who adds hints to SQL statements to specify the appropriate driving table. Some DBAs use the *num_rows* column of DBA_TABLES to get an idea of which table will be the best driving table, but the best way to determine the driving table is to look at the Boolean predicates in the *where* clause.

```
select /*+ rule */
    emp.ename,
    emp.deptno,
    bonus.comm
from
    emp,
    bonus
where
    emp.ename = bonus.ename
;
```

Note that the *bonus* table is the driving table because it appears last in the *from* clause. Let's explain this statement and observe the execution plan.

```
OPERATION
-------------------------------------------------------------------
OPTIONS                          OBJECT_NAME                POSITION
------------------------------   --------------------------  --------
  SELECT STATEMENT
  NESTED LOOPS
                                                                1
    TABLE ACCESS
FULL                             BONUS                          1
    TABLE ACCESS
BY INDEX ROWID                   EMP                            2
      INDEX
RANGE SCAN                       EMP_ENAME                      1
```

Now we reverse the table order, placing the *bonus* table first in the *from* clause.

```
select /*+ rule */
    emp.ename,
    emp.deptno,
    bonus.comm
from
    bonus,
    emp
```

```
where
    emp.ename = bonus.ename
;
```

Now when we reexecute the explain plan utility, we should see that the driving table has been reversed.

```
OPERATION
----------------------------------------------------------------------
OPTIONS                         OBJECT_NAME                  POSITION
----------------------------- --------------------------- ----------
  SELECT STATEMENT
  NESTED LOOPS
                                                                    1
    TABLE ACCESS
FULL                            EMP                                 1
    TABLE ACCESS
BY INDEX ROWID                  BONUS                               2
        INDEX
RANGE SCAN                      BONUS_ENAME                         1
```

Here you see that the driving table has changed, and this is clear evidence that the only factor influencing the driving table with the RBO is the position of the table name in the *where* clause.

The Driving Table and Table Cardinality

Remember, the driving table should be the table that *returns* the smallest number of rows, and this is not always the table with the smallest number of rows. Hence, you should evaluate each table independently and factor any filtering constraints into the *where* clause.

For example, assume we have a *customer* table with 100,000 rows and an *order* table with 500,000 rows.

```
select
    customer_name
from
    customer,
    order,
where
    customer.cust_nbr = order.cust_nbr
and
    order_status = 'backordered';
```

At first blush, it might appear that the *customer* table should be the driving table. However, if there are only 50,000 *order* rows that meet the *order_status='backordered'* criterion, then the *order* table should be made the driving table.

The driving table is important because it is retrieved first, and the rows from the second table are then merged into the result set from the first table. Therefore, it is essential that the second table return the least number of rows in terms of the *where* clause. Note that the driving table should be the table that returns the least number of rows, not always the table with the smallest value for *num_rows* in the DBA_ TABLES view.

With the rule-based optimizer, the indexing of tables, the order of table names in the *from* clause, and Boolean expressions within the SQL statement control the execution plan for the SQL. For the rule-based optimizer, consider the following query:

```
select /*+ rule */
    dname,
    sum(bonus.comm)
from
    emp,
    bonus,
    dept
where
    dept.deptno = emp.deptno
and
    emp.ename = bonus.ename
group by
    dname;
```

Here we expect that a single row will be returned for each department, but hundreds of *emp* and *bonus* rows may be scanned in order to compute the sum of all bonuses by department. Hence, we want the *dept* table to be the driving table for this query, and we have placed it last in the *from* clause.

```
OPERATION
------------------------------------------------------------------
OPTIONS                         OBJECT_NAME                POSITION
--------------------------  ---------------------------  ----------
  SELECT STATEMENT
   SORT
GROUP BY                                                          1
      NESTED LOOPS
                                                                  1
        NESTED LOOPS
                                                                  1
          TABLE ACCESS
FULL                            DEPT                              1
          TABLE ACCESS
BY INDEX ROWID                  EMP                               2
              INDEX
RANGE SCAN                      EMP_DEPTNO                        1
```

```
        TABLE ACCESS
BY INDEX ROWID                  BONUS                          2
        INDEX
RANGE SCAN                      BONUS_ENAME                    1
```

As you can see from this example, the placement of the table names in the *from* clause is critical to the execution plan and the speed of the query.

Tips for Tuning Rule-Based Queries

Unlike cost-based tuning, where your job is to add hints to change the execution plan, the job with the RBO is to rewrite the query to change the execution plan. Here are some tips for effective use of Oracle's rule-based optimizer:

- **Resequence table names** Try changing the order of the tables listed in the *from* clause to change the driving table. Joins should be driven from tables returning fewer rows rather than tables returning more rows. In other words, the table that returns the fewest rows should be listed *last*. This *usually* means that the table with the most rows is listed *first*. If the tables in the statement have indexes, the driving table is determined by the indexes. One Oracle developer recently cut SQL processing time in half by changing the order of the tables in the *from* clause! Another developer had a process shift from running for 5 hours to running in 30 minutes by changing the *from* clause.

- **Resequence Boolean predicates** Try changing the order of the statements in the *where* clause. Oracle parses the SQL from the bottom of the SQL statement in the reverse order with Boolean expressions separated by ANDs. Therefore, the most restrictive Boolean expression should be on the bottom.

- **Add cost-based hints** There are many cases in Oracle8*i* where you will want to override the rule-based default with the *first_rows* hint and analyze all tables and indexes that participate in the query. Remember, you can combine the *first_rows* hints with other cost hints to get exactly the fastest execution plan.

- **Carefully evaluate join methods** If you are using the RBO, you must settle for a nested loop join. Even though a sort merge join is available in the RBO, you should replace all RBO queries that perform sort merge joins with the cost-based equivalent that utilizes Oracle parallel query. In general, a merge join is the most efficient join when the query returns a large number of rows from both tables and you have multiple CPUs, because the sort merge join performs full-table scans against both tables. To use a sort merge join with the

RBO, add a *use_merge* hint combined with a *parallel* hint and be sure to analyze all tables and indexes that participate in the query.

TIP
Remember that the hash join is not available in the RBO. If you suspect your nested loop join will run faster with a hash join, analyze the involved table and indexes and add a use_hash *hint to your query.*

Next, let's take a close look at how the order of predicates in the *where* clause can affect the execution plan for rule-based Oracle SQL.

When the Rule-Based Optimizer Fails

There are cases in which the rule-based optimizer fails to choose an optimal execution plan. In Oracle8*i*, this is most often due to the inability of the RBO to use advanced index structures and parallel query. New features aside, we also see that the RBO will often choose a suboptimal index to service a query. This happens because the rule-based optimizer is not aware of the number of distinct values in tables and indexes but relies on simple heuristics to find an acceptable access path to the data.

Remember, in rule-based optimization, all indexes have an equal ranking. When items have an equal order, the row cache order is used to select the first index. When the RBO detects equally ranked objects, it chooses the first object that it comes to in the row cache. Be aware that row cache order cannot be externally controlled, as it is determined by a internal unpublished algorithm. It is possible that row cache order can be changed by modifying shared pool parameters, or by dropping and re-creating the objects, but this option is seldom as feasible as simply adding a hint and running the query again as a cost-based query.

When the Rule-Based Optimizer Is Best

As I have repeatedly noted, there are many times when the RBO will achieve a faster execution plan than cost-based optimization, especially in the earlier releases of Oracle8. To illustrate these differences, let's use the Oracle demo database for our example. For the following query, assume that we have built a nonunique B-tree index on both the *deptno* and *mgr* columns.

```
select /*+ rule */
    count(*)
from
    emp
where
    mgr = 7902
and
    deptno = 10
;
```

Now, let's take a look at the distribution of distinct values within the *deptno* and *mgr* columns.

```
SQL> select distinct deptno from emp;

    DEPTNO
----------
        10
        20
        30

SQL> select distinct mgr from emp;

       MGR
----------
      7566
      7698
      7782
      7788
      7839
      7902
```

Here you see that the *mgr* column has more than double the selectivity of the *deptno* column because it has far more unique values. We would expect that the most efficient way to service this query would be to use the AND_EQUAL access method, starting with the most selective index. Here is the rule-based execution plan for this query:

```
OPERATION
-----------------------------------------------------------------------
OPTIONS                       OBJECT_NAME                     POSITION
--------------------------    --------------------------    ----------
 SELECT STATEMENT
  SORT
 AGGREGATE                                                            1
     AND-EQUAL
```

```
1
      INDEX
RANGE SCAN                     EMP_MGR                      1
      INDEX
RANGE SCAN                     EMP_DEPTNO                   2
```

The rule-based optimization uses the AND-EQUAL access method to combine the ROWID lists from each index range scan to get only those ROWIDs that meet the selection criteria.

To see the difference between this method and cost-based optimization, here is the same query using the *first_rows* hint.

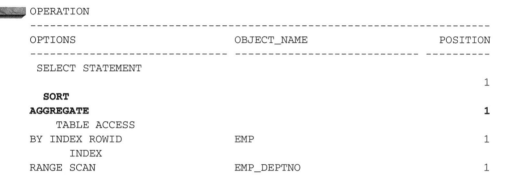

```
OPERATION
--------------------------------------------------------------------------
OPTIONS                        OBJECT_NAME                  POSITION
----------------------------   --------------------------   ----------
  SELECT STATEMENT
                                                            1
  SORT
AGGREGATE                                                   1
    TABLE ACCESS
BY INDEX ROWID                 EMP                          1
      INDEX
RANGE SCAN                     EMP_DEPTNO                   1
```

Unlike under rule-based optimization, the cost-based optimizer wants to perform an index range scan on the *deptno* index and then filter for the rows belonging to the specified *mgr* column. This could take a long time, especially if the tables are large.

NOTE
Remember that the rule-based optimizer does not recognize bitmap or function-based indexes. Adding a rule hint will cause full-table scans in cases where cost-based indexes are used to access the target table.

In sum, you need to pay careful attention to the indexes that are chosen by the rule-based optimizer, and either disable the indexes that you do not want to be used in the query or force the use of the index that you want. To review, indexes can be explicitly specified with the *index* hint, or unwanted indexes can be disabled by mixing data type on the index (i.e., *where numeric_column_value = 123||' '*).

Any perceived index change (whether it really affects the value or not) will defeat the index, so simply adding zero to a number or a null to a character should always disable index access.

Conclusion

The rule-based optimizer remains quite popular in Oracle8*i* despite the attempts by Oracle to improve cost-based optimization to the point where it always outperforms the RBO. The major points in this chapter include these:

- The RBO is very stable and predictable, while the CBO is more intelligent but often unpredictable.

- The number of databases using the RBO falls with each new release of the CBO, but there are still a significant number of databases using a rule-based optimizer default.

- Some shops use a cost-based optimizer default and override selected queries with the *rule* hint.

- Some shops use a rule-based default and tune SQL queries by adding cost-based hints and analyzing selected tables and indexes.

- In the RBO, the order of tables in the *from* clause determines the table join order. The last table in the *from* clause is the driving table, which should be the smallest table.

- The order of the Boolean predicates in the *where* clause can also affect the behavior of the RBO.

- Using *optimizer_mode=choose* can be very dangerous to performance if selected tables or indexes are analyzed.

- The most common error with the RBO is its inability to know the selectivity of each index on a table. Hence, the RBO sometimes uses a nonselective index to access a table.

Next, let's take a look at the single most complex of all SQL tuning operations, the optimization of table joins. If you can master the table join, you are well on your way to being a SQL tuning guru.

CHAPTER
16

Tuning Table Joins

able joins are the heart of SQL tuning and are one of the most complex areas of SQL tuning. When evaluating a table join, we must determine the optimal table join order and the most appropriate table join methods, all while ensuring that the query performs as fast as possible.

This chapter will cover the following topics relating to table joining:

- The table join types

- The basic table join methods

- Determining the optimal table join order

- Tuning distributed SQL joins

We will begin with a review of the basic SQL join types, move on to look at Oracle's implementation of join methods, and then take a look at how Oracle evaluates the table join order for multi-table joins. We will then cover distributed table joins in a net8 environment. Let's begin with a review of the basic table join types.

The Table Join Types

Before we dive into the complex tuning of Oracle table joins, let's begin with a brief review of the different types of table joins within ANSI standard SQL. We need to make the distinction between the theoretical types of SQL joins and the Oracle implementation of the join. In most cases they are somewhat similar, but in several cases the theoretical join type does not have a parallel within Oracle join methods. For example, an outer join has a very clear differentiation from an equi-join, but within Oracle, the nested loops table access plan can be used to drive either of these join types.

Here are the basic SQL join types. Once you understand these theoretical join types, we will move to look at Oracle implementation of these join structures.

- **Equi-join** This is a standard join that pairs the rows between two tables by matching the values in a common column between the two tables. The Oracle table access plan for equi-joins may include NESTED LOOPS, HASH JOIN, or MERGE.

- **Outer join** This is a join that preserves incomplete rows where a matching condition is not found in both tables. Oracle returns all rows that meet the join condition. Oracle also returns all rows from the table without the outer join operator for which there are no matching rows in the table with the outer join operator. Just like an equi-join, the outer join may invoke a NESTED LOOPS Oracle table access.

- **Self-join** This is a special case where a table is joined against itself. This is a common feature in bill-of-materials tables and time-based tables where values are compared over different time periods.

- **Anti-join** This is the type of join we normally see when we use a subquery with a NOT IN or a NOT EXISTS clause. The *anti-join* is normally evidenced by the TABLE ACCESS FULL table access method.

- **Semi-join** A *semi-join* returns rows that match a query with an *exists* clause, without duplicating rows from the left side of the predicate when multiple rows on the right side satisfy the criteria of the subquery. The execution plan most commonly associated with a semi-join is TABLE ACCESS FULL against the driving table and an INDEX RANGE SCAN against the joined table.

Now let's take a look at the details for each of these conceptual join methods. During our discussion, I will show some of the Oracle table access plans that relate to each method.

The Equi-Join

An *equi-join* is any SQL statement that references two or more tables, with an equality predicate in the *where* clause to specify the join condition for the tables (Figure 16-1).

The equi-join is the most common of all of the join types and therefore deserves a closer inspection. For example, what follows is an equi-join to display all employees and their bonuses:

```
select
    emp.ename,
    emp.deptno
    bonus.comm
from
    emp,
    bonus
where
```

FIGURE 16-1. *The SQL equi-join*

```
    emp.ename = bonus.ename
;
```

Here we see the output from this query. Note that the equi-join key (*ename* in this example) does not need to be displayed in the result set to serve as the join key.

```
ENAME          DEPTNO        COMM
----------  ----------  ----------
ALLEN              30          300
WARD               30          500
MARTIN             30         1400
```

The equi-join is the most straightforward of all of the relational join operators, and Oracle offers three join methods for equi-joins, the nested loop join method, the hash join method, and the sort merge join method.

The Outer Join

An *outer join* is a special case of a table join where unmatched columns from a table are still displayed in the output of the query (Figure 16-2).

The outer join is implemented by placing the *plus-sign* (+) operator in the equality predicate of the *where* clause. In the next example, we want to display all employees, not just those who received a bonus. Hence, we place the (+) outer join directive on the side of the equality that references the bonus table to indicate that we also want the nonmatching rows.

```
select
    emp.ename,
    emp.deptno,
    bonus.comm
from
    emp,
    bonus
```

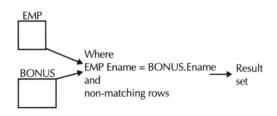

FIGURE 16-2. *An outer join*

```
where
    emp.ename = bonus.ename(+)
;
```

Let's examine the output from this query. As you can see, the (+) directive made
the Oracle SQL include *emp* rows, even where there was no matching row in the
bonus table.

ENAME	DEPTNO	COMM
ALLEN	30	300
WARD	30	500
MARTIN	30	1400
FORD	20	
SCOTT	20	
JAMES	30	
KING	10	
BLAKE	30	
MILLER	10	
TURNER	30	
CLARK	10	
JONES	20	
ADAMS	20	
SMITH	20	

This is the *first_rows* execution plan for this query. Note the use of the NESTED
LOOPS OUTER access method. We must also note that the SQL optimizer
understands that we want to see all of the rows in the *emp* table, and it has wisely
chosen a full-table scan because all of the rows are required.

OPERATION		
OPTIONS	OBJECT_NAME	POSITION
SELECT STATEMENT		
NESTED LOOPS		
OUTER		1
TABLE ACCESS		
FULL	EMP	1
TABLE ACCESS		
BY INDEX ROWID	BONUS	2
INDEX		
RANGE SCAN	**BONUS_ENAME**	1

In this case of an outer join, the RBO and the CBO will always generate an
identical table access method. The only difference is that the position of the tables
in the *where* clause will affect the choice of the driving table in the RBO, while the
CBO will generally use the table with the smallest value for *num_rows* as the
driving table.

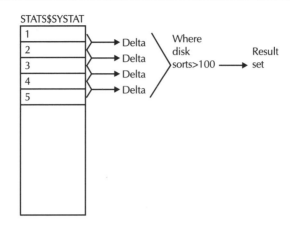

STATS$SYSTAT

FIGURE 16-3. *A self-join for a STATSPACK table*

The Self-Join

A *self-join* is a condition where a table is joined against itself. This is commonly done when you want to compare two time-based values within a table to see the differences between the two times (Figure 16-3).

The STATSPACK tables are an excellent example of time-based tables. Each snapshot has a date column, and you can write STATSPACK queries to compare values between STATSPACK snapshots. In the following example, we join the *stats$sysstat* table against itself to display times where we have more than 100 disk sorts per hour:

```
prompt
prompt
prompt  ************************************************************
prompt  When there are high disk sorts, you should investigate
prompt  increasing sort_area_size, or adding indexes to force
prompt  index_full scans.
prompt
prompt  ************************************************************


column sorts_memory  format 999,999,999
column sorts_disk    format 999,999,999
column ratio format .9999999999999

select
   to_char(snap_time,'dd Mon HH24:mi:ss') mydate,
```

```
      newmem.value-oldmem.value sorts_memory,
      newdsk.value-olddsk.value sorts_disk,
      (newdsk.value-olddsk.value)/(newmem.value-oldmem.value) ratio
from
      perfstat.stats$sysstat oldmem,
      perfstat.stats$sysstat newmem,
      perfstat.stats$sysstat newdsk,
      perfstat.stats$sysstat olddsk,
      perfstat.stats$snapshot   sn
where
-- Where there are more than 100 disk sorts per hour
      newdsk.value-olddsk.value > 100
and
      sn.snap_id = (select max(snap_id) from stats$snapshot)
and
      newdsk.snap_id = sn.snap_id
and
      olddsk.snap_id = sn.snap_id-1
and
      newmem.snap_id = sn.snap_id
and
      oldmem.snap_id = sn.snap_id-1
and
      oldmem.name = 'sorts (memory)'
and
      newmem.name = 'sorts (memory)'
and
      olddsk.name = 'sorts (disk)'
and
      newdsk.name = 'sorts (disk)'
;
```

This report is commonly used to show periods of high sort activity to alert the DBA to check the SQL in the *stats$sql_summary* table for the period of high disk sorts. Here is an actual sample from a production database.

TO_CHAR(SNAP_	SORTS_MEMORY	SORTS_DISK	RATIO
2001-04-09 09	60,404	141	.0023342824978
2001-04-09 14	23,520	251	.0106717687075
2001-04-09 15	17,980	402	.0223581757508
2001-04-10 11	26,451	149	.0056330573513
2001-04-10 14	36,313	2,794	.0769421419326
2001-04-10 16	17,995	132	.0073353709364
2001-04-11 13	22,057	177	.0080246633722
2001-04-11 15	20,274	170	.0083851238039
2001-04-12 14	21,540	2,056	.0954503249768

When joining a table against itself, Oracle normally invokes a nested loops access. Here is the execution plan for the self-join. Note the use of the NESTED LOOPS table access method for each self reference.

```
OPERATION
-----------------------------------------------------------------------
OPTIONS                        OBJECT_NAME                    POSITION
------------------------------ ------------------------------ ----------
SELECT STATEMENT
                                                              25
  NESTED LOOPS
                                                              1
    NESTED LOOPS
                                                              1
      NESTED LOOPS
                                                              1
        NESTED LOOPS
                                                              1
          TABLE ACCESS
BY INDEX ROWID                 STATS$SNAPSHOT                 1
            INDEX
RANGE SCAN                     STATS$SNAPSHOT_PK              1
              SORT
AGGREGATE                                                     1
              INDEX
FULL SCAN (MIN/MAX)            STATS$SNAPSHOT_PK              1
            TABLE ACCESS
BY INDEX ROWID                 STATS$SYSSTAT                  2
            INDEX
RANGE SCAN                     STATS$SYSSTAT_PK               1
          TABLE ACCESS
BY INDEX ROWID                 STATS$SYSSTAT                  2
            INDEX
RANGE SCAN                     STATS$SYSSTAT_PK               1
        TABLE ACCESS
BY INDEX ROWID                 STATS$SYSSTAT                  2
          INDEX
RANGE SCAN                     STATS$SYSSTAT_PK               1
      TABLE ACCESS
BY INDEX ROWID                 STATS$SYSSTAT                  2
        INDEX
RANGE SCAN                     STATS$SYSSTAT_PK               1
```

Despite the complex look of this execution plan, this query runs quite quickly. Also, note the relatively rare INDEX FULL SCAN (MIN/MAX) table access method. In this query, the (MIN/MAX) is used because we are scanning all snapshots within the *stats$snapshot* table.

Next, let's look at a special case of a table join where we use a noncorrelated subquery to filter the selection criteria for the main table. This type is query is known as the anti-join.

The Anti-Join

An *anti-join* operation is a case where we have a noncorrelated subquery with a NOT IN or NOT EXISTS clause. Essentially, an anti-join is a subquery where any rows found in the subquery are not included in the result set. An anti-join returns rows from the left side of the predicate for which there is no corresponding row on the right side of the predicate. That is, it returns rows that fail to match the subquery on the right side (Figure 16-4).

For example, an anti-join can select a list of employees who have not received a bonus.

```
select /*+ first_rows */
    ename,
    deptno
from
    emp
where
    ename NOT IN
    ( select
        ename
        from
        bonus
    )
;
```

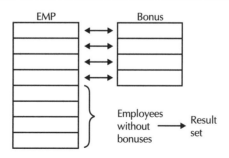

FIGURE 16-4. *An anti-join*

Here is the execution plan for this query. Note that the Oracle CBO recognizes that there is no *where* clause for the subquery and properly invokes a full-table scan because all of the rows in both tables are required to satisfy the query.

```
OPERATION
- - - - - - - - - - - - - - - - - - - - - - - - - - - - - - - - - - - - - - - - - - - - - - - -
OPTIONS                        OBJECT_NAME                 POSITION
- - - - - - - - - - - - - - - - - -   - - - - - - - - - - - - - - - - - - - - - -   - - - - - - - - - -
SELECT STATEMENT
  FILTER
                                                                  1
    TABLE ACCESS
FULL                           EMP                         1
    TABLE ACCESS
FULL                           BONUS                       2
```

Wow, two full-table scans. This would be a very time-consuming query if these were large tables. I mentioned in earlier chapters how the *not in* clause can sometime be replaced by a standard join. In the case of this query, we are interested in a display of those employees who have not received a bonus. We could use a standard join into the bonus table and then eliminate matching rows in the bonus table (i.e., where *comm* is not null). Let's try it:

```
select /*+ first_rows */
    emp.ename,
    emp.deptno
from
    emp,
    bonus
where
    emp.ename = bonus.ename(+)
and
    bonus.comm is null;
```

Here we do a standard outer join, so that we can use an index, and we then remove unwanted rows for the employees who have received a bonus.

```
OPERATION
- - - - - - - - - - - - - - - - - - - - - - - - - - - - - - - - - - - - - - - - - - - - - - - -
OPTIONS                        OBJECT_NAME                 POSITION
- - - - - - - - - - - - - - - - - -   - - - - - - - - - - - - - - - - - - - - - -   - - - - - - - - - -
SELECT STATEMENT
  FILTER
                                                                  1
    NESTED LOOPS
OUTER                                                      1
      TABLE ACCESS
```

FULL	EMP	1
TABLE ACCESS BY INDEX ROWID	BONUS	2
INDEX RANGE SCAN	BONUS_ENAME	1

Here we have greatly improved the overall speed of the query by replacing the NOT IN clause. The optimizer uses a nested loops algorithm for NOT IN subqueries by default, unless the *always_anti_join* initialization parameter is set to *merge* or *hash,* provided that all of the required conditions for merge and hash joins are met as explained in Chapter 12.

Table Anti-Join Hints

Let's take a look at some useful Oracle hints that can aid you in your quest to make anti-joins efficient. For details, see Chapter 12.

However, it is still a good idea to discourage general use of the NOT IN clause (which invokes a subquery) and to prefer NOT EXISTS (which invokes a correlated subquery), since the query returns no rows if *any* rows returned by the subquery contain null values.

The Merge Anti-Join

The *merge anti-join* is performed in a NOT IN subquery to perform an anti-join where full-table access is preferred over index access.

There is an alternative method for evaluating NOT IN subqueries that does not reevaluate the subquery once for each row in the outer query block and should be considered when the outer query block generates a large number of rows. This method can only be used when NOT NULL predicates exist on the subquery column and you have a hint in the subquery query block. The anti-join can be executed as either a *hash_aj* or a *merge_aj* hint depending on the desired join type.

CAUTION

The anti-join hints merge_aj *and* hash_aj *will only work if the column requested in the not in clause has a NOT NULL constraint.*

In sum, the *merge_aj* and *hash_aj* hints may dramatically improve the performance of *not in* subqueries, provided that the subquery column is NOT NULL. Next, let's take a look at how you can direct the Oracle optimizer to use a specific index.

The Semi-Join

A *semi-join* is an operation where the EXISTS clause is used with a subquery. It is called a semi-join because even if duplicate rows are returned in the subquery, only one set of matching values in the outer query is returned. In the case of the EXISTS clause, the subquery is executed, but even if the subquery returned multiple rows, the semi-join will not duplicate the value referenced in the outer query, as show in Figure 16-5.

This is an example of a correlated subquery because the EXISTS references the outer table in the *where* clause. Here we display the names of all departments who have employees who earned more than a $5,000 commission. This is a semi-join because even though the subquery may return many rows for each employee with more than $5,000 in commissions, only one department name will be displayed.

```
select /*+ first_rows */
    dname
from
    dept
where
    exists
    (select
        *
    from
        emp
    where
        dept.deptno = emp.deptno
    and
        emp.comm > 5000
    )
;
```

When you examine this query, it is clear that even though there may be many employees in each department with $5,000 commissions, only one match is required to display the department name. Of course, if we have an index on the

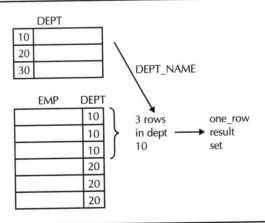

FIGURE 16-5. *A semi-join*

comm column, then a semi-join would not be necessary, because the query could filter all *emp* rows where *comm* > 5000 and then probe into the *dept* table for the names of employees in those departments. If there is no index on the *comm* column in *emp,* then a semi-join can be used to improve query performance.

As you may remember from previous chapters, the CBO always invokes a NESTED LOOPS table access method for all queries with EXISTS clauses when an index is available on both columns (*comm* and *deptno* in this example). However, since we have no index on *comm,* we see the following semi-join plan.

```
OPERATION
------------------------------------------------------------------
OPTIONS                         OBJECT_NAME              POSITION
------------------------------- ------------------------- ----------
  SELECT STATEMENT
                                                                1
    FILTER
                                                                1
      TABLE ACCESS
FULL                            DEPT                          1
      TABLE ACCESS
BY INDEX ROWID                  EMP                           2
        INDEX
RANGE SCAN                      EMP_DEPTNO                    1
```

This makes sense for a semi-join because the query only has the *deptno* index available, and the entire join set must be filtered for those rows where *comm* is greater than $5,000. Next, let's see how the inefficient nature of semi-joins makes them candidates for replacement with equi-joins using the *select distinct* clause.

Alternative Representation for Semi-Joins

If you examined the query carefully, you may notice that it could be rewritten as a standard equi-join. The trick is to eliminate the duplicate rows in the department name, and we can do this in a standard join by specifying the *select distinct* clause. As you may remember from previous chapters, the *distinct* clause invokes a sort to eliminate the duplicate rows from the result set. Here is the rewritten query with an equi-join:

```
select distinct /*+ first_rows */
   dname
from
   dept,
   emp
where
   dept.deptno = emp.deptno
and
   emp.comm > 5000
;
```

Now, look carefully at the new execution plan where there is no index on the *comm* column. Here we see a hash join, with full-table scans being executed against both tables. The presence of the full-table scans indicates that this may not be the fastest execution plan if the query is accessing large tables.

```
OPERATION
-------------------------------------------------------------------
OPTIONS                         OBJECT_NAME                 POSITION
---------------------------     ---------------------------  ----------

 SELECT STATEMENT
                                                                    6

  SORT
UNIQUE                                                              1
     HASH JOIN
                                                                    1

     TABLE ACCESS
FULL                            EMP                                 1
     TABLE ACCESS
FULL                            DEPT                                2
```

This execution plan should raise immediate suspicion because the query is serviced by performing a full-table scan against the *emp* table, and then performing another full-table scan on the *dept* table.

With an index on the *comm* column, we see a very different execution plan because full-table scans are no longer required.

```
OPERATION
-------------------------------------------------------------------
OPTIONS                         OBJECT_NAME                 POSITION
---------------------------     ---------------------------  ----------

 SELECT STATEMENT
                                                                    6

  SORT
UNIQUE                                                              1
     HASH JOIN
                                                                    1

     TABLE ACCESS
BY INDEX ROWID                  EMP                                 1
        INDEX
RANGE SCAN                      EMP_COMM                            1
     TABLE ACCESS
FULL                            DEPT                                2
```

Here you see the HASH JOIN table access method, with the department table acting as the driving table.

TIP
You can usually avoid a semi-join by ensuring that a column index exists on all relevant predicates in the where *clauses of both the outer and inner queries. Also, you can often replace a subquery with the* exists *clause, replacing it with a standard equi-join using the* SELECT DISTINCT *clause.*

Next, let's move away from the theoretical join types and take a look at Oracle implementation of table joining.

Oracle Table Join Methods

Now that you understand the conceptual join methods, let's look at how Oracle joins the tables together. As you will recall from previous chapters, Oracle provides the following methods for joining tables:

- Nested loop
- Sort merge joins
- Hash joins
- Star joins

Oracle also provides parallel partition join methods that are fully described in Chapter 21. The relative performance of these join types as a function of the number of rows in the tables is represented in Figure 16-6.

Of course, Figure 16-6 is a bit misleading because under certain circumstances, each of these join methods may be the fastest for your query. For example, a join where one table is very small will generally be fastest with a hash join, while a join of two very large tables is generally fastest with a nested loop join. Let's take a close look at each method and understand how they work.

Nested Loop Joins

The nested loop join is the oldest and most basic of the table join methods. In a nested loop join, rows are accessed from a driving table (using either TABLE ACCESS FULL or INDEX RANGE SCAN), and then this result set is nested within a probe of the second table, normally using an INDEX RANGE SCAN method.

In Oracle6, there were only two table join methods, the nested loops and the sort merge. Now in Oracle8*i* we have added a hash join and star joins to our list of

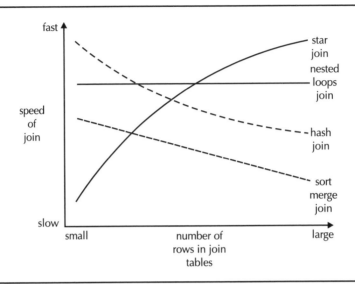

FIGURE 16-6. *The relative speeds of different Oracle join methods*

possible table join mechanisms. The nested loops method works by comparing each key in the outer table to each key in the inner table. There are several subtypes of nested loop joins, which we will examine later in this chapter.

Let's begin by looking at a case where only one of the joined tables possesses an index. This may dramatically increase the overall *cost* because of the exponential growth of the nested loops strategy. In fact, this path will be considered only if at least one support index is present in the joining tables.

Another permutation of nested loops works when both tables possess a selective index. If multiple indexes are present, Oracle will choose the index access for the table (inner table) with the most selective index.

TIP

When performing a nested loop join with incomplete indexes, the SQL optimizer will always make the driving table the table that does not possess an index on the join key.

Under the CBO, the nested loops method takes advantage of differences in table size. The smaller table will generally be chosen as the driving table for the nested loop join. If you are invoking nested loops with the RBO, then you will want to place the smallest table as the last table in the *from* clause to ensure that the smallest table is used to drive the nested loop query.

To start, consider this query that performs a standard equi-join against two tables.

```
select /*+ rule */
    ename,
    dname
from
    emp,
    dept
where
    emp.deptno = dept.deptno;
```

Here we see that the query will select all employees and we have a *rule* hint, so we have properly specified the *dept* table as the last table in the *from* clause to make *dept* the driving table. When reading the execution plan for a nested loop join, the driving table will be the first table displayed after the NESTED LOOPS table access method.

```
OPERATION
---------------------------------------------------------------------
OPTIONS                          OBJECT_NAME              POSITION
----------------------------- -------------------------- ----------
  SELECT STATEMENT
  NESTED LOOPS
                                                                 1
    TABLE ACCESS
FULL                            DEPT                             1
      TABLE ACCESS
BY INDEX ROWID                  EMP                              2
        INDEX
RANGE SCAN                      EMP_DEPTNO                       1
```

As we expected, the nested loop join uses the *dept* table as the driving table.

Now, let's change the query to add a constraint on the *emp* rows, only selecting those employees in department 10.

```
select /*+ rule */
    ename,
    dname
from
    dept,
    emp
where
    emp.deptno = dept.deptno
    and
    emp.deptno = 10
;
```

Here we see the change to the table access using the RBO with an index on *deptno* on both tables. We see that the nested loops access each table with an index range scan.

```
OPERATION
----------------------------------------------------------------------
OPTIONS                          OBJECT_NAME                 POSITION
----------------------------     -------------------------   ----------
SELECT STATEMENT
  NESTED LOOPS
                                                                  1

    TABLE ACCESS
BY INDEX ROWID                   EMP                             1
        INDEX
RANGE SCAN                       EMP_DEPTNO                      1
    TABLE ACCESS
BY INDEX ROWID                   DEPT                            2
        INDEX
RANGE SCAN                       DEPT_DEPTNO                     1
```

As you see, we are using rule-based optimization for this equi-join and the nested loops method takes full advantage of the available indexes.

Next, let's see how we can force a nested loop join with a hint.

The use_nl Hint

The *use_nl* hint forces a nested loop join against the target tables. Unlike the other join hints that specify both tables, the *use_nl* hint only requires the name of the driving table (the first table in the *from* clause when using the CBO with the ordered *hint*). The *use_nl* hint is seldom used in SQL tuning because both the CBO and the RBO tend to favor nested loop joins over hash or merge joins. However, the *use_nl* hint is sometimes useful for changing the driving table without changing the order of the tables in the *from* clause. This is because it is not always evident which table should be the driving table. Sometimes both tables have a comparable distribution of rows, and you can often improve the performance of a nested loop join by changing the driving table for the join. For more details on the *use_nl* hint, see Chapter 12.

The Hash Join

The *hash join* was first introduced in Oracle7.3 as an alternative to nested loop joins. The hash join technique improves the join speed of equi-joins by loading the driving table into RAM and using a hash technique to join into the second table.

A hash join is the recommended join method when the tables are different sizes and the smaller table is close to the available memory in *hash_area_size*. The basic premise of any hash join algorithm is to build an in-memory hash table from the smaller of the input row sources, the *build* input, and use the larger input to *probe* the hash table (Figure 16-7).

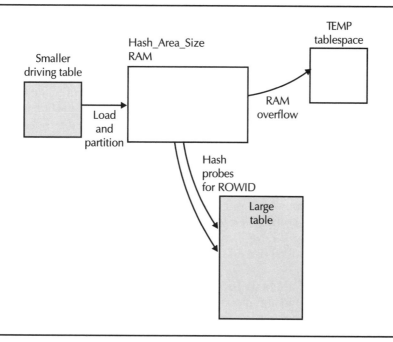

FIGURE 16-7.   *A hash join*

Hash join algorithms work well for simple hash joins when the available hash area memory is large enough to hold the build input, but it is not necessary to fit entire probe input in *hash_area_size* memory. If the smaller driving table in a hash join does not fit into *hash_area_size*, Oracle will partition the hash probes and use temporary segments in the TEMP tablespace to manage the overflow.

TIP
When the smaller driving table is small enough to fit entirely into the RAM allocated by hash_area_size, *then the hash join will generally perform faster than a nested loop join. Remember, you can adjust the* hash_area_size *for your query at the session level using the* alter session *command. Oracle recommends that the* hash_area_size *for the driving table be set at 1.6 times the sum of bytes for the driving table.*

Internally, a hash join involves two phases, the partition phase and the join phase. To fully understand hash joins, let's examine each of these phases.

The Partitioning Phase of a Hash Join

When the driving table cannot fit entirely into the RAM allocated by *hash_area_size,* a hash partition occurs. In a partition, contiguous pieces of the driving table are split into partitions on temporary segments in the TEMP tablespace (Figure 16-8).

This partitioning effectively divides the hash query into many smaller inputs that can be independently processed. However, the problem of partitioning the inputs is not trivial. It is difficult to have a partitioning scheme that will split any data distribution into equal partitions without any skew. To minimize any skew in the partitioning, Oracle relies on column histograms and special bit-vector filtering techniques.

If, after partitioning, the smaller of the two inputs is larger than the size of the memory available to build the hash table, the hash table overflow is dealt with by performing a *nested-loops hash join.* The hash table is created with the build input partition and then the probe phase joins the tables. Then, the remainder of the build input is iteratively retrieved, and the hash table is built and joined with all the probe partitions until all of the build input is consumed.

The Join Phase of a Hash Join

Partition pairs of the build and probe inputs with the same key values are then joined (in what is called the *join* phase). This algorithm, known as the *grace join,* dramatically reduces the search space and key comparisons required for doing the join.

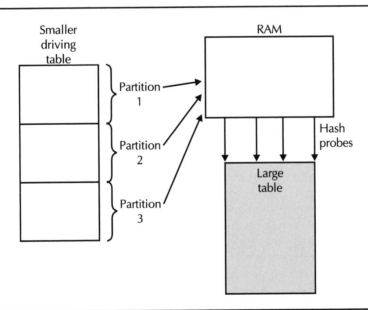

FIGURE 16-8. *Hash query partitioning*

A limitation of the hash join algorithm is that it is based on the assumption that the distribution of join values in the tables is not skewed and that each partition receives approximately the same number of rows.

The hash_area_size and Disk I/O

As we have demonstrated, the hash join is more memory intensive than a nested loop join. To be faster than a nested loop join, we must set the *hash_area_size* large enough to hold the entire hash table in memory (about 1.6 times the sum of the rows in the table). If the hash join overflows the *hash_area_size* memory, the hash join will page into the TEMP tablespace, severely degrading the performance of the hash join. You can use the following script, *hash_area.sql*, to dynamically allocate the proper *hash_area_size* for your SQL query in terms of the size of your target table.

hash_area.sql

```
set heading off;
set feedback off;
set verify off;
set pages 999;

spool run_hash.sql

select
   'alter session set hash_area_size='||trunc(sum(bytes)*1.6)||';'
from
   dba_segments
where
   segment_name = upper('&1');

spool off;

@run_hash
```

Here is the output from this script. As you see, we pass the driving table name, and the script generates the appropriate *alter session* command to ensure that we have enough space in *hash_area_size* RAM to hold the driving table.

```
SQL> @hash_area customer

alter session set hash_area_size=3774873;
```

In addition to seeing the *hash_area_size,* we must also be able to adjust the degree of parallelism in cases where we use a full-table scan to access the tables in a hash join. Let's take a look at how we can combine the *use_hash* and *parallel* hints to improve the performance of hash joins.

The use_hash Hint

The *use_hash* hint requests a hash join against the specified tables. The following query is an example of a query that has been hinted to force a hash join with parallel query:

```
select /*+ ordered use_hash(e,b) parallel(e, 4) parallel(b, 4) */
    e.ename,
    hiredate,
    b.comm
from
    bonus b,
    emp e
where
    e.ename = b.ename
;
```

Here is the execution plan for the hash join. Note that both tables in this join are using parallel query to obtain their rows.

```
OPERATION
-----------------------------------------------------------------
OPTIONS                          OBJECT_NAME                 POSITION
------------------------------   -------------------------   ----------
  SELECT STATEMENT
                                                                    3
    HASH JOIN
                                                                    1
PARALLEL_TO_SERIAL
      TABLE ACCESS
FULL                             BONUS                              1
PARALLEL_TO_PARALLEL
      TABLE ACCESS
FULL                             EMP                                2
```

Finally, we must enable Oracle to invoke the hash join. Since the CBO will naturally favor nested loop joins, we must reset some important parameters to enable hash joining.

Enabling Your Database to Accept the use_hash Hint

The *use_hash* hint is very finicky, and there are many conditions that must be satisfied. It is not uncommon to find that a *use_hash* hint is ignored, and here are some common causes of this problem.

■ **Check initialization parameters** Make sure that you have the proper settings for *optimizer_index_cost_adj* and *optimizer_max_permutations* to limit the number of table join evaluations. Also check your values for *hash_area_size* and *hash_multiblock_io_count.*

■ **Verify the driving Table** Make sure that the smaller table is the driving table (the first table in the *from* clause with the ordered *hint*). This is because a hash join builds the memory array using the driving table.

■ **Analyze CBO statistics** Check that tables and/or columns of the join tables are appropriately analyzed.

■ **Check for skewed columns** Histograms are recommended only for nonuniform column distributions. If necessary, you can override the join order chosen by the cost-based optimizer using the *ordered* hint.

■ **Check RAM region** Ensure that *hash_area_size* is large enough to hold the smaller table in memory. Otherwise, Oracle must write to the TEMP tablespace, slowing down the hash join. Oracle recommends that the *hash_area_size* for the driving table be set at 1.6 times the sum of bytes for the driving table, and you can use the *hash_area.sql* script to set the *hash_area_size* for your query session.

Next, let's take a look at one of the oldest table join methods, the sort merge join.

The Sort Merge Join

The *sort merge join* is among the simplest and oldest implementations of table joins. In a sort merge join, indexes are not used, and both tables are accessed via a full-table scan. Following the full-table scan, the result sets from each scan are independently sorted, and the sorted result sets are then merged to arrive at the query result set (Figure 16-9).

In general, a sort merge join is invoked only under the following circumstances:

■ When no useful indexes exist to join the table columns

■ When the query returns the majority of data blocks from both tables

■ When the CBO determines that a full-table scan is faster than an index access

As a general rule, the sort merge table access method is useful only in rare cases, such as large batch reports that return all of the rows in both tables. Otherwise, a nested loop or hash join is almost always more efficient.

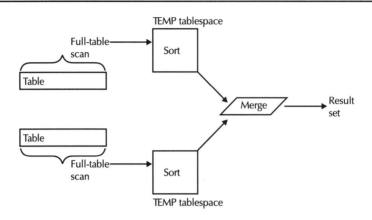

FIGURE 16-9. *A sort merge join*

Here is a rule-based query where no indexes exist on the *EMP* or *dept* tables:

```
select /*+ first_rows */
    ename,
    dname
from
    dept,
    emp
where
    emp.deptno = dept.deptno
and
    emp.deptno = 10
;
```

Now, we see the standard merge join with a full-table scan against both tables.

```
OPERATION
----------------------------------------------------------------------
OPTIONS                         OBJECT_NAME                 POSITION
----------------------------    -------------------------   ----------
 SELECT STATEMENT
  MERGE JOIN
                                                                    1

    SORT
JOIN                                                                1
      TABLE ACCESS
FULL                            EMP                                 1
    SORT
JOIN                                                                2
      TABLE ACCESS
FULL                            DEPT                                1
```

The Cartesian Merge Join

In a special case of the sort merge join, we see another dialect of the merge join that can use indexes to avoid the full-table scan. To illustrate, let's return to our earlier query and use the *first_rows* hint with no indexes on the *deptno* column.

```
OPERATION
----------------------------------------------------------------------
OPTIONS                             OBJECT_NAME                POSITION
-------------------------------     -------------------------  ---------
  SELECT STATEMENT
                                                                      3
    MERGE JOIN
  CARTESIAN                                                           1
      TABLE ACCESS
  FULL                              DEPT                              1
      SORT
  JOIN                                                                2
        TABLE ACCESS
  FULL                              EMP                               1
```

Here we see the sort merge join performing a full-table scan on both tables, and this is a requirement of the Cartesian merge join because it is normally invoked in cases where no join columns exist for the tables.

In the following example, we reexplain the query after adding indexes on *deptno* in both tables. We also have a small number of rows in both tables. Because both tables have a small number of rows, the CBO detects the low cardinality and invokes a sort merge join; it also uses both *deptno* indexes instead of a full-table scan.

```
OPERATION
----------------------------------------------------------------------
OPTIONS                             OBJECT_NAME                POSITION
-------------------------------     -------------------------  ---------
SELECT STATEMENT
                                                                      3
    MERGE JOIN
  CARTESIAN                                                           1
      TABLE ACCESS
  BY INDEX ROWID                    DEPT                              1
        INDEX
  RANGE SCAN                        DEPT_DEPTNO                       1
      SORT
  JOIN                                                                2
        TABLE ACCESS
  BY INDEX ROWID                    EMP                               1
          INDEX
  RANGE SCAN                        EMP_DEPTNO                        1
```

Next, let's look at how we can force a sort merge join with Oracle hints.

The use_merge Hint

The *use_merge* hint forces a sort merge operation. The sort merge operation is often used in conjunction with parallel query because a sort merge join always performs full-table scans against the tables. Sort merge joins are generally best for queries that produce very large result sets such as daily reports and table detail summary queries, or tables that do not possess indexes on the join keys. Here we see a simple query that has been formed to perform a sort merge using parallel query against both tables:

```
select /*+ use_merge(e,b) parallel(e, 4) parallel(b, 4) */
    e.ename,
    hiredate,
    b.comm
from
    emp e,
    bonus b
where
    e.ename = b.ename
;
```

Here is the output of the execution plan for this query. Note the full-table scans and the sort merge operation. Even though a join equality was specified in the *where* clause *(where e.ename = b.ename),* the use of the *parallel* hint told the Oracle optimizer to bypass indexes and invoke parallel full-table scans against both tables.

```
OPERATION
-------------------------------------------------------------------
OPTIONS                          OBJECT_NAME                 POSITION
-------------------------------- --------------------------- ----------
  SELECT STATEMENT
                                                                     5
   MERGE JOIN
                                                                     1
PARALLEL_TO_SERIAL
     SORT
JOIN                                                                 1
PARALLEL_COMBINED_WITH_PARENT
       TABLE ACCESS
FULL                             EMP                                 1
PARALLEL_TO_PARALLEL

     SORT
JOIN                                                                 2
PARALLEL_COMBINED_WITH_PARENT
       TABLE ACCESS
FULL                             BONUS                               1
PARALLEL_TO_PARALLEL
```

It is important to note that a sort merge join does not use indexes to join the tables. In most cases, index access is faster, but a sort merge join may be appropriate for a large table join without a *where* clause, or in queries that do not have indexes to join the tables.

TIP

Remember, there are limitations on the speed of Oracle parallel query. The benefit from a parallel query is heavily dependent on the number of CPUs on the database server and on the distribution of the target data files across multiple disks.

Now let's examine a special type of join that is used in Oracle data warehouse queries.

The Star Join

The *star join* has its roots firmly planted in data warehouse design. Dr. Ralph Kimball, founder of Red Brick Systems, popularized the term *star schema* to describe a denormalization process that simulates the structure of a multidimensional database. With a star schema, the designer can simulate the functions of a multidimensional database without having to purchase expensive third-party software. Dr. Kimball describes the denormalization process as the prejoining of tables, such that the run-time SQL application does not have to join the tables at execution time.

At the heart of the star schema is a *fact table,* a long and wide table that is usually composed entirely of key values and raw facts. A fact table is generally very long and wide and may have millions of rows. Surrounding the fact table are a series of dimension tables that serve to add value to the base information in the fact table. For example, consider the E/R model for a sales database shown in Figure 16-10.

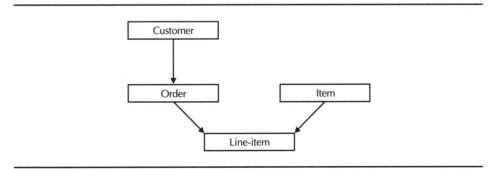

FIGURE 16-10. *An E/R model for a sales database*

Here we see a standard third normal form (3NF) database to represent the sale of items. No redundant information is provided in this design, and aggregated reports such as sales summaries would need to be displayed by joining many tables together.

Clearly, high volumes of queries that summarize information would benefit if we could prejoin the tables into a single table with redundant values. Here we have used the Create Table As Select (CTAS) syntax to de-normalize the third normal form table into a large fact table.

```
create table
    fact
as
select
    sale_date,
    region,
    state,
    salesman,
    product_nbr,
    product_type,
    product_color,
    quantity_sold
    sale_amount.
from
    order,
    item,
    customer
    line_item
where
    item.item_nbr = line_item.iten_nbr
and
    order.product_id = line_item.product_id
and
    customer_cust_nbr = order.cust_nbr;
```

Here we have selected the keys from all of the tables, and we have prejoined a fact table. In this case, the facts are *quantity_sold* and *sale_amount,* and all of the other information exists as keys into the dimension tables. For example, the *product_nbr* would be the key for the product dimension, and we would reference this key to join into the product table for additional details. For example, a data warehouse asking to summarize *sale_amount* by *product_shelf_life* would require a join from the fact table into the product table in order to get the *product_s helf_ life* column.

This massive denormalization of the database structure means that just about any query against the star schema is going to involve the joining of many large tables—including a large "fact" table and many smaller reference tables. Oracle has provided star query joins that employ a special procedure to improve performance of the query. Oracle does not require the use of a *star* hint to invoke a star join. All that is required is the proper index on the fact table, and the Oracle cost-based optimizer will invoke the star join. However, the *star* hint is still allowed in the SQL syntax and is generally a good idea for documentation purposes. Prior to Oracle8*i*, the star query requires that a single concatenated index resides in the fact table for all keys, but this was changed to bitmap indexes in Oracle8*i*.

Requirements for a Star Join

The star join is far faster than the traditional method of joining the smallest reference table against the fact table and then joining each of the other reference tables against the intermediate table. To invoke the star join, the following prerequisites must be present:

- There must be at least three tables being joined, one large fact table and several smaller dimension tables.

- Up until Oracle8, there must be a concatenated index on the fact table with at least three columns, one for each of the table join keys. Starting with Oracle8*i*, bitmap index structures may also be used.

- You must verify with an explain plan that the NESTED LOOPS table access operation is being used to perform the join.

Oracle follows a different procedure for processing star queries, depending on your Oracle version.

Pre-Oracle8i star join execution   As we noted, prior to Oracle8*i* you must have a concatenated index on all columns of the fact table. During the *star* join, Oracle will first service the queries against the smaller dimension tables, combining the result set into a Cartesian product table that is held in Oracle memory. This virtual table will contain all of the columns from all of the participating dimension tables. The primary key for this virtual table will be a composite of all of the keys for the dimension tables. If this key matches the composite index on the fact table, then the query will be able to process very quickly. Once the sum of the reference tables has been addressed, Oracle will perform a nested loop join of the intermediate table against the fact table.

Oracle8i parallel bitmap star join execution   In Oracle8*i*, bitmap indexes are required for all join columns on the fact table, and Oracle8*i* will initially use these bitmap indexes as a path to the fact table. The SQL optimizer will then re-write the original query, replacing the equi-join criteria with sub-queries using the IN clause.

These sub-queries are used as sources of keys to drive the bitmap index accesses, using bitmap key iteration to access the dimension tables. Once the resulting bitmap-ROWID lists are retrieved, Oracle will use a hash join to merge the result sets.

To see how the Oracle SQL optimizer transforms a star query, consider the following query where we sum the sales by region for all southern regions during the months of March and April:

```
select
    store.region,
    time.month,
    sum(sales.sales_amount)
from
    sales,
    store,
    time,
    product
where
    sales.store_key = store.store_key
and
    sales.month = time.month
and
    store.region = `south'
 and
    time.month in (`01-03', `01-04')
group by
    store.region, time.month
;
```

The star optimizer replaces the *where* clauses as follows. Note that the equi-join criterion is replaced by a sub-query using the IN clause.

Region clause before star transformation:

```
    where
        store.region = `south'
    and
        sales.store_key = store.store_key
```

Region clause after star transformation:

```
    where
        sales.store_key in (select store_key from store
                                where region = `south')
```

We see a similar transformation in the join into the time table:

Month clause before star transformation:

```
where
    sales.month = time.month
and
    time.month in (`01-03', `01-04')
```

Month clause after star transformation:

```
where
    sales.month in (select month from time
                where month in (`01-03', `01-04'))
```

As we see, the query is significantly transformed, replacing all *where* clause entries for the dimension table with a single sub-select statement. These IN sub-queries are ideal for the use of bitmap indexes because the bitmap can quickly scan the low-cardinality columns in the bitmap and produce a ROWID list of rows with matching values.

This approach is far faster than the traditional method of joining the smallest reference table against the fact table and then joining each of the other reference tables against the intermediate table. The speed is a result of reducing the physical I/O. The indexes are read to gather the virtual table in memory, and the fact table will not be accessed until the virtual index has everything it requires to go directly to the requested rows via the composite index on the fact table (Figure 16-11).

Starting with Oracle8*i*, the requirement for a concatenated index has changed, and the STAR hint requires bitmap indexes. The bitmap indexes can be joined more efficiently than a concatenated index, and they provide a faster result.

As I have noted, the star query can be very tricky to implement, and careful consideration must be given to the proper placement of indexes. Each dimension table must have an index on the join key, and in Oracle7 and Oracle8, the large fact table must have a composite index consisting of all of the join keys from all of the dimension tables, while in Oracle8*i* you need bitmap indexes on the fact table. In addition, the sequencing of the keys in the fact table composite index must be in the correct order, or Oracle will not be able to use the index to service the query.

Next, let's move on and look at some other important issues surrounding Oracle table joins. As I have noted in earlier chapters, Oracle must go to a great deal of work during the parse phase of a query to determine the optimal table join order when many tables are being joined.

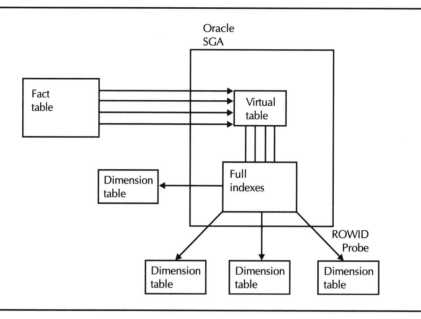

FIGURE 16-11. *Oracle star query processing*

Evaluating Table Join Order

One of the most time-consuming phases of SQL parsing is determining the join order for large n-way table joins. For example, in a 7-way table join, Oracle must evaluate 7! possible table join combinations. Seven factorial is 7*6*5*4*3*2*1 = 5,040 possible table join combinations. It is no wonder that the CBO can often take an entire hour to evaluate the join combinations for large n-way table joins.

When evaluating table join orders, the CBO builds a decision tree (Figure 16-12). For each possible table join combination, Oracle estimates the cost from the CBO statistics.

Once the CBO has completed all permutations (or *optimizer_max_permutations* is exceeded), Oracle will choose the table join orders with the lowest estimated cost.

Of course, the solution is to manually tune the query and resequence the table names in the *from* clause and use the *ordered* hint to direct the CBO to join the tables in the order specified in the *from* clause. If you cannot alter the source code for the SQL because it is being generated from a dynamic SQL generator, you can create a stored outline to join the tables in the fastest order and completely bypass the parsing process. For details on using optimizer plan stability (stored outlines), see Chapter 13.

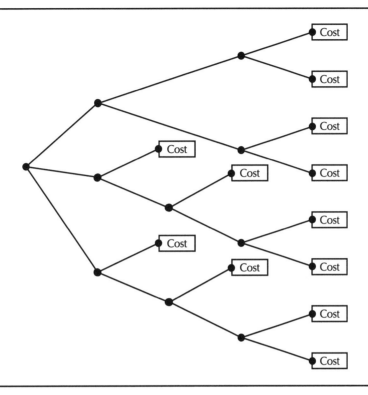

FIGURE 16-12.   *A CBO decision tree for table join ordering*

You can also tweak the *optimizer_max_permutations* parameter to limit the amount of time spent evaluating table join orders, and you can get details on this procedure in Chapter 12. In general, you should manually determine the join order from the size of the result sets from each table.

Tuning Distributed SQL Table Joins

With Oracle databases commonly being distributed across the globe, there are some important considerations regarding table joins for distributed queries. There are two permutations of distributed joins:

■ **Remote-to-remote join**   This is a case where both remote tables reside at the remote site and are joined at the remote site. For these remote joins, you should create a view on the remote database that specifies the join, thereby forcing the remote site to be the driving site for the table join (Figure 16-13).

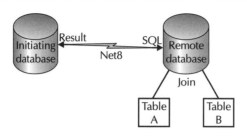

FIGURE 16-13. *A remote-to-remote table join*

■ **Remote-to-local join** This is a case where one table resides locally and the other table resides at a remote site. For this class of queries, we always use the CBO and carefully ensure that an unnecessary full-table scan is not being performed at the remote site. This is most commonly done by ensuring that an index exists on the join column and verifying the execution plan by explaining the subquery on the remote site (Figure 16-14).

To illustrate a distributed join, consider the following query that joins a local table to a remote table using an equi-join condition in the *where* clause:

```
select
    customer_name,
    order_nbr
from
    customer,
    order@new_york
where
    customer.customer_nbr = order.customer_nbr
and
    customer_nbr = :var1
order by
    customer_name,
    order_nbr;
```

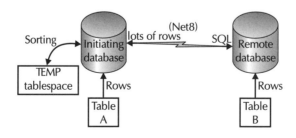

FIGURE 16-14. *A remote-to-local table join*

Here we join a local customer table with a remote table using Net8 and a database link to reference the remote table. Of course, the local database will not be aware of the statistics or dictionary information on the remote table, and we also have the issue of sorting the result set.

In a distributed SQL query, the rows are fetched from the remote database and sorted on the Oracle database that initiated the request. Hence, you may see severe impact on the local TEMP tablespace when many remote queries are issued. You can often circumvent this sorting issue by forcing access against the remote table with an *index* hint.

Always Use the CBO for Distributed Joins

The rule-based optimizer has severe limitations for distributed joins primarily because it does not have information about indexes for remote tables. Therefore, the RBO commonly generates a nested loop join between a local table and a remote table with the local table as the outer table in the join. The RBO uses either a nested loop join with the remote table as the outer table or a sort merge join, depending on the indexes available for the local table.

Remember, the cost-based optimizer can consider more execution plans than the rule-based optimizer. For example, the cost-based optimizer knows whether indexes on remote tables are available and in which cases it makes sense to remote indexes. In addition, the cost-based optimizer considers index access of the remote tables as well as full-table scans, whereas the rule-based optimizer considers only full-table scans.

Viewing the Execution Plan for Distributed Joins

Oracle provides a script to display the execution plan for a remote query. You should note that Oracle uses the *other* column in *plan_table* to hold the remote join information. The *remote_plan.sql* script is used on the initiating database, but you must then extract the remote query and reexplain it on the remote database.

remote_plan.sql

```
set long 2000
set arraysize 1

col operation    format a22
col options      format a8
col object_name  format a10
col object_node  format a5
col other        format a20
col position     format 99999
col optimizer    format a10

select lpad(' ',2*(level-1))||operation operation,options,object_name,
```

```
optimizer,object_node,other
from plan_table
start with id=0 and statement_id='A'
connect by prior id=parent_id and statement_id='A';
set echo on
```

To see how *remote_plan.sql* differs from a standard remote join, consider the following distributed query:

```
select
    e.empno,
    e.ename,
    d.dname,
    l.loc,
    d.deptno
from
    emp@new_york   e,
    dept@san_fran d,
    location      l
where
    d.deptno = e.deptno
and
    d.loc = l.loc
and
    e.empno = 1234;
```

Here is the execution plan from this SQL statement using *remote_plan.sql.*

OPERATION	OPTIONS	OBJECT_NAM	OPTIMIZER	OBJEC	OTHER
SELECT STATEMENT			CHOOSE		
NESTED LOOPS					
NESTED LOOPS					
REMOTE					ROSE. SELECT "EMPNO","ENAM WORLD E","DEPTNO" FROM "EMP" E WHERE "EMPNO"=1234
REMOTE					ROSE. SELECT "DEPTNO","DNA WORLD ME","LOC" FROM "DEPT " D WHERE "DEPTNO"=: 1
TABLE ACCESS	FULL	LOCATION	ANALYZED		

With remote tables, the row with the REMOTE table access method stores the SQL sent the remote node in the *other* column of the *remote_plan.sql* output. It is important to note that we can only see the SQL being transmitted to the remote site and we are not told how the SQL will be executed at the remote site. The solution is to log onto the remote database and evaluate the execution plan on the remote server.

Next, let's review some very important guidelines for tuning distributed SQL joins.

Tuning Guidelines for Distributed Joins

Here is a set of guidelines that is used by SQL tuning experts for tuning distributed joins:

- The overall goal of tuning a distributed join is to minimize the amount of data being transferred across Net8. If possible, consider using advanced replication to replicate the table to the local site to improve join speed.

- The SQL that is passed to the remote instance is available in the *other* column of the plan table. Hence, you can use the enhanced *explain plan* utility *remote_plan.sql* to tune distributed joins. You also must explain the SQL portions on the remote database to get the whole picture.

- The local table should *always* be the driving table for a remote join. Oracle provides the *driving_site* hint for this purpose. The *driving_site* hint tells Oracle to make the site where the referenced table resides the driving site. You want the driving site to be the one that has the larger amount of data, so that the smaller amount of data will be passed over the network.

- For tables that join more than four tables, the parse time to determine the table join order can be excessive because n! table join methods must be evaluated. Joins of more than four tables should be manually tuned for optimal table join order and made permanent by using the *ordered* hint or stored outlines. The use of the *ordered* hint or stored outlines will cause the optimizer to skip the time-consuming table join evaluation, improving overall performance.

- For cases where both tables reside at a remote database, you can force execution to be at the driving site by converting the distributed join into a view that you define at the remote instance and then query from your local instance.

- When the amount of data to be retrieved from the remote instance is small in relation to the local table total size, then converting the join to a correlated subquery can improve performance.

- The entire SQL is not passed to the remote instance; only the remote portion of the query is passed. Since Oracle only sends the piece of the query to the remote site, the remote site is not aware of the full SQL join. Hence, each CBO executes independently of the others in a distributed query.

■ Always verify that the index column for the join condition exists as an index on the remote site. It is very common in untuned distributed joins to see remote table access being performed with a full-table scan.

■ Always use the CBO for distributed queries. The rule-based optimizer cannot generate nested loop joins between remote and local tables when the tables are joined with equi-joins. More importantly, the RBO cannot execute joins remotely, and all joins must be executed at the driving site. This means that Oracle must fetch the rows across Net8 before beginning the join.

■ All sorting of result sets is performed at the initiating database. This can cause a huge impact on the TEMP tablespace, so it is very important to minimize network traffic for incoming result sets from the remote database.

In addition to these guidelines, Oracle has other important limitations on distributed joins:

■ In the CBO, no more than 20 indexes per remote table are considered when generating query plans. The order of the indexes varies; if the 20-index limitation is exceeded, then random variation in query plans can result.

■ Reverse indexes on remote tables are not visible to the optimizer. This can prevent nested loop joins from being used for remote tables if there is an equi-join using a column with only a reverse index.

■ The CBO cannot recognize that a remote object is partitioned. Thus, the optimizer can generate less than optimal plans for remote partitioned objects, particularly when partition pruning would have been possible had the object been local.

■ Remote views are not merged, and the optimizer has no statistics for them. It is best to replicate all mergeable views at all sites to obtain good query plans.

Conclusion

This chapter has been a basic review of the table joins methods and the issues surrounding the optimization of table join operations. The main points of this chapter include these:

■ The RBO can only invoke a sort merge join or a nested loop join. Advanced join methods such as hash joins and star joins are only available to the CBO.

■ A self-join is a common operation against tables where the rows are stored in time series order and you need to compare values between time slices. These queries use a nested loops access method and utilize the column index.

■ Anti-joins subqueries (i.e. subqueries with a *not in* clause) can sometime be replaced by a standard equi-join where you remove the extra values with a *where column is not null* clause.

■ A semi-join subquery (i.e. a subquery with an *exists* clause) can often be rewritten as a standard equi-join using a *select distinct* clause to remove duplicate rows.

■ The hash join can outperform the nested loop join if the driving table is small and fits entirely into the *hash_area_size* RAM region. You can use the *hash_area.sql* script to dynamically generate the *alter session* command to resize your *hash_area_size* for a particular query.

■ The CBO should always be used for remote table joins because the RBO cannot access remote dictionary values.

■ Remote table joins can be explained with the *remote_plan.sql* script, and you must also explain the SQL on the remote database to fully understand the whole execution plan.

■ The goal of tuning a distributed table join is to minimize the amount of data transported over the network.

Next, let's move on and take a look at tuning Oracle DML operations. While DML is relatively straightforward, there are some important tuning mechanisms for improving the performance of DML.

PART
III

Advanced SQL Tuning

CHAPTER
17

Tuning SQL DML
Statements

his chapter is concerned with the tuning of SQL statements that perform data manipulation. Known as data manipulation language, or DML, these are special types of SQL statements that perform update, insert, and delete operations. Unlike standard SQL select statements, DML performance is heavily influenced by the internal Oracle storage parameters, and understanding the relationship between DML and object parameters will be the primary focus of this chapter.

With only a few hints available for DML tuning (such as the *append* hint), the focus of this chapter is on how you can adjust the way you perform DML operations to minimize Oracle overhead. The topics in this chapter include:

- Oracle storage parameters and DML performance

- Freelists and DML performance

- Long data columns and DML behavior

- Setting PCTFREE and PCTUSED according to average row length

- Buffer busy waits and DML contention

- Reducing index overhead with DML operations

Oracle Storage Parameters and DML Performance

Let's begin by making it clear that the SQL insert, update and delete statements are very simple in nature, and by their structure, offer few opportunities for SQL tuning. SQL inserts, for example, only process a single row at a time, and contain no *where* clause.

The largest opportunity for tuning Oracle DML is to exploit the relationship between object storage parameters and SQL performance. Poor SQL performance within Oracle DML is experienced in several areas:

- **Slow inserts**   Insert operations run slowly and have excessive I/O. This happens when blocks on the freelist only have room for a few rows before Oracle is forced to grab another free block.

- **Slow updates**   Update statements run very slowly with double the amount of I/O. This happens when SQL *update* operations expand a VARCHAR or BLOB column and Oracle is forced to chain the row contents onto additional data blocks.

■ **Slow deletes**   Large SQL *delete* statements can run slowly and cause segment header contention. This happens when rows are deleted and Oracle must relink the data block onto the freelist for the table.

As you see, the storage parameters for Oracle tables and indexes can have an important effect on the performance of the database. Let's begin our discussion of object tuning by reviewing the common storage parameters that affect Oracle performance.

The pctfree Storage Parameter

The purpose of *pctfree* is to tell Oracle when to remove a block from the object's freelist. Since the Oracle default is *pctfree*=10, blocks remain on the freelist while they are less than 90 percent full. As shown in Figure 17-1, once an insert makes the block grow beyond 90 percent full, it is removed from the freelist, leaving 10 percent of the block for row expansion. Furthermore, the data block will remain off the freelist even after the space drops below 90 percent. Only *after* subsequent *delete* operations cause the space to fall below the *pctused* threshold of 40 percent will Oracle put the block back onto the freelist.

The pctused Storage Parameter

The *pctused* parameter tells Oracle when to add a previously full block onto the freelist. As rows are deleted from a table, the database blocks become eligible to accept new rows. This happens when the amount of space in a database block falls below *pctused*, and a freelist relink operation is triggered, as shown in Figure 17-2.

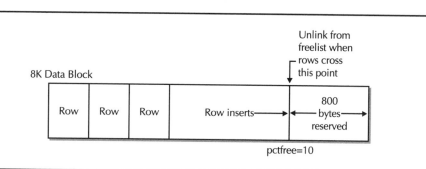

FIGURE 17-1.   *The* pctfree *threshold*

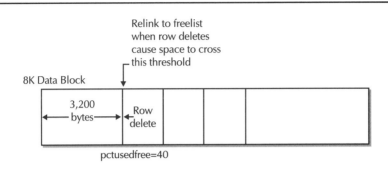

FIGURE 17-2. *The* pctused *threshold*

For example, with *pctused*=60, all database blocks that have less than 60 percent will be on the freelist, as well as other blocks that dropped below *pctused* and have not yet grown to *pctfree*. Once a block deletes a row and becomes less than 60 percent full, the block goes back on the freelist. When rows are deleted, data blocks become available when a block's free space drops below the value of *pctused* for the table, and Oracle relinks the data block onto the freelist chain. As the table has rows inserted into it, it will grow until the space on the block exceeds the threshold *pctfree,* at which time the block is unlinked from the freelist.

The freelists Parameter and DML performance

The *freelists* parameter tells Oracle how many segment header blocks to create for a table or index. Multiple freelists are used to prevent segment header contention when several tasks compete to *insert, update,* or *delete* from the table. The *freelists* parameter should be set to the maximum number of concurrent update operations.

TIP
Prior to Oracle8i, you must reorganize the table to change the freelists *storage parameter. In Oracle8i, you can dynamically add freelists to any table or index with the* alter table *command, as long as the* compatibility *parameter is set to at least 8.1.6. In Oracle8i, adding a freelist reserves a new block in the table to hold the control structures.*

The freelist groups Storage Parameter for OPS

The *freelist groups* parameter is used in Oracle Parallel Server (renamed Real Application Clusters in Oracle9i). When multiple instances access a table, separate freelist groups are allocated in the segment header. The *freelist groups* parameter should be set to the number of instances that access the table.

NOTE
The variables are called pctfree *and* pctused *in the* create table *and* alter table *syntax, but they are called PCT_FREE and PCT_USED in the* dba_tables *view in the Oracle dictionary. The programmer responsible for this mix-up was promoted to senior vice president in recognition of his contribution to the complexity of the Oracle software.*

Summary of Storage Parameter Rules

The following rules govern the settings for the storage parameters *freelists, freelist groups, pctfree,* and *pctused.* As you know, the value of *pctused* and *pctfree* can easily be changed at any time with the *alter table* command, and the observant DBA should be able to develop a methodology for deciding the optimal settings for these parameters. For now, accept these rules, and I will discuss them in detail later in this chapter.

There is a direct trade-off between effective space utilization and high performance, and the table storage parameters control this trade-off:

■ **For efficient space reuse**   A high value for *pctused* will effectively reuse space on data blocks, but at the expense of additional I/O. A high *pctused* means that relatively full blocks are placed on the freelist. Hence, these blocks will be able to accept only a few rows before becoming full again, leading to more I/O.

■ **For high performance**   A low value for *pctused* means that Oracle will not place a data block onto the freelist until it is nearly empty. The block will be able to accept many rows until it becomes full, thereby reducing I/O at insert time. Remember that it is always faster for Oracle to extend into new blocks than to reuse existing blocks. It takes fewer resources for Oracle to extend a table than to manage freelists.

While we will go into the justification for these rules later in this chapter, let's review the general guidelines for setting of object storage parameters:

■ Always set *pctused* to allow enough room to accept a new row. We never want to have free blocks that do not have enough room to accept a row. If we do, this will cause a slowdown, since Oracle will attempt to read five "dead" free blocks before extending the table to get an empty block.

- The presence of chained rows in a table means that *pctfree* is too low or that *db_block_size* is too small. In most cases within Oracle, RAW and LONG RAW columns make huge rows that exceed the maximum block size for Oracle, making chained rows unavoidable.

- If a table has multiple simultaneous *insert* SQL processes, it needs to have multiple simultaneous *delete* processes.

  Running a single purge job will place all of the free blocks on only one freelist, and none of the other freelists will contain any free blocks from the purge.

- The *freelist* parameter should be set to the high-water mark of updates to a table. For example, if the customer table has up to 20 end users performing *insert* operations at any time, the customer table should have *freelists*=20.

- The *freelist groups* parameter should be set for the number of Oracle Parallel Server instances that access the table.

Freelist Management and DML Performance

One of the benefits of having Oracle is that it manages all of the free space within each tablespace. Oracle handles table and index space management for us and insulates humans from the inner workings of the Oracle tables and indexes. However, experienced Oracle tuning professionals need to understand how Oracle manages table extents and free data blocks.

Knowing the internal Oracle table management strategies will help you become successful in managing high-volume performance within Oracle. To be proficient at object tuning, you need to understand the behavior of freelists and freelist groups, and their relationship to the values of the *pctfree* and *pctused* parameters. This knowledge is especially imperative for enterprise resource planning (ERP) applications, where poor table performance is often directly related to improper table settings.

The most common mistake for the beginner is assuming that the default Oracle parameters are optimal for all objects. Unless disk consumption is not a concern, you must consider the average row length and database block size when setting *pctfree* and *pctused* for a table such that empty blocks are efficiently placed back onto the freelists. When these settings are wrong, Oracle may populate freelists with "dead" blocks that do not have enough room to store a row, causing significant processing delays.

This dead block problem occurs when the setting for *pctused* allows a block to relink onto the freelist when it does not have enough free space to accept a new row. I will explain the relationship between average row length and freelist behavior later in this chapter.

Freelists are critical to the effective reuse of space within the Oracle tablespaces and are directly related to the *pctfree* and *pctused* storage parameters. When the database is directed to make blocks available as soon as possible (with a high setting of *pctused*), the reuse of free space is maximized. However, there is a direct trade-off between high performance and efficient reuse of table blocks. When tuning Oracle tables and indexes, you need to consciously decide if you desire high performance or efficient space reuse, and set the table parameters accordingly. Let's take a close look at how these freelists affect the performance of Oracle.

Whenever a request is made to insert a row into a table, Oracle goes to a freelist to find a block with enough space to accept a row. As you may know, the freelist chain is kept in the first block of the table or index, and this block is known as the segment header. The sole purpose of the *pctfree* and *pctused* table allocation parameters is to control the movement of blocks to and from the freelists. While the freelist link and unlink operations are simple Oracle functions, the settings for freelist link *(pctused)* and unlink *(pctfree)* operations can have a dramatic impact on the performance of Oracle DML statements.

The default settings for all Oracle objects are *pctused*=40 and *pctfree*=10. As you may know from DBA basics, the *pctfree* parameter governs freelist unlinks. Setting *pctfree*=10 means that every block reserves 10 percent of the space for row expansion. The *pctused* parameter governs freelist relinks. Setting *pctused*=40 means that a block must become less than 40 percent full before being relinked on the table freelist.

Let's take a closer look at how freelist management works, and how it affects the performance of Oracle. Many neophytes misunderstand what happens when a block is re-added to the freelist. Once a block is relinked onto the freelist after a delete, it will remain on the freelist even when the space exceeds 60 percent. Only reaching *pctfree* will take the database block off of the freelist.

Linking and Unlinking from the Freelists

As you now know, the *pctfree* and *pctused* table parameters are used to govern the movement of database blocks to and from the table freelists. In general, there is a direct trade-off between performance and efficient table utilization because efficient block reuse requires some overhead when linking and unlinking blocks with the freelist. As you may know, linking and unlinking a block requires two writes: one to the segment header for the freelist head node, and the other to the new block to make it participate in the freelist chain. The following general rules apply to freelists:

- **insert** A SQL *insert* may trigger the *pctfree* threshold, causing a freelist unlink. Since *insert* operations always use the free block at the head of the freelist chain, there will be minimal overhead when unlinking this block.

- **update**   A SQL *update* that expands row length is affected by *pctfree,* but it will *not* cause a freelist unlink, since the target block would not be at the head of the freelist chain.

- **delete**   A SQL *delete* of rows may trigger the *pctused* threshold and cause a freelist link.

You also need to understand how new free blocks are added to the freelist chain. At table extension time, the high-water mark for the table is increased, and new blocks are moved onto the master freelist, where they are, in turn, moved to process freelists. For tables that do not contain multiple freelists, the transfer is done five blocks at a time. For tables with multiple freelists, the transfer is done in sizes (5*(number of freelists + 1)). For example, in a table with 20 freelists, 105 blocks will be moved onto the master freelist each time that a table increases its high-water mark.

To see how this works, let's review the mechanisms associated with freelist links and unlinks. For the purposes of the following examples, let's use Figure 17-3.

The segment header contains a space to hold a pointer to the first free block in the table. Inside Oracle, a pointer to a block is called a data block address, or DBA for short. The first block on the freelist chain also has a space in the block header to contain the DBA for the next free block, and so on.

Let's explore what happens internally during row operations.

Freelist Unlinks with SQL *insert* Operations

As new rows are inserted, the block may be removed from the freelist if the free space becomes less than the bytes specified by *pctfree*. Since the block being inserted is always at the head of the freelist chain, only two blocks will be affected.

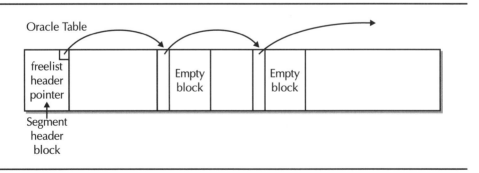

FIGURE 17-3.   *A sample freelist chain*

In our example, let's assume that the *insert* has caused block 106 to be removed from the freelist chain:

1. Oracle detects that free space is less than *pctfree* for block 20 and invokes the unlink operation. Since block 20 is the first block on the freelist chain, Oracle reads the data block address (DBA) inside the block header and sees that the next free block is block 60.

2. Oracle next adjusts the freelist header node and moves the DBA for block 60 to the head of the freelist in the segment header. Block 20 no longer participates in the freelist chain, and the first entry in the freelist is now block 60, as shown in Figure 17-4.

Freelist Relinks with update Statements

As updates to existing rows cause the row to expand, the block may be unlinked from the freelist if the free space in the block becomes less than *pctfree*. Of course, this will only happen if the row contains VARCHAR, RAW, or LONG RAW column datatypes, since these are the only datatypes that could expand upon a SQL *update*. Because the updated block is not at the head of the freelist chain, the prior block's freelist pointer cannot be adjusted to omit the block. Note that the dead block remains on the freelist even though it does not have room to accept a row.

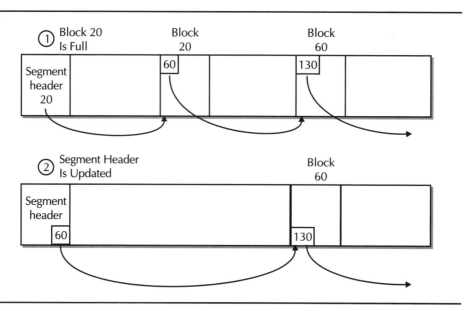

FIGURE 17-4.   *A freelist unlink operation*

The dead block remaining on the list will cause additional Oracle overhead, especially if there are a large number of "unavailable" blocks on the freelist. At run time, Oracle will incur additional I/Os when reading these freelists, and it will try the freelist as many as five times attempting to find a block with enough room to store the new row. After five attempts, Oracle will raise the high-water mark for the table.

Reducing Freelist Relink Operations

Either of these techniques will cause the freelists to be populated largely from new extents. Of course, this approach requires lots of extra disk space, and the table must be reorganized periodically to reclaim the wasted storage. Freelist relinks can be reduced in two ways:

- "Turn down" freelist relinks by setting *pctused* to 1. Setting *pctused* to a low value means that data blocks are not relinked onto the freelist chain unless they are completely empty.

- Use the *append* hint when adding rows. By using *append* with inserts, you tell Oracle to bypass the freelists and raise the high-water mark for the table to grab a fresh, unused data block.

TIP
Remember the cardinal rule of DML tuning. There is a direct trade-off between efficient space reuse and fast performance of insert *statements. If high performance is more important than space reuse, you can use an Oracle8 SQL hint that will bypass freelist checking. By placing* /*+ append */ *immediately after the* insert *keyword, you direct Oracle to increase the high-water mark for the table and place the row into a fresh empty block.*

Now that you understand how freelists operate within each Oracle table and index, you are ready to dig deeper and look at long data columns and DML behavior.

Long Data Columns and DML Behavior

One of the most confounding problems with some Oracle tables is the use of large columns. The main problem with RAW and LONG RAW, BLOB and CLOB datatypes is that they often exceed the block size, and whenever a column is larger than the database block size, the column will fragment onto an adjacent data block. This causes Oracle to incur two I/Os instead of one I/O every time the row is accessed. This block-chaining problem is especially prevalent in tables where column lengths grow to thousands of bytes. Of course, it is a good idea to use the maximum supported *db_block_size* for your version of Oracle (usually 8,192 bytes) in an effort to minimize this chaining.

In order to avoid fragmentation of a row, Oracle will always insert table rows containing a RAW or LONG RAW column onto a completely empty block. Therefore, on insert, Oracle will not attempt to insert below the high-water mark (using freelists) and will always bump the high-water mark, pulling the free blocks from the master freelist. Since Oracle pulls free blocks by raising the high-water mark, Oracle will not reuse blocks once they have been placed on the freelist chain. Actually, free blocks below the high-water mark (i.e., blocks on the freelists) may be used for inserting LONG columns, but only if the block is completely empty. If the block is partially used but still below the *pctused* mark, it will not be used to insert the LONG data.

Remember, multiple freelists can waste a significant amount of disk space. Tables with dozens of freelists may exhibit the "sparse table" phenomenon as the table grows and each freelist contains blocks that are not known to the other freelist chains. If these tables consume too much space, the Oracle administrator faces a tough decision. To maximize space reuse, you would want the table to be placed onto a freelist as soon as it is capable of receiving more than two new rows. Therefore, a fairly high value for *pctused* is desired. On the other hand, this would result in slower run-time performance, since Oracle will be able to insert only a few rows before having to perform an I/O to get another block.

There are cases when large row lengths and an improper setting of *pctfree* can cause performance degradation during SQL *insert* operations. The problem occurs when a block becomes too full to accept another row while the block remains on the freelist. As rows are inserted, Oracle must fetch these blocks from the freelist, only to find that there is not enough room for a row. Fortunately, Oracle will not continue fetching freelist blocks forever. After retrieving five too-small blocks from the freelist, Oracle assumes that there will be no blocks on the freelist that have enough space for the row, and Oracle will grab an empty block from the master freelist, as shown in Figure 17-7.

This problem usually occurs when the row length for the table exceeds the space reserved on the block. For example, with 4K blocks and *pctfree*=10, the reserved space will equal 410 bytes (not counting block header space). Therefore, we may see this problem for any rows that are more than 410 bytes in length.

Now that you understand the internal freelist linking mechanism, let's see how to monitor Oracle to identify when Oracle is waiting because of freelist contention.

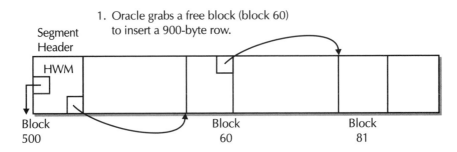

1. Oracle grabs a free block (block 60) to insert a 900-byte row.

2. Block 20 only has 800 free bytes, so Oracle tries the next free block (block 81).

3. Block 81 does not have room for the row.

4. Oracle stops trying the freelists and grabs five empty blocks by raising the table high-water mark.

FIGURE 17-5. *Oracle eventually abandons the freelist and raises the high-water mark*

Setting *pctfree* and *pctused* by Average Row Length

It is very important that the DBA understand how the row length affects setting the values for *pctfree* and *pctused.* You want to set *pctfree* such that room is left on each block for row expansion, and you want to set *pctused* so that newly linked blocks have enough room to accept rows.

Here you see the trade-off between effective space usage and performance. If you set *pctused* to a high value—say, 80—a block will quickly become available to accept new rows, but it will not have room for a lot of rows before it becomes logically full again. Remember the rule for *pctused.* The lower the value for *pctused,* the more space will be available on each data block, and subsequent SQL *insert* operations will run faster. The downside is that a block must be nearly empty before it becomes eligible to accept new rows.

The script shown next will generate the table alteration syntax. Please note that this script only provides general guidelines, and you will want to leave the default *pctused*=40 unless your system is low on disk space, or unless the average row length is very large.

pctused.sql

```
rem pctused.sql
set heading off;
set pages 9999;
set feedback off;

spool pctused.lst;
column db_block_size new_value blksz noprint
select value db_block_size from v$parameter where name='db_block_size';

define spare_rows = 2;

select
   ' alter table '||owner||'.'||table_name||
   ' pctused '||
   least(round(100-((&spare_rows*avg_row_len)/(&blksz/10))),95)||
   ' '||
   ' pctfree '||
   greatest(round((&spare_rows*avg_row_len)/(&blksz/10)),5)||
   ';'
from
   dba_tables
where
avg_row_len > 1
and
avg_row_len < .5*&blksz
and
table_name not in
 (select table_name from dba_tab_columns b
   where
 data_type in ('RAW','LONG RAW','BLOB','CLOB','NCLOB')
 )
order by
   owner,
   table_name
;

spool off;
```

Now that you understand the table storage parameters and their effect on performance, let's talk about buffer busy waits and see how they relate to object parameters.

Buffer Busy Waits and DML Contention

When multiple tasks want to *insert* or *update* rows in a table, there may be contention in the segment header for the table. This contention can manifest itself as a buffer busy wait or a freelist wait. Let's look at some queries that can be run to identify these contention conditions. You are now ready to understand how they occur at the table and index levels.

Oracle keeps a v$ view called *v$waitstat* and the *stats$waitstat* table for monitoring wait events. The following query shows how many times Oracle has waited for a freelist to become available. As you can see, it does not tell you which freelists are experiencing the contention problems:

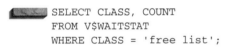

```
SELECT CLASS, COUNT
FROM V$WAITSTAT
WHERE CLASS = 'free list';


     CLASS                          COUNT
  --------------              ------------
    free list                       383
```

The main problem with the *v$waitstat* view and the *stats$waitstat* table is that they only keep the wait statistics for the whole database and do not distinguish waits by table or index name. Here, you can see that Oracle had to wait 383 times for a table freelist to become available. This could represent a wait of 383 times on the same table or perhaps a single wait for 383 separate tables. While 383 seems to be a large number, remember that Oracle can perform hundreds of I/Os each second, so 383 could be quite insignificant to the overall system. In any case, if you suspect that you know which table's freelist is having the contention, the table can be exported, dropped, and redefined to have more freelists. While an extra freelist consumes more of Oracle's memory, additional freelists can help throughput on tables that have lots of *insert* statements. Generally, you should define extra freelists only on those tables that will have many concurrent *update* operations.

Using STATSPACK to Find DML Wait Contention

Now let's look at how STATSPACK can identify these wait conditions for concurrent DML. The *stats$waitstat* table contains a historical listing of all wait events. The *stats$waitstat* contains the following classes:

```
SQL> select distinct class from stats$waitstat

CLASS
------------------
bitmap block
bitmap index block
data block
extent map
free list
save undo block
save undo header
segment header
sort block
system undo block
system undo header
undo block
undo header
unused
```

rpt_waitstat.sql

```
set pages 999;
set lines 80;

column mydate heading 'Yr. Mo Dy Hr'      format a13;
column class                              format a20;
column wait_count                         format 999,999;
column time                               format 999,999,999;
column avg_wait_secs                      format 99,999;

break on to_char(snap_time,'yyyy-mm-dd') skip 1;

select
   to_char(snap_time,'yyyy-mm-dd HH24')              mydate,
   e.class,
   e.wait_count - nvl(b.wait_count,0)               wait_count,
   e.time - nvl(b.time,0)                           time
from
   stats$waitstat       b,
   stats$waitstat       e,
   stats$snapshot       sn
where
   e.snap_id = sn.snap_id
and
   b.snap_id = e.snap_id-1
and
   b.class = e.class
and
(
```

```
        e.wait_count - b.wait_count  > 1
        or
        e.time - b.time > 1
)
;
```

Here is a sample report from this query. Here we see a list of all wait events and the object of the wait. This information can sometimes provide insight into a contention problem within Oracle.

```
Yr. Mo Dy Hr CLASS                    WAIT_COUNT          TIME
------------- --------------------- ---------- ------------
2000-12-20 11 data block                     2             0
2000-12-20 12 data block                    21             0
2000-12-20 12 undo header                    5             0
2000-12-20 13 data block                   407             0
2000-12-20 13 segment header                3             0
2000-12-20 13 undo block                   270             0
2000-12-20 13 undo header                   61             0
2000-12-20 16 data block                    55             0
2000-12-20 16 undo block                     8             0
2000-12-20 16 undo header                    5             0
2000-12-20 17 data block                   252             0
2000-12-20 18 data block                   311             0
2000-12-20 18 undo block                   173             0
2000-12-21 00 data block                 2,268             0
2000-12-21 00 undo block                   744             0
2000-12-21 00 undo header                  132             0
2000-12-21 01 data block                 2,761             0
2000-12-21 01 undo block                 1,078             0
2000-12-21 01 undo header                  419             0
2000-12-21 05 data block                     7             0
2000-12-21 09 data block                    17             0
2000-12-21 09 undo block                     8             0
2000-12-21 10 data block                    30             0
2000-12-21 10 undo block                    29             0
2000-12-21 10 undo header                    4             0
2000-12-21 11 data block                   139             0
2000-12-21 11 undo header                    2             0
2000-12-21 12 data block                    17             0
2000-12-21 13 data block                    11             0
2000-12-21 14 data block                    42             0
2000-12-21 14 undo header                    2             0
2000-12-21 15 data block                    10             0
2000-12-21 15 undo block                     5             0
2000-12-21 16 data block                    23             0
```

```
2000-12-21 17 data block               17              0
2000-12-21 17 undo block                2              0
2000-12-21 18 data block              122              0
2000-12-21 18 undo block              117              0
2000-12-21 18 undo header              19              0
2000-12-21 21 data block               15              0
2000-12-21 22 data block                3              0
2000-12-22 02 data block               59              0
2000-12-22 08 data block               19              0
2000-12-22 09 data block               72              0
2000-12-22 09 undo block                2              0
2000-12-22 10 data block               57              0
2000-12-22 10 undo block                7              0
2000-12-22 10 undo header               3              0
2000-12-22 11 data block              423              0
2000-12-22 11 undo block               10              0
2000-12-22 16 data block                2              0
2000-12-22 17 data block              319              0
2000-12-22 17 undo block              149              0
2000-12-22 17 undo header              44              0
2000-12-22 18 data block                3              0
2000-12-22 18 undo header               2              0
2000-12-22 19 data block               16              0
2000-12-22 20 data block            5,526              0
2000-12-22 20 segment header           30              0
2000-12-22 20 undo block               46              0
```

Note that the segment header and data block waits are often related to competing SQL *update* tasks that have to wait on a single freelist in the segment header.

While this STATSPACK report is useful for summarizing wait conditions within Oracle, it does not tell us the names of the objects that experienced the wait conditions. The following section will show you how to drill down and find the offending data block for buffer busy waits.

Finding Buffer Busy Waits with STATSPACK

I am discussing buffer busy waits now because buffer busy waits are usually associated with segment header contention that can be remedied by adding additional freelists for the table or index. However, buffer busy waits are measured at the instance level and it is to our benefit to look at the instance-wide reports on buffer busy waits.

Before proceeding, let's remember that a buffer busy wait occurs when a database block is found in the data buffer but it is unavailable because another Oracle task is using the data block. What follows is a sample STATSPACK report to display buffer busy waits for each of the three data buffers.

rpt_bbw.sql

```
set pages 9999;

column buffer_busy_wait format 999,999,999
column mydate heading 'yr. mo dy Hr.'

select
   to_char(snap_time,'yyyy-mm-dd HH24')        mydate,
   new.name,
   new.buffer_busy_wait-old.buffer_busy_wait buffer_busy_wait
from
   perfstat.stats$buffer_pool_statistics old,
   perfstat.stats$buffer_pool_statistics new,
   perfstat.stats$snapshot                 sn
where
   new.name = old.name
and
   new.snap_id = sn.snap_id
and
   old.snap_id = sn.snap_id-1
and
   new.buffer_busy_wait-old.buffer_busy_wait > 1
group by
   to_char(snap_time,'yyyy-mm-dd HH24'),
   new.name,
   new.buffer_busy_wait-old.buffer_busy_wait
;
```

Here is a sample of the report from this script. Note that it provides instance-wide buffer busy waits and does not tell us the data blocks where the wait occurred. We will see advanced techniques for finding the blocks in the next section.

```
yr. mo dy Hr NAME                  BUFFER_BUSY_WAIT
------------ -------------------- ----------------
2000-09-21 15 DEFAULT                             3
2000-10-02 15 DEFAULT                            11
2000-12-11 18 DEFAULT                            20
```

We can enhance this report to show times when the number of buffer busy waits is causing a performance problem. The script that follows alerts us when there are more than 400 buffer busy waits between snapshot intervals.

rpt_bbw_alert.sql

```
set pages 9999;

column buffer_busy_wait format 999,999,999
column mydate heading 'Yr. Mo Dy  Hr.' format a16
```

```
select
   to_char(snap_time,'yyyy-mm-dd HH24')          mydate,
   avg(new.buffer_busy_wait-old.buffer_busy_wait) buffer_busy_wait
from
   perfstat.stats$buffer_pool_statistics old,
   perfstat.stats$buffer_pool_statistics new,
   perfstat.stats$snapshot    sn
where
   new.snap_id = sn.snap_id
and
   old.snap_id = sn.snap_id-1
and
   new.buffer_busy_wait-old.buffer_busy_wait > 4000
group by
   to_char(snap_time,'yyyy-mm-dd HH24')
;
```

We can run this script and learn those time periods when buffer busy waits were excessive. This can provide the DBA with valuable clues about the tables and processes that were involved in creating the block wait conditions.

```
SQL> @rpt_bbw_alert.sql

Yr. Mo Dy  Hr. BUFFER_BUSY_WAIT
--------------- ----------------
2001-01-04 01            4,570
2001-01-04 06            4,576
2001-01-04 07            4,582
2001-01-04 11            4,669
2001-01-04 12            4,687
2001-01-04 13            4,692
2001-01-04 14            4,762
2001-01-04 20            4,867
2001-01-04 21            4,875
2001-01-04 23            4,883
2001-01-05 00            4,885
2001-01-07 20            5,462
2001-01-07 21            5,471
2001-01-07 22            5,476
2001-01-07 23            5,482
2001-01-08 00            5,482
2001-01-08 01            5,482
2001-01-08 02            5,484
2001-01-08 03            5,504
2001-01-08 04            5,505
2001-01-08 10            5,365
2001-01-08 11            5,396
2001-01-08 12            5,505
```

```
2001-01-08 13                      5,943
2001-01-08 14                      6,155
2001-01-08 15                      6,226
2001-01-08 16                      6,767
2001-01-08 17                     14,396
2001-01-08 18                     13,958
2001-01-08 19                     13,972
2001-01-08 20                     13,977
2001-01-08 21                     13,979
2001-01-08 22                     13,981
2001-01-08 23                     13,982
2001-01-09 00                     13,986
2001-01-10 23                      4,517
2001-01-11 00                      5,033
2001-01-16 21                      9,048
2001-01-16 22                      9,051
2001-01-16 23                      9,051
```

We can also gain insight into the patterns behind buffer busy waits by averaging them by the hour of the day. The following STATSPACK script can be used to develop a buffer busy wait "signature."

rpt_avg_bbw_hr.sql

```
set pages 9999;

column buffer_busy_wait format 999,999,999
column mydate heading 'Yr. Mo Dy  Hr.' format a16

select
   to_char(snap_time,'HH24')              mydate,
   avg(new.buffer_busy_wait-old.buffer_busy_wait) buffer_busy_wait
from
   perfstat.stats$buffer_pool_statistics old,
   perfstat.stats$buffer_pool_statistics new,
   perfstat.stats$snapshot    sn
where
   new.snap_id = sn.snap_id
and
   old.snap_id = sn.snap_id-1
having
   avg(new.buffer_busy_wait-old.buffer_busy_wait) > 0
group by
   to_char(snap_time,'HH24')
;
```

Here is the output from this script that we can paste into a spreadsheet for charting. We clearly see the average buffer busy waits for each hour of the day.

```
Yr. Mo Dy  Hr. BUFFER_BUSY_WAIT
---------------- ----------------
00                           155
02                            19
03                             0
06                             5
07                             4
08                             8
09                            28
10                            66
11                            28
13                            31
14                            45
15                           169
16                            61
17                           364
18                            48
19                            34
20                            88
22                            17
23                           186
```

The chart in Figure 17-6 shows the plot of buffer busy waits during a typical day. Here we see a clear spike in waits at 3:00 P.M. and again at 5:00 P.M. The next step would be to go to the *stats$sql_summary* table and try to locate the SQL and the underlying tables for these waits.

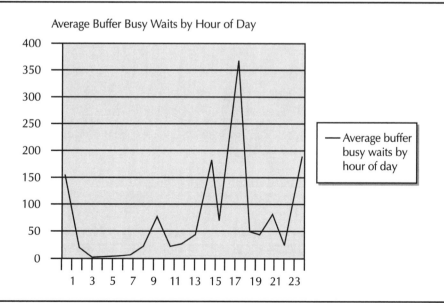

FIGURE 17-6. *Average buffer busy waits by hour of the day*

Now that you understand the general nature of buffer busy waits, let's move on and see how we can find the exact object that caused the buffer busy wait.

Finding the Offending Block for a Buffer Busy Wait

As I discussed, Oracle does not keep an accumulator to track individual buffer busy waits. To see them, you must create a script to detect them and then schedule the task to run frequently on your database server.

get_busy.ksh

```ksh
#!/bin/ksh

# First, we must set the environment . . . .
ORACLE_SID=proderp
export ORACLE_SID
ORACLE_HOME=`cat /var/opt/oracle/oratab|\
    grep \^$ORACLE_SID:|cut -f2 -d':'`
export ORACLE_HOME
PATH=$ORACLE_HOME/bin:$PATH
export PATH

SERVER_NAME=`uname -a|awk '{print $2}'`
typeset -u SERVER_NAME
export SERVER_NAME

# sample every 10 seconds
SAMPLE_TIME=10

while true
do

   #*************************************************************
   # Test to see if Oracle is accepting connections
   #*************************************************************
   $ORACLE_HOME/bin/sqlplus -s /<<! > /tmp/check_$ORACLE_SID.ora
   select * from v\$database;
   exit
 !

   #*************************************************************
   # If not, exit immediately . . .
   #*************************************************************
   check_stat=`cat /tmp/check_$ORACLE_SID.ora|grep -i error|wc -l`;
   oracle_num=`expr $check_stat`
   if [ $oracle_num -gt 0 ]
    then
```

```
  exit 0
 fi

 rm -f /export/home/oracle/statspack/busy.lst

 $ORACLE_HOME/bin/sqlplus -s perfstat/perfstat<<!> /tmp/busy.lst

 set feedback off;
 select
    sysdate,
    event,
    substr(tablespace_name,1,14),
    p2
 from
    v\$session_wait a,
    dba_data_files  b
 where
    a.p1 = b.file_id
;
!

var=`cat /tmp/busy.lst|wc -l`

echo $var
if [[ $var -gt 1 ]];
 then
  echo
*************************************************************"
  echo "There are waits"
  cat /tmp/busy.lst|mailx -s "Prod block wait found"\
  don@remote-dba.net \
  Larry_Ellison@oracle.com
  echo
*************************************************************"
 exit
fi

sleep $SAMPLE_TIME
done
```

As you can see from this script, it probes the database for buffer busy waits every 10 seconds. When a buffer busy wait is found, it mails the date, tablespace name, and block number to the DBA. Here is an example of a block alert e-mail:

```
SYSDATE    SUBSTR(TABLESP P2
--------- -------------- ----------
28-DEC-00 APPLSYSD          25654
```

Here we see that we have a block wait condition at block 25654 in the *applsysd* tablespace. To see the contents of this data block, we have several command options:

```
SQL> alter system dump datafile 1 block 25654;
System altered.
```

or:

```
SQL > alter system dump datafile
SQL > '/u03/oradata/PROD/applsysd01.dbf' block 25654;
System altered.
```

or:

```
SQL> ALTER SESSION SET EVENTS
2>    'IMMEDIATE TRACE NAME BLOCKDUMP LEVEL 25654';
System altered.
```

This will then generate a trace file that contains the detailed information about the contents of the data block. In most cases, this will be the first block in the table (the segment header). Let's go to the udump directory and inspect the trace file.

```
oracle*PROD-/u01/app/oracle/admin/PROD/udump
>ls -alt|head
total 5544
-rw-r--r--   1 oracle       dba          69816 Dec 28 14:16 ora_4443.trc
```

Next, we look at the contents of the trace file using the UNIX *more* command.

```
root> more ora_4443.trc

Dump file /u01/app/oracle/admin/PROD/udump/ora_4443.trc
Oracle8 Enterprise Edition Release 8.0.5.1.0 - Production
 .
 .
 .

Block header dump: rdba: 0x00406436
 Object id on Block? Y
 seg/obj: 0x63  csc: 0x00.d3aa2  itc: 9  flg: -  typ: 2 - INDEX
```

Here we see that the object on this block is an index and the object ID is hex 63. We convert the hex 63 and see that our object ID is number 99.

We can then run a query against dba_objects and see the name of the index.

```
SQL> select object_name, object_type
  2  from dba_objects
  3  where object_id=99;

OBJECT_NAME
-------------------------------------------------------------------
OBJECT_TYPE
---------------
VUST_IDX
INDEX


SQL> select table_name from dba_indexes
  2  where index_name = 'CUST_IDX';

TABLE_NAME
------------------------------
CUSTOMER
```

So, here we see that our wait event was on the root index node for the *cust_idx* index. This index has only a single freelist, and it appears that the contention was caused by multiple tasks competing for an *insert* on the customer table.

Now that you see how to monitor buffer busy waits, let's move on to see how indexes and referential integrity constraints affect Oracle DML.

Update SQL, Subqueries, and Parallel DML

Updates with *where* constraints that contain correlated subqueries are one of the most confounding problems of the SQL update statement. This is because of the rule that an update statement may only contain a single table name. Hence, we do not add a correlated subquery when the values of other table rows influence our update decision.

To illustrate, consider the following SQL that gives a 10 percent raise to all employees who did not receive a bonus last year. To do this, we must execute a NOT IN anti-join against the bonus table.

```
update
    emp
set
    sal= sal+ (sal*.1)
```

```
where
   ename NOT IN
   (select /*+ first_rows */
      ename
   from
      bonus
   where
      emp.ename = bonus.ename
   and
      to_char(bonus_date,'YYYY') = '2000'
   );
```

Now, let's explain the query. We expect to see a full-table scan against the *emp* table.

```
OPERATION
------------------------------------------------------------------------
OPTIONS                          OBJECT_NAME                    POSITION
------------------------------   --------------------------     ----------
 UPDATE STATEMENT
                                                                      1
   UPDATE
                                 EMP                                  1
     FILTER
                                                                      1
       TABLE ACCESS
FULL                             EMP                                  1
         TABLE ACCESS
BY INDEX ROWID                   BONUS                                2
           INDEX
RANGE SCAN                       BONUS_ENAME                          1
```

As we expected, we see a full-table scan against the *emp* table, followed by an index range scan against the *bonus* table.

As you recall from Chapter 16, the NOT IN anti-join is always serviced by a full-table scan against the outer table, and you have learned that a NOT IN subquery can often be replaced with an outer join and a *where bonus IS NULL*. However, since SQL only allows a single table name in the outer query, it is impossible to remove the NOT IN clause by replacing it with a standard outer join.

So, given that we are stuck with a full-table scan, how can we improve the performance of the update statement? If we are on an Oracle server with lots of CPUs, we can add a *parallel* hint to the SQL *update* statement. Here, we invoke 25 parallel processes to partition and update the *emp* rows:

```
update /*+ parallel(emp,35) */
   emp
set
   sal= sal+ (sal*.1)
```

```
where
   ename NOT IN
   (select /*+ first_rows */
      ename
   from
      bonus
   where
      emp.ename = bonus.ename
   and
      to_char(bonus_date,'YYYY') = '2000'
   );
```

Here is the revised execution plan:

```
OPERATION
--------------------------------------------------------------------
OPTIONS                         OBJECT_NAME                 POSITION
------------------------------  --------------------------  ----------
OTHER_TAG
--------------------------------------------------------------------
UPDATE STATEMENT
                                                                   1
   UPDATE
                                EMP                                 1
      FILTER
                                                                   1
         TABLE ACCESS
FULL                            EMP                                 1
PARALLEL_TO_SERIAL
         TABLE ACCESS
BY INDEX ROWID                  BONUS                               2
            INDEX
RANGE SCAN                      BONUS_ENAME                         1
```

It might be tempting to try to improve the speed of the update scan by adding a function-based index on the *bonus_date* column to see if the CBO will choose to use the *bonus_date* instead of the *ename* column.

```
SQL> create index bonus_date_year on bonus
     (to_char(bonus_date,'YYYY'));
```

However, the CBO recognizes that the *ename* index has far more unique values than our *bonus_date,* and this will have no effect of the execution plan for the query.

   The main point of this section is that correlated subqueries are unavoidable for complex DML because of the rule that only one table name can appear in the DML statement. Hence, our only way to improve performance is to add *parallel* DML hints to improve the speed of the required full-table scan.

Oracle also provides parallelism for all SQL *update, insert,* and *insert as select* operations, as well as parallel index re-building. For example, when rebuilding a global partitioned index, Oracle will recognize that the index is partitioned and allow parallel query processes to independently read each partition of the index.

Next, let's take a look at how referential integrity (RI) constraints affect the performance of DML statements.

Overhead of Constraints on DML Performance

Referential integrity constraints are added to table to enforce business rules. The constraints that affect DML can include check constraints, primary key constraints, and foreign key constraints. No matter how good referential integrity is for maintaining the integrity of the application, RI constraints are the bane of DML performance. Specifically, we see the following issues:

- **Check constraints** A check constraint is used to verify that valid values are placed inside specific data columns. For large-volume insert or update operations, a significant amount of time is spent checking the valid values for each column (Figure 17-7).

- **Primary key constraints** The primary key constraint is enforced by a unique B-tree index on the column, and the index overhead on insert and delete operations can slow down large-volume inserts or updates, since each value must be looked up in the index (Figure 17-8).

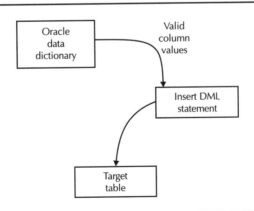

FIGURE 17-7. *Overhead of a check constraint*

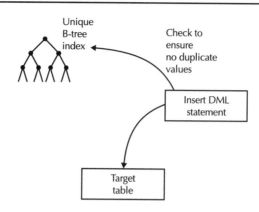

FIGURE 17-8. *Primary key overhead for DML*

■ **Foreign key constraints** These constraints enforce intertable data
relationships. For example, a foreign key constraint could be defined such
that an order row cannot be added unless a matching customer row exists.
The checking of intertable foreign key constraints requires several steps.
The data dictionary must first retrieve the name of the foreign key column
and then access the foreign table to ensure that the required value is
present. Only after this verification is the row added to the target table
(Figure 17-9).

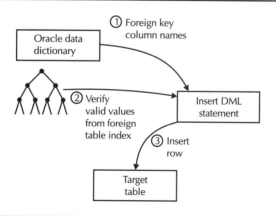

FIGURE 17-9. *Foreign key integrity checking for DML*

It should be obvious that that RI constraints are only meaningful during an insert or update DML statement, and there are some techniques employed by DBAs to make large-volume DML tasks run faster.

When performing large-volume insert or update tasks, it is possible to temporarily disable all constraints that reference the affected table. After the load has been completed, the RI constraints are reenabled, and any errors or exceptions are noted.

This is a well-known performance technique for SQL*Loader, Oracle imports, and large batch inserts and updates. It is far faster to disable the constraints, load the data, and reenable the constraints than it is to perform all of the RI error checking for each row.

It is relatively easy to locate and temporarily disable primary key and check constraints, but it is a bit more tricky to locate foreign key constraints, because they are defined on other tables.

Overhead of Maintaining Indexes with DML

For Oracle systems that are highly indexed, there's an extreme overhead associated with the bulk insertion and updates.

As you may recall from Oracle fundamentals, whenever a row is inserted or modified, all indexes in which that index participates have to be updated in real time. This can often increase the overhead of maintaining batch inserts and updates by an order of magnitude, dramatically slowing down the performance of the system.

In the real world, it is not uncommon for a very large batch DML operation to drop all of the indexes prior to altering the base table. Following the batch update or insert operation, the indexes are rebuilt very quickly through a full-table scan within the Oracle tables. It has been conclusively demonstrated that this kind of approach is often far faster for bulk loading, provided, of course, that all SQL selects are temporarily suspended during the load (Figure 17-10).

An additional problem with updating B-tree indexes in place is that the indexes commonly get out of balance. For example, when a large number of rows are added to a table, Oracle will often have to split and spawn that area of the B-tree index, creating an area within the index that may spawn to four and even five levels deep. We also can see a disproportionate number of unbalanced leaf nodes within the index. By dropping the indexes, loading the data, and rebuilding the indexes, the overall time is reduced and you can be assured of well-balanced B-tree indexes.

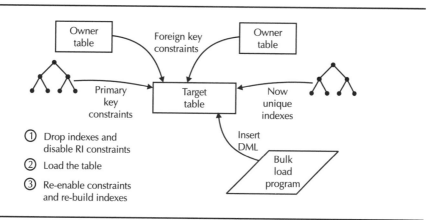

FIGURE 17-10. *Dropping indexes during a bulk DML operation*

Using PL/SQL Bulk Inserts to Improve SQL Insert Speed

One of the inherent issues with SQL inserts is that an individual insert statement must be generated and executed for every row that is added to the database. The PL/SQL language has a procedure where bulk insertions can be done far faster than the traditional row-at-a-time method.

When inserting rows in PL/SQL, developers often place the insert statement inside a FOR loop. To insert 1,000 rows using the FOR loop, there would be 1,000 context switches between PL/SQL and the Oracle library cache. Oracle8*i* allows you to do bulk binds using the PL/SQL FORALL loop, which requires only one context switch. This is achieved by the FORALL statement passing an entire PL/SQL table to the SQL engine in a single step. Internal tests show that this process results in substantial performance increases over traditional methods.

Here's how it works. In this example, assume that a Pro*C program is calling a PL/SQL function for a bulk insert.

   I. In your PL/SQL package, you create some global PL/SQL table variables for each column of your table. Here is an example of the PL/SQL type definition:

```
type
    cust_key_array
is table of
    customer.cust_key%TYPE
INDEX BY BINARY_INTEGER;
```

2. Next, you create a PL/SQL procedure with parameters of type PL/SQL tables:

```
PROCEDURE customer_insert
    (p_cust_key IN              customer.cust_key%TYPE,
     p_current_state IN         current_state_array,
     p_anno_user_category IN anno_user_category_array,
     p_anno_name IN             anno_name_array,
     p_color IN                 color_array)
```

3. To invoke the procedure, you pass a C array for each parameter that is defined in the PL/SQL table.

4. To properly perform the bulk insert you must get the number of items passed in by the Pro*C program. You can do this by checking one of the PL/SQL parameters using the PL/SQL table built-in function COUNT.

```
lv_rowcount := p_cust_key.COUNT;
```

5. Finally, we can insert using the FORALL statement, using the lv_rowcount parameter as the terminator of the FORALL loop.

```
FORALL i IN 1..lv_rowcount
    INSERT INTO customer
              (cust_key,
               page_seq_nbr,
               user_unique_id,
               in_page_seq_nbr,
               date_time,
               posx,
               posy,
               length,
               current_state,
               anno_user_category,
               anno_name,
               color)
    VALUES    (p_cust_key,
               p_page_seq_nbr(i),
               p_user_unique_id,
               p_in_page_seq_nbr(i),
               SYSDATE,
               p_posx(i),
               p_posy(i),
               p_length(i),
               p_current_state(i),
               p_anno_user_category(i),
               p_anno_name(i),
               p_color(i));
```

In sum, the FORALL clause in PL/SQL can speed-up SQL DML that is called from an external programming language such as Pro*C or Pro*Cobol. You can also use the *dbms_sql* package for bulk inserts of Oracle rows.

Conclusion

This chapter has reviewed the fundamentals for tuning Oracle SQL DML statements. The main points of this chapter include these:

■ There is only one SQL hint that assists with the speed of DML, the *append* hint.

■ The *append* hint tells Oracle to bypass the table freelists and place inserted rows on fresh data blocks. This is done by raising the high-water mark for the table, thereby placing the new rows at the end of the table.

■ Oracle DML performance is heavily dependent on the Oracle table storage parameters *pctfree, pctused,* and *freelists.*

■ The *pctfree* parameter controls freelist unlink operations, and a too-high setting for *pctfree* can precipitate row chaining at update time.

■ The *pctused* parameter controls freelist relink operations. A too-high setting for *pctused* will cause data blocks to be relinked when they can only accept a few new rows before being unlinked.

■ The *freelists* parameter controls concurrent DML. The setting for freelists should always be set to the high-water mark for concurrent DML operations against the object.

■ A shortage of freelists commonly causes buffer busy waits because DML tasks must enqueue to access the segment header block.

■ Oracle update DML often requires correlated subqueries. These subqueries cannot be rewritten as standard equi-joins because update statements may only have one table name in the *from* clause. Hence, the *parallel* hint can improve the speed of resulting full-table scans.

■ For large-volume DML with SQL*Loader, Oracle import, or batch loads, referential integrity constraints can be temporarily disabled and later reenabled to improve performance.

■ Oracle indexes are often dropped and rebuilt after bulk inserts, deletes, or updates. This improves the overall speed of the bulk operations and ensures that all B-tree indexes are well balanced following the bulk operation.

Next, let's turn our attention to the tuning of Oracle SQL with the use of temporary tables. By giving your developers the ability to create temporary tables, you can radically improve the speed of certain types of Oracle SQL statements.

CHAPTER
18

Tuning SQL with
Temporary Tables

or certain types of SQL operations, the creation of intermediate result tables can result in stunning performance improvements. This chapter will discuss how you can use the create table as select (CTAS) syntax to improve the speed of queries that perform complex summarization activities, and how to speed up two-stage queries that perform both summarization and comparison activities. This chapter contains the following topics:

- Using CTAS with dictionary views
- Tuning aggregation queries with temporary tables

Let's begin by looking at how the creation of temporary tables can speed noncorrelated subqueries against the Oracle data dictionary.

Using CTAS with Dictionary Views

The prudent use of temporary tables can dramatically improve Oracle SQL performance. To illustrate the concept, consider the following example from the DBA world. In the query that follows, we want to identify all users who exist within Oracle who have not been granted a role. We could formulate the query as an anti-join with a noncorrelated subquery as shown here:

```
select
    username
from
    dba_users
where
    username NOT IN
        (select grantee from dba_role_privs);
```

This query runs in 18 seconds. As you may remember from Chapter 12, these anti-joins can often be replaced with an outer join. However, we have another option by using CTAS. Now, we rewrite the same query to utilize temporary tables by selecting the distinct values from each table.

```
drop table temp1;
drop table temp2;

create table
    temp1
as
  select
      username
```

```
     from
        dba_users;

create table
    temp2
as
  select distinct
        grantee
    from
        dba_role_privs;

select
    username
from
    temp1
where
    username not in
        (select grantee from temp2);
```

With the addition of temporary tables to hold the intermediate results, this query runs in less than three seconds, a 6× performance increase. Again, it is not easy to quantify the reason for this speed increase, since the DBA views do not map directly to Oracle tables, but it is clear that temporary tables show promise for improving the execution speed of certain types of Oracle SQL queries.

Next, let's look at tuning aggregate queries with temporary tables. These types of queries that summarize and compare ranges of values within temporary tables will run far faster if we create intermediate tables for the query.

TIP

If you are using Oracle8i and above, you can use global temporary tables instead of dropping and creating your own temporary tables.

Tuning Aggregation Queries with Temporary Tables

In addition to data dictionary queries, temporary tables can dramatically improve the performance of certain SQL self-join queries that summarize data values.

For example, consider a query that examines the *stats$tab_stats* STATSPACK extension table. Rows for the *stats$tab_stats* table are collected weekly, and one row in this table exists for each table in the schema. This STATSPACK extension table is loaded by collecting the *table_name* and the bytes consumed by the table (from the *dba_segments* view), and we want to use this table-level detail data to summarize our overall size change per week.

Here is the description for this STATSPACK extension table. For details on using this table, refer to *Oracle High-Performance Tuning with STATSPACK,* by Don Burleson (McGraw-Hill Professional Publishing, 2001).

```
SQL> desc stats$tab_stats;
Name                                         Null?      Type
------------------------------------------  --------  ----------------
SNAP_TIME                                               DATE
SERVER_NAME                                             VARCHAR2(20)
DB_NAME                                                 VARCHAR2(9)
TABLESPACE_NAME                                         VARCHAR2(40)
OWNER                                                   VARCHAR2(40)
TABLE_NAME                                              VARCHAR2(40)
NUM_ROWS                                                NUMBER
AVG_ROW_LEN                                             NUMBER
NEXT_EXTENT                                             NUMBER
EXTENTS                                                 NUMBER
BYTES                                                   NUMBER
```

Since each row of this table contains a date *(snap_time),* a table name *(table_name),* and the number of bytes, we need a query that sums up the total size for all tables for one week, and then compares that value to the overall size for the following week (Figure 18-1).

Essentially, we could formulate this comparison of summaries as a single query that summarizes each range of rows.

```
select distinct
    to_char(old_size.snap_time,'yyyy-mm-dd'),  -- The old snapshot date
    sum(old_size.bytes),
    sum(new_size.bytes),
    sum(new_size.bytes) - sum(old_size.bytes)
from
    stats$tab_stats old_size,
    stats$tab_stats new_size
where
    -- This is the highest date in the table
    new_size.snap_time = (select max(snap_time) from stats$tab_stats)
and
    -- This is the prior weeks snapshot
    old_size.snap_time = (select min(snap_time)-7 from stats$tab_stats)
group by
    to_char(old_size.snap_time,'yyyy-mm-dd')
;
```

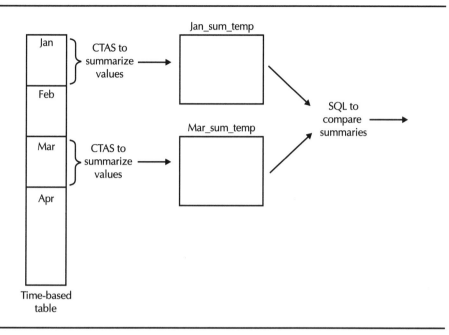

FIGURE 18-1. *Using temporary tables to preaggregate values from
a time-based table*

Here is the execution plan for this query. Because we are summing and comparing
ranges of values within the same table, we see the dreaded MERGE JOIN CARTESIAN
access method. As you know, a Cartesian merge join can run for hours because the
Cartesian products of the tables must be derived.

```
OPERATION
---------------------------------------------------------------------
OPTIONS                          OBJECT_NAME                    POSITION
---------------------------      -------------------------      ----------
SELECT STATEMENT
                                                                    5
  SORT
GROUP BY                                                            1
    MERGE JOIN
CARTESIAN                                                           1
      TABLE ACCESS
```

BY INDEX ROWID	STATS$TAB_STATS	1
INDEX		
RANGE SCAN	TAB_STAT_DATE_IDX	1
SORT		
AGGREGATE		1
INDEX		
FULL SCAN (MIN/MAX)	TAB_STAT_DATE_IDX	1
SORT		
JOIN		2
TABLE ACCESS		
BY INDEX ROWID	STATS$TAB_STATS	1
INDEX		
RANGE SCAN	TAB_STAT_DATE_IDX	1
SORT		
AGGREGATE		1
INDEX		
FULL SCAN (MIN/MAX)	TAB_STAT_DATE_IDX	1

Take a close look at the execution plan for this query, and carefully review the steps:

1. We begin with an index range scan to get the maximum date in the *stats$tab_stats* table.

2. Next, we perform an index range scan to get the sysdate–7 value.

3. Once we have the target data values, we must perform a Cartesian merge join to access the rows and resolve the query.

This query gets tricky where we must compare a range of common dates with another range of common dates. As you can see, these range comparison queries are hard to formulate and hard for Oracle to optimize.

To see an alternative query, let's look at an equivalent query that utilizes temporary tables. This report uses the STATSPACK extension tables for objects to prepare weekly growth reports. The *rpt_object_stats.sql* script is a very useful STATSPACK report that approximates the overall growth of the database over the past week. The DBA can quickly compare table and index counts, and see the total growth for tables and indexes over the past week. This report is often e-mailed to MIS managers.

Let's take a closer look at each section of the report and then see how to formulate the query.

Elapsed-Time Section of the Date Range Report

The first section of the report identifies the snapshots that are used in the comparison. The script identifies the most recent snapshot and compares it to the n–1 snapshot.

```
SQL> @rpt_object_stats
Connected.
'*********************************************'

Mon Jan 22                                                  page   1
                              Object growth
                         Comparing last two snapshots

   Most recent date 2001-01-22

   Older date 2001-01-08

'*********************************************'
```

The Object Count and Bytes Report Output

The next section shows the total counts of tables and indexes in the database. This is a very useful report for the DBA to ensure that no new objects have migrated into the production environment. We also see the total bytes for all tables and indexes and the size change over the past week. Here is the section of the report that shows the total growth of tables and indexes for the past week:

```
Mon Apr 22                                                  page   1
                    Most recent database object counts and sizes

DB_NAME  TAB_COUNT  IDX_COUNT     TAB_BYTES         IDX_BYTES
-------  ---------  ---------  ---------------  ---------------
prodzz1       451        674      330,219,520      242,204,672
              ---        ---  ---------------  ---------------
Total         451        674      330,219,520      242,204,672

Mon Jan 22                                                  page   1
                         Database size change
                  comparing the most recent snapshot dates

DB_NAME      OLD_BYTES          NEW_BYTES           CHANGE
-------  -------------    ---------------    ---------------
prodzz1    467,419,136        572,424,192      105,005,056
           -------------    ---------------    ---------------
Total      467,419,136        572,424,192      105,005,056
```

This is a very sophisticated DBA report, and one that can run for many hours without the use of temporary tables because of Oracle's use of the CARTESIAN access method. However, with the use of temporary tables, the table and index counts can be summarized and saved in the temp tables for fast analysis. We also use the same technique to sum the number of bytes in all tables and indexes into temporary tables, and then quickly interrogate the summary tables for total sizes of our database.

The Report Generation SQL Script

Here is the section of code that computes the date ranges and computes the total table and index counts and bytes. While this query is more verbose than our original query, it runs more than 100 times faster than our first query.

rpt_object.sql

```
set lines 80;
set pages 999;
set feedback off;
set verify off;
set echo off;

--********************************************************
-- This report compares the max(snap_time) to the second-highest date
--********************************************************

--********************************************************
-- First we need to get the second-highest date in tab_stats
--********************************************************
drop table d1;

create table d1 as
select distinct
   to_char(snap_time,'YYYY-MM-DD') mydate
from
   stats$tab_stats
where
   to_char(snap_time,'YYYY-MM-DD') <
     (select max(to_char(snap_time,'YYYY-MM-DD')) from stats$tab_stats)
;

--********************************************************
-- The second highest date is select max(mydate) from d1;
--********************************************************

set heading off;

prompt '*******************************************'
select '  Most recent date '||
        max(to_char(snap_time,'YYYY-MM-DD'))
```

```
from stats$tab_stats;
select '  Older date '||
         max(mydate)
from d1;
prompt '*********************************************'

set heading on;

drop table t1;
drop table t2;
drop table t3;
drop table t4;

--   ****************************************************************
--   Summarize the counts of all tables for the most recent snapshot
--   ****************************************************************

create table t1 as
select db_name, count(*) tab_count, snap_time from stats$tab_stats
where    to_char(snap_time, 'YYYY-MM-DD') =
             (select max(to_char(snap_time,'YYYY-MM-DD'))
                 from stats$tab_stats)
group by db_name, snap_time;

--   ****************************************************************
--   Summarize the counts of all indexes for the most recent snapshot
--   ****************************************************************

create table t2 as
select db_name, count(*) idx_count, snap_time from stats$idx_stats
where    to_char(snap_time, 'YYYY-MM-DD') =
             (select max(to_char(snap_time,'YYYY-MM-DD'))
                 from stats$idx_stats)
group by db_name, snap_time;

--   ****************************************************************
--   Summarize sum of bytes of all tables for the 2nd highest snapshot
--   ****************************************************************

create table t3 as
select db_name, sum(bytes) tab_bytes, snap_time from stats$tab_stats
where    to_char(snap_time, 'YYYY-MM-DD') =
             (select max(to_char(snap_time,'YYYY-MM-DD'))
                 from stats$tab_stats)
group by db_name, snap_time;
```

```
--      ************************************************************
--      Summarize sum of bytes of all indexes for the 2nd highest snapshot
--      ************************************************************

create table t4 as
select db_name, sum(bytes) idx_bytes, snap_time from stats$idx_stats
where    to_char(snap_time, 'YYYY-MM-DD') =
             (select max(to_char(snap_time,'YYYY-MM-DD'))
                 from stats$idx_stats)
group by db_name, snap_time;

--*********************************************************
-- This report displays the most recent counts & size totals
--*********************************************************

column tab_bytes format 999,999,999,999
column idx_bytes format 999,999,999,999
column tab_count format 99,999
column idx_count format 99,999

clear computes;
compute sum label "Total" of tab_count on report;
compute sum label "Total" of idx_count on report;
compute sum label "Total" of tab_bytes on report;
compute sum label "Total" of idx_bytes on report;

break on report;

ttitle 'Most recent database object counts and sizes'

select
   a.db_name,
   tab_count,
   idx_count,
   tab_bytes,
   idx_bytes
from
   perfstat.t1 a,   - table counts
   perfstat.t2 b,   - index counts
   perfstat.t3 c,   - all table bytes
   perfstat.t4 d    - all index bytes
where
   a.db_name = b.db_name
and
   a.db_name = c.db_name
and
   a.db_name = d.db_name
;
```

```
--_**********************************************************
-- These temp tables will compare size growth since last snap
--_**********************************************************
drop table t1;
drop table t2;
drop table t3;
drop table t4;

create table t1 as
select db_name, sum(bytes) new_tab_bytes, snap_time
     from stats$tab_stats
where    to_char(snap_time, 'YYYY-MM-DD') =
            (select max(to_char(snap_time,'YYYY-MM-DD'))
                from stats$tab_stats)
group by db_name, snap_time;

create table t2 as
select db_name, sum(bytes) new_idx_bytes, snap_time
     from stats$idx_stats
where    to_char(snap_time, 'YYYY-MM-DD') =
            (select max(to_char(snap_time,'YYYY-MM-DD'))
                from stats$idx_stats)
group by db_name, snap_time;

create table t3 as
select db_name, sum(bytes) old_tab_bytes, snap_time
     from stats$tab_stats
where    to_char(snap_time, 'YYYY-MM-DD') =
            (select max(mydate) from d1)
group by db_name, snap_time;

create table t4 as
select db_name, sum(bytes) old_idx_bytes, snap_time
     from stats$idx_stats
where    to_char(snap_time, 'YYYY-MM-DD') =
            (select max(mydate) from d1)
group by db_name, snap_time;



--_**********************************************************
-- This is the size comparison report
--_**********************************************************
column old_bytes format 999,999,999,999
column new_bytes format 999,999,999,999
column change    format 999,999,999,999
```

```
compute sum label "Total" of old_bytes on report;
compute sum label "Total" of new_bytes on report;
compute sum label "Total" of change    on report;

break on report;
ttitle 'Database size change|comparing most recent snapshot dates';


select
    a.db_name,
    old_tab_bytes+old_idx_bytes old_bytes,
    new_tab_bytes+new_idx_bytes new_bytes,
    (new_tab_bytes+new_idx_bytes)-(old_tab_bytes+old_idx_bytes) change
from
    perfstat.t1 a,
    perfstat.t2 b,
    perfstat.t3 c,
    perfstat.t4 d
where
    a.db_name = b.db_name
and
    a.db_name = c.db_name
and
    a.db_name = d.db_name
;
```

Upon close examination, we see that we create temporary tables to hold the total counts, and we also create two temporary tables to hold the sum of bytes for each table and index. Once the sums are precalculated, it becomes fast and easy for Oracle SQL to compute the total bytes for the whole database.

Conclusion

The use of temporary table can be an extremely effective mechanism for improving speed of queries that select aggregated information (e.g., *sum, avg*) from a single table. While many other SQL queries may also benefit from this approach, the use of temporary tables is especially suited to time-series tables like those found in a data warehouse.

The only downside to allowing developers to use temporary tables is the requirement to grant them the create table privilege and the extra stress on the user's DEFAULT tablespace.

Next, let's take a look at the techniques involved with the tuning of Oracle subqueries.

CHAPTER
19

Tuning SQL Subqueries

n Chapter 12, we briefly discussed hinting techniques that could be used to tune subqueries, but subquery tuning involves far more than adding hints. In this chapter, we will take a closer look at subqueries and see when they are legitimate, when to replace them with other join methods, and how get the best performance from both correlated and noncorrelated subqueries. This chapter will contain the following topics:

- Basics of Oracle subqueries

- Correlated versus noncorrelated subqueries

- Automatic SQL transformation of subqueries

- Tuning subqueries with the IN and EXISTS clauses

- Tuning queries with the NOT IN and NOT EXISTS clauses

- Tuning queries with nonequality conditions

- Hints to improve subquery execution speed

Let's begin with an overview of the types of subqueries.

Basics of Oracle Subqueries

Whenever possible, the use of a subquery within Oracle SQL should be avoided. In some cases, the subquery can be replaced with a standard join operation, thereby avoiding the overhead that is associated with subqueries. However, there are circumstances when the use of an Oracle subquery is unavoidable, and this section describes the rules for determining the best way to specify a subquery for maximum performance.

One of the shortcomings of Oracle SQL is that there are numerous ways to write most SQL statements, each of which will return identical results, but they may have radically different access paths and execution times. While the Oracle SQL optimizer will often detect "complex" subqueries and decompose them into equivalent join operations, taking the subquery and converting it into a nested loop join, we cannot always count on the optimal access path to service the query.

In cases where we must use subqueries, there are several options that we need to consider. We have the choice of using a correlated or a noncorrelated subquery, and we also have the choice of using either the IN clause or the EXISTS clause as the comparison condition for the subquery.

The summary in Table 19-1 show a summary of techniques for each type of subquery.

From Table 19-1, you see there are four possible forms for the subquery, either correlated or noncorrelated and either standard or anti-join. Let's begin by looking at the basic form of each type of subquery. We will start by comparing a correlated subquery with a noncorrelated one. Here is a noncorrelated subquery:

```
select
    stuff
from
    tablename
where
    key IN
    -- noncorrelated subquery
    (select
       other_stuff
     from
       inner_table
    )
;
```

	Standard Subquery		Anti-Join Subquery	
	In	**Exists**	**Not In**	**Not Exists**
Correlated subquery	Redundant Boolean predicates. Can always be replaced with a standard join.	Automatic Transformation to nested loop join	Rewrite as *select distinct* outer join	Rewrite as *select distinct* outer join
Noncorrelated subquery	Automatic transformation to nested loop join	Never appropriate	Rewrite as nested loop join with *minus* operator	Never appropriate

TABLE 19-1. *Techniques for Each Type of Subquery*

Here is the correlated subquery. Note the reference in the inner query to the column value in the outer query:

```
select
    stuff
from
    tablename
where
    key IN
    -- correlated subquery
    (select
       other_stuff
     from
       inner_table
     where
       tablename.key = inner_table.key
    )
;
```

Next, we can look at the anti-joins. As you know, an anti-join subquery is a subquery that uses the NOT EXISTS or NOT IN clause. Just like standard queries, anti-join queries may be correlated or noncorrelated.

Here is an example of an anti-join, noncorrelated subquery:

```
select stuff
from
    tablename
where
    key NOT IN
    -- noncorrelated subquery
    (select
       other_stuff
     from
       inner_table
    )
;
```

Here is the correlated subquery form of the anti-join.

```
select stuff
from
    tablename
where
    key NOT IN
```

```
-- correlated subquery
(select
   other_stuff
 from
   inner_table
 where
   tablename.key = inner_table.key
)
;
```

Now that you've seen the basic forms of subqueries, let's examine each of these subquery types and look at the most efficient execution plans for Oracle SQL.

Correlated Versus Noncorrelated Subqueries

Since we have the choice of using a correlated subquery or a noncorrelated one, we need to examine the basic properties of these constructs. In essence a "correlated" subquery references the outer table inside the subquery, while the noncorrelated subquery does not reference the outer table. A correlated subquery is evaluated once per row processed by the parent query, while a noncorrelated subquery is only executed once and the result set is kept in memory (if the result set is small), or in an Oracle temporary segment (if the result set is large). A "scalar" subquery is a noncorrelated subquery that returns a single row. Where the subquery only returns one row, the Oracle optimizer will reduce this result to a constant and only execute the subquery one time.

For our example, an identical query could be written either as a correlated subquery or a noncorrelated subquery, and both will return the same result set.

Here is a noncorrelated subquery:

```
select
   count(*)
from
   outer_table
where
   key in
   (select key from inner_table)
;
```

For the purpose of this discussion, we will call the main query (the *select count(*)*) the "outer" query, as opposed to the "inner" subquery that is enclosed in parentheses.

The choice of using a correlated or noncorrelated subquery depends upon the number of rows that are returned by the outer query and the subquery. Given that both of these queries will return the same result, which is the most efficient? Let's begin our answer to this question by exploring the number of rows that we get back from the query.

Issues of Scale and Subqueries

In practice, the choice between a correlated or noncorrelated subquery depends upon the expected number of rows that is returned by both the parent query and the subquery. Our goal is to balance the overhead that is associated with each type of subquery.

- **Correlated subquery overhead** The subquery will be reexecuted once for each row that is returned by the outer query. Hence, we must ensure that the subquery uses an index whenever possible.

- **Noncorrelated subquery overhead** The subquery is executed once, and the result set is usually sorted and kept in an Oracle temporary segment where it is referenced as each row is returned by the parent query. In cases where the subquery returns a large number of rows, a significant overhead will be involved with sorting this result set and storing the temporary segment.

In sum, our choice depends wholly on the number of rows returned by the parent query. If our parent query returns only a few rows, the overhead of reexecuting the subquery is not so great. On the other hand, if the parent query returns a million rows, the subquery would be executed a million times. The same concept applies to the number of rows returned by the subquery. If our subquery returns only a few rows, then there is not much overhead in keeping the result set in memory for the parent query. On the other hand, if the subquery returns a million rows, then Oracle would need to store this result set as a temporary segment on disk, and then sort the segment in order to service each row of the parent query.

Timing Subquery Execution

To see the difference between the execution plans for correlated and noncorrelated subqueries, let's design an experiment where we use the *count(*)* SQL function and take a look at the explain plan for the queries to see which is the most efficient.

In our test, *outer_table* was created with 14,000 rows, and *inner_table* was created with 7,000 rows. A nonunique index was created on the key for both

tables, and we used Oracle's rule-based optimizer to generate the paths to the data.
All of the queries are in the following form:

```
select
    count(*)
from
    outer_table
where
    XXX
(select yyy from inner_table)
;
-- Where XXX=EXISTS, IN, NOT IN, and NOT EXISTS
```

Now, let's take a look at each form of this query, and see the relative differences
in execution speed.

Timing Subqueries with the IN Clause

We expect that each of the *count(*)* queries should return 7,000 rows, one for each
row that exists in *outer_table,* which was found in *inner_table.* To factor out variances
in elapsed times, each query was run three times and the total elapsed time for the
queries was recorded.

Drawing on our previous discussion on issues of scale, we expect the parent
query to return 14,000 rows and the subquery to return 7,000 rows. Consequently,
the correlated subquery would need to execute the inner query 14,000 times to
service all of the rows in the parent table. The noncorrelated subquery will need to
store 7,000 rows in a temporary segment, but the result set is small enough that the
sort can take place in memory, and we will only need to execute the subquery one
time. Therefore, we expect that the noncorrelated subquery would probably run
faster, since there will be fewer fetches. To test the execution speed, we executed
our queries three times, and generated the execution plans for each query.

Speed of Noncorrelated Subqueries with the IN Clause   Here are the output
timings for the noncorrelated subquery using the IN clause:

```
COUNT(*)
----------
      7000

Elapsed: 00:00:01.09
Elapsed: 00:00:01.46
Elapsed: 00:00:01.30
```

Here you see that the query completed in slightly more than one second. The noncorrelated subquery begins by performing a full-table scan on *inner_table* and sorting the table in memory, storing the sorted result in a system view (temporary segment). We next move into nested loops where the index on *outer_table* is used to retrieve the key for *outer_table* and this key is looked up in the temporary segment. As I have noted, the subquery is executed only once, and the result set is kept and used for each test from the parent query.

Speed of Correlated Subqueries with the IN Clause   This is the output for the correlated subquery using the IN clause. Here you see the counts for the query, and the three timings for the query with the *set timing on* SQL*Plus command. Note that the database was stopped and re-started between timings.

```
COUNT(*)
----------
      7000

Elapsed: 00:00:02.82
Elapsed: 00:00:04.72
Elapsed: 00:00:04.83
```

Here you see roughly twice the execution time as with the noncorrelated subquery. As I have discussed, the correlated subquery is executed once for each row that is returned from the parent query. Hence, if we return 14,000 rows from the parent query, the inner query would be executed once for each row. As you see from the execution plan, a full-table scan is invoked for *outer_table*. As each row is fetched, the key column from *outer_table* is used in an index-only merge scan to return the counts from our query.

Timing Subqueries with the EXISTS Clause

The EXISTS clause can sometimes be used instead of the IN clause for subqueries, but there are some important differences in the behavior of the queries. When using EXISTS with a subquery, the Boolean operator in the parent statement becomes true if *any* rows are returned by the subquery, and this may not give the desired result. Consequently, the following query would fail to count the 7,000 matching rows:

```
select
    count(*)
from
    outer_table
where
    exists
    (select key from inner_table)
;
```

Speed of Noncorrelated Subqueries with the EXISTS Clause Here are the output timings for the query as a noncorrelated subquery using the EXISTS clause. Note that we get the wrong answer for our count!

```
COUNT(*)
----------
     14000
```

```
Elapsed: 00:00:00.12
Elapsed: 00:00:00.11
Elapsed: 00:00:00.13
```

Here we note that using the EXISTS clause in a noncorrelated subquery gives us the wrong number of rows. In this noncorrelated subquery, using the EXISTS clause results in returning the number of rows from the parent table (*outer_table* in this case), and the subquery seems to be disregarded.

Speed of Correlated Subqueries with the EXISTS Clause But what about using the EXISTS clause as a part of a correlated subquery? Since the correlated subquery is executed once for each row in the parent table, we would expect that this approach would work in identifying our 7,000 rows:

```
select
    count(*)
from
    outer_table
where
    EXISTS
    (select key from inner_table where outer_table.key = inner_table.key)
;
```

This is the execution timing for our correlated subquery with the EXISTS clause:

```
COUNT(*)
----------
      7000
```

```
Elapsed: 00:00:03.73
Elapsed: 00:00:03.36
Elapsed: 00:00:03.36
```

Basic Characteristics of Subquery Execution

The immediate conclusion about subqueries is that each SQL subquery must be evaluated on an individual basis, with an emphasis on the number of expected rows that will be returned from both the inner table and the outer table. Let's review the conclusions about subqueries:

- When using a correlated subquery, the execution plans are often identical for subqueries that use the IN clause or the EXISTS clause.

- The EXISTS clause is always inappropriate for a noncorrelated subquery.

- When the outer query returns a relatively small number of rows, the correlated subquery will perform faster than the noncorrelated subquery.

- When the subquery returns more than one row, the query cannot be automatically transformed into a join.

- With a small number of rows in the inner query, a noncorrelated subquery will run faster than a correlated subquery.

Now that we have reviewed the basics of subqueries, let's take a closer look and examine the execution plans for each type of subquery.

Automatic SQL Transformation of Subqueries

Oracle has always been transforming SQL into alternative SQL syntax. The simplest example is the conversion of the nested select to a join. However, there are some types of poor SQL syntax that the Oracle SQL optimizer can't transform into a join, and there are also cases where Oracle doesn't transform the SQL as it should. Oracle will transform several types of subqueries into standard joins. These include:

- Noncorrelated subqueries using the IN clause

- Correlated subqueries using the EXISTS clause

However, you must always remember that there are many other factors dictating when the SQL optimizer performs an automatic query transformation of a subquery to a join. Foremost, you generally need to have a unique index on both table join columns. In sum, it is never a good idea to trust Oracle to rewrite malformed SQL statements. You should always rewrite subqueries whenever possible.

Let's take a look at correlated and noncorrelated subqueries and understand the issues surrounding the use of the IN and EXISTS clauses.

Tuning Subqueries with the IN and EXISTS Clauses

There are many cases where we need to compare the values in an outer table with another table using the EXISTS or IN clause. In some cases, the IN and EXISTS clauses can be used interchangeably.

Noncorrelated Subqueries Using the IN Clause

To begin, what does it mean to perform a nested loop join instead of a noncorrelated subquery? The nested loop join extracts one row from one table and then extracts rows from the second table where the join columns evaluate to true. Regarding the noncorrelated subquery, we know that the subquery is completely executed before any comparison is made with the outer query.

Let's illustrate the query rewrite functionality with a simple example. In the query that follows, Oracle must return the complete result set for the subquery of the *bad_credit* table.

```
Select /*+ rule */
    ename
from
    emp
where
    empno IN
    (select
        empno
    from
        bad_credit
    where
        bad_credit_date > sysdate-365
    )
;
```

Because the Oracle SQL optimizer will transform this query, we will simulate the untransformed behavior by removing the *empno* indexes from both tables.

```
OPERATION
-----------------------------------------------------------------------
OPTIONS                      OBJECT_NAME                POSITION
----------------------------- --------------------------- ----------
SELECT STATEMENT
                                                              5
   MERGE JOIN
                                                              1
   VIEW
                             VW_NSO_1                         1
     SORT
UNIQUE                                                        1
       TABLE ACCESS
FULL                         BAD_CREDIT                       1
     SORT
JOIN                                                          2
       TABLE ACCESS
FULL                         EMP                              1
```

When the VIEW execution method exists, the operation represents a nested select. Since no unique key exists on the *empno* column in the *emp* table, Oracle performs the SORT UNIQUE operation and then joins the result set to the *bad_credit* rows. If we had the *empno* indexes in place for these tables, look how the execution plan has changed. Note that the automatic SQL transformation is only appropriate when the columns in the select list of the nested select form a unique key, and the comparison operator is the IN operator.

```
OPERATION
-----------------------------------------------------------------------
OPTIONS                      OBJECT_NAME                POSITION
----------------------------- --------------------------- ----------
SELECT STATEMENT
  NESTED LOOPS
                                                              1
    TABLE ACCESS
FULL                         BAD_CREDIT                       1
    TABLE ACCESS
BY INDEX ROWID               EMP                              2
      INDEX
RANGE SCAN                   EMP_EMPNO                        1
```

Why is the unique key required to transform to a join? The reason is that without a uniqueness guarantee (via the index), it is possible for the transformed query join to produce a different result set. Why? Because when uniqueness isn't guaranteed, multiple rows might be joined to the row in the surrounding query, thus producing a Cartesian product effect. That is why we add the *select distinct* clause to eliminate duplicate rows.

But after the transformation, Oracle now has the choice of whether to drive the query with the *emp* table or the *bad_credit* table. The query transformation is only appropriate when the columns in the select list of the noncorrelated subquery make up a unique key, and the comparison operator is the IN operator. For example, the preceding query returns all employees who have had a bad credit rating in the past year.

Here is the transformed query. Note the standard join and the use of *select distinct* to remove any duplicate rows.

```
Select distinct /*+ rule */
    ename
from
    emp,
    bad_credit
where
    emp.empno = bad_credit.empno
and
    bad_credit_date > sysdate-365
;
```

Here you see the execution plan for this query with a unique index on *empno* in both tables. We also use the *rule* hint to ensure that the index is used.

OPERATION			
OPTIONS		OBJECT_NAME	POSITION
SELECT STATEMENT			
			6
SORT			
UNIQUE			1
HASH JOIN			
			1
TABLE ACCESS			
FULL		BAD_CREDIT	1
TABLE ACCESS			
FULL		EMP	2

Oracle will always make the transformation to a join when the subquery is noncorrelated and the query uses the IN operator. We also see a great benefit in transforming this type of subquery into a join.

However, you should never completely rely on Oracle to transform and optimize the subquery. As we have noted in our example, the Oracle transformation used a NESTED LOOPS join, while our rewritten query uses a faster HASH JOIN. Also, Oracle does not always determine the proper driving table for a transformed query, and you can get even faster performance by using the *ordered* hint to manually specify the driving table for the query.

TIP
Oracle will automatically transform only noncorrelated subqueries that use the IN clause. However, it is always a good idea to rewrite the query manually to take advantage of the use_hash *and* ordered *hints.*

Column Uniqueness and Subquery Transformation

Whenever an Oracle SQL tuning professional sees a subquery in a SQL statement, his or her first inclination is to see if the query can be rewritten as a standard join. However, this can be very dangerous unless you know whether the subquery is querying on unique values.

When the subquery has multiple tables in the *from* clause, explicit uniqueness can only occur when either of the following is true:

- The columns defining a unique key in the lowest table of the hierarchy are on the select list of the subquery.

- At least one of the columns defining the unique key is on the select list, and the other columns defining the unique key have an equality criterion specified, directly or indirectly.

If a subquery is rewritten to specify the subquery table in the *from* clause, the result set had better return only a single row, or otherwise the transformed query will return the wrong answer. Let's illustrate this fact with a simple example. Assume that we want a quick list of all employees who have spent at least one year in the Accounting department. Since the department name is in the *dept* table, the following query could be used:

```
select /*+ first_rows */
   ename,
   hiredate
from
   emp
where
   hiredate < sysdate-365
and
   deptno IN
      (
      select deptno from dept
      where dname = 'ACCOUNTING'
      );
```

Assuming that we have indexes on *dname* in the *dept* table, Oracle will perform a nested loop scan.

```
OPERATION
--------------------------------------------------------------------------
OPTIONS                         OBJECT_NAME                  POSITION
----------------------------  ---------------------------  ----------
SELECT STATEMENT
                                                                   7

   NESTED LOOPS
                                                                   1
      VIEW
                                VW_NSO_1                           1
         SORT
UNIQUE                                                             1
            TABLE ACCESS
FULL                            DEPT                               1
         TABLE ACCESS
BY INDEX ROWID                  EMP                                2
            INDEX
RANGE SCAN                      DEPT_EMP                           1
```

Now, it might be tempting to rewrite this query to replace the subquery with a join:

```
select /*+ first_rows */
    ename,
    hiredate
from
    emp,
    dept
where
    emp.deptno = dept.deptno
and
    hiredate < sysdate-365
and
    dname = 'ACCOUNTING'
;
```

Can you see the problem with this query? Remember, the department name is not unique. Here is the execution plan:

```
OPERATION
------------------------------------------------------------------------
OPTIONS                         OBJECT_NAME                   POSITION
------------------------------  --------------------------  ----------
SELECT STATEMENT
                                                                     5

  NESTED LOOPS
                                                                     1

    TABLE ACCESS
FULL                            DEPT                                 1

    TABLE ACCESS
BY INDEX ROWID                  EMP                                  2

      INDEX
RANGE SCAN                      DEPT_EMP                             1
```

Here we see that the execution plan has changed, but we have a real problem here, because this query might not always return the same result as the subquery. The reason is that the *dname* column is not unique.

Why is the unique key required to transform a subquery into a join? The simple reason is that without the uniqueness guarantee, it is possible for the transformed query to produce a different result set. This is because when uniqueness is not guaranteed, multiple rows may be joined to the row in the surrounding query, thus producing a Cartesian product effect.

Next, let's examine the rare case where a correlated subquery uses the IN clause.

Correlated Subqueries with the IN Clause

This type of query form is redundant because the IN clause is doing exactly the same thing as the correlation in the subquery. To illustrate, consider the following query:

```
select /*+ first_rows */
    ename,
    hiredate
from
    emp
where
    deptno IN
        (
        select deptno from dept
        where emp.deptno = dept.deptno
        );
```

Here we see that this query contains redundant Boolean operators. The *where deptno IN* clause performs the same check as the *where emp.deptno = dept.deptno* clause.

Noncorrelated Subqueries with the EXISTS Clause

As I already noted, it is never appropriate to specify a noncorrelated subquery with the EXISTS clause. This is because a Cartesian product results from the execution.

For example, the following query might be used to attempt to count those employees who have bad credit.

```
select
    ename
from
    emp e
where EXISTS
    (select
        null
    from
        bad_credit b
    )
;
```

However, since each employee may have many *bad_credit* rows, and we do not specify a join condition, Oracle will perform a Cartesian join.

Next, let's look at performing correlated subqueries with the EXISTS clause.

Correlated Subqueries Using the EXISTS Clause

Oracle calls this class of subqueries correlated because a Boolean condition in the *where* clause of the inner query references a corresponding row in the outer query. The restrictions that must be met before Oracle can transform the correlated subquery to a join include these:

- The correlated subquery must use the EXISTS clause.

- The outer query cannot also be a subquery (for example, a nested subquery).

- The correlation criteria in the inner query must use the equality operator, "=".

- The subquery cannot contain a *group by* or *connect by* reference.

- The equality operator in the subquery must only return a single row.

These restrictions greatly limit the number of automatic transformations by the SQL optimizer. Especially limiting is the requirement that the query use the EXISTS clause, such that this transformation will not occur when using the IN clause.

However, just because Oracle does not transform the subquery does not mean that you cannot manually transform your correlated subquery. This type of transformation generally involves moving the subquery to the *from* clause of the surrounding query, thereby changing the subquery into an in-line view. Additionally, some types of correlated subqueries can be directly merged into the surrounding subquery rather than moved to the *from* clause.

The rule for automatically transforming a correlated subquery is simple. The only rule is that only one row is returned from the subquery for the corresponding correlation criteria.

For example, the following query returns all employees with bad credit:

```
select
    ename
from
    emp e
where EXISTS
    (select
        null
    from
        bad_credit b
    where
        e.empno=b.empno
    )
;
```

Here we see the execution plan for this query. Note that the subquery has been removed and the expected VIEW access method is replaced by a full-table scan.

```
OPERATION
------------------------------------------------------------------
OPTIONS                        OBJECT_NAME                POSITION
-----------------------------  -------------------------  ----------
SELECT STATEMENT
                                                              1
   FILTER
                                                              1
     TABLE ACCESS
FULL                           EMP                            1
       INDEX
RANGE SCAN                     BAD_EMPNO                      2
```

However, just as in the case of noncorrelated subqueries using the IN clause, we are better off rewriting the subquery. This is because we are assured that the query is always transformed, and we can also add hints to improve the join method. Here we see the equivalent query, rewritten as a standard join to use the rule hint.

```
select /*+ rule */
    ename
from
    emp e,
    bad_credit b
where
    e.empno=b.empno
;
```

Next we see that the execution plan is different from the automatic query transformation.

```
OPERATION
------------------------------------------------------------------
OPTIONS                        OBJECT_NAME                POSITION
-----------------------------  -------------------------  ----------
SELECT STATEMENT
   NESTED LOOPS
                                                              1
     TABLE ACCESS
FULL                           BAD_CREDIT                     1
     TABLE ACCESS
BY INDEX ROWID                 EMP                            2
         INDEX
RANGE SCAN                     EMP_EMPNO                      1
```

We also see that the standard join is easier to understand and also allows us to alter the execution plan by adding hints.

TIP
*Oracle will automatically transform correlated
subqueries that use the EXISTS clause. However,
you should always manually rewrite this form of
subquery as a standard join so that you can take
advantage of hints.*

Next, let's examine anti-joins, which you know are noncorrelated subqueries
with the NOT IN operator.

Tuning Subqueries with NOT IN and NOT EXISTS Clauses

Now, let's look at using Oracle SQL for queries with the NOT IN and NOT EXISTS
conditions. As you know from Chapter 12, a subquery that has the NOT IN or NOT
EXISTS clause is called an anti-join. It is called an anti-join because the purpose of
the subquery is to eliminate rows from the outer table result set.

Noncorrelated Subqueries Using the NOT IN Operator

There are cases where we need to use a subquery with the NOT IN clause. To
illustrate, consider the following query to show employees who do not have a
bad credit rating in the past year. I also noted in Chapter 12 that a noncorrelated
query with the NOT IN clause can be dangerous. Prior to Oracle 7.3, Oracle
would perform a full-table scan of the *bad_credit* table for each row in the outer
query. So if there were 10,000 employees, Oracle would have to perform 10,000
full-table scans of the *bad_credit* table.

```
Select /*+ rule */
    ename
from
    emp
where
    empno NOT IN
    (select
        empno
    from
        bad_credit
```

```
   where
      bad_credit_date > sysdate-365
   )
;
```

Starting with Oracle 7.3, Oracle will sometimes transform a noncorrelated subquery with a NOT IN into a standard join. In Oracle8, the default is to automatically rewrite anti-joins, and the initialization parameter *always_anti_join* defaults to *nested_loops*. However, you can also explicitly set *always_anti_join=hash* (and sometime *merge*). Here we see the default execution plan in Oracle8*i*, without setting the *always_ anti_ join* parameter.

OPERATION

OPTIONS	OBJECT_NAME	POSITION
SELECT STATEMENT		
		1
FILTER		
		1
TABLE ACCESS		
FULL	EMP	1
TABLE ACCESS		
FULL	BAD_CREDIT	2

The anti-join is the opposite of an equi-join. For example, in the preceding anti-join, Oracle takes an *emp* row and then checks for a matching row in the *bad_credit* table. If a row is found, then that row is eliminated from the result set and the next *emp* row is retrieved. In sum, instead of checking if the outer rows exists in the inner query, the anti-join verifies that the rows do not exist in the inner query.

Another common way to rewrite noncorrelated anti-join subqueries is to utilize the Oracle SQL *minus* clause. To illustrate, here we have changed the NOT IN subquery into an IN subquery:

```
select /*+ rule */
   ename
from
   emp
where
   empno IN
   (select
      empno
   from
      employees
```

```
MINUS
select
    empno
from
    bad_credit
where
    bad_credit_date > sysdate-365
)
;
```

Here is the execution plan for this query. Here we see that Oracle must execute the query against the *emp* table twice, but this is still faster than executing the subquery once for each row in the outer table.

OPERATION OPTIONS	OBJECT_NAME	POSITION
SELECT STATEMENT		1385
NESTED LOOPS		1
VIEW	VW_NSO_1	1
MINUS		1
SORT UNIQUE		1
TABLE ACCESS FULL	EMP	1
SORT UNIQUE		2
TABLE ACCESS FULL	BAD_CREDIT	1
TABLE ACCESS BY INDEX ROWID	EMP	2
INDEX RANGE SCAN	EMP_EMPNO	1

Next let's take a look at subqueries that use the NOT IN operator.

Correlated Subqueries with the NOT IN Operator

Logically, it is very unusual to use a NOT IN subquery with a correlation in the subquery. The NOT is the anti-join that says to filter out matching rows, while the correlation says to specifically match rows in the subquery.

To show this type of subquery, we have created a table called *dependents* that contains the following data columns.

```
SQL> select * from dependents;

    EMPNO DEPENDENT_ RELATION
---------- ---------- ----------
     7902 Sarah      daughter
     7902 Janet      spouse
     7934 Jan        spouse
     7934 William    son
     7934 Bob        son
     7934 Marianne   daughter
```

Here is a query to select all employees without a son.

```
select
    ename
from
    emp
where empno NOT IN
    (select
        empno
    from
        dependents
    where
        emp.empno = dependents.empno
    and
        relation='son'
    )
;
```

These opposing goals will still work, but the best solution is to remove the subquery and use an outer join with the *select distinct* clause.

Correlated Subqueries with the NOT EXISTS Operator

Recall that Oracle doesn't consider transforming correlated subqueries that are interfaced via the NOT EXISTS operator. Here is an example of a noncorrelated subquery with the NOT EXISTS operator.

This query could be used to locate employees who do not have a son. This type of anti-join will evaluate the inner query for each row in the outer query and filter out all rows except those where the employee has no inner table rows *where relation='son'*.

```
select
    ename
from
    emp
where NOT EXISTS
    (select
        null
    from
        dependents
    where
        emp.empno = dependents.empno
    and
        relation='son'
    )
;
```

Here is the execution plan. Note the full-table scan against the *emp* table because the subquery does not use the *empno* index on the *emp* table. This full-table scan could be very time-consuming if the *emp* table had millions of rows.

```
OPERATION
------------------------------------------------------------------
OPTIONS                      OBJECT_NAME                   POSITION
--------------------------   -------------------------   ----------
SELECT STATEMENT
                                                                 1
    FILTER
                                                                 1
    TABLE ACCESS
FULL                         EMP                                 1
    TABLE ACCESS
BY INDEX ROWID               DEPENDENTS                          2
        INDEX
RANGE SCAN                   DEP_EMPNO                           1
```

Now, here it would be tempting to try to rewrite this query as an outer join. In fact, we can reformulate the equivalent query by specifying the outer join conditions in a equi-join, being careful to add the *select distinct* clause to eliminate any duplicate rows.

```
select distinct
    ename
from
    emp,
    dependents
where
    emp.empno = dependents.empno(+)
and
    relation(+)='son'
```

```
and
    dependents.empno is null
;
```

Here we see a faster execution plan using an OUTER access method with the HASH JOIN access method. In a case where the driving table (in this case the outer *emp* table) is small, this query will execute far faster than the original subquery.

```
OPERATION
-----------------------------------------------------------------------
OPTIONS                          OBJECT_NAME                POSITION
-------------------------------  -------------------------  ----------
SELECT STATEMENT
                                                                  6
  SORT
UNIQUE                                                            1
    FILTER
                                                                  1
      HASH JOIN
OUTER                                                             1
        TABLE ACCESS
FULL                             EMP                              1
        TABLE ACCESS
FULL                             DEPENDENTS                       2
```

Next, let's look at noncorrelated subqueries that use the NOT EXISTS operator.

Noncorrelated Subqueries with the NOT EXISTS Operator

It never makes sense to use the NOT EXISTS clause in a noncorrelated subquery, because the query cannot be resolved. To illustrate, consider the query below:

```
select
    ename
from
    emp
where NOT EXISTS
    (select
       null
    from
       bad_credit
    )
;
```

Next, let's examine how Oracle SQL handles nonequality conditions.

Tuning Subqueries with Nonequality Conditions

In addition to subqueries where the inner query is tied to the outer query with an equality operator, you can also specify other conditions before the subquery. This section will examine how Oracle processes subqueries using the ANY, ALL, and standard nonequality conditions such as greater than (>), less than (<), and not equals (<>).

Let's begin by reviewing the ALL and ANY clauses.

Using the ANY or ALL Condition in a Subquery

The ANY and ALL operators are used with subqueries when you want to return matching values from the subquery to the outer query. This is a relatively obscure technique, but it is supported in Oracle SQL, and it is used from time to time when the need arises to compare scalar values in two tables. We will see that the ALL or ANY clause can easily be replaced by in-line views that simplify both the structure of the query and the internal performance of the query. Let's start with the ANY clause.

Using the ANY Clause in a Subquery

For example, consider the "> ANY" operator as shown next. Here our user is trying to display the names of all employees who are younger than any customer born after 1985. Why would a user want to know this information, you ask? The technical term for this types of query is "brain fart," and obtuse queries like this one are generated every day by SQL developers.

```
select
    ename
from
    emp
where
    birthdate > ANY
    (select
        birthdate
    from
        customer
    where
        birthdate > '31-DEC-1985'
    )
;
```

This query will return all employee names where their *birthdate* > any customers born after 1985. Here is the execution plan.

```
OPERATION
------------------------------------------------------------------------
OPTIONS                         OBJECT_NAME                 POSITION
------------------------------ --------------------------- ----------
SELECT STATEMENT
                                                                   1
   FILTER
                                                                   1
      TABLE ACCESS
FULL                            EMP                               1
      TABLE ACCESS
FULL                            CUSTOMER                          2
```

The "> ANY" operator says to return values where *any* returned value in the subquery is true. Note that this is equivalent to returning saying that if the employees' *birthdate* is greater than the minimum customer *birthdate* that is returned from the subquery.

Hence, we can replace the "> ANY" with a nonequality and select the minimum values in an in-line view. As you may recall, an in-line view is a query where a subquery is specified in the *from* clause, just as if it were a table name.

```
select
    ename
from
    emp,
    (select
       min(birthdate) min_bday
     from
       customer
     where
       birthdate > '31-DEC-1985'
    ) in_line_view
where
    emp.birthdate > in_line_view.min_bday
;
```

The ALL operator is a bit different from the ANY operator. To illustrate, look at the following query:

```
select
    ename
from
    emp
where
    birthdate > ALL
    (select
        birthdate
    from
        customer
    where
        birthdate > '31-DEC-1985'
    )
;
```

This query says to display the names of all employees whose *birthdate* is greater than any customers who were born after 1985.

It should now be apparent that the ANY operator returns the minimum value from the in-line view, and the ALL operator returns the maximum value from the in-line view. Here is an equivalent query:

```
select
    ename
from
    emp,
    (select
        max(birthdate) max_bday
     from
        customer
     where
        birthdate > '31-DEC-1985'
    ) in_line_view
where
    emp.birthdate > in_line_view.min_bday
;
```

In sum, the ALL and ANY subquery forms can always be replaced with in-line views, and the in-line view form of the query has far greater performance because it can utilize the indexes on the joined tables.

Next, let's look at other forms of subqueries that have nonequality operators.

Using Nonequality Conditions in Subqueries

For example, consider a subquery where the inner query returns many rows. Here we add the following table to our schema, used to track each employee's salary history:

```
SQL> select * from sal_hist;

    EMPNO     SALARY EFFECTIVE
---------- ---------- ---------
      7369       4000 31-MAR-01
      7499       4000 31-MAR-01
      7369       5000 20-APR-01
      7499       5000 24-APR-01
```

Because each employee may have many rows in the *sal_hist* table, we cannot create a unique index on the *empno* column.

The following query returns the last effective date for a raise, selecting only those employees who have not received a raise in the past 90 days:

```
select
    ename
from
    emp        e,
    sal_hist   s1
where
    e.empno = s1.empno
and
    effective_date <
    (select
       max(effective_date)
    from
       sal_hist s2
    where
       s1.empno=s2.empno
    and
       s2.effective_date <= sysdate-90
    )
;
```

Here is the execution plan. Note that we see the VIEW table access method that is always performed in a subquery.

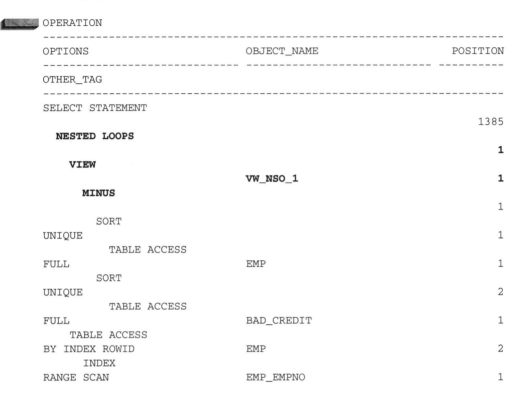

```
OPERATION
------------------------------------------------------------------------
OPTIONS                         OBJECT_NAME                     POSITION
---------------------------     ---------------------------     ----------
OTHER_TAG
------------------------------------------------------------------------
SELECT STATEMENT
                                                                    1385
  NESTED LOOPS
                                                                       1
    VIEW
                                VW_NSO_1                               1
      MINUS
                                                                       1
        SORT
UNIQUE                                                                  1
          TABLE ACCESS
FULL                            EMP                                    1
        SORT
UNIQUE                                                                  2
          TABLE ACCESS
FULL                            BAD_CREDIT                             1
      TABLE ACCESS
BY INDEX ROWID                  EMP                                    2
        INDEX
RANGE SCAN                      EMP_EMPNO                              1
```

Here we see an execution plan using the VIEW access method, and we are doing a complex and time-consuming subquery. Since this correlated subquery returns an aggregate (*max, min, sum,* or *avg*), we can use a temporary table to store the maximum values for each employee's salary *effective_date.* As you will remember from Chapter 18, temporary tables are great for speeding up queries by moving the precomputed aggregation to another table.

TIP
Never underestimate the power of temporary tables. Whenever your SQL is performing multiple aggregations, using temporary tables can often improve the speed of the query by several orders of magnitude. For details on using temporary tables to tune SQL, please see Chapter 18.

```
drop table
    temp;

create table
    temp
as
select
    empno,
    max(effective_date) max_date
from
    sal_hist
group by
    empno
;

select
    ename
from
    emp e,
    temp t
where
    e.empno=t.empno
and
    t.max_date < sysdate-90
;
```

Here we have greatly improved the speed of the overall query, and we have also simplified the query syntax and the execution plan.

```
OPERATION
-----------------------------------------------------------------------
OPTIONS                        OBJECT_NAME                   POSITION
------------------------------ -------------------------- ----------
SELECT STATEMENT
                                                                  19

  NESTED LOOPS
                                                                   1

    TABLE ACCESS
FULL                           TEMP                               1
    TABLE ACCESS
BY INDEX ROWID                 EMP                                2
        INDEX
RANGE SCAN                     EMP_EMPNO                          1
```

Next, let's take a look at how hints are used to improve execution speed for subqueries.

Hints to Improve Subquery Execution Speed

As I noted in detail in Chapter 12, we can add hints to improve the speed of subqueries. These include the *merge_aj* hint to force a merge anti-join and the *hash_aj* hint to force a hash anti-join. For details, see Chapter 12.

- ■ *merge_aj* **hint** The *merge_aj* hint is placed in a NOT IN subquery to perform an anti-join where full-table access is preferred over index access.

- ■ *hash_aj* **hint** The *hash_aj* hint is placed in a NOT IN subquery to perform a hash anti-join in cases where a hash join is desired.

- ■ *push_subq* **hint** The *push_subq* hint causes all subqueries in the query block to be executed at the earliest possible place in the execution plan. Normally, subqueries that are not merged are executed as the last step in the execution plan. If the subquery is relatively inexpensive and reduces the number of rows significantly, then it improves performance to evaluate the subquery earlier. The *push_subq* hint has no effect if the subquery is using a sort merge join, or when the subquery references a remote table.

Conclusion

As should be clear, there are only a few legitimate conditions for performing a subquery. Many other subqueries can be rewritten to utilize standard joins or in-line views. One of the first things that a Oracle professional learns is to carefully evaluate the legitimacy of all subqueries and re-write them whenever possible.

Next, let's take a look at how queries can be tuned to use indexes.

CHAPTER
20

Tuning SQL
with Indexes

ne of the most common techniques for removing an unwanted large-table full-table scan is to add a new index to a table. Of course, we must be cautious when adding indexes because a new index may change the execution plan for many other SQL statements. It is always a good idea to make all SQL tuning changes by using optimizer plan stability or by adding hints to the SQL. If we determine that the query is accessing a small portion of the table rows (less than 40 percent of a row-sequenced table, or 12 percent of an unordered table), then adding an index will almost always improve the speed of the query. Of course, the overall speed of the index range scan as opposed to the full-table scan is not always easy to determine and is influenced by the *db_block_size,* the *avg_ row_ len,* and the degree of parallelism for the full-table scan. I will present a more detailed description of the estimation of query speed later in this chapter.

When tuning by adding indexes, there are two special cases of indexes that are especially useful:

- **Function-based indexes**   Whenever a SQL query must use a function (e.g., *where upper(last_name)='JONES'),* a function-based index can remove a full-table scan. We also see a great improvement of index access of DATE datatypes by indexing DATE columns with the *to_char* function. One of the shortcoming of Oracle SQL is that using a built-in function on an index will make the index unusable, and function-based indexes are a godsend for improving the access speed of queries that reference a built-in function in the SQL.

- **Bitmap indexes**   It was a common misconception that bitmap indexes were only appropriate for columns with a very small number of distinct values—say, less than 50. Current research in Oracle8*i* has shown that bitmap indexes can substantially improve the speed of queries using columns with up to 1,000 distinct values, because retrieval from a bitmap index is done in RAM and is almost always faster than using a traditional B-tree index. Most experienced DBAs will look for columns with fewer than 1,000 distinct values, build a bitmap index on this column, and then see if the query is faster.

Finding Indexing Opportunities

The process of locating opportunities for indexing is an easy and rewarding activity. Because most SQL developers do not look to see if indexes are available, there are many opportunities for speeding up queries by adding indexes. Better still, adding new indexes is easy and requires no changes to the existing SQL (unless you are using optimizer plan stability).

In general, searching for indexing opportunities involves the following steps:

1. **Go fishing for large-table full-table scans** You can check the *v$sqlarea* view or the *stats$sql_summary* table to identify tables that experience large-table full-table scans. This is done by executing the *access.sql* script to explain all of the SQL and generate the full-table scan report. This report will show you the table names, the number of full-table scans, and the number of blocks in the table. As a general rule, tables with full-table scans that have more than 100 blocks warrant investigation.

2. **Extract the SQL statement** Once a table name is identified as having large-table full-table scans, you can extract the SQL that accesses these tables.

3. **Add the index** Add the index to the database in a test environment. Remember, adding an index could affect the execution plans of many SQL statements, and the index should not be added into the production environment until the speed improvement has been verified.

4. **Evaluate the legitimacy of the full-table scan** Next, we test the number of data blocks returned from the query to determine if the query would run faster with an index.

5. **Test the execution speed** If the large-table full-table scan has a nonindexed column, create an index on the column and time the query using the *set timing on* SQL*Plus command.

6. **Predict the benefit to the whole database** Once the index is created in the test environment, you can use the STATSPACK historical SQL table, to see how the new index would affect the whole database.

The first step in looking for indexing opportunities is to locate those large tables that experience frequent full-table scans. Using the *access.sql* script from Chapter 5, we can begin by observing the full-table scan report that was produced by analyzing all of the SQL that was in the library cache. From this report, we can check the number of rows returned from each SQL statement to see if the large-table full-table scan is legitimate.

```
Mon Jan 29                                                        page    1
                         full table scans and counts
                 Note that "C" indicates the table is cached.
                 The "K" indicates that the table in the KEEP pool.

OWNER           NAME                          NUM_ROWS C K   BLOCKS   NBR_FTS
-------------   -----------------------       ------------ - -  --------  --------
SYS             DUAL                                   N        2    97,237
EMPDB1          PAGER                      3,450,209 N    932,120     9,999
EMPDB1          RWU_PAGE                         434 N          8     7,355
EMPDB1          STAR_IMAGE                    18,067 N      1,104     5,368
EMPDB1          SUBSCRIPTION                     476 N K      192     2,087
EMPDB1          PRINT_PAGE_RANGE                  10 N K       32       874
ARSD            JANET_BOOKS                       20 N          8        64
PERFSTAT        STATS$TAB_STATS                     N         65        10
```

Here, we must make the subjective judgment about what tables warrant further investigation. As you know, small-table full-table scan tables are placed in the KEEP pool, so we are only concerned with large tables.

In the preceding example, you see that the *pager* and *star_image* tables consist of more than 1000 data blocks, and both have more than 5000 full-table scans. These are clear candidates for further investigation, and our next step is to extract these SQL statements and evaluate the legitimacy of the full-table scans.

Extract the SQL Statement

Once we have located a table that has large-table full-table scans, the next step is to extract all SQL statements that reference the query. If you were using *access.sql* to explain all of the SQL in your library cache, you can run a query against the *v$sqlarea* view to extract the SQL statements that reference the table.

```
set lines 2000;

select
    sql_text
from
    v$sqlarea
where
    sql_text like '% pager %';
```

The *set lines 2000;* SQL*Plus command will allow most SQL statements to be displayed, and you can easily cut and paste the SQL statements into a file for further evaluation. Now that we have the SQL, we must evaluate the legitimacy of the SQL statement.

Add the Index

You will next add the index that you think will aid the query in your test environment. Remember, adding an index can change the execution plans for many other SQL statements, so this is always best done in the test environment. The main reason for creating the index is to obtain the *clustering_factor* from *dba_indexes* for the index.

When comparing the costs of a full-table scan and an index range scan, it is important to know the *clustering_factor* of our index to the table. As you know, a low value for *clustering_factor* (near the number of blocks in the table) means that more sequential data rows will be accessed in each block read (Figure 20-1).

Conversely, a high *clustering_factor,* where the value approaches the number of rows in the table *(num_rows),* indicates that the rows are not in the same sequence as the index, and additional I/O will be required for index range scans (Figure 20-2).

Next, let's look at how to evaluate the legitimacy of a full-table scan.

Evaluate the Legitimacy of the Full-Table Scan

As you should know by now, a full-table scan may be faster than an index range scan if a minority of the table blocks are retrieved by the query. We say "able blocks" instead of the number of rows, because it is the number of data blocks, and not the number of table rows, that most influences the decision to perform a full-table scan over an index range scan. For an unsequenced table with small row lengths and a large block size, a random retrieval of 10 percent of the rows can access well over 50 percent of the table blocks in the table.

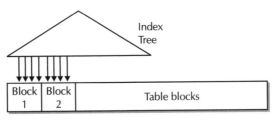

FIGURE 20-1.   *An index with a low* clustering_factor

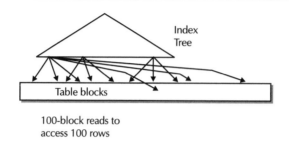

FIGURE 20-2. *An index with a high* clustering_factor

Since the number of rows returned is heavily dependent on the row length and the block size, there is no firm percentage that can be used to determine the threshold for a full-table scan. If the query retrieves fewer data blocks using an index range scan than the full-table scan, then the index access will generally be a faster alternative.

The goal is to compare the number of blocks returned by the full-table scan with the number of data blocks returned by the index range scan. Computing the number of blocks accessed by a full-table scan can be done by going to the Oracle data dictionary and summing the number of blocks from the *dba_segments* view:

```
select
    sum(blocks)
from
    dba_segments
where
    table_name = 'CUSTOMER';

SUM(BLOCKS)
----------------------
152392
```

Now, we need to compare the number of blocks retrieved by the full-table scan with the blocks retrieved from an index range scan. Since the number of blocks retrieved by the query is the most important, the following equation can be used to determine the approximate number of blocks retrieved by the query. To use this equation, you need the following information:

- The number of rows returned by the query. This is determined by executing the query

- The database blocksize (the *db_block_size* initialization parameter)

- The average row length (the *avg_row_len* in the *dba_tables* view)

- The *clustering_factor* in the *dba_indexes* view for the index you plan to use

Let's look at two methods for comparing an indexed SQL query against the block I/O for a full-table scan.

Estimating Blocks Retrieved by an Indexed Table Query

This is an equation to compute the number of blocks retrieved by a row-sequenced table. We discussed the method for using CTAS to resequence rows. You can tell if your table is row-sequenced by checking the *clustering_factor* column of the *dba_indexes* view for the index that you are using to retrieve your rows.

- If *clustering_factor* is close to the number of data blocks in your table (the *blocks* column of *dba_segments*), then your table is row-sequenced.

- If *clustering_factor* is close to the number of rows (the *num_rows* column of the *dba_tables* view), then your table rows are not in index sequence. Hence, we must perform lots of additional block accesses to retrieve our rows.

Next, let's look at a way to estimate the number of data blocks retrieved by a query. If your *clustering_factor* is close to the number of blocks in the table, then you can use this method to estimate the number of blocks retrieved by the query. Here is a great way to estimate the number of blocks retrieved by your query:

```
                                    number of rows retrieved
Number of blocks retrieved = ----------------------------------------------------
                               db_block_size       dba.segments.blocks
                               -------------   x   -------------------------
                               avg_row_len         dba_indexes.clustering_factor
```

To see how this works, assume that you have collected the following information about the table and index in your query.

- number of rows retrieved = 600

- *db_block_size* = 16K (rounded to 16,000 for estimation purposes)

- *dba_tables.avg_row_len* = 80

- *dba_segments.blocks* = 1000

- *dba_indexes.clustering_factor* = 20,000

When we plug numbers into the equation, we see that this index range scan causes about 60 data blocks to be retrieved by Oracle. Of course, a block request does not always result in a disk I/O, because of the buffering in the DEFAULT, KEEP, and RECYCLE pools.

$$\frac{600}{200 \times .05} = \frac{600}{10} = 60 \text{ data blocks retrieved}$$

Note that as the *clustering_factor* increases from the number of blocks in the table to the number of rows in the table, the number of disk accesses will increase. For example, when we change the clustering factor from 1,000 to 2,000, we see that Oracle must retrieve twice the number of blocks.

NOTE
Be sure to completely reanalyze the table and the index to get accurate dictionary statistics for this equation.

Now that you know the number of data blocks retrieved by the query, we can accurately compare the number of blocks retrieved as a percentage of the number of blocks in the table.

Determining the Block Threshold Percentage

Remember, when considering the total number of blocks accessed, you must also consider the index block accesses, and we generally add a 20 percent overhead for block access. The generally recognized threshold for block access is about 40 percent, meaning that any query that accesses over 40 percent of the table blocks will be faster with a nonparallel full-table scan.

We also have to account for Oracle parallel query, which speeds the full-table scan by 60 percent for each parallel query slave process. This 60 percent gain is based on the number of CPUs on your database server and the distribution of your data blocks across disk devices, but 60 percent provides a good starting point.

For example, if a full-table scan has a parallel degree of 16, the full-table scan will run about 60 percent of 16, or about 10 times faster than a nonparallel full-table scan.

When the starting block access threshold for a table is 40 percent, we must reduce this percentage based on our optimal degree of parallelism for the table. For details on computing the optimal degree of parallelism for a table, see Chapter 10. The goal is to compare the estimated number of blocks retrieved by the index range scan with our threshold.

Concluding the Estimate

In our example, we retrieved about 60 blocks of our 1000-block table. This is about 17 percent of the table blocks, and it is safe to assume that the index range scan would be faster than a full-table scan, unless we have a very large database server with dozens of CPUs, and we can get a high degree of full-table scan performance improvements with Oracle parallel query.

As you can see from the preceding section, empirically estimating the benefit of an index range scan versus a full-table scan depends on many factors. Hence, most SQL tuning professionals dispense with the equations except to get a general idea of the threshold.

In the real world, the only way to verify that an index outperforms a full-table scan is to set timing on and test the execution speed in SQL*Plus. There is no substitute for timing your query.

Time the Query with the New Index

When all is said and done, the only real measure is the execution speed of the query. To make the test realistic, many people will restart the Oracle test database immediately preceding the query to ensure that the data buffer caching does not affect the query response time.

Predict the Benefit for the Whole Database

When adding a new index, one additional step that is commonly performed is predicting the overall benefit to the database. To do this, you begin by going to the historical STATSPACK tables and reexplaining all of the SQL from the *stats$sql_summary* table. Once in your plan table, you can run the *access_report.sql* script to get the table access report for each snapshot period.

One perplexing problem is that it is not easy to predict how often an index is used. By modifying the *access.sql* script from the Web site for this book, you can explain all of the SQL for a specified STATSPACK snapshot and see how often your index would be used at that time. This allows your DBA to weigh the costs of the index storage with the speed improvements resulting from the new index.

From the report, you should see a reduction in full-table scans against the target table. In addition, you will also see your new index being used in the index range scan report.

Next, let explore methods for removing time-consuming SQL disk sorts by adding indexes.

Removing Sorts by Adding Indexes

One of the best ways to remove disk sorts is by adding indexes. When operating in *first_rows* mode, Oracle will always try to resolve an *order by* clause by using an index in lieu of a sort operation. However, you must always remember that while an index will retrieve the rows far faster than a sort, the index scan will have less throughput than the sort operation.

As you may know, Oracle will sometimes use an index-full scan in place of a disk sort operation. As part of the determination of whether to use an index, the Oracle optimizer considers the number of rows returned by the query and weighs the costs of the sort versus the costs of retrieving the rows via the index. In most cases, Oracle will only consider an index-full scan in cases where a large number of rows are being retrieved and a disk sort would be required to satisfy the query.

Unnecessary Sorts

There are many cases where Oracle performs a sort operation even though a sort is not required. This generally happens when one of the following conditions is present:

- **Missing index**   Many DBAs are not aware that a column index is required for a query until they begin SQL tuning.

- **Sort merge join**   Anytime a sort merge join is requested, a sort will be performed to join the key values. In many cases, a nested loop join is a better choice because it is more efficient and does not require sorting or full-table scans.

- **Using the *distinct* clause**   Using the *select distinct* clause on a query will always invoke a sort to remove the duplicate rows. There are many documented cases of SQL that has a distinct clause even though there can never be duplicate rows in the result set.

Index Predicates

As a general rule, indexes will always increase the performance of a database query when it is able to utilize the index, and if there is a small subset of rows required by the query. For Oracle, indexes are recommended for two reasons: to speed the retrieval of a small set of rows from a table, and to "presort" result sets so that the SQL *order by* clause does not cause an internal sort.

In order to use an index, the SQL optimizer must recognize that the column has a valid value for index use. This is called a *sargable predicate,* and the data types in the column and the predicates must match to allow Oracle to use index access. The term *sargable* refers to the ability of the SQL optimizer to utilize the index.

Here are some examples of invalid predicates. Note that the data types are mixed, and numeric columns are compared to character strings, and vice versa.

```
select * from employee
where
    emp_no = "123";
```

Performing a math function in the *where* clause can also invalidate an index.

```
select * from employee
where
    salary * 2 < 50000;
```

Also, using the not equal operator (<>) will invalidate the index.

```
select * from employee
where
    dept_no <> 10;
```

Whenever a transformation to a field value takes place, the Oracle database will not be able to use the index for that column. In the examples that follow, the use of an Oracle built-in function invalidates the standard index:

```
select * from employee
where
    to_char(hire_date,'YYYY')=1998;
```

Using a substring function can also invalidate an index.

```
select * from employee
where
    substr(last_name,1,4) = 'FRED';
```

Conversion of columns to uppercase or lowercase can also invalidate the index. This use of the *upper* function is very common on systems that perform row access on test strings, where the end-users do not want the end users to be concerned with case sensitivity:

```
select * from employee
where
    upper(last_name) = 'JONES';
select * from employee
where
    lower(book_title) = 'war and peace';
```

In these cases, a function-based index can be used to allow corresponding access to the columns.

```
create index
    emp_upper_last_name
on
    emp
    (
        upper(last_name)
    )
;

create index
    book_title_lower
on
    book
    (
        lower(book_title)
    )
;
```

You can also combine the use of function-based indexes with bitmap indexes. In the example that follows, we convert a low-cardinality column such as *item_color* (which has fewer than 20 distinct values) into a bitmap index. To ensure easy retrieval, we index on the color in lowercase:

```
create bitmap index
    item_color_lower
on
    book
    (
        lower(item_color)
    )
;
```

Oracle date datatypes are also problematical, and the *to_char* function is sometimes needed in SQL to select dates within specific ranges. For example, our SQL may use the *to_char* function to extract dates for specific years and months. Hence, we can index on the *to_char* function to specify years and month-year combinations:

```
select * from customer
where
    to_char(order_date,'YYYY')='1999';

select * from customer
where
    to_char(order_date,'MON-YY')='JAN-01'
;
```

Here we match the function-based indexes with the date format string in the SQL statements:

```
create index
    cust_order_year
on
    customer
    (
        to_char(order_date,'YYYY')
    )
;
create index
    cust_order_mon_year
on
    customer
    (
        to_char(order_date,'MON-YY')
    )
;
```

Next, let's look at issues surrounding the *like* parameter in SQL statements.

Problems with the *like* Parameter

You cannot create a function-based index using the *like* parameter, because you cannot create a function-based index on a column mask. Of course, using a *like* clause will invalidate the index if the high-order item is specified with the percent (%) wildcard:

```
select * from employee
where
    last_name like '%SON';
```

The preceding query will not be able to use the index because it begins with the "%" mask. Next, let's explore index usage within Oracle when a column has an uneven distribution of values.

Evaluating Index Usage for Skewed Column Values

Even within a specific column value, the value of the column can impact the execution plan. For example, assume that a student table has 1,000 rows, representing 900 undergraduate students and 100 graduate students. A nonunique index has been built on the *student_level* field that indicates UNDERGRAD or GRAD. The same query will benefit from different access methods depending upon the value of the literal in the *where* clause. The following query will retrieve 90 percent of the rows in the table, and it will run faster with a full-table scan than it will if the SQL optimizer chooses to use an index:

```
select
    *
from
    student
where
    student_level = 'UNDERGRAD';
```

This next query will access only 10 percent of the table rows, and it will run faster by using the index on the *student_level* column:

```
select
    *
from
    student
where
    student_level = 'GRAD';
```

Without histograms, the Oracle database cannot predict in advance the number of rows that will be returned from a query. Often the SQL optimizer will invoke an index access even though it may not always be the fastest access method.

Oracle, for example, allows the concatenation of a null string to the field name in the *where* clause to suppress index access. The previous query could be rewritten in Oracle SQL to bypass the *student_level* index as follows:

```
select
    *
from
    student
where
    student_level||'' = 'UNDERGRAD';
```

The concatenation (||) of a null string to the field tells the Oracle SQL optimizer to bypass index processing for this field, instead invoking a faster-running full-table scan.

This is a very important point. While the Oracle9*i* SQL optimizer is becoming more intelligent about the best access plan, it still cannot always estimate the number of rows returned by a specific Boolean predicate and will not always choose the best access path.

For example, the not equal (<>) operator will cause an index to be bypassed and the query "show all undergrads who are not computer science majors" will cause a full-table scan:

```
select
    *
from
    student
where
     student_level = 'UNDERGRAD'
and
     major <> 'computer science';
```

Here, the <> condition cannot utilize an index, and this query will invoke a full-table scan. In sum, there are many query conditions that can invalidate the index, and you must always explain the SQL to see the execution plan to ensure that your query is using the expected indexes.

Oracle9*i* and Index Usage for Skewed Columns
A new feature in Oracle9*i* allows the CBO to change execution plans even when optimizer plan stability is used. This is called "peeking" and allows the CBO to change execution plans when the value of a bind variable would cause a significant change to the execution plan for the SQL.

When using cursor sharing, the CBO changes any literal values in the SQL to bind variables. In Oracle9*i*, the CBO "peeks" at the values of user-defined bind variables on the first invocation of a cursor. This lets the optimizer determine the selectivity of the *where* clause operator and change the execution plan whenever the *south* value appears in the SQL.

This enhancement greatly improves the performance of cursor sharing when a bind variable is used against a highly skewed column.

Indexing Alternatives to B-Tree Indexes

As you may know, Oracle offers several alternative indexing methods to enhance the standard B-tree indexes. These include bitmap indexes, function-based indexes, and reverse-key indexes.

Bitmap Indexes

It was a common misconception that bitmap indexes were only appropriate for columns with a very small number of distinct values—say, fewer than 50. Current research in Oracle8*i* has shown that bitmap indexes can substantially improve the speed of queries using columns with up to 1,000 distinct values, because retrieval from a bitmap index is done in RAM and is almost always faster than using a traditional B-tree index. Most experienced DBAs will look for tables that contain columns with fewer than 1,000 distinct values, build a bitmap index on these columns, and then see if the query is faster.

Function-Based Indexes

To use the alternative indexing structures, you must first identify SQL statements that are using the BIF. In the next example, we can search the *v$sqlarea* view to find all SQL statements that are using the *to_char* BIF.

```
select
    sql_text
from
    v$sqlarea  -- or stats$sql_summary
where
    sql_text like '%to_char%';
```

Once identified, function-based indexes can be created to remove the full-table scans and replace them with index-range scans. For details on tuning with function-based indexes, see Chapter 23.

Reverse-Key Indexes and SQL Performance

There is, however, a major scalability danger with automatically generated synthetic keys. Every insertion to a table requires a corresponding insertion to its primary key index. If the primary key values are being generated in ascending order, then all inserts will need to change the high-order leaf block in the B-tree. There is an obvious danger here of contention for that block of the index, if several users attempt concurrent inserts (whereas the inserts to the table itself can easily be distributed to a variety of blocks by using multiple process freelists).

Prior to Oracle8, the standard strategy to avoid this problem was to ensure that the synthetic key values were not generated in order. This was done by permuting the values generated by the sequence number generator before using them. Various permutation schemes such as adding a leading check digit, or reversing the order of the digits, have been used. These schemes have the effect of distributing inserts evenly over the range of values in the index, thus preventing leaf block contention. In Oracle8, the same effect may be obtained by using a reverse-key index.

The major disadvantage of distributing inserts in this way is that the data density of index leaf blocks will be typically only 75 percent of capacity rather than almost 100 percent, making fast full-index scans on the primary key index less efficient. However, this access path is not typical and is seldom performance critical when used. So, reverse-key indexes should be used in general for synthetic primary key indexes.

Index Usage for Queries with IN Conditions

When a query has an IN condition to evaluate multiple expressions, the SQL optimizer will often perform a full-table scan, but with many variant execution plans. Queries that evaluate multiple conditions can execute with TABLE ACCESS FULL, CONCATENATION, INLIST ITERATOR, and UNION, which all perform the exact same function of returning rows with multiple values.

To illustrate, consider the following simple query.

```
select
    ename
from
    emp
where
    job IN ('MANAGER','PRESIDENT')
;
```

Here you see the execution plan. Note the use of the CONCATENATION operator.

```
OPERATION
----------------------------------------------------------------------------
OPTIONS                          OBJECT_NAME                  POSITION
-------------------------------  ---------------------------  ----------
SELECT STATEMENT
   CONCATENATION
                                                                      1
      TABLE ACCESS
BY INDEX ROWID                   EMP                                  1
         INDEX
RANGE SCAN                       JOB_IDX                              1
      TABLE ACCESS
BY INDEX ROWID                   EMP                                  2
         INDEX
RANGE SCAN                       JOB_IDX                              1
```

Now we change to the CBO by adding a *first_rows* hint, and we see an entirely different execution plan.

```
OPERATION
----------------------------------------------------------------------------
OPTIONS                          OBJECT_NAME                  POSITION
-------------------------------  ---------------------------  ----------
SELECT STATEMENT
                                                                      1
   INLIST ITERATOR
                                                                      1
      TABLE ACCESS
BY INDEX ROWID                   EMP                                  1
         INDEX
RANGE SCAN                       JOB_IDX                              1
```

Of course, this query can also be rewritten to utilize the *union* SQL operator. Here is an equivalent query.

```
select /*+ first_rows */
   ename
from
   emp
where
   job = 'MANAGER'
union
select ename from emp
where
   job = 'PRESIDENT'
;
```

Here you see the execution plan using the UNION-ALL table access method.

```
OPERATION
-------------------------------------------------------------------------------
OPTIONS                         OBJECT_NAME                     POSITION
--------------------------  ----------------------------  ----------
SELECT STATEMENT
                                                                   6
  SORT
UNIQUE                                                             1
    UNION-ALL
                                                                   1
      TABLE ACCESS
BY INDEX ROWID                  EMP                               1
        INDEX
RANGE SCAN                      JOB_IDX                           1
      TABLE ACCESS
BY INDEX ROWID                  EMP                               2
        INDEX
RANGE SCAN                      JOB_IDX                           1
```

Here you see three alternative execution plans for the exact same result set. The point is that there are many opportunities to change the execution plan for queries that evaluate for multiple conditions, and in most cases you must actually time the queries to see which execution plan is fastest for your specific query.

Conclusion

This chapter has been concerned with the appropriate use of indexes to service Oracle queries. The main points of this chapter include these:

■ The number of table blocks accessed by a query determines whether to use an index range scan or a full-table scan. You must evaluate the number of blocks returned by each form of the query to determine the fastest execution path.

■ Using BIFs in a query or performing computations on an index column can sometimes invalidate the index and cause a full-table scan.

■ When using the RBO, bitmap and function-based indexes will be ignored.

■ Oracle bitmap indexes have been enhanced to allow for columns that possess up to 1000 distinct values.

■ Oracle provides alternative indexing methods including bitmap indexes, function-based indexes, and reverse-key indexes to provide performance improvements for specialized queries.

Next, let's move on and look at how to tune queries that maximize performance for Oracle data warehouses.

CHAPTER
21

Tuning Data Warehouse
SQL

ne of the most important enhancements to Oracle8 was improving the scalability of the Oracle database software. Starting with Oracle8, Oracle made a commitment to supporting very large databases and developed sophisticated partitioning schemes and enhancements directly targeted to data warehouse queries, and now Oracle databases can easily support data warehouses with terabytes of data. Along with this support of very large databases came changes to Oracle SQL to support very large queries.

For data warehouse SQL, we see several features that are germane to SQL and the tuning of SQL. These include:

- **Large table join tuning** This relates to the use of the *star* and *ordered* hints to improve the throughput of join operations against very large tables.

- **Oracle partitioning and SQL tuning** Oracle provides internal methods to allow specific partitions of tables and indexes to be accessed during execution of an SQL query. In most cases, however, this use of partitions is transparent to the SQL.

- **Oracle parallel query and SQL tuning** Oracle has enhanced Oracle parallel query to speed up large-table full-table scans and make aggregation operations faster.

- **Oracle optimization and data warehouse queries** The parse phase of data warehouse SQL can be very time-consuming, and Oracle provides several initialization parameters and techniques for limiting the amount of parsing performed for data warehouse queries.

In addition to the data warehouse features, we will also explore techniques that can be used to identify those SQL queries that might benefit from data warehouse features.

Let's begin with a review of large tables and see how Oracle8*i* and Oracle9*i* handle very large tables with SQL.

Large Table Join Tuning

One of the foremost characteristics of data warehouse SQL queries is the presence of many tables in the SQL select statements. In standard star schema design, a central fact table is joined with numerous dimension tables.

As a matter of SQL tuning, we see the following SQL tuning techniques to improve the speed of data warehouse SQL statements:

- **The *ordered* hint** The *ordered* hint specifies the optimal way to join the tables together. This bypasses the expensive parse phase of data warehouse SQL and ensures that the tables are always joined in the same order. For details on tuning n-way joins, see Chapter 16.

- **The *star* hint** For queries of a fact table or a dimension table, the *star* hint can greatly improve the join speed of data warehouse queries. A permutation of the hash join, the star join techniques builds a hash index on the fact table indexes. For details on the *star* join, see Chapter 16.

- **Optimizer plan stability** The use of stored outlines also speeds up data warehouse queries and is a technique commonly used to bypass SQL join order parsing and ensure that SQL tuning changes are permanent. For details on stored outlines, see Chapter 13.

The ordered Hint

As I noted in detail in Chapter 12, Oracle must spend a great deal of time parsing n-way table joins to determine the optimal order to join the tables. The *ordered* hint can be used to reduce the parse time for queries that join more than five tables, and the *ordered* hint tells the CBO to join the tables in the same order in which they appear in the *from* clause. Hence, the first table after the *from* clause becomes the driving table, and the driving table should be the table that returns the smallest number of rows.

In the cost-based optimizer, the *ordered* hint requests that the tables should be joined in the order specified in the *from* clause, with the first table in the *from* clause specifying the driving table.

The *ordered* hint is commonly used in conjunction with other hints to ensure that multiple tables are joined in their proper order. For example, we may have a query that joins five tables together, and we want several of the joins to use a hash join and other tables to use a nested loop join. The *ordered* hint is very common in tuning data warehouse queries that join more than four tables together.

TIP
Large n-way table joins with seven or more tables can often take more than 30 minutes to parse the SQL. This is because Oracle must evaluate all possible table join orders. For example, with eight tables, Oracle must evaluate 8!, or 40,320, possible join combinations. Most people use the ordered hint to bypass this very expensive and time-consuming SQL parsing operation.

The ordered_predicates Hint

The *ordered_predicates* hint is a specialized hint that is specified in the *where* clause of a query; it directs the order in which the Boolean predicates in the *where* clause are evaluated. As we may know, Oracle should always evaluate the most restrictive predicate first, thereby reducing the size of the intermediate result sets.

Without the *ordered_predicates* hint, Oracle uses the following steps to evaluate the order of SQL predicates.

1. Subqueries are evaluated before the outer Boolean conditions in the *where* clause.

2. All Boolean conditions without built-in functions or subqueries are evaluated in their reverse order in the *where* clause, going from bottom-up, with the last predicate being evaluated first.

3. With Boolean predicates with built-in functions, the optimizer computes the cost of each predicate and evaluates them in increasing order of their costs.

Whenever the CBO makes a mistake in the evaluation order of your predicates, these default evaluation rules can be overridden by using the *ordered_predicates* hint. This hint is the equivalent of resequencing Booleans in the *where* clause for the RBO, where the *where* clause items are evaluated in the order that they appear in the query. This hint is very useful in cases where you know the most restrictive predicates and you want to control the order in which Oracle evaluates conditions in the where clause.

The *ordered_predicates* hint is commonly used in cases where a PL/SQL function is used inside the *where* clause of a query.

Oracle Partitioning and Oracle SQL Tuning

In order to improve the manageability of large tables and indexes in Oracle8, Oracle introduced the concept of *object partitioning*. Once a table or index is defined as partitioned , Oracle SQL automatically detects the partition segments and determines the appropriate segment to access during a SQL query.

CAUTION
You should always ensure that you are using the cost-based optimizer when using partitions because the rule-based optimizer will not use the performance enhancements of partition-wise joins and exclusive partition access. Make sure that your optimizer_ mode is set to first_rows *or* all_rows.

Partitioning and SQL Table Joining

The use of partitioned Tables and indexes will also improve the speed of table join operations in a special case of a join called a partition-wise join.

In a partition-wise join, Oracle divides the join into smaller joins that occur between each of the partitions on which the tables reside, completing the overall join in less time.

There are two types of partition-wise joins. The first variation requires that both tables reside in partitions, but Oracle also supports a partial partition-wise join, whereby only one of the tables is partitioned. Of course, the access of the partitions is transparent to the SQL, and the only way to see the partition access is to view the execution plan for the SQL.

In cases of partitioned full-table scans, parallelism can also be combined with partitioning. When parallelism is combined such that each partition has a parallel query process, the dividing of the table becomes faster and the overall execution time is faster.

Partitioning and SQL Execution Speed

When a partitioned index is analyzed with the analyze command, the Oracle data dictionary is populated with information about the ranges of values within each partition. This information is used by Oracle to include only those partitions that are relevant to the SQL query.

For example, suppose you have defined a partitioned index and an SQL statement requests an index range scan within a single index partition. Oracle will only access that index partition and can invoke an index fast-full scan against the partition, thereby improving the query speed because the entire index did not need to be accessed. Oracle calls this feature *partition-aware optimization*. At the heart of partition-aware optimization is the requirement that Oracle only access those partitions that are required to service the SQL query.

If you know the partition that contains your data you can explicitly reference it in your SQL query. While the CBO should be intelligent enough to recognize that a single partition is required, the partition clause makes it very clear which partition is being referenced.

```
Select /*+ full */
    sum(sales)
from
    fact PARTITION ( march_2001_sales )
where
    sales_month = '2001-03'
;
```

Next, let's examine how Oracle parallel query can be used with data warehouse SQL.

Oracle Parallel Query and Oracle SQL Tuning

For Oracle SQL queries that perform large-table full-table scans, Oracle parallel query can greatly improve the access speed for data warehouse queries.

There are several *init.ora* parameters that are set when using Oracle parallel query. Many of these are default values and are set by Oracle when your database is created. Oracle parallel query can be turned on in several ways. You can turn it on permanently for a table, or you can isolate the parallel query to a single table.

Method 1—Permanent Parallelism (not recommended)

```
Alter table customer parallel degree 35;
```

Method 2—Single-Query Parallelism

```
select /*+ FULL(emp) PARALLEL(emp, 35) */
        emp_name
    from
      emp;
```

Note the use of the double hints in the preceding query. Most Oracle DBAs always use the FULL hint with the PARALLEL hint because they are both required to use Oracle parallel query.

CAUTION
Setting a table for parallel query with the alter table xxx parallel degree nn *command can be very dangerous to Oracle SQL performance. If you are using the CBO and you set table-level parallelism, the optimizer may reevaluate the execution plans for SQL statements and change many statements from index range scans to full-table scans. This can cause serious performance degradations for an entire database, and the parallel hint is a far better choice for implementing parallelism because you will never have unintended side effects.*

Most Oracle DBAs identify those tables that perform full-table scans and then alter those tables to specify the degree of parallelism. This way, all full-table scans against the tables will invoke Oracle parallel query.

parallel Query init.ora Parameters

There are several important *init.ora* parameters that have a direct impact on the behavior of Oracle parallel query:

- *sort_area_size*   The higher the value, the more memory is available for individual sorts on each parallel process. Note that the *sort_area_size* parameter allocates memory for every query on the system that invokes a sort. For example, if a single query needs more memory, and you increase the *sort_area_size* parameter, *all* Oracle tasks will allocate the new amount of sort area, regardless of whether they will use all of the space. It is also possible to dynamically change *sort_area_size* for a specific session with the *alter session* command. This technique can be used when a specific transaction requires a larger sort area than the default for the database.

- *parallel_min_servers*   This value specifies the minimum number of query servers that will be active on the instance. There are system resources involved in starting a query server, and having the query server started and waiting for requests will accelerate processing. Note that if the actual number of required servers is less than the values of *parallel_min_servers,* the idle query servers will be consuming unnecessary overhead, and the value should be decreased.

- ***parallel_max_servers***   This value specifies the maximum number of query servers allowed on the instance. This parameter will prevent Oracle from starting so many query servers that the instance cannot service all of them properly.

- ***optimizer_percent_parallel***   This parameter defines the amount of parallelism that the optimizer uses in its cost functions. The default of 0 means that the optimizer chooses the best serial plan. A value of 100 means that the optimizer uses each object's degree of parallelism in computing the cost of a full-table scan operation.

NOTE
Cost-based optimization will always be used for any query that references an object with a nonzero degree of parallelism. Hence, you should be careful when setting parallelism if your default is optimizer_mode=RULE.

Setting the Optimal Degree of Parallelism

Determining the optimal degree of parallelism for Oracle tasks is not easy. Because of the highly volatile nature of most SMP systems, there is no general rule that will apply to all situations. As you may know, the degree of parallelism is the number of operating system processes that are created by Oracle to service the query.

Oracle states that the optimal degree of parallelism for a query is based on several factors. These factors are presented in decreasing order of importance:

- The number of CPUs on the server

- The number of physical disks that the table resides upon

- For parallelizing by partition, the number of partitions that will be accessed, based upon partition pruning (if appropriate)

- For parallel DML operations with global index maintenance, the minimum number of transaction freelists among all the global indexes to be updated. The minimum number of transaction freelists for a partitioned global index is the minimum number across all index partitions. This is a requirement in order to prevent self-deadlock.

For example, if your system has 20 CPUs and you issue a parallel query on a table that is stored on 15 disk drives, the default degree of parallelism for your query is 15 query servers.

There has been a great deal of debate about what number of parallel processes results in the fastest response time. As a general rule, the optimal degree of parallelism can be safely set to N–1, where N is the number of processors in your SMP or MPP cluster.

In practice, the best method is a trial-and-error approach. When tuning a specific query, the DBA can set the query to force a full-table scan and then experiment with different degrees of parallelism until the fastest response time is achieved.

Finding the Number of CPUs on Your Database Server

Sometimes the Oracle DBA does not know the number of CPUs on the database server. The following UNIX commands can be issued to report on the number of CPUs on the database server.

Windows NT   If you are using MS-Windows NT, you can find the number of CPUs by entering the Control Panel and choosing the System icon.

Linux   To see the number of CPUs on a Linux server, you can *cat* the */proc/cpuinfo* file. In the example that follows, we see that our Linux server has four CPUs:

```
>cat /proc/cpuinfo|grep processor|wc -l
     4
```

Solaris   In Sun Solaris, the *prsinfo* command can be used to count the number of CPUs on the processor.

```
>psrinfo -v|grep "Status of processor"|wc -l
      24
```

IBM-AIX   The following example, taken from an AIX server, shows that the server has four CPUs:

```
>lsdev -C|grep Process|wc -l

     36
```

HP/UX   In HP UNIX, you can use the glance or top utilities to display the number of CPUs.

NOTE
Parallel hints will often speed up index creation even on single-processor machines. This is not because there is more processing power available, but because there is less I/O wait contention with multiple processes. On the other end of the spectrum, we generally see diminishing elapsed time when the degree of parallelism exceeds the number of processors in the cluster.

There are several formulas for computing the optimal parallelism. Oracle provides a formula for computing the optimal parallelism based on the number of CPUs and the number of disks that the file is striped onto. Assume that D is the number of devices that P is striped across (either SQL*loader striping or OS striping). Assume that C is the number of CPUs available:

 `P = ceil(D/max(floor(D/C), 1))`

Simply put, the degree of parallelism for a table should generally be the number of devices on which the table is loaded, scaled down so that it isn't too much greater than the number of CPUs. For example, with ten devices and eight CPUs, a good choice for the degree of parallelism is ten. With only four CPUs, a better choice of parallelism might be five.

However, this complex rule is not always suitable for the real world. A better rule for setting the degree of parallelism is to simply use the number of CPUs:

 `P=(number of CPUs)-1`

As a general rule, you can set the degree of parallelism to the number of CPUs on your server, minus one. This is because one processor will be required to handle the parallel query.

Using parallel query Hints

Invoking the parallel query with hints requires several steps. The most important is that the execution plan for the query must specify a full-table scan. If the output of the execution plan does not indicate a full-table scan, the query can be forced to ignore the index by using the *full* hint. There are two permutations of parallel hints, the *parallel* hint and the *pq_distribute* hint. Let's take a look at each and see how they work.

The parallel Hint

The number of processors dedicated to service a SQL request is ultimately determined by Oracle Query Manager, but the programmer can specify the upper limit on the number of simultaneous processes. When using the cost-based optimizer, the *parallel* hint can be embedded into the SQL to specify the number of processes. For instance:

```
select /*+ FULL(employee_table) PARALLEL(employee_table, 35) */
employee_name
from
employee_table
where
emp_type = 'SALARIED';
```

If you are using an SMP or MPP database server with many CPUs, you can issue a parallel request and leave it up to each Oracle instance to use its default degree of parallelism. For example:

```
select /*+ FULL(employee_table) PARALLEL(employee_table, DEFAULT,
DEFAULT) */
employee_name
from
employee_table
where
emp_type = 'SALARIED';
```

In most cases, it is better for the Oracle DBA to determine the optimal degree of parallelism and then set that degree in the data dictionary with the following command:

```
Alter table employee_table parallel degree 35;
```

This way, the DBA can always be sure of the degree of parallelism for any particular table.

Oracle also provides the *parallel_automatic_tuning init.ora* parameter to assist in setting the best degree of parallelism. When setting *parallel_automatic_tuning,* you only need to specify parallelism for a table, and Oracle will dynamically change the *parallel_adaptive_multi_user* parameter to override the execution plan in favor of maintaining an acceptable overall load on the database. You should also note that setting *parallel_automatic_tuning* will cause extra storage in the large pool because Oracle will allocate message buffers from the large pool instead of the shared pool.

The pq_distribute Hint

The *pq_distribute* hint is used in data warehouses to improve parallel join operation performance when using partitioned tables. The *pq_distribute* hint allows you to specify how rows of joined tables should be distributed among producer and consumer parallel query servers. The *pq_distribute* hint accepts three parameters: the table name, the outer distribution, and the inner distribution.

As I discussed in Chapter 10, we always want to avoid the PARALLEL_TO_PARALLEL execution plan when performing a parallel query join. Performing a PARALLEL_TO_PARALLEL operation means the incoming and outgoing data streams are parallelized, resulting in slow join performance. On the other hand, invoking the PARALLEL_COMBINED_WITH_PARENT operation means that sort and merge operations are combined into one operation.

Prior to the use of the *pq_distribute* hint, Oracle DBAs would often fake out the SQL optimizer by deleting the CBO statistics on the inner table to force the PARALLEL_COMBINED_WITH_PARENT operation. This is because the SQL optimizer evaluates the size of candidate broadcast tables according to the CBO statistics. If a table is above a threshold value, the table will be joined via the PARALLEL_ TO_ PARALLEL execution mode, resulting in very slow execution times.

There are six acceptable combinations for table distribution with the *pq_distribute* hint. We use the *emp* table in these examples. Remember that the order of the parameters is outer distribution followed by inner distribution.

- **pq_distribute(emp, hash, hash)** This maps the rows of each table to consumer parallel query servers using a hash function on the join keys. When mapping is complete, each query server performs the join between a pair of resulting partitions. This hint is recommended when the tables are comparable in size and the join operation is implemented by hash join or sort merge join.

- **pq_distribute(emp, broadcast, none)** This ensures that all rows of the outer table are broadcast to each parallel query server, while the inner table rows are randomly partitioned. This hint is recommended when the outer table is very small compared to the inner table. A rule of thumb is to use the Broadcast/None hint if the size of the inner table times the number of parallel query servers is greater than the size of the outer table.

- **pq_distribute(emp, none, broadcast)** This forces all rows of the inner table to be broadcast to each consumer parallel query server. The outer table rows are randomly partitioned. This hint is recommended when the inner table is very small compared to the outer table. A rule of thumb is to use the None/Broadcast hint if the size of the inner table times the number of parallel query servers is less than the size of the outer table.

- **pq_distribute(emp, partition, none)** This maps the rows of the outer table using the partitioning of the inner table. The inner table must be partitioned on the join keys. This hint is recommended when the number of partitions of the outer table is equal to or nearly equal to a multiple of the number of parallel query servers.

- **pq_distribute(emp, none, partition)** This combination maps the rows of the inner table using the partitioning of the outer table. The outer table must be partitioned on the join keys. This hint is recommended when the number of partitions of the outer table is equal to or nearly equal to a multiple of the number of query servers.

- **pq_distribute(emp, none, none)** Each parallel query server performs the join operation between a pair of matching partitions, one from each table. Both tables must be equi-partitioned on the join keys.

Oracle Optimization of Data Warehouse Queries

Oracle provides initialization parameters to control the amount of work performed by the cost-based optimizer when evaluating a query. While parsing is quite fast for simple queries, complex queries with more than six tables can parse for many minutes while Oracle evaluates every possible table join combination.

Sometimes, data warehouse DBAs are perplexed when they find that a 15-way table join takes 30 minutes to parse! This is because there are 15 factorial possible permutations of the query and over one trillion (1,307,674,368,000) query permutations.

While the ultimate solution is to employ stored outlines to remove the parsing phase, Oracle has two important initialization parameters that work together to control the number of possible execution plans generated by the Oracle optimizer.

TIP
If you do not have complex SQL queries that join five or more tables together, you need not be concerned with the optimizer_search_limit *or* optimizer_max_permutations *parameters. These only apply when Oracle is computing possible table join combinations for queries with large numbers of tables.*

The optimizer_search_limit Parameter

The *optimizer_search_limit* parameter specifies the maximum number of table join combinations that will be evaluated by the CBO when deciding the best way to join multiple tables. The reason is to prevent the optimizer from spending an inordinate amount of time on every possible join ordering. The *optimizer_search_limit* parameter also controls the threshold for invoking a star join hint, and a star hint will be honored when the number of tables in the query is less than the *optimizer_search_limit*. The default value is 5.

If the number of tables in the query is less than *optimizer_search_limit,* the optimizer examines all possible table join combinations. The number of join orders is the factorial value of the number of tables in the query. For example, a query joining five tables would have 5! = 5*4*3*2*1 = 120 possible combinations of table join orders. The number of possible evaluations is the factorial of the *optimizer_search_limit,* so with the default value for *optimizer_search_limit* of 5, the cost-based optimizer will evaluate up to 120 table join orders.

The *optimizer_search_limit* and *optimizer_max_permutations* parameters work together, and the optimizer will generate possible table join permutations until the higher of these two values is met. When the optimizer stops evaluating table join combinations, it will choose the combination with the lowest cost. For example, queries joining six tables will exceed the *optimizer_search_limit* but still may spend expensive time evaluating all 6! (720) possible table join orders because the *optimizer_max_permutations* parameter has not been exceeded with its default value of 80,000.

However, when tuning a SQL statement when you plan to use optimizer plan stability to make the execution plan permanent, it is acceptable to temporarily set the *optimizer_search_limit* up to the number of tables in your query, tune the query by reordering the table names in the *where* clause, and then using the *ordered* hint with stored outlines to make the change permanent.

NOTE
The use of the ordered *hint overrides the* optimizer_search_limit *and* optimizer_max_permutations *parameters. This is because the ordered hint requests that the tables be joined in their specified order in the* from *clause of the query. The* ordered *hint is the way most SQL tuning professionals disable table join evaluation, once the optimal join order has been determined.*

The optimizer_max_permutations Parameter

The *optimizer_max_permutations* initialization parameter defines the upper boundary for the maximum number of permutations considered by the cost-based optimizer. Unfortunately, with large numbers of tables, the time spent evaluating a single permutation can be significantly greater than with fewer tables. This means that 50,000 permutations with a 15-way table join can take significantly longer than a query with an 8-way table join. The *optimizer_max_permutations* value is dependent on the *optimizer_search_limit* initialization parameter; the default value for *optimizer_max_permutations* is 80,000.

When determining the upper boundary for the number of query permutations to evaluate, the CBO uses the following rule. If the number of non–single row tables in a query is less than *optimizer_search_limit*+1, then the maximum number of permutations is the larger of

```
        optimizer_max_permutations
    -----------------------------------
    (number of possible start tables + 1)
```

or

```
      optimizer_search_limit factorial
    -----------------------------------
    (number of possible start tables + 1)
```

For example, if we are joining five tables, we get the following values:

```
Maximum permutations = 80,000/6 = 13,333

Search Limit = 5!/6 = 120/6 = 20
```

The large of these values is 13,333, and this is the maximum number of permutations that will be considered by the optimizer. It should be readily apparent at this point that the CBO will be quite slow if it must evaluate 13,333 possible query permutations.

TIP

In your large data warehouse environment with n-way table joins, make sure you use optimizer plan stability to avoid the time-consuming parse phase. For new production queries, try setting the optimizer_max_permutations to a low value such as 500. For queries with more than six tables, the parse phase can take up to 20 minutes to evaluate more than 100,000 possible query permutations. The best advice is to always use stored outlines with data warehouse SQL queries to bypass the long parse times.

Even with a very high value of 80,000 allowed permutation evaluations, there is still a chance that the optimizer may stop before it has located the optimal join order for a large data warehouse query. Consider a 15-way table join with 15!, or over one trillion (1,307,674,368,000), possible query permutations. By cutting off the maximum permutations at 80,000, there is a good chance that the optimizer will give up too early.

The following list is intended to indicate total permutations and what percentage 80,000 is of this number. This may give an idea of how accurate or not the evaluation of a particular plan may or may not be.

Number of tables (n)	Total number of possible permutations (n!)	Proportion of total represented by 80,000 permutations (80,000 / n! * 100)
1	1	Not Relevant
2	2	Not Relevant
3	6	Not Relevant
4	24	Not Relevant
5	120	Not Relevant
6	720	Not Relevant
7	5040	Not Relevant
8	40320	Not Relevant
9	362880	22%
10	3628800	2.2%
11	39916800	0.2%
12	479001600	0.016%
13	6226020800	0.001284%
14	87178291200	0.000092%
15	1307674368000	0.000006%

Clearly, there is a problem when submitting queries where the parse phase must evaluate over 80,000 possible permutations.

In the real world, most DBAs size down *optimizer_max_permutations* in their production environment and *always* use optimizer plan stability (stored outlines) to prevent time-consuming reparsing of the large n-way table joins. Once the best table join order has been found, you can make it permanent by manually specifying the join order for the tables by adding the *ordered* hint to the query and saving the stored outline for the hinted query. See Chapter 13 for details on this procedure.

Before Oracle8*i* (release 8.1.7), the optimizer often did not make enough permutations to find the optimal table join order. A fix is created in Oracle8*i* (8.1.7) to change the algorithm used to choose the initial join orders in an attempt to improve the chance of finding the best plan. To enable the fix in 8.1.7, a new hidden initialization parameter called *_new_initial_join_orders=true* must be added to your *init.ora* file.

Conclusion

Data warehouse SQL queries are like all other queries, except that they experience performance issues at parse time and at execution time. The main points of this chapter include these:

- Oracle partitioning can greatly improve the performance and manageability of data warehouse queries by only accessing the partitions that contain the required data.

- There are several Oracle hints to improve the performance of data warehouse queries.

- The *ordered* hint can be used to bypass the expensive evaluation of table join orders by allowing you to manually specify the table join order in the *from* clause.

- Parallel query can greatly improve response time for legitimate full-table scans.

- You should never set a table to parallel with the *alter table* command because the CBO can wrongly reevaluate many queries to perform full-table scans.

- Oracle parallel query performance depends on the number of CPUs on your database server and the distribution of the data files across multiple disks.

Next, let's take a look at how the STATSPACK utility can be used to assist in Oracle SQL tuning.

CHAPTER
22

SQL Tuning with
STATSPACK

he Oracle STATSPACK utility was first introduced in Oracle8*i*, with a back-port to Oracle8. Introduced with little fanfare, the STATSPACK utility is one of the most powerful Oracle utilities for system tuning and for Oracle SQL tuning.

The tuning of individual SQL statements is the most time-consuming of all of the processes in Oracle tuning. While Oracle SQL tuning is a very time-consuming job, the tuning of SQL also promises the most benefits in the overall performance of the Oracle system. It is not uncommon to increase performance by an order of magnitude by using the proper Oracle SQL tuning techniques.

This chapter will also show how to use Oracle STATSPACK utility in order to monitor the behavior of SQL within your library cache and periodically alert the Oracle professional to SQL statements that may not be optimized for maximum performance. This is done by examining the SQL source in the *stats$sql_summary* table.

There is also a section on managing SQL statements within the library cache. As every Oracle professional knows, SQL statements are very transient within the Oracle instance and may only reside in the library cache for a short period of time. At any given point in time, information with the library cache may change. SQL statements that enter the library cache remain in the library cache until they age out and are no longer available to the Oracle instance. I will show you how to capture information from the library cache in a way that will build the foundation for using special scripts that will interrogate the library cache at a given point in time and prepare detailed reports showing the execution plans for all of the important SQL statements that are in the Oracle library cache.

The STATSPACK utility monitors the library cache information and can be used to create automated alert reports that will show whenever poorly tuned SQL statements are being executed within the Oracle instance.

The tuning of individual SQL statements will show how to change the execution plans with the use of SQL hints. We will examine actual examples for SQL tuning and show how the execution time of SQL statements can be reduced from hours down to only a few minutes.

In addition to storing system statistics, STATSPACK is also very useful for the tuning of Oracle SQL statements. Because STATSPACK stored all SQL statements that meet the snapshot selection criteria, you can create a historical record of all of the important SQL statements that were in the library cache at the time of the snapshot. Because most shops take STATSPACK snapshots hourly, you can quickly develop a complete picture of all historical SQL statements.

From this database of SQL statements, you can write STATSPACK extraction utilities to extract and reexplain all SQL statements after making changes to important

Oracle initialization parameters or adding indexes. In this fashion, you can accurately predict the performance benefit of a SQL tuning change without impacting the production database.

This chapter contains the following topics:

- Setting the STATSPACK SQL collection thresholds

- Querying the historical STATSPACK table to extract SQL

- Extracting specific SQL statements from STATSPACK

Let's begin by reviewing the Oracle STATSPACK utility and review how STATSPACK collects and stores historical SQL statements.

STATSPACK and SQL Data Collection

The STATSPACK utility collects historical SQL information in a table called *stats$sql_summary*. The *stats$sql_summary* table contains the following values:

```
SQL> desc stats$sql_summary;
 Name                                     Null?    Type
 ---------------------------------------- -------- ---------------------------
 SNAP_ID                                  NOT NULL NUMBER(6)
 DBID                                     NOT NULL NUMBER
 INSTANCE_NUMBER                          NOT NULL NUMBER
 SQL_TEXT                                          VARCHAR2(1000)
 SHARABLE_MEM                                      NUMBER
 SORTS                                             NUMBER
 MODULE                                            VARCHAR2(64)
 LOADED_VERSIONS                                   NUMBER
 EXECUTIONS                                        NUMBER
 LOADS                                             NUMBER
 INVALIDATIONS                                     NUMBER
 PARSE_CALLS                                       NUMBER
 DISK_READS                                        NUMBER
 BUFFER_GETS                                       NUMBER
 ROWS_PROCESSED                                    NUMBER
 ADDRESS                                  NOT NULL RAW(8)
 HASH_VALUE                               NOT NULL NUMBER
 VERSION_COUNT                                     NUMBER
```

Note that in addition to the SQL source statement, we also have valuable information about the number of times the SQL statement was parsed and executed, as well as the number of disk reads, buffer gets, and rows processed for the SQL statement. These attributes allow us to quickly locate the offensive SQL for tuning.

In addition, STATSPACK also collects systemwide performance statistics in the *stats$sysstat* table, and many DBAs correlate the execution of an offensive SQL statement with the overall performance of the database. We can track the total sorting activity of our database over time and take a close look at times when SQL *order by* clauses are causing high sort activity, and we might examine *disk_sorts* for our database and correlate the period of high disk sorts to specific SQL statements.

Let's take a close look at tracking SQL sorting with STATSPACK.

Tuning Oracle SQL Sorting with STATSPACK

As a small but very important component of SQL syntax, sorting is a frequently overlooked aspect of Oracle tuning. In general, an Oracle database will automatically perform sorting operations on row data as requested by a *create index* or a SQL *order by* or *group by* statement. In general, Oracle sorting occurs under the following circumstances:

- SQL using the ORDER BY clause

- SQL using the GROUP BY clause

- When an index is created

- When a MERGE SORT is invoked by the SQL optimizer because inadequate indexes exist for a table join

At the time a session is established with Oracle, a private sort area is allocated in RAM for use by the session for sorting. If the connection is via a dedicated connection, a Program Global Area (PGA) is allocated according to the *sort_area_size init.ora* parameter. For connections via the multithreaded server, sort space is allocated in the *large_pool*. Unfortunately, the amount of memory used in sorting must be the same for all sessions, and it is not possible to add additional sort areas for tasks that require large sort operations. Therefore, the designer must strike a balance between allocating enough sort area to avoid disk sorts for the large sorting tasks and keeping in mind that the extra sort area will be allocated and not used by tasks that do not require intensive sorting. Of course, sorts that cannot fit into the *sort_area_size* will be paged out into the TEMP tablespaces for a disk sort. Disk sorts are about 14,000 times slower than memory sorts.

TIP
When using SQL*Plus, or when a user knows that he or she will perform a large sort, the alter session set sort_area_size *command can be used to enlarge the sort area.*

As I noted, the size of the private sort area is determined by the *sort_area_size init.ora* parameter. The size for each individual sort is specified by the *sort_area_retained_size init.ora* parameter. Whenever a sort cannot be completed within the assigned space, a disk sort is invoked using the temporary tablespace for the Oracle instance.

Disk sorts are expensive for several reasons. First, they are extremely slow when compared to an in-memory sort. Also, a disk sort consumes resources in the temporary tablespace. Oracle must also allocate buffer pool blocks to hold the blocks in the temporary tablespace. In-memory sorts are always preferable to disk sorts, and disk sorts will surely slow down an individual task as well as impact concurrent tasks on the Oracle instance. Also, excessive disk sorting will cause a high value for free buffer waits, paging other tasks' data blocks out of the buffer.

The following STATSPACK query uses the *stats$sysstat* table. From this table we can get an accurate picture of memory and disk sorts.

rpt_sorts_alert.sql

```
set pages 9999;

column mydate    heading 'Yr.  Mo Dy  Hr.' format a16
column sorts_memory  format 999,999,999
column sorts_disk    format 999,999,999
column ratio         format .99999

select
   to_char(snap_time,'yyyy-mm-dd HH24') mydate,
   newmem.value-oldmem.value sorts_memory,
   newdsk.value-olddsk.value sorts_disk,
   ((newdsk.value-olddsk.value)/(newmem.value-oldmem.value)) ratio
from
   perfstat.stats$sysstat oldmem,
   perfstat.stats$sysstat newmem,
   perfstat.stats$sysstat newdsk,
   perfstat.stats$sysstat olddsk,
   perfstat.stats$snapshot   sn
where
   newdsk.snap_id = sn.snap_id
```

```
and
   olddsk.snap_id = sn.snap_id-1
and
   newmem.snap_id = sn.snap_id
and
   oldmem.snap_id = sn.snap_id-1
and
   oldmem.name = 'sorts (memory)'
and
   newmem.name = 'sorts (memory)'
and
   olddsk.name = 'sorts (disk)'
and
   newdsk.name = 'sorts (disk)'
and
   newmem.value-oldmem.value > 0
   and
   newdsk.value-olddsk.value > 100
;
```

Here is the output from the script. Here, you can clearly see the number of memory sorts and disk sorts, and the ratio of disk to memory sorts.

Yr. Mo Dy Hr.	SORTS_MEMORY	SORTS_DISK	RATIO
2000-12-20 12	13,166	166	.01261
2000-12-20 16	25,694	223	.00868
2000-12-21 10	99,183	215	.00217
2000-12-21 15	13,662	130	.00952
2000-12-21 16	17,004	192	.01129
2000-12-22 10	18,900	141	.00746
2000-12-22 11	19,487	131	.00672
2000-12-26 12	12,502	147	.01176
2000-12-27 13	20,338	118	.00580
2000-12-27 18	11,032	119	.01079
2000-12-28 16	16,514	205	.01241
2000-12-29 10	17,327	242	.01397
2000-12-29 16	50,874	167	.00328
2001-01-02 08	15,574	108	.00693
2001-01-02 10	39,052	136	.00348
2001-01-03 11	13,193	153	.01160
2001-01-03 13	19,901	104	.00523
2001-01-03 15	19,929	130	.00652

This report can be changed to send an alert when the number of disk sorts exceeds a predefined threshold, and we can also modify it to plot average sorts by hour of the day and day of the week. The script that follows computes average sorts, ordered by hour of the day.

rpt_avg_sorts_hr.sql

```
set pages 9999;

column sorts_memory   format 999,999,999
column sorts_disk     format 999,999,999
column ratio          format .99999

select
   to_char(snap_time,'HH24'),
   avg(newmem.value-oldmem.value) sorts_memory,
   avg(newdsk.value-olddsk.value) sorts_disk
from
   perfstat.stats$sysstat oldmem,
   perfstat.stats$sysstat newmem,
   perfstat.stats$sysstat newdsk,
   perfstat.stats$sysstat olddsk,
   perfstat.stats$snapshot    sn
where
   newdsk.snap_id = sn.snap_id
and
   olddsk.snap_id = sn.snap_id-1
and
   newmem.snap_id = sn.snap_id
and
   oldmem.snap_id = sn.snap_id-1
and
   oldmem.name = 'sorts (memory)'
and
   newmem.name = 'sorts (memory)'
and
   olddsk.name = 'sorts (disk)'
and
   newdsk.name = 'sorts (disk)'
and
   newmem.value-oldmem.value > 0
group by
   to_char(snap_time,'HH24')
;
```

Here is the output from the script. We can now take this data and create a graph in a spreadsheet.

```
TO  SORTS_MEMORY    SORTS_DISK
--  ------------   ------------
00        18,855            11
01        19,546            15
02        10,128             5
03         6,503             8
04        10,410             4
05         8,920             5
06         8,302             7
07         9,124            27
08        13,492            71
09        19,449            55
10        19,812           106
11        17,332            78
12        20,566            76
13        17,130            46
14        19,071            61
15        19,494            68
16        20,701            79
17        19,478            44
18        23,364            29
19        13,626            20
20        11,937            17
21         8,467             7
22         8,432            10
23        11,587            10
```

Figure 22-1 shows the plot from the output. Here you see a typical increase in sort activity during the online period of the day. Sorts rise at about 8:00 A.M. and then go down after 6:00 P.M.

Now, let's run the script to compute the averages by the day of the week.

rpt_avg_sorts_dy.sql

```
set pages 9999;

column sorts_memory   format 999,999,999
column sorts_disk     format 999,999,999
column ratio          format .99999

select
    to_char(snap_time,'day')        DAY,
    avg(newmem.value-oldmem.value)  sorts_memory,
    avg(newdsk.value-olddsk.value)  sorts_disk
```

```
from
   perfstat.stats$sysstat oldmem,
   perfstat.stats$sysstat newmem,
   perfstat.stats$sysstat newdsk,
   perfstat.stats$sysstat olddsk,
   perfstat.stats$snapshot    sn
where
   newdsk.snap_id = sn.snap_id
and
   olddsk.snap_id = sn.snap_id-1
and
   newmem.snap_id = sn.snap_id
and
   oldmem.snap_id = sn.snap_id-1
and
   oldmem.name = 'sorts (memory)'
and
   newmem.name = 'sorts (memory)'
and
   olddsk.name = 'sorts (disk)'
and
   newdsk.name = 'sorts (disk)'
and
   newmem.value-oldmem.value > 0
group by
   to_char(snap_time,'day')
;
```

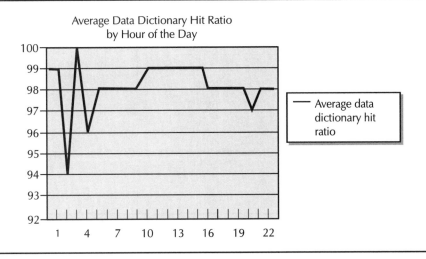

FIGURE 22-1. *Average memory sorts by hour of the day*

Again, we will take the result set and plot it in a chart. This time, let's plot the disk sorts.

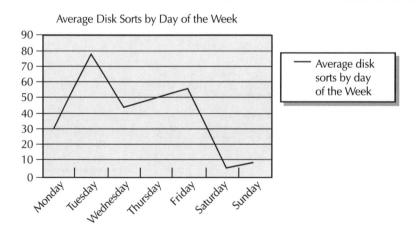

```
DAY           SORTS_MEMORY   SORTS_DISK
---------     ------------   ------------
friday              12,545           54
monday              14,352           29
saturday            12,430            2
sunday              13,807            4
thursday            17,042           47
tuesday             15,172           78
wednesday           14,650           43
```

Figure 22-2 shows the graph. In this database, the activity pattern on Tuesday shows a large number of disk sorts, with another smaller spike on Thursday. For this database, the DBA may want to pay careful attention to the TEMP tablespaces on these days, and perhaps issue an *alter session* command to create continuous extents in the TEMP tablespace.

To do this, you may need a special command using events:

```
rem Used to clean up temp segments in temporary tablespace
rem x is the temp tablespace number in TS$ plus
rem
ALTER SESSION SET EVENTS 'IMMEDIATE TRACENAME DROP_SEGMENTS LEVEL &x';
```

FIGURE 22-2.   *Average disk sorts by day of the week*

At the risk of being redundant, I need to reemphasize that the single most important factor in the performance of any Oracle database is the minimization of disk I/O. Hence, the tuning of the Oracle sorting remains one of the most important considerations in the tuning of any Oracle database.

Tracking SQL with STATSPACK

Because most shops collect STATSPACK snapshots hourly, the *stats$sql_summary* table can grow very large. For example, if the library cache has 5000 SQL statements in the library cache, each snapshot would capture all 5000 SQL statements in the *stats$sql_summary* table. To limit the collection of SQL statements to only the most important statements, Oracle has created STATSPACK to allow SQL collection to be constrained with thresholds. Let's take a closer look at how this works.

SQL Snapshot Thresholds

The snapshot thresholds only apply to the SQL statements that are captured in the *stats$sql_summary* table. The *stats$sql_summary* table can easily become the largest table in STATSPACK schema because each snapshot might collect several hundred rows, one for each SQL statement that was in the library cache at the time of the snapshot.

The thresholds are stored in the *stats$statspack_parameter* table. Let's take a look at each threshold:

- executions_th This is the number of executions of the SQL statement (default 100).

- disk_reads_th This is the number of disk reads performed by the SQL statement (default 1000).

- parse_calls_th This is the number of parse calls performed by the SQL statement (default 1000).

- buffer_gets_th This is the number of buffer gets performed by the SQL statement (default 10,000).

It is important to understand that each SQL statement will be evaluated against all of these thresholds, and the SQL statement will be included in the *stats$sql_summary* table if *any one* of the thresholds is exceeded. In other words, these thresholds are not AND'ed together as we might expect, but they are OR'ed together such that any value exceeding any of the thresholds will cause a row to be populated.

The main purpose of these thresholds is to control the rapid growth of the *stats$sql_summary* table that will occur when a highly active database has hundreds of SQL statements in the library cache. In the next chapter, we will be discussing clean-up strategies for removing unwanted snapshots from the database.

You can change the threshold defaults by calling the *statspack.modify_statspack_parameter* function. In the example that follows, we change the default threshold for buffer_gets and disk_reads to 100,000. In all subsequent snapshots, we will only see SQL that exceeds 100,000 buffer gets or disk reads.

```
SQL>  execute statspack.modify_statspack_parameter -
              (i_buffer_gets_th=>100000, i_disk_reads_th=>100000);
```

STATSPACK SQL Top-10 Report

What follows is an easy-to-use Korn shell script that can be run against the STATSPACK tables to identify high-use SQL statements.

rpt_sql.ksh

```
#!/bin/ksh

# First, we must set the environment . . . .
ORACLE_SID=readtest
export ORACLE_SID
ORACLE_HOME=`cat /var/opt/oracle/oratab|grep ^$ORACLE_SID:|cut -f2 -d':'`
export ORACLE_HOME
PATH=$ORACLE_HOME/bin:$PATH
export PATH

echo "How many days back to search?"
read days_back

echo executions
echo loads
echo parse_calls
echo disk_reads
echo buffer_gets
echo rows_processed
echo sorts
echo
echo "Enter sort key:"
read sortkey

$ORACLE_HOME/bin/sqlplus perfstat/perfstat<<!
```

```
set array 1;
set lines 80;
set wrap on;
set pages 999;
set echo off;
set feedback off;

column mydate        format a8
column exec          format 9,999,999
column loads         format 999,999
column parse         format 999,999
column reads         format 9,999,999
column gets          format 9,999,999
column rows_proc     format 9,999,999
column inval         format 9,999
column sorts         format 999,999

drop table temp1;
create table temp1 as
    select min(snap_id) min_snap
    from stats\$snapshot where snap_time > sysdate-$days_back;

drop table temp2;

create table temp2 as
select
    to_char(snap_time,'dd Mon HH24:mi:ss') mydate,
    executions                             exec,
    loads                                  loads,
    parse_calls                            parse,
    disk_reads                             reads,
    buffer_gets                            gets,
    rows_processed                         rows_proc,
    sorts                                  sorts,
    sql_text
from
    perfstat.stats\$sql_summary sql,
    perfstat.stats\$snapshot     sn
where
    sql.snap_id >
    (select min_snap from temp1)
and
    sql.snap_id = sn.snap_id
order by $sortkey desc
;
spool off;

select * from temp2 where rownum < 11;

exit
!
```

Here is the listing from running this valuable script. Note that the DBA is prompted as to how many days back to search, and the sort key for extracting the SQL.

rpt_sql.ksh

```
How many days back to search?
7
executions
loads
parse_calls
disk_reads
buffer_gets
rows_processed
sorts

Enter sort key:
disk_reads

SQL*Plus: Release 8.1.6.0.0 - Production on Thu Dec 14 09:14:46 2000

(c) Copyright 1999 Oracle Corporation. All rights reserved.


Connected to:
Oracle8i Enterprise Edition Release 8.1.6.1.0 - 64bit Production
With the Partitioning option
JServer Release 8.1.6.1.0 - 64bit Production

MYDATE         EXEC      LOADS    PARSE      READS        GETS  ROWS_PROC    SORTS
--------  ----------  --------  --------  ----------  ----------  ----------  --------
SQL_TEXT
---------------------------------------------------------------------------------
11 Dec 1       866         1       866    246,877  2,795,211        865         0
4:00:09
DECLARE job BINARY_INTEGER := :job; next_date DATE := :mydate;  broken BOOLEAN :
= FALSE; BEGIN statspack.snap; :mydate := next_date; IF broken THEN :b := 1; ELS
E :b := 0; END IF; END;

11 Dec 1       863         1       863    245,768  2,784,834        862         0
1:00:29
DECLARE job BINARY_INTEGER := :job; next_date DATE := :mydate;  broken BOOLEAN :
= FALSE; BEGIN statspack.snap; :mydate := next_date; IF broken THEN :b := 1; ELS
E :b := 0; END IF; END;

11 Dec 1       866         1       866    245,325    597,647    129,993        866
4:00:09
INSERT INTO STATS$SQL_SUMMARY ( SNAP_ID,DBID,INSTANCE_NUMBER,SQL_TEXT,SHARABLE_M
EM,SORTS,MODULE,LOADED_VERSIONS,EXECUTIONS,LOADS,INVALIDATIONS,PARSE_CALLS,DISK_
READS,BUFFER_GETS,ROWS_PROCESSED,ADDRESS,HASH_VALUE,VERSION_COUNT )   SELECT MIN(
:b1),MIN(:b2),MIN(:b3),MIN(SQL_TEXT),SUM(SHARABLE_MEM),SUM(SORTS),MIN(MODULE),SU
M(LOADED_VERSIONS),SUM(EXECUTIONS),SUM(LOADS),SUM(INVALIDATIONS),SUM(PARSE_CALLS
),SUM(DISK_READS),SUM(BUFFER_GETS),SUM(ROWS_PROCESSED),ADDRESS,HASH_VALUE,COUNT(
1)    FROM V$SQL  GROUP BY ADDRESS,HASH_VALUE  HAVING (SUM(BUFFER_GETS) > :b4  OR
 SUM(DISK_READS) > :b5  OR SUM(PARSE_CALLS) > :b6  OR SUM(EXECUTIONS) > :b7 )
```

```
11 Dec 0      861       1      861    245,029  2,778,052      860        0
9:00:24
DECLARE job BINARY_INTEGER := :job; next_date DATE := :mydate;  broken BOOLEAN :
= FALSE; BEGIN statspack.snap; :mydate := next_date; IF broken THEN :b := 1; ELS
E :b := 0; END IF; END;

11 Dec 1      864       1      864    244,587    595,861   129,605      864
2:00:02
INSERT INTO STATS$SQL_SUMMARY ( SNAP_ID,DBID,INSTANCE_NUMBER,SQL_TEXT,SHARABLE_M
EM,SORTS,MODULE,LOADED_VERSIONS,EXECUTIONS,LOADS,INVALIDATIONS,PARSE_CALLS,DISK_
READS,BUFFER_GETS,ROWS_PROCESSED,ADDRESS,HASH_VALUE,VERSION_COUNT )   SELECT MIN(
:b1),MIN(:b2),MIN(:b3),MIN(SQL_TEXT),SUM(SHARABLE_MEM),SUM(SORTS),MIN(MODULE),SU
M(LOADED_VERSIONS),SUM(EXECUTIONS),SUM(LOADS),SUM(INVALIDATIONS),SUM(PARSE_CALLS
),SUM(DISK_READS),SUM(BUFFER_GETS),SUM(ROWS_PROCESSED),ADDRESS,HASH_VALUE,COUNT(
1)   FROM V$SQL  GROUP BY ADDRESS,HASH_VALUE  HAVING (SUM(BUFFER_GETS) > :b4  OR
SUM(DISK_READS) > :b5  OR SUM(PARSE_CALLS) > :b6  OR SUM(EXECUTIONS) > :b7 )
```

It is interesting to note in the preceding output that we see the STATSPACK insert statement for the *stats$sql_summary* table.

Conclusion

The STATSPACK utility can be very useful for extracting historical SQL statements and tuning the SQL. Because you may not have the location of the original source SQL statement, optimizer plan stability can be used to tune the SQL without changing the original SQL statement. The main points in this chapter include these:

■ The *stats$sql_summary* table collects all SQL statements that meet any one of the STATSPACK threshold values.

■ The *access.sql* script can be easily modified to extract historical SQL by specifying the *stats$sql_summary* table. You can then run *access_reports.sql* to get a picture of all full-table scans and table sizes.

■ Once a table that is experiencing large-table full-table scans is located, you can extract the SQL statements from the *stats$sql_summary* table.

Next, let's conclude this text by taking a look at how to tune SQL statements that utilize built-in functions.

CHAPTER
23

Tuning SQL with Built-in Functions and Special Operators

racle provides a wealth of non-ANSI built-in functions to improve the functionality of SQL statements to transform datatypes. These built-in functions, commonly called BIFs, are widely used to improve the ability of SQL to transform column datatypes for easier table access.

As you will learn, the main problem with the use of BIFs in SQL statements is that they can cause unnecessary full-table scans. The remedy to this problem is to rewrite the SQL without BIFs or add a function-based index to remove the large-table full-table scan.

This chapter has two areas, the use of the like and case statements, and the section on Oracle BIFs. Both of these areas are very important for a full knowledge of Oracle SQL tuning.

Using the like and case Clauses in SQL

While the case and like operators are not built-in functions, they are closely related and serve many of the same purposes as BIFs. You already know that BIFs can be made to use an index by creating a matching function-based index, but the behaviors of the *like* and *case* clauses are very subtle.

Let's begin by looking at one of the most popular string conversion clauses, the *like* clause.

Using the like Clause in Oracle Queries

The *like* clause is one of the most popular SQL clauses because it can be used to easily extract a string anywhere in a text column. Because the *like* parameter is used so frequently, it is a great benefit to understand how Oracle can use indexes and alternative execution plans to service these types of queries.

As you know, the percent (%) operator is used with the *like* clause as a mask, and the % will match any character. For example, if we wanted all names containing "smith," we could issue a query as follows:

```
select
    ename
from
    emp
where
    ename like '%smith%'
;
```

Here is the output. Note that "smith" can appear anywhere in the output. As you see, the *like* clause is a very useful tool for extracting substrings from textual column output.

```
ENAME
----------
smith
smithson
havensmith
nesmith
```

But how can we get good Oracle SQL performance using the *like* clause? To answer this question, we must evaluate how the Oracle SQL optimizer uses indexes with the *like* clause.

Let's begin by looking at a query that uses the *like* clause to find all employee names beginning with an "S".

```
select
    ename
from
    emp
where
    ename like 'S%'
;
```

Here is the execution plan, and you see that our query was able to utilize the *emp_ename* index to service the query. This means that the Oracle SQL optimizer will recognize the *like* clause for indexing so long as the leading edge of the query is a literal value.

```
OPERATION
---------------------------------------------------------------------
OPTIONS                          OBJECT_NAME                 POSITION
-----------------------------   --------------------------  ----------
SELECT STATEMENT
                                                                  1
   INDEX
RANGE SCAN                       EMP_ENAME                        1
```

However, the *like* operator will not work if a % is placed in the left-hand side of the query. Hence, the query that follows should not be able to use the index because there is a wildcard at the leading edge of the *like* clause format mask.

```
select
    ename
from
    emp
where
    ename like '%TH%'
;
```

Here is a surprise. While we might expect a full-table scan, we see an index full scan. This is because even though the SQL optimizer was not able to read the leading edge of the index, the index full scan can be used because the index nodes contain everything required to answer the query.

```
OPERATION
----------------------------------------------------------------------
OPTIONS                          OBJECT_NAME                  POSITION
--------------------------       -------------------------   ----------
SELECT STATEMENT
                                                                     1
    INDEX
FULL SCAN                        EMP_ENAME                            1
```

Next, let's look at the SQL case statement and see how it can reduce the number of full-table scans.

Combining Multiples Scans with CASE Statements

It is often necessary to calculate different aggregates on various sets of tables. This is generally done with multiple scans on the table, but it is easy to calculate all the aggregates with one single scan. Eliminating n–1 scans can greatly improve performance.

Combining multiple scans into one scan can be done by moving the *where* condition of each scan into a *case* statement, which filters the data for the aggregation. For each aggregation, there could be another column that retrieves the data.

The following example asks for the count of all employees who earn less than $1000 per month, all those who earn between $1000 and $5000 per month, and the DBAs who earn more than $5000 each month. This can be done with three separate queries:

```
select
   count(*)
from
   emp
where
   sal < 1000;

select
   count(*)
from
   emp
where
```

```
  sal between 1000 and 5000;

select
   count (*)
from
   emp
where
   sal > 5000;
```

Here is the output:

```
  COUNT(*)
----------
         1


  COUNT(*)
----------
        12


  COUNT(*)
----------
         1
```

Of course, because each of these queries does a count(*), there will be three full-table scans against the *emp* table.

However, it is more efficient to run the entire query in a single statement using the *case* function. Each number is calculated as one column. The count uses a filter with the *case* statement to count only the rows where the condition is valid. For example:

```
select
   count (case when sal < 1000
        then 1 else null end)                    count_poor,
   count (case when sal between 1001 and 5000
        then 1 else null end)                    count_blue_collar,
   count (case when sal > 5001
         then 1 else null end)                   count_dba
from
   emp;
```

Here is the output from this query. Note that we get our counts on a single line of output.

```
COUNT_POOR COUNT_BLUE_COLLAR  COUNT_DBA
---------- -----------------  ----------
         1                12           1
```

Now let's examine the execution plan for this query to see how the *case* clause improves the original SQL execution of three full-table scans:

```
OPERATION
--------------------------------------------------------------------
OPTIONS                         OBJECT_NAME                 POSITION
----------------------------  -------------------------  ----------
 SELECT STATEMENT
                                                                  1
  SORT
AGGREGATE                                                         1
    TABLE ACCESS
FULL                          EMP                                 1
```

Here you see that we have replaced three full-table scans with a single full-table scan, resulting in a 3x performance improvement.

The moral of this story is that the *case* statement can be used to speed up multiple counting operations when a common column is involved.

Next, let's look at the true built-in functions of Oracle SQL and see how they behave.

Tuning SQL with BIFs

Let's begin with a review of the basic BIFs and see how they are used. Oracle BIFs are especially useful for retrieving Oracle table columns where a transformation is required. We generally see a BIF under the following conditions:

- **Transforming characters** Oracle provides the *to_number, to_date, upper, lower,* and *substr* BIFs for transforming character data at retrieval time.

- **Transforming dates** The *to_char* BIF is extremely useful for transforming Oracle date datatypes. The *to_char* BIF is used with dates to extract specific days, months, and years.

Of course, you know that the remedy for the problem of non-index usage when a query contains a BIF is to create a function-based index to match the predicate in the *where* clause of the SQL. However, there are some subtle surprises when using BIFs. Let's take a closer look at each of these transformation types and see how they change SQL execution.

Using BIFs with Character Datatypes

With character datatypes, we commonly see BIFs used to transform character strings to remove case sensitivity. For example, here we can query on the *last_name* column without being concerned about case sensitivity:

```
select
   customer_stuff
from
   customer
where
   upper(last_name) = 'JONES'
;
```

Using BIFs with Date Datatypes

One of the most common uses of Oracle BIFs is the transformation of the Oracle date datatype. As you know, the Oracle date datatype stores both the date and the time down to the hundredths of a second. Because of this high degree of precision, it is difficult to convert the date datatype to a character. However, we do have the *nls_date_format* session variable, which can be used to change an Oracle SQL statement's display format for all dates. Surprisingly, the *nls_date_format* also affects the execution plan for SQL statements. To see, examine the following query to display all employees hired in January.

```
select
   ename
from
   emp
where
   to_char(hiredate,'MON') = 'JAN'
;
```

Here is the execution plan, and we see the expected full-table scan.

```
OPERATION
---------------------------------------------------------------------
OPTIONS                         OBJECT_NAME                  POSITION
------------------------------- ---------------------------- ----------
SELECT STATEMENT
                                                                      1
  TABLE ACCESS
FULL                            EMP                                  1
```

Now, if we change the *nls_date_format,* we can rewrite the query to specify the numeric month.

```
SQL> alter session set nls_date_format='MM';

Session altered.
```

Now we change the query from the character month (MON) to the numeric month (MM), and we remove the *to_char* BIF.

```
select
   ename
from
   emp
where
hiredate = '01';
```

Here is the execution plan for the preceding SQL. Here you see that by removing the *to_char* BIF, we are able to utilize the index to service our query.

```
OPERATION
-----------------------------------------------------------------
OPTIONS                        OBJECT_NAME                POSITION
-----------------------------  -------------------------  --------
SELECT STATEMENT
                                                               64
  TABLE ACCESS
BY INDEX ROWID                 EMP                              1
    INDEX
RANGE SCAN                     EMP_HIREDATE                     1
```

However, please note that we are looking for the character '01'. When we try to do a numeric comparison for a date, we have other issues because of a datatype mismatch.

To illustrate, here is another query that uses the *to_number* BIF to transform a date to pull all employees hired after 1996.

```
select
   ename
from
   emp
where
   to_number(to_char(hiredate,'YYYY')) > 1996
;
```

Here is the execution plan for this SQL. As we expect, without a function-based index on *hiredate,* we see the full_table scan.

```
OPERATION
--------------------------------------------------------------------
OPTIONS                         OBJECT_NAME                 POSITION
---------------------------- --------------------------- ----------
SELECT STATEMENT
                                                                  1
    TABLE ACCESS
FULL                            EMP                               1
```

Now, it might be tempting to change the *nls_date_format* to see if we can remove the full-table scan by changing the date display to a four-digit numeric year value. Let's try it and watch what happens.

alter session set nls_date_format='YYYY';

```
explain plan set statement_id='test3' for
select
    ename
from
    emp
where
    hiredate > 1956
;
```

Here you see an inconsistent datatypes message. This is because the date datatype is not numeric, even if we manipulate the *nls_date_format* to make the result look like a number.

```
    hiredate > 1956
            *
ERROR at line 7:
ORA-00932: inconsistent datatypes
```

Hence, we are forced to use the *to_number* BIF to convert the date year to a number. Now, we should be comparing two numeric values.

```
select
    ename
from
    emp
where
    to_number(hiredate) > 1956
;
```

Here is the execution plan for this query, and as we expect, adding the *to_number* BIF has make our date index unusable, resulting in a full-table scan.

```
OPERATION
-----------------------------------------------------------------
OPTIONS                         OBJECT_NAME               POSITION
------------------------------- ------------------------- ---------
SELECT STATEMENT
                                                                 1
  TABLE ACCESS
FULL                            EMP                              1
```

Now, let's add a function-based index to the *emp* table, using the same nested BIFs that we used in our query.

```
create index
    emp_hiredate_year
on
    emp
(
    to_number(to_char(hiredate,'YYYY'))
)
;
```

Now, there is no need to reset the *nls_date_format,* and our original query should use our new function-based index:

```
select
    ename
from
    emp
where
    to_number(to_char(hiredate,'YYYY')) > 1956
;
```

Here is the execution plan, and as we expected, our new index has removed the full-table scan.

```
OPERATION
-----------------------------------------------------------------
OPTIONS                         OBJECT_NAME               POSITION
------------------------------- ------------------------- ---------
SELECT STATEMENT
                                                                 1
  TABLE ACCESS
BY INDEX ROWID                  EMP                              1
    INDEX
RANGE SCAN                      EMP_HIREDATE_YEAR                1
```

Using the substr BIF

There are many times when we want our query to select a subset of a column. In these cases, many SQL developers will use the substr BIF to transform the SQL statement. In the next example, we select all employees whose names begin with "SM".

```
select
   ename
from
   emp
where
   substr(ename,1,2)='SM'
;
```

Here is the execution plan.

```
OPERATION
----------------------------------------------------------------------
OPTIONS                        OBJECT_NAME                 POSITION
------------------------------ --------------------------- ----------
SELECT STATEMENT
                                                                   1
   TABLE ACCESS
FULL                           EMP                               1
```

Now let's create a function-based index with the substr function, just like the one in our query.

```
create index
   emp_ename_substr
on
   emp
(
   substr(ename,1,2)
)
;
```

Now, we expect that the function-based indexes will be used:

```
----------------------------------------------------------------------
OPTIONS                        OBJECT_NAME                 POSITION
------------------------------ --------------------------- ----------
SELECT STATEMENT
                                                                   1
  TABLE ACCESS
BY INDEX ROWID                 EMP                               1
     INDEX
RANGE SCAN                     EMP_ENAME_SUBSTR                  1
```

Since we have a function-based index on the first two characters of our substring, can Oracle use this index when we want only the first character? Let's see if this index can be used with the first character of the substring. Here we try to select all employees whose names begin with an "S".

```
select
   ename
from
   emp
where
   substr(ename,1,1)='S'
;
```

Here is the execution plan, and we see that our index could not be used by Oracle to service this query.

```
OPERATION
-----------------------------------------------------------------
OPTIONS                         OBJECT_NAME                POSITION
------------------------------- -------------------------- ----------
SELECT STATEMENT
                                                                  1
   TABLE ACCESS
   FULL                         EMP                               1
```

Hence, function-based indexes will be used on substring BIFs only when the columns match identically.

Next, let's take a look at some new BIFs that are introduced with Oracle9*i*.

Oracle9i BIF Enhancements

Oracle Structured Query Language (SQL) has changed significantly over the past four years. Oracle Corporation has been struggling to find a balance between making SQL adhere to the ANSI standard and providing robust built-in functions to improve Oracle SQL performance. Oracle 9*i* has deliberately chosen to vary from the ANSI standard for SQL and provide a wealth of built-in functions that can improve the performance of the Oracle database.

Oracle has also improved the responsiveness of SQL by providing Java-based interfaces directly to their OLAP engine for data warehousing. This makes SQL more accessible to external portals within the Internet world.

In keeping with this commitment to extending Oracle SQL, Oracle has provided some exciting new features for the analysis of large volumes of data:

- **LEAD and LAG functions** These SQL extensions enable complex time-series analysis of data warehouse information and allow for the easy aggregation of rolling time periods.

- **Ranking functions** Oracle9*i* SQL includes ranking functions that provide support for common OLAP rankings, such as the top 10, bottom 10, top 10 percent, and bottom 10 percent.

- **Advanced grouping functions** Oracle9*i* now provides categorization functions that group values into buckets, such as age groups or income brackets.

- **Statistical functions** Oracle9*i* offers statistical functions, including support for correlation, standard deviation, linear regressions, and other common calculations.

In addition to these SQL enhancements, Oracle9*i* has improved its OLAP engine and offers tools that simplify the complex task of loading Oracle data warehouses.

Conclusion

The use of the *like* clause, the *case* clause, and Oracle BIFs have an impact on the execution plans for Oracle SQL, and the SQL tuning expert must understand how the SQL optimizer chooses indexes for these functions. This chapter contains the following points.

- Multiple *count(*)* SQL statements can be combined using the *case* clause, to perform all counts in a single full-table scan.

- The *like* operator will use an index on the leading edge of the column.

- The *like* operator can use a full-index scan in place of a full-table scan, even when the leading edge of the query is a wildcard (%) value.

- All queries using BIFs can have a function-based index created to remove the full-table scan.

- The *to_char* BIF is commonly used to transform date datatypes.

- The *nls_date_format* can sometimes be used to select subsets of date datatypes using an existing date index.

- The *substr* BIF can only use a function-based index when the query substring exactly matches the function-based index.

Book Conclusion

It has been a tremendous challenge to write this text, and with Oracle SQL in a constant state of flux, there will undoubtedly be many more opportunities to revise and enhance this book. I love tuning Oracle SQL, and because I do it for a living, I am always excited to hear about new SQL tuning techniques and tips.

I always feedback, and I invite all readers to e-mail me at **don@burleson.cc**. I sincerely hope that you enjoy reading this book as much as I have enjoyed writing it, and I wish you the best of luck in your SQL tuning endeavors.

Index

J

K

L

M

S

W

INTERNATIONAL CONTACT INFORMATION

AUSTRALIA
McGraw-Hill Book Company Australia Pty. Ltd.
TEL +61-2-9417-9899
FAX +61-2-9417-5687
http://www.mcgraw-hill.com.au
books-it_sydney@mcgraw-hill.com

CANADA
McGraw-Hill Ryerson Ltd.
TEL +905-430-5000
FAX +905-430-5020
http://www.mcgrawhill.ca

GREECE, MIDDLE EAST,
NORTHERN AFRICA
McGraw-Hill Hellas
TEL +30-1-656-0990-3-4
FAX +30-1-654-5525

MEXICO (Also serving Latin America)
McGraw-Hill Interamericana Editores S.A. de C.V.
TEL +525-117-1583
FAX +525-117-1589
http://www.mcgraw-hill.com.mx
fernando_castellanos@mcgraw-hill.com

SINGAPORE (Serving Asia)
McGraw-Hill Book Company
TEL +65-863-1580
FAX +65-862-3354
http://www.mcgraw-hill.com.sg
mghasia@mcgraw-hill.com

SOUTH AFRICA
McGraw-Hill South Africa
TEL +27-11-622-7512
FAX +27-11-622-9045
robyn_swanepoel@mcgraw-hill.com

UNITED KINGDOM & EUROPE
(Excluding Southern Europe)
McGraw-Hill Education Europe
TEL +44-1-628-502500
FAX +44-1-628-770224
http://www.mcgraw-hill.co.uk
computing_neurope@mcgraw-hill.com

ALL OTHER INQUIRIES Contact:
Osborne/McGraw-Hill
TEL +1-510-549-6600
FAX +1-510-883-7600
http://www.osborne.com
omg_international@mcgraw-hill.com

Get Your FREE Subscription to *Oracle Magazine*

Oracle Magazine is essential gear for today's information technology professionals. Stay informed and increase your productivity with every issue of *Oracle Magazine*. Inside each **FREE,** bimonthly issue you'll get:

- Up-to-date information on Oracle Database Server, Oracle Applications, Internet Computing, and tools
- Third-party news and announcements
- Technical articles on Oracle products and operating environments
- Development and administration tips
- Real-world customer stories

Three easy ways to subscribe:

1. Web
**Visit our Web site at www.oracle.com/oramag/.
You'll find a subscription form there, plus much more!**

2. Fax
Complete the questionnaire on the back of this card and fax the questionnaire side only to **+1.847.647.9735.**

3. Mail
Complete the questionnaire on the back of this card and mail it to P.O. Box 1263, Skokie, IL 60076-8263.

If there are other Oracle users at your location who would like to receive their own subscription to *Oracle Magazine*, please photocopy this form and pass it along.

Knowledge is power. To which we say,

crank up the power.

Are you ready for a power surge?

 Accelerate your career—become an **Oracle Certified Professional** (OCP). With Oracle's cutting-edge *Instructor-Led Training*, *Technology-Based Training*, and this *guide*, you can prepare for certification faster than ever. Set your own trajectory by logging your personal training plan with us. Go to **http://education.oracle.com/tpb**, where we'll help you pick a training path, select your courses, and track your progress. We'll even send you an email when your courses are offered in your area. If you don't have access to the Web, call us at 1-800-441-3541 (Outside the U.S. call +1-310-335-2403).
Power learning has never been easier.

U n i v e r s i t y